Grumman F-14
TOMCAT

Grumman F-14

TOMCAT

EDITOR: JON LAKE

Aerospace Publishing London
AIRtime Publishing USA

Published by
Aerospace Publishing Ltd
179 Dalling Road
London W6 0ES
England

Published under licence in USA and
Canada by
AIRtime Publishing Inc.
10 Bay Street
Westport, CT 06880
USA

Aerospace **ISBN: 1 874023 41 7**
AIRtime **ISBN: 1-880588-13-7**

Distributed in the UK,
Commonwealth and Europe by
Airlife Publishing Ltd
101 Longden Road
Shrewsbury SY3 9EB
England
Telephone: 01743 235651
Fax: 01743 232944

Distributed to retail bookstores in the
USA and Canada by
AIRtime Publishing Inc.
10 Bay Street
Westport, CT 06880
USA
Telephone: (203) 838-7979
Fax: (203) 838-7344

US readers wishing to order by mail,
please contact
AIRtime Publishing Inc. toll-free at
1 800 359-3003

Publisher:	Stan Morse
Managing Editor:	David Donald
Editor:	Jon Lake
Sub Editors:	Chris Chant
	Karen Leverington
Design:	Dean A. Morris
Authors:	Jon Lake
	David Donald
	Robert F. Dorr
	Bill Gunston
	Robert Hewson
	Julian Lake
	Peter B. Mersky
	Lt Todd Parker
	Lt Sam Platt
	Warren Thompson
Artists:	Mike Badrocke
	Chris Davey
	Keith Fretwell
	Rob Garrard
	Grant Race
	Mark Styling
	John Weal

Origination by
Imago Publishing Ltd

Printed in Italy

WORLD AIR POWER JOURNAL
is published quarterly and
provides an in-depth analysis
of contemporary military
aircraft and their worldwide
operators. Superbly produced
and filled with extensive colour
photography, *World Air Power
Journal* is available by
subscription from:

UK, Europe and
Commonwealth:
Aerospace Publishing Ltd
PO Box 2822
London, W6 0BR
UK

Telephone: 0181-740 9554
Fax: 0181-746 2556

USA and Canada:
AIRtime Publishing Inc.
Subscription Dept
10 Bay Street
Westport, CT 06880
USA
Telephone: (203) 838-7979
Toll-free number in USA:
1 800 359-3003

For subscription information
and details of other products,
visit the new *World Air Power*
web site
http://www.airpower.co.uk

CONTENTS

Acknowledgments

The editor would like to express his sincere gratitude to the following individuals for all their assistance during the production of this book.

Vice Admiral Bill Hauser, USN retired, Rear Admiral Julian Lake, USN retired, Commander Lewis Scott Lamoreaux, USN retired, Admiral Thomas Moorer, USN retired, Commander Dave Parsons, USN retired, Lieutenant Commander Joseph T. Stanik, USN retired

Commander Ian Anderson, Lieutenant Jim Bartelloni, VF-101, Lieutenant Tom Bau, No. 226 OCU, Royal Air Force, Commander Bob Brauer, VF-41, Colonel William T. Bridgham, Jr. USMC retired, Lieutenant Stuart Broce, Commander Mark Clemente, VF-213 Commander Dave Cully, CO VF-31, Commander Jim Green, XO VF-103, Commander Kirby Miller, Lieutenant Jim Muse, VF-101, Lieutenant Todd Parker, SWATSLANT, Lieutenant Commander Samuel M. Platt, COMSEVENTHFLT

Robert F. Dorr, Warren E. Thompson, Peter B. Mersky, Vernon Pugh, Mike Benolkin, P. Donen, Paul Hart, Tom Kaminski, Michael Anselmo

John Aris, Bob Bionde, Kurt Hofman, Harry Janiesch, Vice President F-14 Programs, Lois Lovisolo, Bill McDonald, Roger Seybel, John Vosilla

Picture acknowledgments

The publishers would like to thank the following individuals and organisations for supplying photographs for this book:

Front cover: US Navy (two). **8-9:** Rick Llinares/Dash 2 Photography. **10-11:** George Hall/Check Six, Darryl L. Glubczynski via Peter B. Mersky. **12:** Jerry Wilkins via Phil Wallick, Grumman via Robert F. Dorr. **13:** Grumman via Robert F. Dorr, Grumman. **14:** Grumman (two), US Navy. **15:** Grumman. **16:** Grumman, via Paul F. Crickmore. **17:** General Dynamics, Hughes. **18:** Hughes. **19:** Hughes, US Navy via Peter B. Mersky. **20:** Grumman, Tom Kaminski. **21:** Grumman, Paul Hart via Robert F. Dorr. **22:** Grumman (two), US Navy. **23:** US Navy (two). **25:** Grumman, Paul Hart via Robert F. Dorr. **26:** Paul Hart via Robert F. Dorr, Tom Kaminski. **27:** US Navy via M. Anselmo (three). **28:** US Navy (two). **29:** US Navy (two). **30:** Aerospace. **31:** Hughes, Aerospace. **32:** Aerospace, Vance Vasquez/US Navy. **33:** George Hall/Check Six, Grumman. **34:** Grumman, US Navy. **35:** Grumman. **36:** Grumman, Jeff Rankin-Lowe/Sirius Productions. **37:** Dave Parsons, Grumman. **38:** Ted Carlson/Fotodynamics, Grumman. **39:** Grumman, via Peter B. Mersky, US Navy. **40:** Steven D. Eisner, US Navy (two). **42:** Steve Mansfield, George Hall/Check Six. **43:** Tony Holmes, US Navy, Peter B. Mersky. **44:** George Hall/Check Six, Dave Parsons via Peter B. Mersky, Steve Mansfield. **45:** via Peter B. Mersky, Dave Baranek. **46:** George Hall/Check Six, US Navy via Peter B. Mersky, Robert L. Lawson. **47:** Robbie Shaw, George Hall/Check Six, Robert L. Lawson. **51:** Robert L. Lawson, Steven D. Eisner, Dave Baranek via Peter B. Mersky. **54:** Robert L. Lawson, Tony Holmes, via Peter B. Mersky. **55:** VF-101/US Navy, US Navy. **56:** Robert L. Lawson, Tony Holmes, Jeff Rankin-Lowe/Sirius Productions. **57:** US Navy via Peter B. Mersky (two), PMTC via Robert F. Dorr. **58:** George Hall/Check Six, Richard Gennis. **59:** Stephen J. Brennan, Steve Mansfield, George Hall/Check Six. **60:** Vance Vasquez via Robert L. Lawson, Robert L. Lawson. **61:** Robert L. Lawson (two). **62:** US Navy via Jon Lake (two). **64:** Grumman (two), Robert L. Lawson. **65:** Joe Cupido. **66:** Ted Carlson/Fotodynamics (two). **67:** Rick Llinares/Dash 2 Photography. **68:** Rick Llinares/Dash 2 Photography, Joe Cupido. **69:** Chuck Lloyd/Dash 2 Photography, via Jon Lake, Ted Carlson/Fotodynamics. **70:** Grumman (two), **71:** Ted Carlson/Fotodynamics, Dave Parsons via Robert L. Lawson. **72:** US Navy via Jon Lake. **73:** Carl Richards. **74:** US Navy via Jon Lake. **75:** US Navy. **78:** Dave Baranek. **79:** via Jon Lake, Hughes. **80:** US Navy (two), General Dynamics. **81:** US Navy via Jon Lake, US Navy, Grumman. **82:** US Navy via Jon Lake (two). **83:** US Navy via Joetey Attariwala, Jim Condy via Tom Kaminski, Robbie Shaw, Vance Vasquez/US Navy. **84:** David Donald, Paul Bennett, Vance Vasquez/US Navy. **85:** Steven D. Eisner (two), Vance Vasquez/US Navy. **86:** US Navy via Peter B. Mersky, US Navy (two). **87:** Hughes (three). **88:** US Navy (two). **89:** Hughes (two). **90-91:** via Simon Watson (four). **94:** US Navy via Joseph Stanik (two), US Navy. **95:** US Navy via Joseph Stanik. **96:** US Navy via Joseph Stanik (two). **97:** US Navy (two), via Jon Lake. **98:** US Navy. **100:** US Navy via Jon Lake, Dave Parsons via Jon Lake. **101:** via Peter B. Mersky, US Navy. **102:** VF-1/US Navy. **103:** VF-1/US Navy. **104:** US Navy, Sam Platt, via Peter B. Mersky. **105-106:** via Peter B. Mersky. **107:** via Peter B. Mersky, Stephen J. Brennan, Michael M. Anselmo. **108:** Ian Anderson via Jon Lake, US Navy. **109:** US Navy, US Navy via Jon Lake. **110:** US Navy via Jon Lake, Ian Anderson via Jon Lake. **111:** Ian Anderson via Jon Lake. **112:** Dave Baranek, Ian Anderson via Jon Lake. **113-115:** Ian Anderson via Jon Lake. **116:** US Navy via Jon Lake, Sam Platt via Peter B. Mersky. **117:** Sam Platt (three). **118:** Sam Platt. **119:** US Navy via Jon Lake, Sam Platt. **120:** Robert L. Lawson, Dave Parsons via Robert L. Lawson. **121:** Ian Anderson, via M. Anselmo. **122:** US Navy via Jon Lake, Kirby Miller via Jon Lake, Ted Carlson/Fotodynamics. **123:** Ian Anderson via Jon Lake, Ted Carlson/Fotodynamics. **124:** Ian Anderson via Jon Lake (two). **125:** Ian Anderson via Jon Lake. **126:** US Navy via Jon Lake (two). **127:** US Navy via Jose M. Ramos. **128:** US Navy via Jon Lake, US Navy via Jose M. Ramos (two). **129:** US Navy via Jose M. Ramos. **130:** Jose M. Ramos (three), US Navy via Jon Lake. **131:** Robert L. Lawson, US Navy via Jon Lake (two). **132:** US Navy via Jon Lake, US Navy via Jose M. Ramos, Peter B. Mersky via Jon Lake. **133:** Peter B. Mersky via Jon Lake, Matt Olafsen. **134:** Peter B. Mersky via Jon Lake. **135:** US Navy via Jon Lake. **136:** Tim Ripley, Jose M. Ramos. **137:** Jose M. Ramos (two). **138:** Tim Ripley (two). **139:** US Navy via Tim Ripley, Tim Ripley. **140-141:** Tim Ripley. **142:** Rick Llinares/Dash

2 Photography, Lt Don Slavin via Robert L. Lawson. **143:** Lt John Martin via Robert L. Lawson, Robert L. Lawson (two), Michael Grove via Robert L. Lawson. **144:** Doug Olson via Robert L. Lawson, Dave Baranek via Robert L. Lawson (two). **145:** Peter B. Mersky via Jon Lake, Robbie Shaw (two), Tom Twomey via Peter B. Mersky. **146:** Joe Cupido, via Robert L. Lawson, Dave Baranek via Robert L. Lawson. **147:** Peter Wilson, Tom Kaminski, via Jon Lake. **148:** via Robert L. Lawson, Doug Olson via Robert L. Lawson. **149:** Robert L. Lawson, Grumman, Richard Gennis, Tom Prochilo via Peter B. Mersky, US Navy via Jon Lake. **150:** Michael Grove via Robert L. Lawson, Rick Morgan via Robert L. Lawson, via Robert L. Lawson. **151:** Robert L. Lawson, Michael Grove via Robert L. Lawson, Doug Olson via Robert L. Lawson. **152:** Robert L. Lawson (two), Ian Anderson via Jon Lake, Peter R. Foster, David Donald. **153:** Robert L. Lawson, Dave Parsons via Robert L. Lawson, Grumman via Robert L. Lawson, Hans Nijhuis, Dave Parsons via Peter B. Mersky, Robbie Shaw. **154:** Robert L. Lawson, Joe Cupido, Ted Carlson/Fotodynamics. **155:** Robert L. Lawson, Rick Morgan via Robert L. Lawson, Joe Cupido. **156:** Robbie Shaw (two), Tom Ross, Sam Platt via Peter B. Mersky, US Navy via Jon Lake. **157:** Robert F. Dorr, Doug Olson via Robert L. Lawson. **158:** Grumman, Peter Wilson, Jeff Puzzullo. **159:** Bruce Trombecky via Robert L. Lawson, Robert L. Lawson, Geoff Pearce/Avia Graphics. **160:** via Robert L. Lawson, Doug Olson via Robert L. Lawson, Dave Baranek via Robert L. Lawson. **161:** Robert L. Lawson, Michael Grove via Robert L. Lawson, Peter B. Mersky Collection. **162:** Robert L. Lawson (two), Dave Ostrowski via Robert L. Lawson. **163:** Jeff Rankin-Lowe/Sirius Productions, Robert L. Lawson, Stan Morse, US Navy via Jon Lake (two). **164:** Pete Clayton via Robert L. Lawson, Dave Parsons via Robert L. Lawson, Joe Cupido. **165:** David Donald, Peter Wilson (two), Tom Kaminski, Peter B. Mersky Collection. **166:** US Navy via Jon Lake, Peter Wilson, VF-103. **167:** Tom Kaminski, Grumman, Michael Grove via Robert L. Lawson. **168:** Robert L. Lawson (two), Michael Grove via Robert L. Lawson, Dr J.G. Handlemann via Robert L. Lawson. **169:** US Navy via Peter B. Mersky, R. Housden via Paul Bennett, Steven D. Eisner, Robert L. Lawson. **170:** John Martin via Robert L. Lawson, Michael Grove via Robert L. Lawson. **171:** Robert L. Lawson, Bruce Trombecky via Robert L. Lawson, Ted Carlson/Fotodynamics. **172:** Peter R. Foster, VF-124, Ian Anderson via Jon Lake. **173:** Robert L. Lawson, Michael Grove via Robert L. Lawson. **174:** Robbie Shaw, Richard Gennis, US Navy, Grumman. **175:** David Donald, Robbie Shaw, Ted Carlson/Fotodynamics, Steven H. Miller via Robert L. Lawson. **176:** Robert L. Lawson, US Navy. **177:** Kirby Miller, Ted Carlson/Fotodynamics, via Peter B. Mersky, Robert L. Lawson. **178:** US Navy via Peter B. Mersky, Robert L. Lawson. **179:** Robert L. Lawson, Peter Wilson (two), David Donald. **180:** Keith Snyder via Robert L. Lawson (two), Peter Wilson, Richard Gennis. **181:** Jeff Puzzullo, Dave Baranek via Peter B. Mersky, Pete Clayton via Robert L. Lawson, Michael Grove via Robert L. Lawson, Joe Cupido. **182:** US Navy via Robert L. Lawson, Dave Swoboda via Robert L. Lawson. **183:** Jan C. Jacobs via Robert L. Lawson (two), US Navy, Richard Gennis. **184:** Bruce Trombecky via Robert L. Lawson, Joe Cupido, Stephen J. Brennan, VF-302. **185:** George Hall/Check Six. **186:** Robert L. Lawson (two), Ted Carlson/Fotodynamics, Michael Grove via Robert L. Lawson. **187:** Michael Grove via Robert L. Lawson, Jan C. Jacobs via Robert L. Lawson, Bruce Trombecky via Robert L. Lawson. **188:** Tom Kaminski, US Navy via Robert L. Lawson. **189:** Ted Carlson/Fotodynamics, Bruce Trombecky via Robert L. Lawson, Robert L. Lawson. **190:** Grumman (two), Paul Hart Collection via Robert F. Dorr. **191:** US Navy (two), Ian Anderson via Jon Lake, US Navy via Peter B. Mersky. **192:** Tom Kaminski, Robert L. Lawson (two), Grumman (three). **193:** US Navy, Robert L. Lawson. **194:** Grumman (two), Robert L. Lawson. **195:** Ted Carlson/Fotodynamics. **196:** Grumman, Jan C. Jacobs via Robert L. Lawson, Bruce Trombecky via Robert L. Lawson, Ted Carlson/Fotodynamics, Geoffrey Pearce/Aviagraphics. **197:** Robert L. Lawson (four). **198:** Paul Hart via Robert F. Dorr (two), Ted Carlson/Fotodynamics, Marty J. Isham via Robert L. Lawson, Robert L. Lawson. **199:** Grumman, Robert L. Lawson, Tom Kaminski. **200:** Robert L. Lawson. **201:** Ted Carlson/Fotodynamics, Mike Grove via Robert L. Lawson, Douglas Olson via Robert L. Lawson. **202:** Joe Cupido, Ted Carlson/Fotodynamics. **204:** Joe Cupido, Ted Carlson/Fotodynamics (two). **205:** Tom Twomey via Robert L. Lawson (three). **206:** Rick Morgan via Robert L. Lawson. **207:** Ted Carlson/Fotodynamics (three). **208:** Ted Carlson/Fotodynamics, Rick Morgan via Robert L. Lawson. **209:** Tom Kaminski, Vance Vasquez via Robert L. Lawson, Robert L. Lawson. **219:** US Navy, Gary Bihary. **220:** Dave Baranek, Robert L. Lawson, M. Anselmo, Grumman, Vernon Pugh. **221:** Robert L. Lawson, Joetey Attariwala, Vance Vasquez/US Navy. **Back cover:** Grumman, Randy Jolly, US Navy via Jon Lake

Foreword

Never before has a single airplane affected world history like the F-14 Tomcat. Untold acts of aggression have undoubtedly been averted when leaders of various nations and their military advisors considered the awesome power of the F-14 Tomcat and its Phoenix missile system. It helps that the Tomcat's air base can approach just about any coastline in a matter of days, but the 100-mile 'death dot' the Tomcat aircrew can place on a radar contact has been, and will continue to be, a driving factor in policy decisions around the world.

Since its inception, the F-14 has exuded lethal power. Its sleek, purposeful lines, powerful wide-set engines, and large bubble canopy make the Tomcat one of the most aggressive-looking aircraft ever built. In spite of its stark businesslike appearance – and maybe as a result – the Tomcat is still one of the most beautiful aircraft flying. An F-14 rocketing off the carrier in full afterburner is one of the most impressive, soul-stirring sights in the world.

The world knows the Tomcat. When an F-14 makes the headlines, the event typically dominates the news for several days. Video footage of the F-14 often adorns the evening news even when the jet isn't directly involved with the story. Any major story that involves a United States carrier battle group – and many do – is usually accompanied by at least one sequence of a Tomcat slamming into a carrier's flight deck or rocketing off the catapult. Film and television producers and Navy recruiters, among others, have also repeatedly capitalised on the Tomcat's strikingly powerful image.

Fate, and training, brought me to the F-14 community. The United States Naval Academy tried to recruit me for their football team while I was in high school. One of their recruiting tactics was to send two Tomcat pilots to visit me in my home after I had expressed an interest in naval aviation. It almost worked; by the time they left, I was convinced that Naval Aviators were some of the coolest people on Earth and that flying F-14s off of aircraft-carriers was the best job in the word.

I didn't end up attending Annapolis, but several years after that seed was planted, I found myself circling the USS *Ranger* in an F-14A, awaiting my recovery window after a combat air patrol flight over southern Iraq. As I watched several squadron mates catapult off the deck for flights in-country, I had the sudden and overwhelming realisation that we were part of a big, incredible machine called the carrier battle group. The thrill and challenges of simply flying the Tomcat pale compared to what it takes to fly in the carrier environment.

The F-14, despite its astounding agility, isn't easy to handle. The flight controls were designed with the best that the 1960s had to offer. 'Digital flight controls' and 'ergonomics' were just obscure concepts when the first Tomcat took to the air, but, at the time, it was the king of the fighter world. With no true 'fly-by-wire' flight control system, F-14 pilots must directly control nearly every movement of major control surfaces, truly earning their flight pay whether pushing the edge of the envelope in a dogfight or simply trying to get aboard a pitching flight deck on the darkest of nights. Despite perceptions in the 1970s and 1980s that the jet was susceptible to uncontrollable flat spins, the Tomcat has very few nasty manners and is a joy to fly at its limits. Nevertheless, the jet's handling is a long shot from surgical, and F-14 pilots must learn to anticipate the jet's quirks; something deferred to computers on more modern aircraft designs.

Handling aside, the President, policy-makers, Joint Chiefs of Staff, admirals and air wing commanders have always taken the tremendous capabilities of the F-14 Tomcat for granted. The F-14 has scored kills nearly every time a hostile aircraft has entered its weapons envelope. Four times against Libyan jets and once against an Iraqi helicopter during Operation Desert Storm. No losses. No missed opportunities. The F-14 entered the combat air-to-ground arena during strikes launched into Bosnia with equally impressive results. With a loadout of laser-guided bombs, long-range missiles and fuel to deliver its ordnance several hundred miles from the carrier, the Tomcat exhibits a lethality no other single aircraft can approach. Send them out in groups of four and there will be hell to pay.

One of the F-14 Tomcat's most important missions, and one rarely covered in the news, is photo-reconnaissance. For decades, Tomcats have launched from carriers with, in addition to lethal missile loads, a large Tactical Air Reconnaissance Pod System or 'TARPS' pod bolted underneath. These missions have taken F-14s over hostile territories all over the world to take high-resolution photographs of civilian and military installations and, as was repeated many times during the Gulf War and in the skies over Bosnia, to gather targeting information for air strikes. Tomcat crews have also taken on the unenviable task of returning to recently-attacked sites to record battle damage for combat planners. The Pentagon and Capitol Hill have, more than once, come to a halt, waiting for a Tomcat to return from hostile territory with essential footage.

Sometime in the mid-1990s, the Navy realised the potential of the F-14 as a true 'strike/fighter' complete with precision bombing capability. This potential has been with the Tomcat since it first rolled off the Grumman lines in the early 1970s, but for various reasons, mostly political, the F-14 remained a 'pure' air-to-air fighter for its first two decades; a situation akin to using a Swiss army knife solely as a letter opener.

When the A-6 Intruder retired recently from the fleet, a huge void opened in the long-range, medium-attack department that only the F-14 can fill. The Navy bought in to the F/A-18 Hornet – a strike/fighter plagued by an anaemic fuel capacity – so heavily that it came up with a new doctrine that portrays a future of short-range 'littoral' conflicts with carriers skirting the beaches of hostile lands; presumably to get the Hornets close enough to strike. Time will tell if that doctrine is realistic, but in its new strike/fighter role, the Tomcat will continue to be a vital element in the United States' projection of power overseas well into the next millennium.

Grumman F-14 Tomcat, possibly the most complete work of its kind, is a precious source of historical and technical information on the history of the F-14. Replete with beautiful illustrations and photographs, *Grumman F-14 Tomcat* is a wonderful tribute to the F-14 Tomcat and should be 'required reading' for Tomcat aircrews and maintenance personnel, and anyone sharing an interest in combat aviation.

Brave men and women continue to patrol the skies in their F-14 Tomcats, in hostile airspace around the world, day and night, in any weather, off the decks of aircraft-carriers. Others work long, dangerous hours on crowded flight decks to prepare the fighters for future missions. They all make tremendous sacrifices to be out there, and they're all proud of the Tomcat. This book is about an exceptional aircraft.

D. Stuart Broce, Lieutenant Commander, United States Navy

Lieutenant Stuart Broce (left) joined the exclusive club of fliers with aerial victories to their name on 6 February 1991, when he and his RIO, squadron CO Commander Ron McElraft, downed a Mil Mi-8 with an AIM-9 Sidewinder missile. They were flying F-14A BuNo. 162603, modex NE-103, from USS Ranger. The aircraft is shown above shortly afterwards, complete with black silhouette kill marking beneath the cockpit rail.

INTRODUCTION

In the post-Cold War world, the aircraft-carrier has assumed a new importance in America's peacekeeping and power projection roles. Wherever it goes, the US Navy carrier is protected by one superbly equipped aircraft type, the Grumman F-14 Tomcat. This is nothing new; the F-14 has been fulfilling the same role for more than 20 years. What is different is that, today, Grumman F-14 Tomcats also fly ground attack and precision bombing missions, with almost equal facility.

Nearly 30 years after its first flight, the Grumman F-14 Tomcat remains the most potent interceptor in service worldwide, and the US Navy's Tomcat squadrons are widely regarded as an élite within an élite, fulfilling a vital role with supreme confidence and great competence. In recent years, the Tomcat community has expanded the scope of its operations and today regards itself as 'King Kong' in the demanding air-to-ground role.

It is in the fleet air defence role that the F-14 remains unique. The F-14's AWG-9 (Air Weapons Group 9) fire-control system and long-range AIM-54 Phoenix missiles allow it to destroy hostile aircraft at enormous ranges, simultaneously engaging targets at different altitudes. Crucially, the F-14 does not need to illuminate its target for the whole of the missile's flight time, being able to turn away when the Phoenix's own active terminal radar takes over. This dramatically reduces the vulnerability of the Tomcat to a return missile shot, giving the previously unknown ability to fire and (later) forget.

The F-14 is much more than a lumbering, missile-armed bomber-destroyer, however. From the start, Grumman was determined to produce a fighter aircraft that would be able to out-fight aircraft like the MiG-21 and MiG-23 in close-quarter combat, and it succeeded in producing an aircraft whose agility was a quantum improvement over that of the F-4 Phantom which it replaced.

Like many aircraft, the Tomcat has vices as well as virtues, and its development and deployment has seen a fascinating and frustrating mix of triumph and tragedy. Handling limitations imposed by the engines

and the widely-spaced intakes severely constrained the aircraft's carefree handling characteristics, while the spinning accidents which prompted their imposition reportedly resulted in an estimated 40 aircraft losses. Even more of a problem were TF30 fan-blade failures in the compressor section, which caused many aircraft losses and prompted some pilots to distrust their engine, and treat it with exaggerated caution. Against a modern agile fighter like an F-15, F-16, MiG-29 or Su-27, or even against a well-flown F-5 or Sea Harrier, the F-14 pilot would thus find himself at something of a disadvantage. Sometimes a good backseater can erode the advantage enjoyed by the more agile single-seat fighter, but the Tomcat's 'ace up the sleeve' remains its ability to destroy multiple targets at an unparalleled distance, downing missile carriers before they can launch their weapons, or fighters before they can close to become a threat.

Long-standing engine problems were only resolved on the F-14A(Plus) (F-14B) and F-14D, whose production has now been radically cut back. Northrop Grumman (Northrop acquired Grumman in 1994) remains positive about the aircraft, though, and is today battling to gain acceptance for advanced Tomcat versions.

Whatever further development takes place, the Tomcat community is today enjoying a renaissance. A rapid and painful contraction of the force, accompanied by the disestablishment of numerous historic squadrons, is now finally over, and the remaining units are playing an increasingly vital role in US Naval air operations. Being an F-14 pilot or RIO is both supremely important and fun once more, and morale is sky high. "The Cat," they boast, "is back!"

Chapter One
Forging the Tomcat

The F-14 Tomcat emerged as a direct result of the failure of its manufacturer's previous attempt to meet virtually the same requirement. In fairness, Grumman's failure with the F-111B was an inevitable side effect of the politicians' misbegotten insistence on commonality with the US Air Force's TFX. The Tomcat's conception was complex, its birth was difficult, and its early years were troubled, yet the aircraft came to be known as the world's greatest interceptor fighter, ever.

Both pictures: The F-14 enjoys superb performance, excellent manoeuvrability and a weapons system which is still unrivalled in its highly specialised primary role. The Tomcat is optimised to be launched from an aircraft-carrier, by day or night, whatever the weather, and to intercept incoming targets before they can threaten the carrier. There is still no finer carrierborne interceptor than the F-14 Tomcat.

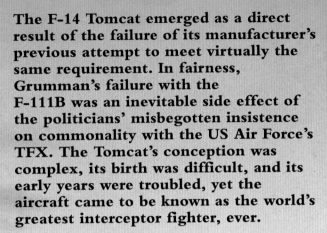

Above: The F-14 Tomcat is the latest in a long line of Grumman-built naval fighters, all those of monoplane layout being named after cats. The F6F Hellcat seen here was probably the best naval fighter of World War II, agile, fast and packing a deadly punch. Other Grumman cats have included the F4F Wildcat, the F7F Tigercat, the F8F Bearcat, the F9F Panther and Cougar, and the F11F Tiger. The family members have all been renowned for their rugged dependability and fighting ability.

Above right: These are just four of the configurations examined by Grumman before it arrived at the Design 303E, which eventually became the Tomcat. Various combinations of fixed- and swing-wings, single or twin fins and podded or buried engines were examined.

During the 1950s, the US Navy began to seek a fleet defence interceptor – a requirement eventually fulfilled by the F-14. The successful aircraft would defend its carrier battle groups against long-range bombers carrying stand-off missiles, and would destroy threats at a safe distance from the ships themselves. Missiles were regarded as a particularly difficult target, and the solution adopted was the interception of the launch aircraft before it could release its weapons. This implied making an interception at a vast distance from the carrier, which in turn would demand a long range and long loiter time. The solution was to accept a large and relatively unmanoeuvrable fighter, with large missile-carrying plus long-range target detection capabilities. The only critical parameter was that the aircraft had to be small enough and light enough to operate from an aircraft-carrier. The interceptor's missile would do the hard work.

A request for proposals to produce a suitable missile for the interceptor was issued in the summer of 1957, a competition that was won by Bendix with its AAM-N-10 Eagle. This weapon was 16 ft (4.9 m) long, and weighed 1,284 lb (582 kg). Tandem motors gave it a Mach-4, 110-nm (126-mile; 203-km) performance. A Westinghouse pulse-Doppler seeker was fitted, derived from the DPN-53

seeker in the Bomarc SAM. The Navy's requirement was paralleled by the USAF's Project Aerie, which envisaged the use of C-135As (each armed with 24 Eagle missiles) as long-range interceptors.

Long-range, long-loiter missile defender

Douglas Aircraft began work in early 1960 on an aircraft to fulfil this requirement, under the designation D-790, and using the name Missileer. This aircraft was one of a number of fighter derivatives of the company's Skywarrior carrier-borne attack aircraft, and differed little from the basic A3D-2 but for having a bulbous nose housing a new AN/APN-122(V) radar. The aircraft carried four of the new Bendix AAM-N-10 missiles in its modified bomb bay, with four more underwing as an overload option with the missile pylons mounted inboard and outboard of the engine nacelles. The aircraft was designed around a pair of 12,000-lb st (53.38-kN) Pratt & Whitney JT3C-14 turbojets, but these were subsequently replaced by 11,650-lb st (51.82-kN) General Electric J79MJ98Cs. The latter gave the aircraft an estimated performance of 635 mph (1010 km/h) clean, or 588 mph (945 km/h) with underwing missiles. Design weight was 55,942 lb (25375 kg), with a maximum take-off weight of 79,410 lb (36020 kg). The aircraft was estimated to have a 4.5-hour loiter capability 150 nm (170 miles; 280 km) from the carrier, including 10 minutes of combat at full power. The first Missileer was abandoned when the DoD circulated a request for proposals for a new fleet air defence aircraft to industry. Douglas decided that a warmed-over Skywarrior, in service since 1956, would not be suitable, and proceeded to design an entirely new aircraft, the D-976, which used the same radar and missiles as the D-790, and which retained the same Missileer name.

After a long competition between six companies, the Navy awarded Douglas a contract to build two prototypes of its design as the XF6D-1 Missileer, on 15 December 1960. The F6D-1 (Model D-976) was an anachronistic-looking aircraft similar in appearance to the earlier but smaller F3D-1 Skyknight. It looked considerably more old fashioned than the swept-wing F3D-3, or the slightly-swept original D-790 Missileer. The new Missileer was designed to protect aircraft-carriers using six Bendix XAAM-N-10

Eagle two-stage air-to-air missiles (though some sources give a total of eight, perhaps by counting the stated 'future overload option' of adding a pair of missiles under the forward fuselage). It was envisaged that the Missileer would typically loiter (for up to six or even 10 hours) 130 nm (150 miles; 240 km) from its carrier and at 35,000 ft (10670 m). If a target was detected, an Eagle would be launched, accelerating to Mach 4 and climbing to 100,000 ft (30480 m) before using its lock-on cruise and homing radar guidance system to engage its target, at ranges of up to 87 nm (100 miles; 160 km). The missile was now even larger, 2,000 lb (907 kg) in weight and 20 ft (6 m) in length. It could pack a conventional or nuclear warhead, the latter making pinpoint accuracy less important. Crucially, it was intended that the Missileer would be able to engage multiple targets simultaneously with its track-while-scan radar. The aircraft carried a crew of three: pilot, co-pilot and missile control operator.

Contract and cancellation

The Missileer would have been adequate for the narrow mission of intercepting enemy bombers, but lacked agility and was unarmed apart from its long-range Eagle AAMs, so it could not have defended itself, although its two 10,000-lb st (44.48-kN) Pratt & Whitney TF30-P-2 turbofans did give a maximum speed of 472 kt (543 mph; 875 km/h). Nevertheless, Douglas received an order for 120 production aircraft, worth $60 million. There were developmental problems with the Eagle, however, and it never reached service. The stand-off concept had always been controversial and, after a review, the contracts were withdrawn on 25 April 1961.

One survivor of the programme was the Hughes AN/AWG-9 fire-control system, which was to continue in development (though it only gained Sidewinder and Sparrow compatibility after the death of the F-111B) until it eventually found a home in the Tomcat. The AN/AWG-9 was much more than a radar, being an integrated target detection and weapons control system with a long-range radar, IR detection system, lightweight solid-state computers (which represented the state of high technology in the pre-transistor days), advanced cockpit displays and a two-way datalink to allow aircraft and ship or ground station or even other aircraft to be linked together. The Eagle missile was also reborn as the AAM-N-11 Phoenix (later AIM-54), after technology was transferred from Bendix to Hughes. Both systems benefited from the incorporation of technology from the Air Force's ASG-18 radar and GAR-9 missile developed for the abandoned Mach 3 F-108 Rapier interceptor and (as the AIM-47) for the experimental Lockheed YF-12A. Before they could be incorporated in the purpose-built airframe which became the F-14, both the radar and the missile had a part to play in another stillborn naval interceptor, the F-111B. This ill-fated aircraft played a crucial role in shaping the Navy's attitude to industry for the next decade, and directly led to the F-14 we know today.

USAF/USN common fighter

The inauguration of President John F. Kennedy marked a new era for America, though not always in the way that history remembers. The new Secretary of Defense, Robert S. McNamara, entered politics from the Ford Motor Company, and surrounded himself with a team of predominantly civilian advisers: analysts, accountants, lawyers and even the odd engineer. He is today remembered by many as America's worst ever Defense Secretary. He was certainly determined to make his mark. McNamara and his so-called 'whiz-kid' advisers were hell-bent on saving money and improving efficiency, and decided that the US Air Force and Navy should adopt a common fighter, called TFX (Tactical Fighter

Despite its single tailfin and outward-folding ventral fins, this full-scale mock-up of the Design 303E is unmistakably a Tomcat. This mock-up was later modified to resemble the final Tomcat configuration, retaining the same spurious BuNo. of 00303. Although Sparrow missiles can be seen below the belly, the aircraft was designed around the AIM-54 Phoenix.

The first F-14 made its maiden flight one month ahead of schedule, on 21 December 1970. Nine days later, on 30 December, William Miller and Robert Smythe took off for the second flight, which ended in disaster. The aircraft is seen during that second flight, trailing a plume of hydraulic fluid as it raced back to Grumman's Calverton facility.

Forging the Tomcat

Experimental, the acronym originally applied to the USAF's requirement). The Air Force was looking for a long-range fighter-bomber (TFX) and the Navy was still searching for a fighter capable of both long-range and close-in combat (the FADF, or Fleet Air Defense Fighter). The Navy placed some emphasis on the need for air combat capability and did not want the virtual pure interceptor which the F-111B (and arguably the F-14) became.

'McNamara's Bow-Tie Bastards'

McNamara was not a specialist, and believed that the USAF's requirement for long ferry range and heavy weapon load fitted in well with the Navy's need for an extended patrol endurance and for the ability to carry a heavy load of fuel and missiles. He ignored the conflicting elements of the two requirements, including the USAF's demand for Mach 1.3 performance at low level, and the Navy's very-high-speed dash capability at high altitude. Both services initially rejected the idea of a common TFX, but their protests were ignored. After weeks of analysing a host of compromise designs, the respective Secretaries of the Navy and Air Force, Paul Fay and Eugene Zuckert, told McNamara on 22 August 1961 that it was "not technically feasible" to build a compromise aircraft which could meet the requirements of both services. The Navy was particularly scathing, estimating that the best compromise aircraft would enjoy only 37 per cent effectiveness in the crucial CAP mission. There were, quite simply, too many directly conflicting requirements. The Air Force wanted tandem seats and a long, narrow nose, while the Navy specified side-by-side seating and a short, fat nose. The Air Force envisaged a heavyweight aircraft spending most of its life at high subsonic speed at very low level, while the Navy wanted a lighter aircraft optimised for Mach 1 to Mach 2 performance at high level. The Air Force's insis-

tence on Mach 1.3 capability at low level actually made the aircraft far heavier than the Navy wanted, while the Navy's demands for an encapsulated escape system, internal carriage for its Phoenix missiles and a 3.5-hour loiter time were irrelevant to the USAF.

In the end, the 'whiz kids' had McNamara's ear and won the argument (gaining a new epithet in the process, becoming 'McNamara's Bow-tie Bastards'). On 1 September McNamara directed that, "A single aircraft for both the Air Force tactical mission and the Navy fleet air defence mission shall be undertaken: the Air Force shall proceed with the development of such an aircraft."

McNamara specified that the Air Force aircraft would have a nose capable of accommodating a 36-in (91-cm) radar dish despite the Navy's requirement for 48 in (122 cm), and a maximum length of 73 ft (22.25 m) regardless of the Navy's specified maximum of 56 ft (17.07 m).

Second best and higher cost

A request for proposals was issued on 1 October 1961, drawing responses from Boeing, General Dynamics, Lockheed, McDonnell, North American and Republic. None was judged acceptable, but the submissions by Boeing and General Dynamics were given paid study contracts for further refinement. Fresh submissions were made by the two companies on 2 April 1962. The Navy found both proposals unacceptable, since neither offered adequate CAP loiter endurance, and neither looked as though it could ever be made compatible with operation from a carrier. Third and fourth submissions were made to refine the designs further and correct the deficiencies, the slightly cheaper Boeing design proving to be the better at each stage. Finally, on 8 November 1962, the Chief of the Navy BuWeps, the commander of TAC, and the commanders of Air Force Systems and Logistics Commands found themselves in agreement and backed an Air Force council statement which declared that "There is a clear and sub-

stantial advantage in the Boeing proposal...magnified by the austere conditions usually inherent in limited war actions." On 24 November McNamara declared General Dynamics winner of the TFX competition, and after allegations of corruption, malpractice and fraud had been worked over, the hapless company set about designing its F-111 to fulfil both roles. In the end, General Dynamics had proposed a greater degree of commonality than Boeing, whose naval and air force variants were angrily condemned by McNamara: "In the two Boeing versions less than half of the structural components of the wing, fuselage and tail were the same. In fact, the evaluation group concluded that Boeing is, in effect, proposing two different airplanes." This was the ultimate heresy, and had to be punished. Senator McClellan's Permanent Sub-Committee on Investigations commented later that, "The Secretary of Defense bought the second-best airplane at the higher price."

F-111B gets under way

The General Dynamics TFX bid had been made in association with Grumman, whose experience as a naval contractor was thought to be invaluable. Grumman was charged with the design and production of the rear fuselage and landing gear of all F-111s, and of the TFX-N naval version (or 'naval deviant' according to critics), the F-111B. This promised to offer advantages of commonality with the Air Force's new aircraft, and held out the lure of a reduced unit price due to the larger production run. The Navy had been pressured into stating a requirement for an eventual 267 F-111Bs, to add to the USAF's orders and the possibility of large orders from overseas. The huge size of the aircraft and its lack of agility did not cause McNamara and his analysts any real worries. In the rarefied atmosphere in which they were working it seemed logical and cost-effective to put the performance into the missile and not the airframe. Their figures showed that long-range missile duels would allow the Missileer-like F-111B to emerge unscathed, and operational concerns that missile combat inevitably degenerated into close-quarter dogfights were ignored as the ravings of hidebound traditionalists who could not see that dogfighting had died with the F-86 and MiG-15. No-one seemed even to consider that politically imposed rules of engagement could also have a critical effect on the range at which an enemy aircraft might be engaged.

Grumman had done much work on the variable-sweep wing with its XF10F-1 Jaguar. First flown on 19 May 1952 and cancelled before it could enter service, the XF10F-1 is memorable, if for anything, as being one of the ugliest aircraft ever built. It was not flown enough to be categorised as one of the worst aircraft built. Fortunately, the Navy did have the good sense to cancel the aircraft – though it was also one of the first with a key feature of the later Tomcat, the variable-geometry (VG) wing. The Jaguar had already become a footnote to history by the time the 'swing' wing and Phoenix missile were incorporated into the navalised Grumman F-111B, which also featured a nose shortened by 10 ft (3.05 m) to allow the aircraft to fit onto a standard carrier lift. Other changes to the F-111B included a redesigned nose gear, wingtips each extended by 3 ft 6 in (1.07 m), a shorter tailfin, new tyres and an upgraded arrester hook. The aircraft was designed to carry six Phoenix missiles on swivelling underwing pylons, with two more on a trapeze inside the weapons bay.

The nautical F-111B prototype was first flown on 18 May 1965, by Ralph H. Donnell and Ernest von der Heyden, after an 11 May roll-out. The first three aircraft were fitted with conventional ejection seats, but the production naval version was always intended to have the McDonnell escape capsule later used by service USAF F-111s. Seven F-111B prototypes were eventually constructed, the fourth and fifth being re-engined with the Pratt & Whitney TF30-P-3 in place of the lower-powered TF30-P-1.

Too big and too heavy

The fuselage of the F-111B was still 66 ft 9 in (20.35 m) long, despite the relocation of avionics behind the cockpit (which displaced much-needed internal fuel tankage). Meanwhile, the aircraft's weight continued to grow, from the design maximum of 62,788 lb (28480 kg) and past 75,000 lb (34020 kg). Captain Scotty Lamoreaux remembers that, "The F-111B was not necessarily too large for carrier operation, but it was too heavy. The F-14 ended up pretty close to it in size. Carrier suitability (particularly cockpit visibility on approach) was the main complaint. Both the F-111 and the F-14 were plagued with the same engine, the TF30, which gave both types many problems." To illustrate the longevity of the engine, it could be added that an earlier incarnation of the same engine had originally featured in the stillborn Douglas F6D Missileer. "Weight growth was a major concern with the F-111 and it was even worse than reported, but perhaps above all the Navy was emotionally opposed to the F-111B and was determined to kill it."

The F-111B was too complex, too heavy, and too slow, never right for the carrier mission and unlikely to be rendered so despite Herculean efforts. Quite apart from the inadequate view from the cockpit, the aircraft was judged to be 'grossly underpowered' and 44 per cent deficient in range, while the engine's inclination to stall was rated a 'safety-of-flight' issue. The landing gear was too far forward for carrier operation, giving the aircraft too great a propensity to tip back onto its tail. The swivelling wing pylons for the Phoenix missiles were judged to be too heavy, complex and unreliable. Some felt that the lack of

The F-111B was an impressive looking aircraft, of vast size and considerable bulk. Expecting it to be carrier-suitable was, in many ways, a triumph of optimism over common sense. Apart from being far too heavy, the aircraft's reliance on spoilers for roll control made it tricky to fly on approach, even in calm weather by day.

ailerons and reliance on spoilers gave insufficient roll control on approach.

Correction of these deficiencies added to airframe weight, with increased internal fuel and new high-lift devices on the wings. Not even a costly Super Weight Improvement Program (incorporated on the fourth and fifth aircraft), and a subsequent, even costlier, Colossal Weight Improvement Program (CWIP) could transform this aircraft into a shipboard interceptor, though the fourth prototype (the first SWIP aircraft) had an empty weight of 43,505 lb (19733 kg) compared with the target weight of 38,804 lb (17601 kg) and the actual weights of the first three F-111Bs (from 46,000 to 47,000 lb/20866 to 21319 kg). The fifth (the second SWIP aircraft) weighed in at 43,478 lb (19721 kg) empty. Empty weights did not tell the full story, and one prototype weighed in at 75,300 lb (34156 kg) during tests, without even being fully laden. This was more than a fully laden Rockwell RA-5C Vigilante, then the Navy's heaviest carrierborne aircraft. Three further weight reduction programmes (CWIP I to

CWIP III) were eventually undertaken, reducing airframe commonality between Air Force and Navy versions from a claimed 84 per cent to an estimated 29 per cent. The Navy even relaxed its requirement to allow the aircraft to fly a CAP with only two missiles, but even this was insufficient to bring the weight to within acceptable limits. The secondary ground-attack role, which envisaged using conventional or nuclear Bullpup missiles and a range of other weapons, was quietly dropped.

Fatal crash

F-111B development was never smooth. The fourth prototype was lost on 21 April 1967 when both engines flamed out at 200 ft (60 m) after take-off. The aircraft crashed, killing pilots Ralph Donnell (the F-111B project pilot) and the recently recruited Charles Wangeman. The four remaining F-111Bs were immediately grounded while the causes of the crash were thoroughly investigated. The DoD's FY68 request for $287 million to fund 20 F-111Bs was denied, and instead Grumman received funding for only eight aircraft ($32.9 million), for test purposes only. On a more positive note, guided trials of the Phoenix missile began in March 1967, with an F-111B flying from Point Mugu for the tests. This made a supersonic Phoenix launch on 18 January 1968. Even more significantly, the fifth F-111B was briefly tested on a dummy carrier deck at Calverton as part of Grumman's Glideslope Controllability Program. Two hundred and sixteen landings were made by seven pilots, five of them 'experts' from the Navy, plus one each from Grumman and General Dynamics.

The same aircraft was then actually taken aboard a carrier by two very brave airmen, who rapidly confirmed that on approach it was all too easy to lose sight of the carrier below the still over-long nose. Lieutenant Commander R. A. Barnes and Lieutenant Roy Buehler of the Naval Flight Test Center flew the fifth F-111B for its first landings and take-offs aboard the USS *Coral Sea* (CV-43), each having only about 12 hours of flying time on the aircraft. Some of the landings were made at weights equivalent to a load of six missiles and several thousand pounds of fuel, while the aircraft lacked the more powerful engines, improved high-

The Mighty Rapier

Once supersonic fighters were in front-line service, with Mach 2 interceptors under development, the USA began looking at developing a new generation of Mach 3 fighters, in anticipation of a growing high-speed bomber threat. As bomber speeds and stand-off range increased, it became increasingly important to intercept them farther and farther from their targets. This implied a very long range for the interceptor itself, with long-range sensors and weapons. In 1955 Northrop,

North American and Lockheed were awarded study contracts to develop Mach 3 interceptors under the designation Weapons System 202.

In June 1957 North American was given a contract to develop its study into an operational fighter, which would be the F-108 Rapier. The aircraft had a fuselage and engine nacelles similar to those of the A3J Vigilante carrierborne bomber but used advanced stainless steel honeycomb construction, and had an enormous double-delta wing, with no

horizontal tail surfaces. The aircraft was effectively a mobile missile launch platform, designed to launch a long-range weapon from a point over 870 nm (1,000 miles; 1610 km) from base, flying at Mach 3 and at altitudes of up to 70,000 ft (21335 m).

The F-108 was cancelled on 23 September 1959, a victim of rising costs and competition from guided missiles. Its Hughes ASG-18 fire control system was saved, however, and Hughes teamed with Lockheed to produce the YF-12, an interceptor derivative of the A-12 reconnaissance aircraft. The company had already

received a Convair B-58 to use as a radar and weapons system testbed, and this was fitted with the ASG-18 radar in a recontoured nose radome, with a new belly pod carrying a GAR-9 missile, tracking and telemetry equipment.

Live firings were made from the YB-58 until the YF-12 itself (which first flew on 7 August 1963) was mature enough to take over. Trials were extraordinarily successful. The first YF-12/GAR-9 firing on 28 September 1965 resulted in a miss distance of only 6 ft 6 in (1.98 m) – after a 36-mile (58-km) flight – while another in April 1966 resulted in a hit. The missile had been fired from a YF-12 travelling at Mach 3.2 at 75,000 ft (22860 m), while the target (a B-47) flew head-on at only 1,500 ft (460 m). The project was formally terminated, on economic grounds, on 1 February 1968. However, essentially the same radar had already found its way into the Douglas Missileer, the naval TFX and eventually the VFX, and the Phoenix missile owed a great deal to the GAR-9, to the extent that the original weapon served as a de facto AIM-54 testbed.

This is the mock-up of the F-108. Due to fly in March 1961, the aircraft was cancelled on 23 September 1959, while still in the mock-up stage. The type would have had virtually the same weapons system as the eventual F-14 Tomcat but with GAR-9 missiles.

This is the F-111B in flight with a full load of AIM-54s. Two were stowed internally, in the capacious weapons bay, with four on complex pylons which swivelled as the wing was swept. From a weapons system point of view the F-111B was just what the Navy wanted, and the AWG-9 was repackaged to form the heart of the lighter F-14.

lift devices and redesigned cockpit then planned for the production F-111B. Press releases made light of the difficulties, and painted the trials as an endorsement of the aircraft's carrier suitability, but behind the scenes the story was different. Deck crews were terrified by the big aircraft, which had an alarming tendency to wallow and to dip its wings on landing. Many felt that landing it on a carrier – even in fine weather – was like waiting for an accident to happen, and few were sanguine that it could ever cope with a pitching, rolling deck. The aircraft then remained overnight aboard the carrier (which was somewhat smaller than the 'Forrestal'-class ships from which it was designed to operate), allowing its deck handling, elevator compatibility and other features to be examined.

The sixth F-111B was the first to be powered by the intended production TF30-P-12 engine (with a reheated rating of 20,250 lb st/90.08 kN), and made its maiden flight on 29 June 1968. This aircraft also had improved high-lift devices.

The F-111B was eventually entirely redesigned on paper, but fortunately more money was not wasted in producing further prototypes. The new design, catchily named Navy II F-111B, reduced airframe commonality with the USAF's F-111A even further. The nose was redesigned, with avionics relocated ahead of the cockpit (giving better access but further reducing forward/downward visibility) to add 2,000 lb (907 kg) of extra fuel behind it. The main gear was moved aft, and the underwing Phoenix pylons were replaced by fixed, non-swivelling pylons under the wing gloves. Weight was better distributed (though not significantly reduced, being estimated at 43,162 lb/ 19619 kg empty for production F-111Bs) and a new canopy, windscreen and raised pilot's seat finally improved the view forward on approach. Although this work represented a major redesign, its effects were limited, and most judged it to be far too little, far too late. The eighth F-111B would have flown with these features incorporated (in January 1970), had it been built.

Death of the F-111B

Most seriously, it became increasingly clear that neither the F-111B nor the Navy II F-111B offered any improvement whatever over the aircraft it was supposed to replace, the F-4 Phantom. Unit cost had tripled from the

original estimates, while the aircraft's eventual carrier suitability was described as being "marginal at best, if ever attained." After a disastrous session in which the CNO, DCNO and Secretary of the Navy were asked to testify to the Senate Armed Services Committee, Admiral Tom Connolly, DCNO (Air), was asked directly, by committee chairman John Stennis, whether the F-111B needed a more powerful engine. "Mr Chairman, all the thrust in Christendom couldn't make a fighter out of that airplane," was Connolly's blunt response. His answer reportedly prevented his promotion to four-star rank, but also killed the F-111B stone dead, after $377.7 million had been spent. The Armed Services Committees of both houses refused to authorise further funding, and on 10 July 1968 the Pentagon issued a stop-work order, agreeing a formal contract termination on 14 December. Work on the seventh prototype (with revised 'Superplow' intakes) continued even after the project's termination. McNamara had by now departed his office to take up the presidency of the World Bank, while the new Secretary of the Navy, Paul Ignatius, was less committed to the F-111B than Paul Nitze, his predecessor, had been. The cease-work order effectively killed the TFX, the notion of commonality, and the F-111B programme, although the US Air Force version of the 'One-eleven' then matured into a potent low-level, long-range bomber. In 1968, though, it was a major blow to General Dynamics, coming hard on the heels of the cancellation of an RAF order for the aircraft.

Some of the F-111Bs remained in use: nos 2 and 3 flew as development aircraft for the AIM-54 Phoenix missile and

An AIM-54 test round is seen on the inboard underwing pylon of one of the F-111Bs. The missile was developed directly from the XAAM-M-10 Eagle designed for the Douglas Missileer. Continuing intensive development during the F-111B programme meant that the weapon was fairly mature by the time the F-14 arrived on the scene.

the AN/AWG-9 weapons system, and no. 1 was used for barrier engagement trials at Lakehurst before scrapping in December 1969. The no. 2 F-111B crashed into the Pacific on 11 September 1968, killing Hughes pilot Barton Warren and his RIO, Anthony Byland. The no. 5 aircraft was damaged beyond repair in a heavy landing exactly one month later. By the time the last aircraft were retired from the programme in May 1971, three had crashed, at the cost of four aircrew killed. The final three survivors were unceremoniously relegated to various naval airfield dumps. The F-111B development programme was estimated to have cost at least $251.1 million, with another $352 million spent on the AIM-54.

Many people were surprised by the cancellation, having listened to the optimistic noises made in the Department of Defense. Others were surprised only that it had taken so long. Shortly before the cancellation, Senator Robert McClellan made a speech to the Senate, in which he pointed out that "for more than five years, notwithstanding the known difficulties associated with this 'commonality concept' and the major inadequacies in performance, the Defense Department, year after year, gave reassurances about the future successful development of the Navy plane. It contended that the aircraft's admitted deficiencies had either been or were in the process of being corrected. Those reassurances have not materialised; those prophecies have not been fulfilled. It is now conclusive that all of the tinkering, fixing, engineering patching and the exorbitant spending of funds for research and development have not produced a Navy plane that is capable of performing the combat missions required by the Navy. In fact, the plane so far produced is not even carrier suitable." He concluded with the hope that "in the future, critical problems will be resolved with less arbitrariness and that the judgement of experts in the military and in the field of aviation will be given proper consideration and greater weight in the making of judgements involving national defence and security."

The Navy's requirement remains

Although the F-111B was entirely discredited, it was clear that the US Navy still needed a new fighter to serve aboard its carriers. By 1969 the F-8 had been in service for 11 years, and the Phantom nine, and both were regarded as approaching obsolescence. A memorandum from Admiral Thomas Moorer, Chairman of the JCS, to the Secretary of the Navy pointed this out, along with the fact that the Soviets had introduced eight new fighter types during the same period, four of which had superior performance to the F-4. Moreover, it was highlighted that the F-4 had only achieved a 1:1 kill ratio against the older model MiG-21s encountered in Vietnam, and that it would "almost certainly not be adequate" against late model MiG-21s and newer Soviet fighters. Moorer candidly admitted that, "Its performance in aerial combat became marginal with respect to the MiG-21 just before the bombing pause...The ratio of MiG-21s downed by F-4s diminished sharply between April 1966 and August 1967. Since then the F-4 has had a 1:1 kill ratio against the older MiG-21s. In a confrontation with late model MiG-21s, and particularly against the newer USSR fighters, the F-4J would be inadequate."

He also drew the Secretary's attention to other weapons systems designed to attack naval targets, including 'Badger' and 'Blinder' bombers armed with five types of stand-off missile and a range of surface-to-surface missiles deployed on ships and submarines. "We must have a new fighter superior in air combat to present and postulated Soviet fighters, for close-in visual encounters and for stand-off

The Phoenix Skywarriors

The A-3 Skywarrior played a major role in the development of the Tomcat's weapons system. An NRA-3B (144825) was modified by Grumman in 1960 with a huge bulbous nose radome to carry the AN/AWG-9 radar and AAM-N-10 missiles of the Missileer, with a huge bulbous nose radome. This aircraft was augmented by two NA-3As (135411 and 135427), another NRA-3B (142667) and a TA-3B (144867). These aircraft were operated by the PMTC at Point Mugu, and were also bailed at various times to Grumman and Hughes. One of the NA-3As (135427) was fitted with the radome of the F-111B in 1964, and had missile pylons fitted alongside the weapons bay. This aircraft became the Primary Phoenix Missile System testbed, and the TA-3B (144867) became a Phoenix Missile System testbed later in the programme, flying with an F-14-type radome. This aircraft subsequently became the testbed for the F-14D's APG-71 and was bailed to Grumman from March 1985. These examples were not the only A-3s closely associated with the F-14 development programme; tankers of VAK-208 lent tanker support above and beyond that provided by Grumman's own four A-6s.

One of the Douglas NA-3A Skywarriors lets fly with an AIM-54 Phoenix, watched (from a discreet distance) by a Grumman F9F chase plane. This aircraft (BuNo. 135427) was fitted with an F-111B radome and radar, and became the Primary Phoenix Missile System testbed. The Phoenix programme was an ambitious step into the unknown for Hughes, but was ultimately successful.

Left: With the failure of the F-111B, the F-14 was accorded a very high priority, and the need to replace the F-4 was seen as being most urgent. A large fleet of development F-14s was funded, in order to speed development and to achieve the earliest possible in-service date. Most of the prototypes carried large areas of Dayglo to increase conspicuity and enhance optical tracking by ground-based observers.

Below: The No. 17 aircraft is seen here landing aboard the USS Enterprise (CVAN-65) during carrier qualification trials by the Naval Air Test Center, based at NAS Patuxent River. Ranged on the deck is a pair of Lockheed T-1A SeaStars, navalised, carrier-capable derivatives of the T-33 Shooting Star.

all-weather conditions. In addition, the new fighter must be able to defeat the enemy air threats to naval forces: bombers and missiles. The threat is serious now. It will become more serious in the future. We are already very late with a new fighter programme to counter superior Soviet capabilities. The F-14/Phoenix system will meet our fighter needs through the 1970s and into the 1980s. Delay in the present funding profile will seriously delay achieving the required high capability as well as raise programme costs markedly.

"Advanced Soviet surface-to-surface and air-to-surface missile threats already exist. They will certainly become more advanced. New 'Foxbat', 'Fiddler' and 'Flagon' fighters have long-range escort capabilities with advanced avionics and missiles, adding to the threat. Advanced Soviet fighters are expected to be armed with missiles of greater range than US missiles except Phoenix. We must be able to counter the full present and future threat, not the past. New missiles are the weapons of concern; they must be countered.

"The F-14 is designed for air superiority, and is the weapon system that can destroy long-range, multiple-raid targets, aircraft and missiles. It can destroy enemy escort fighters in close-in combat."

F-14 genesis

In October 1967, at the height of the war in Vietnam, Grumman had proposed that an entirely new airframe be developed to accommodate the avionics, missile, engines and weapon system of the discredited F-111B. The company found no resistance from the Navy, which was heartily sick of the F-111B but had no real problem with its weapons and systems. The Vietnam experience had subtly changed the Navy's perception of what it required from a new fighter. A pure bomber-destroyer in the mould of the Missileer or F-111B was no longer required; instead, a fighter capable of dealing with the same threats would also have to deal with an agile fighter threat. Grumman started by designing and building (at its own expense) a new wing box of welded titanium, designed for an optimised naval fighter. It was the largest electron beam-welded titanium structure fabricated up to that time, incorporating 45 machined parts and using 100 welds. A new airframe offered opportunities to save weight and to optimise the

design for agility, acceleration and high roll rates; and to carry the right amount of fuel for the naval role rather than the Air Force's interdictor mission. The new airframe promised to be vastly superior to the F-111B in all regimes. Although some suggested that the F-4 could be improved to make it equal in performance to the proposed F-14 (then still more properly known by its VFX acronym), the Navy pointed out that this would be impossible without a major redesign costing millions of dollars, and that it would result in an aircraft which would still be inferior to the latest Soviet fighters. As an aircraft designed to destroy high-altitude bombers, many doubted that the McDonnell F-4 Phantom could ever be agile enough for air superiority close-in combat.

Three Tomcat prototypes in flight show three different wing sweep angles and some of the different colour schemes applied to the pre-production batch. The aircraft nearest the camera was the 12th prototype, redesignated Tomcat 1X and used to replace the first prototype, especially in expanding the upper end of the performance envelope. Aircraft 4 was used primarily for AWG-9/AIM-54 system integration, and aircraft 2 leads the formation.

In this busy scene of the flight test shed at Calverton, the aircraft nearest the camera was being used for aerodynamic trials, and was broadly representative of the initial production configuration. The large fleet of prototypes allowed much testing to be conducted in parallel, while the use of inflight refuelling and telemetry squeezed the maximum benefit from every sortie.

Others thought that the aircraft needed by the US Navy would be an even more direct antithesis of the heavyweight F-111B and a more direct replacement for the lightweight, agile and relatively unsophisticated F-8 Crusader. The USAF's lightweight fighter 'Mafia' already had its followers in the Navy, who wanted a light, agile, cheap and uncomplicated fighter. Some even wanted the new fighter to return to the single-seat configuration of the F-8. Former F-4 aircrew and VFX adherents like Admiral Moorer countered the single-seat case by pointing out that although there was "a weight and cost penalty associated with the requirement for two men, these disadvantages were more than offset by the much greater capability of the two-man airplane, particularly under adverse conditions. Today, electronic warfare developments have made the tactical environment much more demanding, re-emphasising the necessity for a two-man crew. F-4 and A-6 experience in Southeast Asia has confirmed that the help provided by the second man with his sensors is invaluable." The insistence on a second seat, and the absolute necessity for all-weather capability and carrier operation, meant that the VFX was never going to be an agile lightweight in the F-16/YF-17 sense of the word, but there was a perception that a larger aircraft could share many of the same attributes. Any carrier aircraft has to be able to withstand the stresses of catapult launch and arrested landings, and has to have heavy tailhook and tie-down points, so it will inevitably be heavier than an equivalent land-based aircraft. The more far-sighted observers understood that the VFX could share many lightweight fighter attributes, especially agility and acceleration, given the right airframe and engines.

Moorer refuted the size/weight argument by saying, "The F-14 is that kind of aircraft to the extent that it will be highly manoeuvrable, and, while it will have a sophisticated weapons control system, it will also have a higher degree of reliability, manoeuvrability and weapons versatility than we have ever achieved. The key to a good fighter is to have a balanced, well-proportioned aircraft with a good thrust-to-weight ratio to provide high speed, good range, outstanding acceleration and the aerodynamic characteristics to ensure the best possible manoeuvrability. These attributes are essential to beat the enemy. The 'lightweight is better than heavyweight' argument is irrelevant and largely untrue. When the F4U Corsair was developed, there was no decision to build a heavier fighter. Rather, an aircraft was designed to meet the needs of a possible war in the Pacific; that is, an aircraft with range and high performance. The result was a fighter heavier than had ever been seen before, anywhere. It also had a longer service life than any other fighter. The F8F, on the other

Tomcat 1X was built as Tomcat 12 but was rushed into the air to replace the first aircraft, flying on 30 August 1971, a mere eight months after Tomcat 1's crash. The aircraft is seen here with its wings fully swept, in clean configuration. High-speed testing was one of the responsibilities assigned to 1X. The original shape of the 'beaver tail' between the engines is noteworthy.

hand, was developed to out-duel the Japanese Zero. Even though it was a 'pilot's dream' it had little potential and a short service life." Moorer was being somewhat disingenuous, since the lightweight F6F Hellcat (let alone the F8F Bearcat) was, despite the hype, a far better (and more successful) fighter than the ponderous F4U. The Hellcat outlasted the Corsair in the fighter role, but not in the fighter-bomber role to which the F4U was relegated at the dawn of the jet age. It was, nevertheless, a convincing argument, although it is interesting to note that a fully armed F-14 has about the same total weight as a wartime B-24 Liberator bomber.

A new airframe for the old system

Concentrating on the design of the VFX airframe was a sensible step for Grumman, since there was nothing inherently wrong with the F-111B's weapons or radar, and no-one could have predicted how insoluble the TF30 engine's problems would prove to be. The original AWG-9 demonstrated a simultaneous AIM-54 Phoenix dual kill capability as early as March 1969, destroying two widely spaced drone targets. By May 1970, 29 Phoenixes had been fired from the F-111Bs and some of the fleet of five modified Skywarriors used in support of the F-111B programme. Twenty-two of the missiles scored direct hits, passed within lethal distance or otherwise successfully met their test objectives. One Phoenix had already hit a target 68 nm (78 miles; 125 km) from the launch point. The test Skywarriors were particularly important in these trials, launching the first unguided Phoenix on 27 April 1966 and conducting the first guided test on 12 May the same year. Between its use in the F-111B installation and the installation for the new VFX proposal, the AN/AWG-9 had picked up new fighter-attack modes to give enhanced dogfight capability, and had gained in flexibility while simultaneously losing a staggering 660 lb (300 kg) in weight. The new 1,340-lb (608-kg) radar-based fire-control system eventually took to the air in a modified TA-3B Skywarrior during April 1970. This weight reduction took total F-14/AWG-9 system weight to within 1 per cent of the estimated weight of an F-14 fitted with the considerably less capable upgraded digital version of the F-4J's AWG-10, and maintained unit cost at 110 per cent of such an aircraft. Radar system volume was reduced from 46 to 30 cu ft (1.3 to 0.85 m³).

Radar development did more than produce a smaller and lighter fire-control system. More extensive use was made of micro-circuitry, and the new radar used a new gridded travelling wave tube which reduced modulator requirements and boosted power output. The fire-control system controls had to be reconfigured for use in the F-14's

tandem cockpits. The higher-g environment demanded simplification and relocation of the backseater's hand controls, but the main Phoenix displays from the F-111B were retained. They comprised a 5-in (127-mm) multi-mode detail data display, presenting raw Doppler radar or infra-red images, with a 10-in (254-mm) CRT display giving tactical information and including the computer's recommended target priorities.

Moreover, the Tomcat's AWG-9 incorporated a passive infra-red search and acquisition system gimbal-mounted in an undernose chin pod. This could gather sufficient information (including rough range data) to allow a Phoenix or Sidewinder to be fired without the radar. The system could work independently or be slaved to slew with the radar, allowing the F-14 crew to search one volume of airspace with radar and another with the IRST. When slaved to the radar, the IRST gives a high-definition picture of a narrow slice of the total radar view, its higher resolution permitting better target discrimination. Radar system changes for the F-14 cost $129 million, of a total R&D bill for the AWG-9 and Phoenix of $414 million. These changes included the addition of new modes and hardware to make the radar fully compatible with the AIM-7 Sparrow and AIM-9 Sidewinder.

RFP issued

The Grumman proposal came just as the Navy was restating its requirement for a fleet interceptor. The VFX-1 requirement was formulated around the new design, with the contemporary VFX-2 requirement describing the same

This head-on view shows one of the prototypes (probably Tomcat 5, the systems instrumentation test aircraft) high above the Atlantic. The F-14 was designed to be agile as well as long-ranged, to be a fighter as well as a long-range interceptor. Despite its large size, the F-14 is a surprisingly graceful aircraft, conforming to the old adage: 'If it looks right...' Certainly the F-14 has always been popular with its pilots, who defend its reputation with an almost aggressive loyalty.

Inset above: BuNo. 158613 was the 14th Tomcat built, and served as part of the 19-aircraft development fleet. It is seen here in normal balanced flight, with both wings swept forward.

Right: The 24th Tomcat (BuNo. 158623) was delivered to the US Navy's West Coast Tomcat training squadron, VF-124, in October 1972. The aircraft was delivered with an 'Anytime, Baby' decal on its pylons.

Main picture above: The presence of a star and bar on both wings led some to believe that this was a cleverly-faked piece of photographic trickery, but in fact the photo really does show Tomcat 3 with its wings swept differentially, with the starboard wing locked fully forward, and the port wing swept fully aft. This was a deliberate test, undertaken as part of a series of six asymmetric wing sweep trials conducted between 19 December 1985 and 28 February 1986. Landings were made with the aft-swept wing at up to 60°, but not at 68°. The trial was flown after four fleet aircraft found themselves in this predicament.

aircraft with advanced-technology engines. Fighter Study II compared VFX-1 and VFX-2 with the existing F-111B and with the proposed Navy II F-111B, but there was simply no contest. Even the modest VFX-1 promised to better the F-4 by the same margin that the F-4 out-performed the Navy II F-111B.

VFX go-ahead

Go-ahead for the VFX programme was given simultaneously with the cancellation of the naval TFX, and in a pleasing piece of symmetry the F-14 emerged from the ashes of the F-111B programme. But there had to be evidence of competition, so the Navy could not simply turn to Grumman and say, "Right, we like that. Build us a production version of your VFX." Other companies were eager for a production order, and had to be given the chance to submit their own designs. When a Request for Proposals (RFP) went out to the aerospace industry on 21 June 1968, calling for a two-seat, twin-engined, Phoenix-armed carrier interceptor, North American, LTV, McDonnell and General Dynamics all submitted designs. The McDonnell submission was the Model 225 (in 225A and 225D forms for

the VFX-1 and -2 requirements respectively), although the company was also still promoting the swing-wing F-4J(FV)S Phantom which had been proposed as an alternative to the F-111B. This mated a new shoulder-mounted variable-geometry wing and enlarged, zero-dihedral tailplane to the airframe of the F-4J. The new version had 59 per cent parts commonality with the basic Phantom but offered a new level of capability. (That aircraft was described in detail in *McDonnell F-4 Phantom – Spirit in the Skies*, Aerospace Publishing, 1992). The various proposals were submitted on 1 October, and were then reviewed between 1 October and 10 December. On 17 December 1968, Admiral I. J. Galantin, the Source Selection Authority and Chief of Naval Material, announced that the submissions by Grumman and McDonnell had been selected for final consideration. Further refinements were incorporated into the two companies' proposals before they were submitted to Naval Systems Command in early January 1969.

The two successful McDonnell Model 225 variants were both similar in appearance to the later F-15 Eagle, albeit with a low-set variable-geometry wing, tandem cockpits, and shorter, broader-chord, slightly canted twin tailfins. This was an unusual feature, since the Grumman VFX submission then still featured a single tailfin, as did the General Dynamics, North American and Vought proposals. The Tomcat's adoption of twin fins came very late – the F-14 mock-up was originally built with a single fin. The cockpits were covered by heavily-framed canopies, reminiscent of the Phantom's.

Grumman's long record of development with the XF10F-1 Jaguar, F11F-1 Tiger and F-111B gave the manufacturer – long the US Navy's key supplier of carrier-based warplanes – a significant advantage over any other manufacturer who might want to produce a new-generation fighter/interceptor for the US Navy, especially one using a VG wing. Grumman's Design 303 was always considered to be a front-runner in the VFX competition. A VG wing was regarded as being absolutely

essential in order to combine benign approach, agility, high-speed and acceleration characteristics. Grumman chose a fully variable swing wing that was able to withstand high *g* at each wing sweep setting, and was able to sweep quickly from position to position without unduly affecting stability. Grumman got the automatic sweep so right that crews seldom use the manual wing-sweep selector option, except for parade-type formation flying or for inflight refuelling. Automatic wing sweep is even used for air-to-air gunnery. The ability to sweep the wing gives rapid acceleration, even with the original TF30 engine, and with wings swept the wing loading is very low. NASA demonstrated that the aircraft could fly safely with one wing locked fully forward, and with the other in any sweep position. Test pilot Chuck Sewell was reported to be "sanguine that a carrier landing approach could be made safely in a 20/68° configuration of asymmetry."

Front-line crews are less optimistic about such severe conditions of asymmetry. "Despite what a test pilot might say over beer, I am not going to land a 20/68° split wing bird on the boat, EVER. I'm either diverting, or going swimming," said one current F-14 pilot. Remarkably, though, even he acknowledged the real possibility of landing an aircraft at a ground airfield with such an out-of-balance configuration.

Grumman's winning design

Although the LTV, GD, McDonnell and Grumman VFX contenders featured VG wings, Grumman did also look at a more conventional design (the Design 303F), using boundary-layer control and huge double-slotted flaps to obtain the necessary slow-speed, take-off and landing performance. This aircraft would have been about 4,900 lb (2225 kg) heavier than the F-14 as built, and was unable to meet the US Navy's requirement when carrying six Phoenix missiles.

The Grumman design was built around a simple box-construction fuselage giving strength and low weight, with extensive use of titanium to maximise weight savings. The fuselage was designed as a lifting body to augment the lift generated by the wings, but contained a large internal fuel load for maximum range/endurance performance. The engines were housed in widely separated pods, which allowed the use of simple straight-through intakes and inlet ducts and provided the best possible access to the powerplants. They also left a large area free for the carriage of stores, and moved the wing pivots farther outboard. The engines were designed to be removed rearwards without jacking the aircraft, or from the side by jacking only one main gear unit.

Design 303 was primarily designed as an air superiority fighter for use in the fighter sweep and escort roles. Then-Commander L. S. 'Scotty' Lamoreaux outlined the requirement in 1970. "Although it still retains some growth potential, the F-4 will not have the manoeuvrability to fight the new fighters the Russians have developed during the last decade. The MiG-21 'Fishbed' has been exported to satellite countries, and has manoeuvrability better than our F-4. The Su-11 [sic] 'Flagon' has an all-weather, long-range advanced fire control system and a deadly air-to-air capability. The MiG-23 [sic] 'Foxbat' is a new high-performance fighter with speed and altitude performance exceeding the Phantom's. In addition, air-to-surface missiles carried by 'Blinder' and 'Badger' bombers can be launched from stand-off ranges of up to 150 miles (240 km). Soviet warships and shore installations are equipped with both surface-to-surface and surface-to-

Above: Tomcat 11 was used for deck trials aboard the USS Independence. They were conducted while the carrier was laid-up in port, and involved no flying operations. The aircraft was, however, taxied and towed around the deck, positioned on the catapults, and moved down to the hangar deck via the carrier's elevators.

Tomcat 11 is seen here being hoisted aboard the Independence for deck compatibility testing. This took place on 22 March 1972, and was attended by Congressional sceptics and the press. The F-14 was going through a bad patch in terms of political hostility, and Grumman and the Navy were eager to give the impression that the aircraft was close to being ready for service, and suitable for carrier use. A high-profile event which would result in photos of a Tomcat on a carrier was felt to be just what the doctor ordered.

air missiles, an ever-present threat to our ships and aircraft. We won the air war in Vietnam with the F-4 Phantom and the F-8 Crusader – mainly due to the skill of our pilots. Today, advances in Soviet technology are rapidly closing the gap. The time has come to provide our air wings with a fighter designed from scratch for air superiority."

High performance and agility were stressed, with modern avionics suitable for the detection and engagement of targets at long and short ranges. The F-14 was therefore originally drawn up around a basic armament of four AIM-7 missiles and a 20-mm gun, with the AIM-9 and AIM-54 considered only as secondary options. Interestingly, the Tomcat carried a smaller load than either the F6D Missileer or the F-111B, with six instead of eight AIM-54s. The AIM-54 Phoenix steadily grew in importance, especially after the development of low-drag pallet carriage for the big missiles. These removable pallets contained all fleet air defence role equipment, in addition to all AIM-54-specific systems, and were designed to be loaded or unloaded very quickly. Lamoreaux claimed that the aircraft could be loaded "with six Phoenix missiles in 18 minutes with standard Aero 21A skids." The impact of Phoenix compatibility on the aircraft's capabilities was therefore minimised in the basic fighter role. The aircraft was designed as a multi-role aircraft, but most emphasis was placed on the primary air superiority role. This was reflected in the importance that Grumman placed on the provision of a one-piece bubble canopy, which aimed to give the pilot and missile control officer (as he was then called) the best possible all-around field of vision. The view

forward was also stressed, to give the frontseater the best possible approach picture. Grumman pointed out that the A-6 had set a fleet record of over 22,000 accident-free carrier landings, attributing this in no small measure to the excellent view from the Intruder's cockpit.

Tomcat versatility

In his 1969 memo to the Secretary of the Navy, Admiral Moorer stated: "Navy aircraft are designed to meet one primary task. But fighters are also used for fleet defence and for air-to-surface attack as additional tasks. Long experience has shown this plan to be sound, effective and efficient. It provides a tactical commander with greater choice and flexibility. As a battle or conflict progresses, needs constantly change: initially the requirement may be for large numbers of fighters, later for large numbers of attackers. Once air superiority is attained only a portion of the fighters are required for air defence. Fighters with an air-to-ground feature are effectively used in the destruction of many targets. Weight-reducing micro-miniaturisation of avionics, balanced by airframe and engine design, has eliminated performance penalties previously associated with multi-mission fighters. In the F-14, 1 per cent of aircraft weight makes it possible to use Phoenix, Sparrow, Sidewinder Agile, a gun and air-to-surface weapons. A large part of that weight is in removable pallets not fitted for the dogfight configuration."

The fleet air defence role, using six AIM-54s, was originally considered to be a subsidiary role, to be achieved without degrading fighter performance for the basic air

The fighter that nearly broke Grumman

The Tomcat's career has been dogged by problems – financial, technical and political. The cost of the aircraft almost led to cancellation on several occasions, and the original plan to procure 722 F-14s was soon downscaled to 301. This actually did little to silence the Tomcat's critics, since, although it reduced total programme cost by 38 per cent, unit cost rose by 43 per cent. Many observers chose to regard this as scandalous. This hike in the unit cost was, of course, a direct result of having to spread the $1.4 billion R&D cost and the almost constant infrastructure and support equipment costs over a smaller total number of aircraft. In fact, cost increases in the F-14 programme were not out of line for a new advanced-technology fighter. Each new fighter programme experienced similar cost growth during the same period. Charges of excessive costs were easily made by detractors or outright opponents, and there were plenty of those. Unfortunately, they were readily believed by media which were willing to seize the cudgel with a vengeance.

There was no smoke without fire, however, and a tight, fixed-price incentive fee R&D contract conspired with raging inflation to destroy the manufacturer's profits on the programme; at one stage, Grumman was losing $1 million on each Tomcat it delivered. Failure to agree a revised price at one stage left FY74 contracts unsigned, and Grumman, faced with bankruptcy, threatened to cease production and to

not deliver Lot V aircraft at all.

The root cause of Grumman's financial difficulties with the F-14 was not the array of technical difficulties that the aircraft suffered (which were no worse than those suffered by other contemporary programmes). The problem lay in the tight fixed-price contract negotiated during the company's boom years in the 1960s, which proved unrealistic in the harsher economic climate of the early 1970s.

Lewis Scott Lamoreaux, former Phantom squadron commander and VFX (F-14) Program Co-ordinator at CNO, who later was employed by Hughes to support the F-14 programme, explained the disadvantages of the contract system used: "This was a difficult way to produce a complex aircraft that is undergoing constant changes in specification and configuration during the formative R&D phase of the contract. The fixed-price R&D contract was widely used and widely condemned, but little has been done to change the practice. Additionally, the contract stipulated an inflation rate that was far below the actual rate experienced at the time. The crisis was not that the cost had escalated that much, but that it had escalated to a point that exceeded Grumman's contract ceiling price, which had allowed only a 10 per cent profit. When the inflation rate gap was subtracted from the profit it did not take much of a price increase to put Grumman into a loss position well below ceiling. The result was that Grumman was forced into a position

where it actually lost money on every aircraft delivered." The target price for the F-14 R&D contract was $388 million, consisting of a target cost of $352.8 million and a target profit of $35.3 million. Ceiling price was set at $440.9 million (125 per cent of target cost), with ceiling price options for seven additional production lots. Penalties were detailed for failure to meet certain performance parameters, and for late delivery of trials aircraft.

The fixed-price contract signed in January 1969 was part of a 'total package' instituted by Robert McNamara, other elements of which were quickly discarded. Although Grumman made a small profit on the first 38 aircraft from Lots I-III, it had been warning that the contract should be renegotiated late in 1969, and general inflation had steadily increased until it was 5 per cent higher than the most pessimistic predictions when the contract had been signed. Other costs had risen even more sharply, the cost of titanium, for example, having risen by between 40 and 50 per cent. (The F-14 used a higher proportion of titanium in its construction than any other aircraft, with the exception of the SR-71.)

The contract was a severe one for both parties, with Grumman given the option to refuse deliveries if funding was not received at specific key dates. The US Navy could have fallen foul of the contract when it had to delay payment for the six aircraft of Lot II by three months. In the event, Grumman chose to honour its side of the contract despite the delay. The

Navy's inability to pay this 'bill' on time reflected a wider problem. Grumman felt that it was not receiving the high-priority funds which had been stipulated, while the company's other programmes had been cut back far more radically than could have been reasonably expected, dramatically reducing the stability of the company's business base. Navy projections had, for example, led Grumman to expect that it would be producing three A-6s per month, whereas in the lean times of 1971 it actually produced only one per month.

After what the Navy chose to see as informal warnings, the company formally notified the Navy that it could not fulfil the Lot IV contract on 1 April 1971, despite closing down 250,000 sq ft (23225 m²) of office and manufacturing space, and slashing the workforce from 36,000 to 26,000. The man-hours required for the F-14 did not rise, but inflation and other factors outside the control of the company had made the original contract impracticable. The number of man-hours required for the F-14 programme were within 1.5 per cent of Grumman's initial estimates, but the cost of those man-hours escalated steadily.

Legally, however, the $806 million price for the FY 1972 buy of 48 aircraft forming Lot IV was binding (as long as the US Navy exercised its option by 1 October 1971). Grumman estimated that at least $35 million extra would be required simply to avoid making a loss on the batch.

For a while it looked as though Congressional opposition to the F-14 might prevent the Navy from placing

Above: The F-14's ability to carry six AIM-54s made it a considerably more useful carrierborne interceptor than any F-4 variant. The mighty Phantom could carry only four BVR weapons, and these were, in any case, the medium-range AIM-7 Sparrow. To the Navy, the Tomcat represented a bargain, almost regardless of its price tag. The aircraft meant survival for the carrier and was a priority programme.

A pair of unmarked early F-14As is seen prior to its delivery to the US Navy. Pilots loved the aircraft, but every early F-14 produced under the original fixed-price contract represented a major financial loss to the manufacturer.

an order for the full 48 aircraft, and a rearguard action was prepared to justify a buy of 28 F-14As in FY 72. This was judged to be the minimum number required to equip an initial carrier air group.

In the end, Grumman accepted the Lot IV contract, which was nearly lost when hostile Senators attempted to remove $806 million from the 1971 procurement allocations, and the Navy ordered the full 48 aircraft. Negotiations on the cost of the Lot III and Lot IV aircraft continued into 1972, when Grumman was estimating a $110 million loss on the production of the first 86 aircraft. The overall programme loss was only $65 million when profits from research and development were taken into consideration, however.

With the Navy set to order 48 more F-14s in Lot V under FY73 (and with 88 more planned for Lot VI/FY74 and 91 more for Lot VII/FY75), Grumman warned that a US Navy exercise of its Lot V option would actually put the company out

of business, and again requested a contract renegotiation. It estimated a total loss of $405 million if the Navy went ahead with its full planned procurement, which then stood at 313 aircraft, and actually claimed to have made a $21.7 million loss on Lot I, a $2.9 million profit on Lot II, a $1.5 million loss on Lot III and a $45 million loss on Lot IV.

Grumman was in deep financial trouble with the F-14 programme. E. Clinton Towl, Grumman Corporation's board chairman, told the Senate's tactical air power sub-committee that, "if the Government exercises Lot V, we will close our doors. There is no other way." He revealed that Grumman's leading bankers had refused to extend the company's unsecured line of credit until the F-14 pricing problem was resolved in a way which "will not impair the financial viability of your company." Towl estimated that the company would require an additional $545 million to complete production of the remaining 227

Tomcats, this including a $140 million fee for Grumman, but still leaving the company with an overall programme loss of $23 million. This would have been 20 per cent higher than the original $2.4 billion ceiling, and raised programme unit cost of each F-14 from $16.8 million to $19 million.

Lot V was the last production batch funded under the original arrangements, after which the Navy handled procurement through separate annual contracts. The batch consisted of 48 aircraft (although long lead-time items for Lot VI were also included) and cost $570.1 million. It brought production to 134 aircraft. Although Lots VI and VII were actually cancelled, the DoD had already directed the Navy to prepare a System Acquisition Report covering the procurement of 48 aircraft from each of what would have been the cancelled Lots, bringing planned production to 240 aircraft. Even then, Grumman was asked to prepare unit cost details

based on a total of 722 F-14s. The programme was back on track.

A compromise was reached in March 1973, under which Grumman accepted the fixed-price contract for the first 134 aircraft (thereby accepting what was agreed to be a $220 million loss). In return the US Navy agreed to renegotiate the price of follow-on orders and to provide a $200 million loan to tide the company over. This loan was terminated when it was discovered that Grumman had invested the money in short-term securities to net a profit of $2.8 million, a reasonable enough step since Grumman could not spend the funding immediately but intended to use it to settle bills as they came due. Fortunately, the Iranian Melli bank stepped in with $75 million, and this gesture of confidence persuaded a syndicate of nine US banks to loan the remainder of the money. Finally, Grumman started to see profits again, and in 1975 even the F-14 began to net a profit!

Forging the Tomcat

Above: Tomcats 46, 47, 48, 49, 53 and 54 line up on the Calverton ramp, awaiting delivery to the US Navy. Early F-14As were delivered in much the same glossy gull grey and white colour scheme as was worn by the F-4 Phantom and F-8 Crusader, and early squadron markings were gaudy and large.

Below: If the tailhook or arrester wire break, the F-14 pilot is faced with a simple choice – to overshoot or to take the barrier. Although designed to stop an aircraft with minimal damage, a barrier engagement inevitably causes minor damage, and barrier trials are a necessary prelude to the aircraft entering service.

superiority mission. The role was defined as defending a carrier task force through maintenance of a long-range CAP or by reacting to a threat with a quick-reaction deck-launched intercept. It required a long loiter time, good supersonic dash capability and the ability to cover distances quickly. Air-to-surface attack would be a secondary role, with the Navy requiring an A-7E level of capability without degrading performance in the fighter role. Rapid conversion to and from all roles was specified.

The F-14's payload/range capability gave it an enormous latent multi-role capability, and one of the tragedies of the aircraft has been the US Navy's failure to exploit this. In the period 1969-71, things looked different, and Grumman was keen to promote a variety of multi-role options. One favourite option was to 'expand the capability base of the F-14 through Podularisation', using a real-time reconnaissance strike pod (rather than alteration or replacement of internal components and/or structure) to house the necessary sensors and avionics. The pod envisaged by Grumman would have contained FLIR, LLLTV, laser designators and TISEO, giving a degree of day/night all-weather attack and reconnaissance capability. Grumman hoped that the use of such a pod might lead to the adoption of an air wing with three F-14 squadrons, in

which the aircraft acted as multi-role fighter-bombers.

The intention was that the aircraft should be able to return to the primary air superiority role from either fleet air defence or attack duties immediately after release of its air-to-ground or fleet air defence ordnance. Carriage of the Phoenix was regarded as an overload, and reduced load factor limits from 6.5 g to 6 g when carried, thereby saving weight and cost, while retaining agility in the basic air superiority configuration. The 0.5 g reduction when carrying the AIM-54 was insignificant, since the fleet air defence role did not call for high-g manoeuvring. The F-14 was not designed with any one specific parameter emphasised. Instead, the aircraft was a carefully balanced combination of parameters. Moorer explained that, "A high-performance fighter should be judged as a 'balanced' weapons system, and the overemphasis of any single parameter can lead to erroneous conclusions as to relative merit. For example, maximising thrust to weight leads to a rocket-like solution; maximising low wing-loading leads to a glider; maximising visibility leads to a slow observation platform; and maximising speed and altitude leads to interceptor-like performance. A comparison and evaluation of tactical fighter capability is at best extremely complex, and requires insight and experience in the balance of total weapon system parameters."

Design team

No aircraft is ever 'designed' by one person. Too many disciplines are harnessed, too many conflicting demands reconciled. A modern warplane is the creation of many minds. Many people contributed to design work on the F-14 Tomcat. Larry Mead, better known for his work on the Intruder, played a vital role, as did engineering manager Bob Kress and pilot/deputy programme manager Joe Rees. In his book on the F-14, Rear Admiral Paul T. Gillcrist particularly lauded Bob Kress: "More than any other single person, he is the one who came up with the unique combination of elements: the AWG-9 weapons system, the variable-geometry wing design, the twin turbofan engines and the unique tandem-seat airframe design." In the US Navy, then-Commander Scott Lamoreaux was OPNAV programme co-ordinator from 1968 to 1972, when he became Commander Fleet Air at Miramar, ready to oversee fleet introduction of the aircraft. Commander Mike Ames was the BuWeps Program Manager.

Despite this, it remains true that to an uncommon extent the Grumman F-14 Tomcat is the brainchild and offspring of a single man – Mike Pelehach, who became Grumman's vice president and F-14 programme director. By the time he became project director for the future Tomcat, then called VFX, in September 1968, Pelehach had amassed years of solid experience, ideally suiting him to the task of developing a new carrier aircraft for the United States Navy. Pelehach had spent 26 years in aircraft system design and analysis, 18 of them with Grumman, and had been a key player in developing the F11F-1 Tiger, the A2F-1 Intruder and the ill-fated F-111B. By September 1969, Pelehach's engineers had settled on the definitive Design 303E and began transforming it from blueprint to actual aircraft. Although Grumman had extensive experience in integrating the Pratt & Whitney TF30-P-12 engine into the F-111B, more than four years of further engineering and wind tunnel work went into developing the F-14 air inlet and exhaust nozzle system.

McDonnell's Model 225 was deemed 'acceptable', but the Grumman Design 303 was preferred. Unfortunately, Grumman's bid for the contract was a massive $400 million higher than McDonnell's, and at the Navy's request Grumman reduced its bid to within a 'mere' $100 million of its competitor. This was enough, although it is interesting to note that Grumman's early $367-410 million losses on the F-14 were similar to the amount by which it had reduced its VFX bid. Grumman's design was selected in preference to the McDonnell submission, and this selection was then reviewed and approved by the Chief of Naval Operations, the Secretary of the Navy and the Secretary of Defense.

Grumman wins VFX

On 14 January 1969 a development contract was awarded, covering six prototypes and providing for the subsequent purchase of 463 production aircraft. Grumman's Design 303E became the VFX winner under the designation F-14. The first 67 (including prototypes) were to be TF30-P-412-powered F-14As operational by April 1973; subsequent aircraft were to be built to VFX-2 standard, powered by a new, more powerful advanced technology engine (with 37 per cent more thrust, 29 per cent better specific fuel consumption, 25 per cent less weight and possessing much greater stall resistance) and designated F-14B. This phased development programme

Although use of a ski-jump can enable a conventional fixed-wing aircraft to take off from an aircraft-carrier, the most efficient method of launching such aircraft is to use a steam catapult, which can accelerate the fighter to flying speed in a relatively short distance. Before a new naval aircraft can operate from US Navy carriers, extensive land-based tests are needed in order to determine the aircraft's catapault requirements, and to develop the correct launch technique. Here a Naval Missile Center F-14A uses a shore-based catapult during clearance trials. The F-14A always launches using afterburner, whereas the F-14D can launch with maximum dry power.

did not include attrition replacements. The 716 aircraft did include aircraft for four Marine fighter squadrons. Many of the 716, it was felt, would be of the advanced multi-mission F-14C variant with further improved avionics taking advantage of solid state technology and micro-miniaturisation. The F-14C was expected to increase the F-14's air-to-ground capabilities to include all-weather attack. The 469 aircraft initially contracted for were to have been procured in eight lots, of six, six, 30, 96, 96, 96, 96 and 43 aircraft. On this basis, unit cost, programme cost was set at $12.4 million (1970 dollars) – unit flyaway cost was $8.1 million. R&D was estimated in 1969 at $731 million (in escalated dollars) with another $243 million for Advanced Technology Engine R&D. Many within the Navy expected an eventual programme total of over 1,200 aircraft, in line with the F-4 and F-8, which was expected to reduce unit cost from $13.6 million for 469 to $10.4 million for the full 1,200.

"Tom's Cat? But which Tom?"

The promised availability of the improved F-14B and F-14C led some to question why the F-14A should be procured at all. In his memo to the Secretary of the Navy, Moorer explained that, "Proceeding by means of evolution from the F-14A to the F-14B reduces risk and provides distinct and substantial savings in cost and time. It also provides flexibility to meet other military objectives. The F-14A represents a comparatively low-risk development programme which would produce at an early time an advanced fighter fully capable of countering the threat. Stopping the F-14A programme and proceeding only with the F-14B would result in additional programme costs of $340 million. These increases do not include TF30-P-412 engine termination, but do reflect sustaining manpower over a longer development period, adding flight testing, changing GFE requirements and timing, and adjusting for inflation due to delay."

Admiral Thomas Moorer was a strong supporter of the F-14 and actually sponsored the development of the aircraft – as did another 'Tom', Admiral Thomas Connolly. The 'Tomcat' name – last in a long line of Grumman 'cats' – was said by some to be a shameless ploy to flatter those two key US Navy decision makers. Others perceived the name to be a sincere tribute to the two men, while yet others nominated different candidates who they believed were being honoured.

The first F-14s procured were the initial six prototypes (which became Lot I) and a subsequent six prototypes became Lot II. Some 26 production F-14As were ordered

Actual 'for real' carrier trials were conducted aboard USS Forrestal *(CV-59) off the Virginia Capes at the end of November 1973, following successful completion of BIS trials in October. Three F-14s participated in the sea trials, notching up 54 launches, 56 traps and 124 'bolters' during a seven-day period. Minimum wind-over-deck requirements were confirmed and the Approach Power Compensator was demonstrated.*

Below: The 14th Tomcat was one of the three aircraft which participated in the sea trials aboard the Forrestal. *It is seen here, hook down, ready to take the wire. It was also used for carrier trials onboard the* Enterprise.

teamed a new airframe with existing engines and avionics to minimise risk, while offering the opportunity for the new airframe to be subsequently teamed with new engines and avionics to provide the ultimate in growth potential and flexibility.

Radar development went remarkably smoothly, which was hardly unexpected after all the testing conducted aboard the F-111Bs and test Skywarrior. On 23 February 1970, Hughes was able to announce the delivery of the first AWG-9 weapon control system configured for the F-14A. The company was also pleased to be able to make a simultaneous claim for the longest-radar range performance ever achieved in a fighter.

The new-generation engine was cancelled but later reinstated, and VFX-2 eventually resulted in the F401-engined F-14B. The F401 engine subsequently went into the F-15, which was about two years behind the F-14. The F-14B was to have entered service from December 1973. Existing F-14As would then have been re-engined with the new powerplant. Moorer boasted that, "Retrofit costs are minimal, approximately $6,000 per aircraft." That option was never exercised, not least because the F-14B was itself cancelled and because it would have further delayed the F-15. This caused the USAF to worry that it might have the Navy's aircraft forced upon them. The eventual projected total was for 716 F-14s, although this

in FY 1971 as Lot III for $274 million, but a request for $5.2 million for F-14C avionics development was denied, effectively killing off the advanced Tomcat version.

There were at least two full-scale mock-ups before the first actual F-14 fighter was built. The original mock-up had a single tailfin. A later version introduced the now-familiar twin fins, shortly before the design was frozen in March 1969. Development was expedited through use of a uniquely detailed mock-up, known as EMMA (Engineering Mock-up Manufacturing Aid), which was built like a real aircraft albeit without external skinning, but since it would never fly it used cheaper manufacturing methods. Thus bulkheads were sand-cast instead of milled, but they were aluminium, and they were real bulkheads. This allowed Grumman engineers to locate hydraulic lines, electrical wires and systems, and to use EMMA to produce patterns and even to fit-check the TF30 engines. The first prototype itself was rolled out at the Grumman plant in December 1972.

Development

The US Navy's ambitious programme for testing and putting the F-14 into service called for a first flight by 31 January 1971, with Board of Inspection and Survey (BIS) trials just 17 months later – not as quickly as the F6F Hellcat or P-51 Mustang had been pushed forward in the heat of war, but an incredibly brief span for a modern jet fighter.

Taxi trials began at Calverton on 14 December 1970, with high-speed taxi trials starting six days later. On 21 December, company chief test pilot Robert Smythe and (in the back seat) project test pilot William (Bill) Miller made the first flight, two wide circuits of the airfield with the wings in the forward position, and laden with four dummy Sparrow missiles. The flight was abbreviated by approaching darkness and a threatening weather front, but was long enough to show that the aircraft had great potential. A more definitive 'first' flight was begun by Miller and Smythe on 30 December 1970 but was disastrous, with the Tomcat experiencing a primary hydraulic system failure. Miller was manoeuvring cautiously back towards a landing, using the nitrogen bottle to blow down the landing gear, when the secondary hydraulic system failed, too. This supplied control power to the rudders and tailplanes only, and, once it failed, the pilot had no control at all over the aircraft's flight path. The two men ejected only 25 ft (7.6 m) above the trees and suffered minor injuries – yet the first Grumman Tomcat was destroyed. Smythe ejected so low that his chute opened directly above the burning wreckage, but the heat

generated by this conflagration lifted him and then carried him clear.

Curing the hydraulic problem

A correction to the Tomcat's hydraulic systems proved relatively easy to accomplish. The cause of the breakdown had been a fatigue failure of both titanium main hydraulic lines caused by a combination of pump resonance (described as a high-pressure ripple) and a loose connector, and by the eventual failure of the third, electrically powered but hydraulically driven emergency back-up flight control module when the fluid leaked away during the transit back to Calverton. Modifications were simple and straightforward, the main change being a switch from titanium to stainless steel hydraulic lines. The loss of the first aircraft caused a delay in envelope-expansion tests and high-speed developmental flying, but the programme moved forward with almost its original momentum. On 24 May 1971, Smythe took the second Tomcat aloft.

Twelve prototype Tomcats were built in the initial run for flight trials. The no. 2 aircraft was assigned the low-speed regime, and also the critical stall/spin trials. For the latter the aircraft was fitted with retractable downward-folding long-chord foreplane vanes on the

Tomcat 4 was the first to be fitted with the AWG-9 fire-control system, and wore the Phoenix programme badge on its tailfin. The aircraft was initially used for integration of the weapons system, and went on (with the ninth aircraft) to fly the 357-hour live missile firing programme, during which the two aircraft fired 11 AIM-54s, four AIM-7s and two AIM-9Gs. On 20 December 1972, one of the aircraft downed five target drones in one engagement, with near-simultaneous launch of five AIM-54s!

upper sides of the nose, ahead of the windscreen, and at first the wings were locked at 20° and the intakes were locked open. This aircraft already had an anti-spin parachute fitted to the boat tail fairing and incorporated a Sundstrand hydrazine-powered turbine which drove an emergency hydraulic pump for the flight controls and an emergency electrical generator. The emergency pump and generator were added because the aircraft was thought most likely to suffer a double flameout at high angles of attack. Wind tunnel tests (carried out in NASA Langley's spin tunnel), trials of models dropped from helicopters, and computer analysis had shown a tendency towards flat spins, with very high rates of rotation, so Grumman was not prepared to take chances. The aircraft initially flew 'stiff-winged' with no wing sweep mechanism installed, and with the wing locked permanently in the fully forward position.

Prototype duties

No. 2 later received wing sweep and eventually tested the F-14's gun. No. 3 flew envelope-expanding trials with steadily increasing loads and speeds, and acted as the structural test vehicle. Nos 4, 5 and 6 went to NAS Point Mugu, the fourth for integration of the AWG-9/AIM-54 system, the fifth for systems, instrumentation and compatibility tests, and the sixth for weapons system and missile separation work. Of these, No. 5 was lost during a Sparrow separation on 20 June 1973.

With six prototypes flying, the aircraft underwent its first Navy Preliminary Evaluation (NPE1) between 2 and 16 December 1971. The first NPE examined flying qualities, carrier compatibility, maintainability and human factors considerations, with an envelope stretching to Mach 0.9 at sea level, to Mach 1.6 at 27,500 ft (8380 m) and to Mach 1.8 at 35,000 ft (10670 m). The aircraft involved flew 73.9 hours in 39 flights. The NPE pilots were enthusiastic about the aircraft, exhilarated by the aircraft's pure performance. Emory Brown, the F-14 OPEVAL Manager, later recalled, "The sheer excitement of strapping on the most advanced tactical fighter aircraft in the world, going from brake release to lift-off in 1,200 ft (365 m), rotating immediately to 70° nose up, then looking back over your shoulder as you pass through 15,000 ft (4570 m) and seeing that you are still within the airport boundaries ... well, that's exhilarating. I had to stifle the urge to leave her in zone five afterburner and to recite 'High Flight' over and over and over again. At that moment there was no man in

the world with whom I would have traded jobs."

Tomcat No. 7 became the test ship for the F-14B with F401 engines, its first flight being delayed, and No. 8 was used to test the production configuration and to provide contractual guarantee data. Nos 9 and 11 went to Point Mugu for radar evaluation and auxiliary system trials (including ACLS) respectively. No. 11 also flew air-to-ground gunnery trials.

No. 10 was delivered to the Naval Air Test Center at Patuxent River, and from there it was flown on structural trials and then carrier-compatibility work. On 15 June 1972 this aircraft made the F-14's first shipborne catapult launch, from the USS Forrestal, and made the first 'live' arrested landing aboard the same ship on 28 June 1972. Emory Brown, the fourth Navy pilot to fly the F-14, was the first pilot to land the type aboard a carrier. There was much ill-informed talk in the US Congress that the F-14 was not suitable for carrier operation, and the first carrier landings were thus conducted in an unusual degree of high-profile interest. The trials were filmed and the film was then flown directly to Andrews AFB for processing at Anacostia and a subsequent screening for influential Congressmen, to prove that the F-14 could do what its supporters said.

Another loss

During preparation for an air display, the no. 10 aircraft crashed into the sea, killing the pilot, Bob Miller, who was flying the aircraft solo. No. 17 replaced this aircraft on carrier-compatibility tests just as No. 12 (redesignated No. 1X) had replaced the first prototype on high-speed flight trials. This aircraft was the most comprehensively instrumented of the test Tomcats, able to transmit up to 647 measurements back to the ground, and fitted with hydraulic 'shakers' for flutter testing. 1X – actually the third F-14 to fly – had exceeded Mach 2.25 by December 1972.

The second phase of the Navy Preliminary Evaluation took place in two parts, NPE2A being conducted at Calverton by a team from Patuxent River under the leadership of Commander George White. This was achieved in 35 flights, totalling 77.7 hours, concluding on 15 August 1972. NPE2B was undertaken at Point Mugu, with a team led by Commander Frank Schluntz evaluating the avionics and weapons systems in 37 flights (totalling 100.6 hours), finishing on 9 August 1972. The NPE flights were augmented by a seven-flight mini OPEVAL conducted at Point Mugu between 29 September and 20 October 1972, and a simultaneous 20-flight R&M

demonstration at Calverton.

Completing the trials fleet were various aircraft from the initial F-14A production batch: No. 13 (anechoic chamber work for compatibility of the electromagnetic systems), No. 20 (climatic trials at Point Mugu) and Nos 15, 16, 18 and 19 (pilot conversion). These extra airframes were allocated to the trials programme to shorten development time, and to bring forward the service entry date. Although only the first 12 Tomcats were officially funded as prototypes, the first 16 were built in prototype jigs at Grumman's Bethpage facility. Subsequent aircraft, starting with No. 17, were built on a modular basis and consisted of separate forward, mid and aft fuselage section modules, intake ducts, tail section and a glove module. Adoption of the new method of construction allowed the production rate to rise from two to three aircraft per month, and paved the way for the transfer of production from Bethpage to Calverton by February 1973, with the 36th aircraft.

Telemetry proves its worth

Throughout the trials period, Grumman was able to maintain rapid progress by using an automated telemetry system (ATS) which relayed data directly to the ground for evaluation. This was originally developed for the A-6 Intruder flight test programme, and proved its worth repeatedly. Most importantly, the use of ATS allowed the aircraft to fly a test point, have it immediately analysed, and repeat it if required, or be cleared to go on to the next point on the same sortie. It obviated the need to land and wait for data to be downloaded and analysed before a second flight was launched to repeat the test point or move on to a simply expanded new test point. Integrated test blocks could be flown, incorporating a series of test points, each of which might previously have required a separate 40-minute flight. Trials were also expedited by the availability of four early A-6A Intruders, modified to virtual KA-6 tanker standards under the designation NA-6A. The NA-6As carried McDonnell Douglas refuelling stores (also quoted as Sargent Fletcher buddy stores) under the fuselage, with four 300-US gal (1136-litre) tanks underwing and up to 20,000 lb (9072 kg) of transferable fuel. They were used to extend Tomcat missions through inflight refuelling, and as low-speed chase aircraft. Some test flights entailed as many as five inflight-refuelling contacts, and the average sortie length was an impressive 2.9 hours. Even quite early in the programme, the test aircraft were totalling 12 or more flying hours per day. One of the support A-6s was also fitted with a smoke generator to aid high-altitude air-speed calibration, and three F-4s performed as high-speed photo-chase platforms.

The AN/AWG-9 fire-control system had already reached a high degree of maturity through trials in the F-111B and a trials TA-3B (as previously recounted). Such trials had included live missile firings, most of which had been judged successful. Once the No. 4 Tomcat had flown with AN/AWG-9 fitted (from early 1972), it was only a matter of time before missiles were fired from the F-14 itself. The fourth prototype F-14A was joined by the ninth, and the two aircraft together flew 357 hours (in 184 sorties) during 1972, firing 11 Phoenix, four AIM-7E Sparrow and two AIM-9G Sidewinder missiles. The bailed TA-3B Skywarrior was even busier, amassing 323 hours in 144 flights, including crucial ECCM demonstrations. In early December 1972, a Tomcat made the first multiple Phoenix launch, firing two missiles at targets representing an enemy bomber and the ASM it had just fired. The missile target was successfully destroyed, but the second missile developed a fault and missed its target. An even more ambitious demonstration was mounted. On 20 December 1972, a Tomcat flying at Mach 0.7 and 31,500 ft (9600 m) successfully engaged a formation of five target drones flying at Mach 0.6 and between 20,000 and 25,000 ft (6095 and 7620 m), shooting down four of them with its

four Phoenix missiles. The three QT-33s and two BQM-34s were destroyed at relatively short range (the missiles were fired at ranges of between 25 and 30 miles/40 and 48 km) and in quick succession, not simultaneously. This was nevertheless a very convincing demonstration of the Tomcat's capability. By the end of 1972, 53 Phoenix missiles had been fired, with a 70 per cent success rate, and only seven more were fired to complete the manufacturer's own test series.

Cutting development time

Clever management integrated development, service trials and operational instruction for crews, the factors together producing an 18-month cut in development time, with a consequent reduction in cost. F-14 development flights were estimated to cost $14,000 each. Weapons system trials were especially successful, demonstrating the F-14's unique qualities and capabilities in a very convincing manner. The fifth Tomcat was sent to sea aboard the USS

The use of telemetry allowed flight test data to be relayed automatically to the ground for near-real time interpretation and evaluation. This proved particularly useful during the live missile firings.

Although it is a naval aircraft through and through, great care was taken to ensure that the F-14 can operate successfully with USAF assets in joint force scenarios. Here an early F-14A refuels from a new USAF KC-10A Extender.

Forging the Tomcat

The Playboy bunny insignia of VX-4 is carried on the fin-band of this 'XF'-coded F-14A. VX-4 was the US Navy's operational test and evaluation squadron for fighter and fighter-attack aircraft types, weapons and tactics. The squadron's role has now been taken over by VX-9 Det Point Mugu, a new unit which also swallowed the air-to-ground OT&E unit, VX-5.

aircraft's approach characteristics, specifically stating that its stability was "better than a production F-4." Even the aircraft's supporters, who claimed adequacy, did not claim superiority over the F-4 in this aspect.

While development continued unabated throughout 1972 and 1973, behind the scenes the Tomcat faced considerable difficulties. From March 1973 the F-14A was compared with a number of cheaper alternatives, including the F-15N, the swing-wing F-4(FVS) Phantom, and a plethora of downgraded Tomcat derivatives. The F-14D retained the AWG-9 weapons system, though with simultaneous target tracking capability cut from 24 to 12, and with simultaneous engagement capability cut from six to four. The glove vanes, direct lift control and approach power compensator were removed to save weight and cost. The F-14 Optimod was the next cheapest option, incorporating three different computer options intended to reduce cost, but retaining the AWG-9 and Phoenix. The F-14X designation covered a number of configurations, with radar options including the Westinghouse WX-200 or -250 or the Hughes APG-64. The first proposal, and the cheapest, was the F-14T, which was a Sparrow-armed austere Tomcat hardly more capable than a late-model Phantom. These various downgraded Tomcats were dropped in May 1974, when evaluation of the Arab-Israeli wars persuaded the USA that it could not afford high attrition, and that the best possible F-14 would be worth the price.

More than a pilot's plaything

Independence for 10 days during March 1973 to obtain preliminary data for full integration of the Carrier Airborne INS system; 160 hours of system tests were conducted, with 20 full alignments of the equipment. Catapult trials were undertaken at Patuxent River and NAS Lakehurst to check CAINS (Carrier Alignment of INS, now known as SINS, or Ship's INS) alignment, and to ensure compatibility with the new flush-deck catapult and modified jet blast deflectors. After steam ingestion problems with the turbofan-powered A-7, there were worries that the F-14 might be similarly afflicted, but the aircraft was able to complete a gruelling 30-launch demonstration in one day. These tests indicated that with four Sparrows loaded, the aircraft would even be able to operate with a 10-kt (12-mph; 18-km/h) tailwind. The 252-flight/529.3-hour BIS trials with the NATC and NMC started on 13 November 1972 and were completed in October 1973, while full sea trials, involving three aircraft, were flown from the USS *Forrestal*, amassing 54 catapult launches, 56 traps (arrested recoveries) and 124 bolters in a seven-day period from 26 November 1973. The BIS team was led by Commander George White, and included six pilots, two each from the carrier suitability, flying qualities and performance (flight test) divisions of the NATC, with two more from the fighter branch of the service test division. Minimum wind-over-deck requirements were explored, and the approach power compensator was thoroughly wrung out. Surprisingly, in view of subsequent criticisms by fleet aviators, Grumman professed complete satisfaction with the

Most pilots loved the F-14's flying characteristics, but a military aircraft had to be more than a mere pilot's plaything. The sweetest handling in the world was useless unless a fighter could fight and win. Success could only be gauged by the ability to fulfil the mission. For the Tomcat, that mission was to intercept and engage multiple targets — incoming bombers and cruise missiles — a considerable distance from the carrier battle group that it was charged with protecting. In addition, the Tomcat was expected to be capable of close-in manoeuvring combat with enemy fighters. The aircraft had a required combat radius of 500 nm (575 miles; 925 km) when armed with four Sparrows and the internal gun, or a 200-nm (230-mile; 370-km) radius when carrying six Phoenix and two Sidewinder missiles for the fleet air defence mission, with a two-hour loiter and five minutes of combat.

Early plans called for an effective operating radius of 480 miles (770 km), a service ceiling of 50,000 ft (15240 m), and the ability to employ radar-guided or heat-seeking missiles, and (after a lesson learned the hard way in Vietnam) a gun. The new fighter would have a radar range of 156 nm (180 miles; 290 km) and be able to fire up to six

A new squadron, VX-9, has combined the roles of the hitherto separate air-to-air and air-to-mud Operational Test and Evaluation Squadrons, VX-4 and VX-5. The new squadron maintains detachments at both Point Mugu and China Lake and uses the bat insignia of VX-5 ('Vampires') on its aircraft, including this F-14 Tomcat. Although the Tomcat is now a mature aircraft, ongoing improvements and developments necessitate a constant OT&E effort, most recently with the Bombcat, LANTIRN and digital TARPS projects.

missiles almost simultaneously at targets 100 miles (160 km) away. All of this had to be achieved in both good and bad weather, at night, and while operating from aircraft-carrier decks. Most of all, the F-14 had to be capable of fulfilling its mission reliably, and at the specified contract price, and it was in these areas that the F-14 was to be found most wanting.

There were technical problems, of course. Quite apart from the catastrophic loss of the first prototype on only its second flight, the Navy reported 43 major and 75 minor deficiencies after an evaluation in November/December 1971. The deficiencies were not described in detail, but were said to have included "engine compressor stalls, throttle quadrant design, nose gear steering status light, rolling performance and so forth."

One area which should have been completely trouble-free was the AN/AWG-9/XN-3 fire-control system, since it had undergone a great deal of testing in the F-111B and had originally been derived from the fire control system developed for the unbuilt Missileer. In fact, technical problems encountered were minor, although the system's very high cost was a serious deficiency in the hostile political and economic climate. By March 1973 it was being reported that Grumman was considering the use of a simpler, cheaper weapons system based on that of the USAF's F-15. It was estimated that this would have saved $1 million per aircraft, although it would have removed AIM-54 compatibility and would have reduced radar range quite dramatically.

Cost overruns and technical problems

It was the cost overruns and technical problems with the F-14A that prompted a sharp reminder to Grumman from the DoD on 7 April 1971. This message pointed out that the project would have excess cost problems, and was followed by a hostile report by Democratic Senators Vance Hartke and Jonathan Bingham of the anti-war MCPL (Members of Congress for Peace through Law) group, which disputed whether the Navy needed the F-14, and which averred that the aircraft was too expensive and not

much better than the F-4. They recommended that Congress should reject the request for $806 million for 48 F-14s in 1972, should deny the $104 million requested for the AIM-54 and the $228 million requested for F-14B/C development, and that it should instead cancel the F-14 and the AIM-54. One suggestion was that the US Navy could take 48 F-4Ks or F-4Ms like those built for Britain, or another advanced F-4 derivative. The report also recommended finding a lower-cost alternative for the USAF's F-15, but intended allowing development to continue while a lower-cost fighter to replace or augment the F-15 could be defined and developed. The senators were motivated primarily by the high cost of the Phoenix, and by the perceived low level of capability of the F-14 without the AIM-54, but they also seemed scandalised by the fact that the aircraft had only a 2 per cent speed advantage over the MiG-21. The F-14's cost overruns and technical difficulties made the aircraft an obvious and easy target, and even a popular one. They foresaw an eventual $13.5 billion saving by axing both projects, or even as much as $25 billion taking into account whole programme

Above: The TF30-engined F-14A was always regarded as an interim aircraft, and the intention had been to build all but the first 67 aircraft as VFX-2 (F-14B) aircraft, powered by the Pratt & Whitney F401-PW-400. Unfortunately, the engine ran into difficulties and the No. 7 YF-14 was the only F-14B to fly, subsequently becoming the Super Tomcat with F101-DFEs and eventually F110-GE-400 engines.

Top: The RIO's view is partially blocked by the F-14's huge intakes, but generally the all-round view is superb, as can be seen in this photo of three VF-301 Tomcats.

The F-14's TARPS pod was originally designed for the subsonic A-7 Corsair, and was only ever intended as an interim solution to the US Navy's shortfall in recce capability following the retirement of the RA-5C Vigilante, and pending the introduction of a reconnaissance version of the F/A-18 Hornet. This pod, carried by the fifth prototype below the starboard engine intake, was a pure aerodynamic dummy, ballasted to represent an operational pod. In fact, by the time TARPS was flying in a functional form there had been many changes, with the operational pod losing the tailfins and gaining various sensor windows.

costs, with immediate FY72 savings of $538 million to $776 million.

The F-14 earned the opprobrium of more than just left-wing and pacifist anti-war politicians. Some naval officers and aircrew were alarmed that the aircraft was over-specified, overweight and far too costly, and that this threatened the maintenance of a sufficiently large force of fleet fighters. Such people wanted a lighter, cheaper fighter, with a lighter, cheaper radar, and, if necessary, a shorter range. "A fighter only needs legs long enough to reach the fight," they claimed, pointing out that long range was useless if the fighter was too heavy and too cumbersome to win the fight when it arrived. Above all, there was great concern that the US Navy would not be able to afford a sufficient number of the new fighters, and that an outnumbered force of F-14s would be easy prey to larger numbers of arguably less effective and cheaper fighters. One former F-4 pilot with combat experience in Vietnam wrote anonymously to the magazine *Aviation Week and Space Technology*, and pointed out that, "For the same price as one F-14, the Navy can have at least five F-4s, eight F-8s or 10 A-4Ms. If Lieutenant Commander Hohlstein [a pro-F-14 correspondent] takes one F-14 and engages 10 A-4Ms he is going to lose, even if every one of his missiles works

perfectly. As compared to the enemy, a single F-14 is equal in cost to a squadron (a big one) of MiG-21s. One F-14 versus a squadron of MiG-21s is a poor bet for the US Navy. Werner Voss engaged a squadron of British fighters once...but only once. The Germans rate him in the 'Ace of the Base' category, and he still lost. Let's face it, the average joker needs a wingman, and he can sure use numerical parity in a fight. The F-14 puts the Navy well along the road to 'let's buy one aircraft and let everybody take turns flying it'."

The Tomcat even drew fire from within the Defense Department, with the Office of Systems Analysis drawing up a report which recommended stretching out the F-14 development and production schedule to spread the costs, and even to cancel the basic TF30-powered F-14A, while pacing development of the F-14B to the development of the USAF's 29,000-lb (129-kN) class engine. This study reportedly enjoyed the backing of the Deputy Defense Secretary, David Packard.

In the red

A Defense Systems Acquisition Council review of the entire F-14 programme followed on 27 May 1971. It was revealed that the project was $400 million in the red, but

An operational TARPS pod is seen below the belly of a VF-102 F-14A. Some 17 ft (5.18 m) long and weighing more than 1,600 lb (726 kg), TARPS contains a KS-87 forward oblique camera, a KA-99 panoramic camera and an AN/AAD-5 IR reconnaissance set. Only a handful of Tomcats are wired to carry the pod, and for many years only one squadron in each two-squadron air wing was trained in its use. The 65 TARPS-modified F-14As carry the pod on Station 5, as do all F-14Ds (all of which are TARPS compatible). The 'interim' TARPS pod entered service with VF-84 aboard the USS Nimitz in 1981 and remains in use today, though it has recently been upgraded with digital-based sensors.

that the Navy still intended to press on with its planned FY 1972 buy of the full Lot IV in apparent ignorance of the likely Congressional refusal to fund the purchase, and Grumman's likely refusal to deliver the aircraft at the originally agreed price. This prompted the Deputy Secretary of Defense to direct Navy Secretary John Chafee to re-examine F-14 procurement plans, and to produce recommendations of how to reduce or cope with the rising costs. At a heated high-level meeting, Packard was reportedly moved to point at the Secretary of the Navy with the words "I should fire you," before pointing at the CNO and his deputy and repeating, "and you, and you." The MCPL group enjoyed some influence, and the Senate only narrowly defeated the amendment which would have knocked $801 million earmarked for Lot IV F-14A production from the military procurement bill.

The project was dramatically pruned, with procurement being slashed from the planned total of 722 F-14s to only 313. Fortunately, the AIM-54 Phoenix missile survived the axe, although some observers expected it to be cancelled. The TF100 advanced technology engine was cancelled, at least insofar as the F-14 was concerned, thereby killing off the F-14B. The engine had been suffering technical problems and cost overruns, and to proceed with it, according to one senior officer, would have been like "throwing money down a rat hole." As if all this were not enough, development of the new variant of the Sparrow was also suffering technical and price difficulties. The last 20 aircraft of Lot IV were to have been F-14Bs, but they were replaced by F-14As.

Ill-informed criticism

Subsequently, politicians frequently attempted to downscale the F-14 programme, although it was never again in danger of outright termination. In 1973, for example, the Navy was directed to look at a number of alternatives to the purchase of further F-14As, including the navalised F-15N and the F-4M as well as a stripped and simplified Tomcat known as the F-14D, but plans to produce two prototypes of each were cancelled, and the projects quietly died. None would have carried the Phoenix, and all would have been equipped with avionics with a production cost not in excess of the Hughes APG-63 in the F-15. In the same year, it was proposed that 301 full-standard, Phoenix-equipped F-14s should be augmented by a naval lightweight fighter, either the YF-16 or the YF-17, though a stripped F-14 (the F-14D again, this time inevitably, though unofficially, dubbed

'Tomkitten') was also suggested. Radars proposed for this variant included the APG-63, and also the 350-lb (159-kg) Westinghouse WX-200, whose capability could be enhanced by adding modules.

Not all of the F-14's detractors were well briefed, and the aircraft was surrounded by ill-informed criticism. In November 1973 Senators Thomas Eagleton and William Proxmire were reported to have alleged that there were serious deficiencies in the aircraft. They included a 3,750-lb (1701-kg) weight overrun, a failure to meet speed, ceiling and payload requirements, repeated failures of the AWG-9, and a poor showing in a fly-off between the F-14 and F-15. No such fly-off ever occurred, and the rest of the criticisms drew the exasperated response from Grumman chairman J. G. Gavin that the senators' "comments indicate insufficient staff work to warrant reply."

Cost-saving modifications

The F-14 had a powerful ally in the person of the Chief of Naval Operations, Admiral Elmo R. Zumwalt, Jr, who was determined to keep Phoenix capability in all fleet Tomcats, and who strove to ensure that any stripped version of the aircraft would be as close as possible to the service F-14A. Under his direction, Grumman and the Navy came up with a series of minor modifications to the basic F-14A which would have saved money. They included a redesigned main landing gear which would have been only 6 lb (2.7 kg) heavier, but which would have saved $5,000 per aircraft in FY 73 dollars. Replacing beryllium in the landing gear with steel would have offered a further $9,000 saving, but would have increased weight by 100 lb (45 kg). Similarly, a change to a different gauge of aluminium honeycomb would have increased aircraft weight by 88 lb (40 kg) while saving $13,800 per aircraft. Grumman showed that removing the backup analog wing sweep channel from the central data computer would save $3,000, while a package of inlet door modifications held out the lure of an $8,000 saving, with a slight reduction in weight and an improvement in drag and stall margin. Deleting the Mach hold autopilot function was estimated as a potential $6,000 per aircraft saving, and deletion of the outboard spoiler modules promised a saving of $5,600, with a weight reduction of 15 lb (6.8 kg). Replacement of the existing vertical display system with the F-15's HUD and automatic direction indicator would reduce weight by 34 lb (15 kg) and also save $90,000 per aircraft.

Grumman also proposed a redesign of the beaver tail to reduce drag. It would add 68 lb (31 kg) to the aircraft

The F-14B prototype became the 'Super Tomcat' when re-engined with F101-DFEs. The new Derivative Fighter Engine improved performance (and especially CAP radius) and paved the way for installation of the derived F110-GE-400 to produce the F-14A Plus (later redesignated F-14B) and the F-14D.

Above: This F-14B wears the markings of VX-4, 'The Evaluators', and shows to advantage the larger-diameter jetpipes associated with the F110-GE-400 engine fitted to the production F-14B and to the F-14D. Although intended as an interim aircraft, more F-14Bs were built or produced by conversion than the total number of F-14Ds produced.

Top: The F-14D has an all-new digital avionics suite, with a powerful new AN/APG-71 radar, which combines the best features of the AWG-9 and of the APG-70 used by the F-15E Strike Eagle. This aircraft was used by VX-4 at Point Mugu.

weight, but could also generate a $15,900 saving per aircraft. Grumman further proposed deleting the glove vanes (saving $100,000 per aircraft and saving 212 lb/96 kg) but admitted that this would reduce the aircraft's maximum speed and supersonic manoeuvrability. At Mach 1.6, a modified F-14 would be able to pull only 1.3 g. A final cost-saving measure put forward depended on continuing production. This was to return manufacture of the nacelle, glove and rear fuselage from sub-contractors (Rohr Industries and Fairchild Industries) to Grumman's Calverton plant. These changes would save $170,000 per aircraft, though the cost of switching production would mean that savings would not become available for two years. The goal of the entire package of modifications was to save $2 million per aircraft in escalated dollars (1973 dollar savings are used throughout in the description of changes above).

F-14 versus F-4

By 1973, the growing number of F-14s flying in the development programme was beginning to win the aircraft new allies and friends, despite the continuing cost escalation and technical problems. In early 1973 Grumman flew a brief series of eight flights which proved particularly influential. In these flights, an F-14 flown by Chuck Sewell flew pre-briefed dogfight manoeuvres against a slatted F-4J flown by Lieutenant D. Walker of the NATC. Backseat 'umpires' were Commander L. White in the F-14, and Captain L. Walker, USMC, in the F-4. The two aircraft took it in turns to begin the engagements in trail, and entered the engagements at speeds between Mach 0.6 and Mach 1.25, and at altitudes between 18,000 and 35,000 ft (5485 and 10670 m). The Tomcat demonstrated superior performance throughout. When the F-14 began in front of the F-4 it always escaped, pulling out of gun range

immediately, and out of the F-4's missile launch range within seconds, and always turning the tables to get on the Phantom's tail and track it. The F-4 was never able to escape the Tomcat, which used its superior turn performance and specific energy to score a quick simulated kill. The F-14 regularly pulled more than 7 g in initial breaks, and demonstrated the ability to simulate kills while flying at angles of attack of up to 48° and at speeds down to 160 kt (184 mph; 295 km/h). The aircraft's ability to decelerate very quickly also proved extremely useful in forcing the F-4 to turn outside it. During the fights the F-4J stalled out twice and suffered one flameout, while the F-14's engines performed flawlessly. During a similar flight conducted for the benefit of *Aviation Week and Space Technology*, the F-14 followed an F-4B which tried to evade by flying a 30-unit AoA, 8-g spiral. This tore off the F-4's fibreglass wingtip fairings, but did not prevent the F-14 from tracking its target throughout the manoeuvre.

Performance was always accorded a high priority in the design of the F-14, which was never intended to be an equipment- and weapon-packed lumbering bomber-destroyer in the mould of the Douglas Missileer, or even the F-111B. Among the earliest achievements advertised by Grumman was the aircraft's ability to reach Mach 2 at high level, and an 850-kt (975-mph; 1570-km/h) low-level limiting IAS, even with the pitch channel stability augmentation system turned off. During relatively early flight tests the aircraft actually reached speeds in excess of Mach 2.2 and 857 kt (984 mph; 1583 km/h) in level flight. Later the Tomcat exceeded its Mach 2.4 limit, the pilot chopping the throttles to decelerate when he reached a reported Mach 2.41, still accelerating. The aircraft had superb acceleration, and was able to go from loiter to Mach 1.8 in only 75 seconds.

Engine problems

The original engine for the F-14A was the 12,350-lb (54.94-kN) thrust Pratt & Whitney TF30-P-412 which introduced minor improvements over the TF30-P-12 tested exhaustively in the F-111B, and adopted for the F-111D. This engine had caused severe problems in the F-111, and was destined to prove equally troublesome in the F-14.

As Pelehach and others on the Tomcat project knew before the prototype F-14A rolled out, the engine had its drawbacks. Even with thrust increasing to 20,900 lb (92.97 kN) in afterburning power, the TF30-powered F-14A was underpowered, and the engine was notably intolerant of disturbed airflow in the intake and embarrassingly prone to compressor stalls. These two main problems were much more serious than had ever been anticipated, however, and their full extent did not become apparent until the F-14 entered service. The engine problems directly led to the loss of 40 aircraft, worth over $1 billion ($1.5 billion, if an average price of $36 million per aircraft is assumed). From the beginning, it was determined that the TF30 would have to be followed by a different, more powerful engine. Some believed that the F-14 should have waited for the new engine, and that the

TF30-engined Tomcat should never have been built. In the end, the threat was felt to be too urgent to allow such a delay. No-one would have been able to foresee how slowly this would happen.

The TF30 remains the powerplant for the bulk of the fleet's F-14As even today, and remains the Tomcat's only real Achilles heel. Had early plans been followed, the TF30 problem would have been a minor inconvenience, since only the first 67 Tomcats had been scheduled to be powered by this engine, and even these aircraft were then to have been re-engined as F-14Bs. Although well equipped to carry out its mission in all other respects, the F-14A Tomcat would be a decidedly underpowered and, above all, an interim aircraft. Production was to have shifted to the original F-14B in the early 1970s.

The advanced F-14B

The original F-14B was to have been powered by the General Electric F401-PW-400. This engine was a derivative of the JTF-22, which also spawned the USAF's advanced-technology fighter engine, the F100. It offered much higher thrust and maintainability than the TF30, with lower fuel consumption, but development proved trouble-prone and costly at a time when the F-14 programme was itself under threat. To test the original F-14B, Grumman had intended to modify two aircraft to F-14B standard to fly the Pratt & Whitney F401 turbofan engine. A test ship bailed to Grumman – hard-working aircraft 157986 – was actually modified and flown with the F401, beginning 12 September 1973. Problems with the highly advanced new engine led to the cancellation of plans to build 400 F-14Bs and to the termination of work on the F401 itself in April 1974. The second test aircraft, 158260, was nearly completed to F-14B standard when the programme was cancelled, and this aircraft reverted to F-14A configuration without ever even flying as a B model.

Looking for a new engine

Given the benefit of a crystal ball, or 20-20 hindsight, many might have preferred to stick with the F401 (whose USAF equivalent suffered similar problems in the F-15 and F-16, but which eventually came good) rather than stay with an engine which was both troublesome and severely lacking in thrust. Instead, the US Navy abandoned its participation in the F401 programme, which had hitherto been shared with the USAF on a 60 per cent/40 per cent

basis. The Navy continued with production of the F-14A variant, but ongoing dissatisfaction with the F-14's performance and continuing problems with the TF30 powerplant kept Grumman looking hard for alternative engines, examining reheated and non-afterburning versions of the A-7's Allison TF41 (a licence-built Rolls-Royce Spey), the F401-PW-26C (refined and developed since abandonment of the original F-14B's F401-PW-400) and the General Electric F101X.

In the end, a new powerplant for the F-14 eventually emerged from US Navy participation in the USAF's Derivative Fighter Engine programme, launched primarily to find a new engine for the F-15 and F-16, producing an engine which combined features from the engines of the B-1 bomber and the F/A-18 Hornet strike fighter. This resulted in the F110-engined F-14B and F-14D, described in later chapters. **Julian Lake, Peter B. Mersky and Jon Lake**

To this day, the TF30-powered F-14A remains partially hamstrung by its engine, which lacks thrust and is alarmingly prone to stalls and surges. Even as recently as Operation Desert Storm, the F-14A was restricted by reliability problems with its engine.

The dual side-by-side undernose sensor pods identify this aircraft as an F-14D. This remarkably obvious modification put a Northrop AN/AXX-1 TCS and a GE AN/AAS IRST together in a dual sensor pod, with the TCS to starboard and the IRST to port. Less obvious equipment changes include new EW equipment, including provision for the ASPJ (Advanced Self-Protection Jammer). This was cancelled after failing to meet some of its specified performance parameters, but still proved an improvement over current systems, and the sets already delivered found their way into the F-14Ds.

Chapter Two

Deployment & Further Development

VF-32 was to become one of only three US Navy Tomcat squadrons to score confirmed air-to-air victories, accounting for a pair of Libyan MiG-23s.

Below: The first Tomcats in service wore much the same colour scheme as had been applied to the Phantoms and Crusaders that had gone before: glossy gull grey with white undersides and control surfaces.

The US Navy originally hoped to replace all fleet F-4 Phantoms with F-14 Tomcats, one-for-one. Following the contract renegotiations of the early 1970s, the total number required was calculated at 522, to equip two squadrons on each of 12 carriers, plus 12 spare aircraft. Including aircraft for the US Marine Corps, the full number could reach 722. The total number of aircraft to be funded fluctuated wildly, from 134 to 240 to 313 and more, eventually rising to 899.

The aircraft began to enter service long before the final quantity was settled. The first Navy squadron to receive the F-14 was VX-4 at Point Mugu, which undertook operational evaluation of the aircraft from September 1972. The first example of the original TF30-engined F-14A Tomcat to reach a fleet squadron was BuNo. 158617, which went to VF-124 at NAS Miramar on 8 October 1972, just 21 months after the type's first flight. VF-124 had previously served as the West Coast F-8 Crusader training unit, for more than 15 years. Crews for each US Navy aircraft type receive their type conversion training prior to fleet service, with a fleet replacement (or replenishment) squadron (FRS). These training squadrons were formerly known as replacement air groups and are still often called 'RAGs'. Each aircraft type usually has one FRS on each side of the American continent to train crews for the Atlantic and Pacific Fleets. In due course, a second RAG for the Tomcat, VF-101 'Grim Reapers', began training crews at NAS Oceana, Virginia.

Establishing the RAGs

Since it must begin by training instructors, and then remains to train new crews, the fleet replenishment squadron is an essential element in the transition to a new aircraft type and, later, in assuring a flow of operational personnel. By 1973, VF-124 was ready to begin training crews who would fly the Tomcat in the first operational fleet squadrons – VF-1 'Wolf Pack' and VF-2 'Bounty Hunters', which had officially been commissioned in October 1972. The FRS converted two squadrons at a time, allowing air wings to convert from the F-4 to the F-14 at one time. Thus F-14s and F-4s never operated together as part of the same air wing, except when Reserve or Marine Phantoms deployed aboard a carrier. By November 1973, there were still only 12 operational F-14As operational at Miramar, with VF-124, VF-1 and VF-2.

The process of producing a first-rate front-line fighter was slow. While Grumman was coming to realise that it was likely to lose money on every Tomcat delivered, there was little incentive to produce the aircraft as quickly as was required. By mid-1973 only 27 aircraft had been delivered, and there seemed little likelihood that the company would

meet its contractually obliged total of 54 aircraft delivered (and 58 flying) by the year's end. In fact, these targets were achieved, on the last day before the Christmas shutdown, although few aircraft were actually delivered to the units at Miramar. VF-1 and VF-2 began their carrier qualifications in the spring of 1974, with Lieutenant Commander Grover Giles and his RIO, Lieutenant Commander Roger McFillen, gaining the honour of becoming the first crew to carqual successfully. On 2 January 1975 the same crew clocked up a less enviable distinction: they became the first fleet crew to eject from an F-14.

The Atlantic Fleet began converting its fleet air defence squadrons to the F-14 in June 1974, with the delivery of the first F-14A (159019) to VF-14 at NAS Oceana. The squadron's ground and aircrew (and those from VF-32) were trained with VF-124 at NAS Miramar, since the East Coast FRS had not then stood up. The first Tomcat units to convert required a great deal of training before they were truly operational and ready to deploy, of course. VF-14, for example, had to run through a squadron-designed datalink training syllabus, much of which involved having a squadron Tomcat sitting on the ramp linked to a VAW-125 E-2C Hawkeye sitting alongside. The hard work paid dividends, however, and F-14 crews were soon able to make intercepts in total radio silence.

The Tomcat's first cruise

The 24 Tomcats of VF-1 and VF-2 left Miramar for loading aboard the USS *Enterprise* at Alameda on 12 September 1974. The *Enterprise* slipped its moorings at 10.00 on 17 September, marking the first carrier deployment by a 'Grumman Cat' since VF-111's Tigers had returned to the USA aboard the *Hancock* in March 1961. The F-14 was Grumman's eighth 'cat', following the Wildcat, Hellcat, Tigercat, Bearcat, Panther, Cougar and Tiger, and found itself deploying aboard the eighth US Navy ship to bear the name *Enterprise*. The two squadrons formed the defensive shield for CVW-14 (commanded by Commander G. M. 'Skip' Furlong), which

was the *raison d'être* of the carrier itself, commanded by Captain C. C. Smith. *Enterprise* was the flagship of Rear Admiral Owen Oberg, the commander of Carrier Group Seven. About one hour and five minutes after it cast off, the 85,000-ton 'Big E' cleared San Francisco's Golden Gate bridge, increased its speed and headed out to sea.

The logistics system lagged behind the aircraft, and initial squadrons were forced to cannibalise many aircraft in order to keep others airworthy. On one day, Miramar had 132 NOR (Not Operationally Ready) aircraft, 29 without one or the other engine, and 30 which had been grounded for maintenance for more than 30 days. In the air, buffeting was experienced when the flaps were deployed, and fatigue cracking affected the boat tail fairing, although both problems were easily cured. Vibration and fatigue also necessitated strengthening the fin-caps. Morale problems were indicated by a 28 per cent pilot retention rate, and niggling complaints about why couldn't pilots wear their leather flight jackets away from the flight line and hangar areas, and why couldn't flying suits be worn in O-Club on Friday night 'Happy Hours'? They were symptoms of a more serious problem. Crews were not flying enough, and were not confident in their new aircraft. Under the newly-promoted Rear Admiral Paul Gillcrist, new Commander Fighter Airborne Early Warning Wings,

Above: A VF-2 'Bounty Hunters' F-14A waits its turn as a VF-1 Tomcat is gently lifted aboard the USS Enterprise *for the Tomcat's first operational cruise. This was to the Western Pacific, where the carrier participated in the final evacuation of Saigon.*

Above left: Seven of the 'Wolfpack's' original F-14As fly a neat formation during work-ups for the Tomcat's first cruise. During this cruise F-14As flew operational sorties covering Operation Frequent Wind, the evacuation of Saigon, but encountered no enemy aircraft.

If a carrier pilot cannot take the wire, perhaps as a result of a hook malfunction, and cannot divert to a land-based airfield, the last remaining option is to make a barrier engagement. The barrier consists of canvas strops mounted between a pair of horizontal cables. It will stop a Tomcat, but not without causing some damage, and not without some risk to the crew.

Above: Tomcats line up on Miramar's ramp. Most of the gaps in the early days were not aircraft which were airborne but rather a reflection of a serviceability rate which was little short of scandalous.

Right: On land as on the carrier deck, Tomcats were often parked nose-to-tail in an effort to save space. When not deployed, Pacific Fleet F-14s were shore-based at NAS Miramar.

Below: Hook down, a VF-2 Tomcat enters the landing pattern to recover aboard the USS Ranger. Even with only two AIM-54s aboard, this will be a heavyweight landing.

US Pacific Fleet, these problems were solved and morale improved markedly. The number of NOR aircraft reached zero, and levelled at below 20, and Gillcrist swore to lock the engineering hangar and buy the beer the day there were no 'bare firewall' aircraft. He did not have to wait long to be separated from his money. He also set up no-notice missile shoots, gunnery meets and fighter derbies, and morale skyrocketed.

The TF30 powerplant proved troublesome, especially at high angles of attack, and engine problems proved harder to beat than poor morale in the Pacific Fleet. In January 1975 two VF-1 aircraft were lost in similar circumstances, with the crews ejecting after experiencing a 'loud thump' followed by a rapid and irreversible loss of power. The cause proved to be uncontrollable inflight fires caused by fan blade failures. They happened during the Tomcat's first fleet deployment, and there were fears that the Tomcat's service life might be marred by frustration and failure, the same fate having befallen several fighter types which had entered service in the 1950s, including the F7U-3 Cutlass and F3H-2 Demon. The handful of Tomcats in service were grounded, and the blame was placed on a vendor, whose blades failed to meet Pratt & Whitney's specifications. The aircraft were soon flying (albeit with severe restrictions) but CVAN-65 was presently able to complete engine inspections, and the restrictions were lifted in March. All seemed to be well and Rear Admiral 'Swoose' Snead, Commander of the Fighter and Airborne Early Warning Wing Pacific, described the F-14's introduction as "the most singularly successful fleet introduction programme of a sophisticated aircraft that the Navy has ever had."

Inflight engine explosions

Unfortunately, another inflight explosion occurred in an East Coast F-14 operating from Oceana, leading to another grounding in June 1975. The crew had managed to limp back to Oceana after extinguishing the fire, and the engine was inspected. The grounding was lifted in July, but the engine clearly had serious problems, and losses began to mount. Most early F-14 pilots experienced engine flame-outs or even inflight explosions, and Lieutenant Spencer Rawlins of VF-14 was by no means unique in having four engine failures during his 1,000 flying hours on the aircraft. Engine problems emerged in service which had gone undetected in development since the test pilots and engineers had not subjected the aircraft to the 'mishandling' which proved part and parcel of its service life. Daily excursions to 30° Alpha were the norm in the dogfighting F-14, together with regular throttle slams from idle to burner and back. It had been estimated that 1,000 hours might include 597 burner light-ups and 1,165 engine cycles, whereas the actual in-service figures were 2,250 afterburner light-ups and 10,549 engine cycles.

The TF30 was then still regarded as an interim powerplant, so its problems were deemed acceptable. Although testing had demonstrated vice-free handling and virtually no AoA limits, problems with spinning were encountered. The original aileron rudder interconnect (ARI), which fed in rudder instead of aileron at high angles of attack to generate roll, had to be disconnected since it made entering a spin all too easy. Aircraft 1X, already at Edwards following spin trials and speed runs, was later bailed to NASA (as NASA 991) and undertook a major three-year trials programme at Dryden which eventually led to the design of a new ARI, but these trials did not even begin until 1979. They were conducted by Dick Gray, a former USN F-14 pilot from the AIMVAL demonstrations. The lessons were learned, however, and the problems were not sufficient to halt the relentless tide of squadron conversions from Crusaders and Phantoms to Tomcats, though the ARI remained disconnected until a cure could be designed. By 30 April 1975 Enterprise's Tomcats were

Grumman F-14A, VF-1 'Wolfpack' Air Wing Fourteen, US Navy USS *Enterprise*, 1976

This 'Wolfpack' F-14A wears the original F-14 colour scheme, with light gull grey topsides and gloss white undersurfaces and control surfaces. Like all the early F-14 squadrons, VF-1 added huge areas of colour to the basic scheme, with red fin tips and ventral fins, a red fuselage stripe or 'cheat line' and a red fin badge. 'NK' tailcodes were carried on the inner faces of the tailfins (again in red), trailed by a red stripe like that applied behind the wolf's head badge. The aircraft is portrayed as it appeared during the squadron's second fleet deployment, which took place between 30 July 1976 and March 1977.

able to claim status as Vietnam veterans by flying top cover for Operation Frequent Wind, the evacuation of Saigon, though North Vietnamese MiGs chose not to interfere with the evacuation. One F-14 even received damage by ground fire.

The Tomcat had some tricky handling characteristics, but was generally an easier aircraft to master than its predecessor, the F-4 Phantom. In take-off configuration the aircraft would display severe wing rock (rolling to up to 90°) and yaw (up to 25°) at angles of attack of more than 28°, though recovery was straightforward and rapid once Alpha was reduced below 15°. The F-14's adverse yaw problems have sometimes been overstated.

Remembering the rudders

As Rear Admiral Julian Lake explained, "Most jet pilots, particularly the ones that never flew props, forget that the rudders are there. The Americans use them to steer the nosewheel on the deck. I had the misfortune to fly the F4D Skyray, a delta-winged monster that caused the invention of the term aileron adverse yaw. It was a carrier-based all-weather interceptor, we flew day and night, on and off the boat, in lots of bad weather. These were all things that it had no business doing. In the PA configuration, if you

put the stick all the way over to the right the nose would yaw so badly to the left that all you would get, beside flying sideways, was about 10° of right bank. The solution was to manually feed in right rudder, but you would still get a lot of sensations very conducive to vertigo. A night instrument approach with a 100-ft ceiling was sheer terror in the Skyray. I instinctively used the rudders when I flew the Tomcat and it was a piece of cake. If you don't use the rudders it flops around all over the place, though. Today's pilots have been spoiled by automatic stability augmentation devices, almost autopilots. The autothrottle is another landing aid that some pilots can almost not do without. It took a long time for the aileron–rudder interconnect to become mandatory. ACLS is seldom used because pilots quickly lose their touch for manual carrier landings."

Automated approaches

Coupled Mode I approaches are not allowed in the F-14A or F-14B because the aircraft's throttle computer is too slow. ACLS is still used for every night landing, and the needles are coupled to give a wind-corrected heading. Throttles have to be disconnected at 200 ft (60 m), however, and because of this they are rarely coupled in the first place. F/A-18s can fly automatic passes right down to touch-down, and the F-14D's improved throttle computer is similarly certified for full automatic Mode I approaches.

The first two Atlantic Fleet squadrons equipped with the new Grumman fighter, VF-14 and VF-32 of CVW-1, undertook carrier qualification in small groups aboard the *Kitty Hawk* and *Kennedy* during December 1974 and February and March 1975. The first two Atlantic Fleet squadrons passed their ORE (Operational Readiness Evaluation) inspections with flying colours in May 1975, then undertook missile shoots at Eglin AFB. On 5 May

In moist air, a transonic pass can generate an impressive and very visible shock wave. This can be a favourite Tomcat air show trick, when conditions are suitable. In service, the F-14's ability to accelerate very rapidly gives it a decisive edge in BVR combat, imparting extra velocity to its missile armament.

Inset left: Preparing a dew-soaked F-14 for flight, one of the ground crew winds down the cockpit access ladder, having already opened the massive clamshell canopy.

1975 Lieutenant Commander Andrews and Lieutenant (jg) Earl Kraay of VF-32 became the first Atlantic Fleet crew to successfully fire an AIM-54 Phoenix, destroying their target (a Bomarc missile flying at 746 kt/856 mph/1380 km/h and 72,000 ft/21950 m). They were followed by Lieutenants Mike Bucchi and Phil McKinney of VF-14. The two units put to sea aboard USS *John F. Kennedy* in June 1975, and were the first F-14 squadrons to work with the Grumman E-2C version of the Hawkeye, and the first units to have all their aircraft equipped with the Northrop TCS (TSU). Their first Sixth Fleet Mediterranean deployment was more successful than the WestPac cruise by VF-1 and VF-2, with only one aircraft being lost, and that through no fault of its own. The aircraft ran off the deck when an arrester gear motor failed. Despite a collision between the *Kennedy* and the USS *Belknap*, the cruise proved to be a success; the Tomcats gained valuable experience in intercepting low-level fighter-bombers during mock attacks by Armée de l'Air Jaguars, Mirages and Vautours, and undertaking successful Sparrow missile shoots at Suda Bay, Crete. Subsequently, the members of CVW-6's VF-142 and VF-143 converted to the Tomcat at Miramar during 1976, with VF-41 and VF-84 of CVW-8 becoming the first Atlantic Fleet units actually converted at Oceana in 1977. Between these units, CVW-9's two squadrons (VF-24 and VF-211) and the units from CVW-11 (VF-114 and VF-213) also transitioned at Miramar. By the late 1970s the Tomcat was fast replacing the F-4 Phantom as the US Navy's shipboard fighter, but its troubles continued.

Indications that rivets in the engine mounts had weakened led to the imposition of major operating restrictions while engines were modified, and to a complete ban on ACM training during the first half of 1976. Cruises during the latter part of 1976 were severely restricted, with F-14 crews flying an average of only 20 missions per crew in a full cruise. The ban was lifted late in 1976, allowing Atlantic Fleet squadrons to send their first crews to 'Top Gun'.

Early plans for purchase of the Tomcat for four US Marine Corps squadrons were abandoned because of cost, but not before the first 'Grunt' aircrews and ground crews had started training with VF-124, incurring costs which reportedly totalled US $6.1 million.

Tomcat for the Corps

The Marines had not originally been included in the F-14 programme, and the Corps' FY 1974 budget request included $130.7 million for the purchase of 10 F-4J Phantoms, plus spares. They were to have been the first of a planned 138 F-4J Phantoms, which were to have cost $891.1 million (initially estimated as $1.73 billion). General Robert E. Cushman, Jr preferred to acquire 138 F-4Js rather than a significantly smaller number of F-14s, and had thought that his service could only afford about 50 F-14s for the same price as the 138 F-4Js. However, because Marine Tomcat procurement could be added to batches of Navy aircraft, the Navy could pay Grumman's overhead, and the Marines would get the aircraft very cheaply. This was demonstrated when Grumman offered 100 F-14s for the same funding as had been contained in the request for 138 F-4Js ($891.1 million, including spares and ground equipment). This undoubtedly represented a very good buy. This offer was made soon after the DoD released the results of a NASA simulation profiling the F-4 (with and without slats) and F-14 against a range of Soviet threat aircraft. The F-14 outfought all of them, while the F-4J struggled. The simulator dogfights were rigorously

A VF-102 'Diamondbacks' F-14A reaches the end of the USS America's waist catapult, tailerons deflected fully to raise the nose. The way in which the very front of the catapult narrows and slopes away is clearly shown, as is the proximity of the aircraft to members of the deck crew. Even when markings were toned down, VF-102's aircraft usually remained fairly colourful, as seen here. The squadron is now equipped with the F110-powered F-14B.

Right: This VF-202
Tomcat is almost
entirely shrouded by the
smoke trail left by its
fast-departing AIM-9
Sidewinder. The AIM-9
remains the F-14's short-
range missile, though
the aircraft has been
equipped with
successively more
capable variants of the
missile. Opportunities
to fire a live missile are
fought for jealously.

*Inset above: This VF-32
F-14A, seen breaking
into the landing pattern
during Operation Desert
Storm, carries one AIM-
54, two AIM-7s, two
tanks and two
Sidewinders, a fairly
typical operational
loadout.*

*Above: In recent years,
the importance of the
F-14 has declined, and
nowadays, most carriers
deploy with only one
Tomcat squadron, but
with three of F/A-18s.
This is an F-14B of
VF-143 'Pukin' Dogs'.*

conducted, although they were slightly artificial in that all were fought on a one-vs-one basis. Six front-line pilots (one a Marine) were selected for the trial, and each received a week of simulator training before flying four times against each simulated enemy aircraft type. "It was no contest. The F-14 just outflew everything we programmed for it to fight," said a senior programme insider. Marine objections to the F-14 rapidly evaporated.

The first all-Marine crew comprised Lieutenant Colonel Don Keast (CO of the Marine detachment) and his RIO, Captain Nellie Dye, who was in charge of Marine F-14 training. They made their first historic flight together in a VF-124 aircraft, Modex 412. The first Marine squadron would reportedly have been VMFA-122, which was undergoing conversion to the Tomcat soon after the successful conversion of VF-14 and VF-31, but, as far as is known, no F-14 ever wore Marine markings. The first USMC F-14s were to have been delivered at the end of

1975. On the day in July 1975 that the decision to axe the Marine Tomcats was announced, the Marines reportedly 'went ape' in the Miramar O-Club, disappointed that they were not going to be getting the new fighters. Instead, it was announced that the USMC would receive four extra F/A-18 Hornet squadrons, and that the Corps' Phantoms would be upgraded for service in the interim. The decision proved to be a good one in the long run, since the F/A-18 promised to better meet the Marines' needs for a tough and robust, versatile and above all simple and cheap warplane. At the time, the decision allowed an estimated saving of 50 maintenance personnel per squadron (while also halving the number of aircrew required in the longer term). Ironically, the Marines eventually developed an operational F/A-18 two-seater to perform FAC-A and other roles which the F-14 could have undertaken without modification.

More F-14s for the Navy

The Marines' loss was the Navy's gain, however, and the number of USN F-14 squadrons was increased by four. This was not always a foregone conclusion, since many observers initially expected the F-14 buy to be reduced by the 80 aircraft originally destined for the Marines. When it was determined that the aircraft would still be procured for the US Navy, it was decided that the Navy would have to give up four F/A-18 units (from 10 to six), but for many this was no sacrifice, since fighter/fleet air defence aircraft then had a more glamorous image than fighter/attack aircraft. In any event, the number of Navy F/A-18 squadrons was soon restored, and even expanded. Arguably even more significant was the transfer of two mobile maintenance facilities to the Navy. They allowed 12 carriers to be Tomcat-compatible, instead of the 10 originally planned.

Another 'customer that might have been' was the US Air Force. In early 1971 it was suggested that Aerospace Defense Command might order a limited number of F-14s if flight tests showed that the aircraft met range and endurance specifications. There were reportedly worries that the F-15 might lack sufficient range for certain missions, and that it would not be ready for service for some time after the F-14 entered service. The F-14 thus

An AIM-7 Sparrow streaks away from an F-14A of VF-213 'Black Lions'. At one time it was believed that the Sparrow would be replaced by the more capable AIM-120 AMRAAM, which has a limited, though significant, fire-and-forget capability.

became a contender for the USAF's Follow-On Interceptor (later Improved Manned Interceptor) requirement, to replace the F-106. Some suggested that the USAF could repurchase F-14As from Iran.

At the end of the day, procurement of even a few F-14s would have threatened the entire F-15 programme, and was not allowed to happen. For many years the two services were careful not to encourage comparison of the two aircraft types, each fearing that they might lose funding for their own aircraft and be forced to accept an appropriate variant of the other. By 1973 the F-15 seemed safe, but it began to threaten the future of the F-14, with proposals that the Navy should examine the acquisition of cheaper F-15Ns (or Phoenix-armed F-15N-PHXs) instead of additional F-14s. Grumman retaliated by persuading the DoD that if the Navy were to be directed to look at the F-15 to meet its requirements, then the USAF's Aerospace Defense Command should be required to re-examine the F-14 as a contender to fulfil its IMI (Improved Manned Interceptor) requirement. In fact, apart from the unacceptable political dimension of buying a US Navy aircraft, the F-14 was probably the best of the three main IMI contenders, the others being a stretched F-111 and an F-15 derivative. The Commander of NORAD, General Daniel James, recommended that the F-14 be purchased in 1977, and his successor, General James Hill, formally asked the Pentagon to consider the aircraft two years later.

F-14s for the USAF?

It was estimated that 170 F-14s would be required, at a cost of US $4.3 billion. An equivalent number of F-15s would cost only $3.9 billion, but it was estimated that 290 F-15s would actually be needed to give the same level of capability, since they scored 50 per cent fewer kills in the USAF's simulations. Changes to the F-14 to allow USAF operation would be relatively minor, including the provision of a USAF-style refuelling receptacle, an HF radio, and a medium PRF mode for the radar. An IMI F-14 with these features even reached the mock-up stage. Much existing USAF ground support equipment was Tomcat-compatible, and the TF30 engine was already in

the USAF inventory with the F-111.

Eventually, both programmes were far enough advanced to be safe from cancellation, but direct comparison was still discouraged. Eventually the two fighters did meet, during Exercise Display Determination in 1978, and then again during a port visit by the USS *Kennedy* to Barcelona in 1978. F-14s from VF-14 and VF-32 were deployed to Zaragosa where they flew DACT sorties against F-15s from Bitburg. The two aircraft were closely matched, with the F-14's RIO giving it the edge in complex multi-bogey engagements, and with the F-15 able to sustain higher turn rates above 15,000 ft (4570 m).

Air superiority

Regardless of how the F-14 shaped up against the contemporary F-15, it certainly marked a considerable improvement over the F-4 Phantom. When service F-14s met F-4s in DACM training they swiftly confirmed the experiences of the test aircrew involved in F-4/F-14 comparitive air combat trials in 1973, described in the 'Forging the Tomcat' chapter of this book. In mid-June 1975, for example, USAF F-4Es visited NAS Oceana for DACT with the Tomcats of VF-14, and proved unable to turn, climb or even keep up with the F-14As. In one engagement, one section of two F-14s was able to beat eight F-4s in simulated air combat. Compared to the F-4 Phantom, the F-14 enjoyed a 40 per cent better turn radius, a 27 per cent better manoeuvre climb, 21 per cent better acceleration and sustained g capability, a 21 per cent better roll rate and a 20 per cent better rate of climb. The

A huge variety of temporary camouflage schemes has been applied to Tomcats for exercises or for temporary use in the adversary role. These aircraft, wearing a disruptive air superiority scheme, were drawn from VF-11, the 'Red Rippers'.

Tomcat's superiority was even more marked in other areas. Radar range was more than 200 per cent better, missile range 250 per cent greater, and combat radius with internal fuel was 80 per cent higher. Loiter times were between 50 per cent higher (with six Phoenix on the F-14) and 100 per cent higher (when both aircraft carried four Sparrows).

Export Tomcats

From the beginning, Grumman had searched for other customers for the Tomcat and first proposed a long-range interceptor version to the US Air Force. Grumman subsequently promoted the F-14 to a number of friendly nations who required a long-range interceptor, including Canada, Australia, Japan and Great Britain. Unfortunately, the aircraft was judged to be too expensive with its AWG-9 and Phoenix, and not sufficiently attractive without it. There were customers, however, for whom the aircraft's high price-tag was no obstacle. In the 1970s, when the Shah of Iran (himself a pilot, infatuated with high-tech hardware and determined to have the very best for his country) was striving to become the dominant force in the

Persian Gulf, Tehran exhibited considerable interest in the Tomcat and other Western fighters. Iran also looked seriously at the F-15 Eagle and, soon afterwards, placed firm orders for the F-16 Fighting Falcon and the Northrop F-18L, land-based version of the F/A-18 Hornet. A few voices were warning that the Shah's fascination for top-of-the-line weaponry was growing excessive and that rumbles of discontent within his populace threatened turmoil ahead. But, Iran was a long-term ally which directly bordered on what was later dubbed 'the evil empire', and was a major supplier of oil to the USA. In any event, arms sales were decided in personal conversations between the Shah and President Nixon, and Imperial Iran's ambitious armament programme forged ahead.

In the competition for the Shah's favour, the Tomcat gained an edge when a strong showing was made by the CO of VF-2, Commander Jim Taylor, and his RIO, Lieutenant Kurt Strauss, at the 1973 Paris air show, and by a personal demonstration for the Shah at Andrews AFB in late 1973. Grumman also hired the Shah's brother-in-law, Houshang Lavi (a close friend of the Iranian air force commander, General Khatami), as a lobbyist for the aircraft. Lamoreaux conducted the briefing for the Shah, whose enthusiasm for the aircraft was such that one scheduled hour turned into seven actual hours. At a later demonstration of the F-14 and F-15, in which a very lightweight F-14 was demonstrated in spectacular fashion, the US Air Force filed a violation against the F-14 crew for "conducting low-level aerobatics over a crowd," and Air Force F-15 programme manager Major General Ben Bellis condemned the F-14 display as "a hot-dogging stunt." It sold the Shah on the naval aircraft, however. Iran's case was not hindered when in August 1974 the Iranian Melli bank stepped in with a loan when the GAO (General Accounting Office) asked Grumman to repay advance performance payments (on the grounds that they were fraudulent or illegal because the necessary progress had not been made). The cheque was ceremonially paid to the Deputy Secretary of Defense by a phalanx of senior Navy officers and Grumman personnel. The deal was nearly scuppered when Lavi's role (and payments by Grumman totalling $28 million) was revealed. Motivated in part by incursions by Soviet MiG-25 'Foxbats' flying from bases on its northern border, the Imperial Iranian Air Force (IIAF) became the first and only foreign purchaser of the Tomcat, ordering 40 aircraft in June 1974 and 40 more in January 1975. The Iranian Tomcats were virtually identical to US Navy F-14As (with different harness locks and a diluter demand oxygen system) and their Phoenix missiles almost identical, except for deletion of the ECCM (electronic counter-countermeasures) suite. At the time, the

General Accounting Office and other watchdog agencies were accusing Grumman of cost overruns in the Tomcat programme.

Iran's F-14s were virtually identical to US Navy F-14As (with different harness locks and a diluter demand oxygen system). The first Iranian Tomcats were delivered to Mehrabad air base on 27 January 1976, and eventually equipped a peak of four squadrons at Khatami and Shiraz. During the summer of 1977, a MiG-25 was tracked by an F-14 while crossing Iran at Mach 2 at 65,000 ft (19820 m). This incident prompted Iran to conduct a live Phoenix firing (at a BQM-34E drone, flying at 50,000 ft/15245 m) as a warning to cease the MiG-25 overflights. The intrusions ceased immediately. After 79 of the 80 Tomcats had been delivered, aircraft No. 80 being retained for trials, the Persian state was swept by revolution, culminating in the fall of the Shah. The 80th Iranian F-14 had been nominated to serve as the prototype for a USAF-style boom-and-receptacle inflight-refuelling kit, which Iran intended to retrofit to all of its F-14s. The revolution killed off all prospects for the repeat order for 70 more F-14s which had been discussed, and for the supply of 400 Phoenix missiles which had already been ordered. The revolution also halted deliveries of 60 F-16s, seven E-3A Sentries and 16 RF-4E Phantoms, and led to dramatic changes for the Imperial Iranian Air Force, which became the Islamic Republic of Iran Air Force (IRIAF). Many pilots went into exile, including most instructors and senior officers, other pilots and ground crew were purged, and the force was suddenly cut off from its prime source of equipment, spares, support and training. It managed to keep most of its F-4D and F-4E Phantoms operational during the 1980-88 war with Iraq, but this was largely due to clandestine assistance from Israel, which also operated Phantoms.

The Tomcat force never proved very effective, since only a small number could be kept airworthy, many aircraft being grounded through shortages of such routine items as brakes and tyres. They did see some action, however, often in a mini-AWACS role. Several were lost. Iraq claimed that

Far left: Ground crew (or, perhaps more accurately, deck crew) manhandle an AIM-54C Phoenix into position, to load it onto an F-14 aboard the USS Forrestal. The limitations imposed by the size, weight and cost of the AIM-54 are such that more than two are seldom carried.

With the checkerboards on the back of his helmet matching those applied to the rudder of his wingman's F-14, a RIO of VF-211 'Fighting Checkmates' demonstrates the superb all-round view afforded by the Tomcat's huge blown canopy. Unusually, the aircraft in the background carries six AIM-54s, a configuration which would rule out landing back on a carrier, without jettisoning two or more of the multi-million dollar missiles.

Air-to-air armament
This Iranian Tomcat is armed with a fairly conventional mix of AIM-7 Sparrows and AIM-9 Sidewinders. There is some evidence to suggest that these missiles have continued to be supplied via countries like Israel, whereas the AIM-54 Phoenix has proved more difficult for Iran to obtain, and is therefore carried less often. Only 284 of the AIM-54s ordered by Iran were actually delivered. The sophisticated AIM-54 is also less easy to keep serviceable, and spare parts are a problem, in the face of US sanctions.

Air-to-ground armament
Although this F-14 is seen loaded for air-to-air duties, the Iranian F-14As do have a significant air-to-ground capability, using dumb bombs and a range of indigenous or indigenously modified air-to-surface weapons. These may include Israeli Popeye missiles, and perhaps even an air-launched derivative of the HAWK SAM.

This F-14A is seen in the unique three-tone green and brown camouflage in which Iran's Tomcats were delivered, and which some Iranian F-14As retain to this day. Other Iranian aircraft have been repainted in a number of new camouflage schemes, similar to those worn by other IRIAF types.

Grumman F-14A
Islamic Republic of Iran Air Force
Shiraz, Iran, 1985

Service
Although many Western observers expected the Iranians to be quite unable to keep their F-14s serviceable, the numbers in use have actually risen. This is almost certainly the result of support from Israel and other nations who are ignoring the arms embargoes imposed by the USA.

Powerplant
Iranian Tomcats use the Pratt & Whitney TF30-P-414 turbofan engine as fitted to many US Navy F-14As, and are thus as handicapped by engine limitations as the US Navy has traditionally been. In fact, the situation is worse, since their engines have never been modified by the manufacturer.

Markings
IRIAF aircraft wear almost the same markings as did those of the Imperial Iranian Air Force, with red, white and green roundels and a similarly coloured tricolour flag.

its fighters (mainly Mirage F1s armed with MATRA 530s and Magics) downed between 12 and 14 Iranian F-14s. Two are known to have been downed by Iraqi Mirage F1s, and another definitely fell to a MiG-21. One was claimed on 4 October 1983, another on 21 November, and more single examples on 24 February and 1 July 1984, while on 11 August 1984 Iraq claimed to have shot down three F-14As. Iranian F-14s are known to have claimed at least three (and perhaps as many as 10) Iraqi fighters in return, including a MiG-21 and two Mirage F1s. A rumour persists, despite the revolution's anti-Communist bent, that one F-14 was secretly whisked from Iran to the Soviet Union for study. Other stories suggest that this aircraft was flown to the USSR by a disaffected pilot. Perhaps more damagingly, Iran received 284 of the 714 AIM-54 Phoenix missiles it had ordered; some of them were almost certainly delivered to the USSR, where they proved of inestimable value to development of the AA-9 'Amos' missile.

Many observers believe that after Iran could no longer receive arms from the West, it exchanged several Tomcats complete with AIM-54A Phoenix and AWG-9 weapon systems to the Soviets in a trade for other arms assistance. These missiles and airframes were supposedly stripped and examined, and would have helped the Soviets in the development of the MiG-31 'Foxhound' and its weapon system. Said one Washington analyst, "Except for some minor changes to the cruciform wings [on the 'Amos'], you could practically pantograph an AIM-54A missile body off it. And I would be hard-pressed to not believe that [the 'Amos'] is a 'Chinese copy' of the birds that were delivered to [the Soviets] by the Iranians." The AA-9 does certainly look just like the AIM-54, but it is generally considered to have a much shorter range and more primitive guidance systems. The Soviet missile is thus something of an enigma: an airframe apparently copied from the AIM-54, married to systems of indigenous origin. Was the AA-9 made to look like the Phoenix in the hope that enemies would assume its performance was similar? Or was the AA-9 actually a direct copy, with the same level of performance? One theory is that the R-33 was an interim missile, which led to the R-37, which may be regarded as a full-up AIM-54 copy. Whether or not the Soviets copied the AIM-54, access to the missile was of great value. Simply having the Phoenix in hand enabled the Soviets to improve their own defensive measures against it.

Iranian Tomcats

It is easy to underestimate the number of F-14s remaining active with the IRIAF. Even as early as 1985, 25 were available for a mass flypast over Tehran, and serviceability and spares supply have probably improved since then. Iran instituted several programmes to manufacture parts and spares for its US-supplied aircraft, and by 1982 was claiming to be able to supply 80 per cent of F-14 components from domestic sources. This was almost certainly an exaggeration, but did reflect a growing self-sufficiency. In July 1985, a US Navy auditor attempted to delay the sailing of the USS *Kitty Hawk* by sending a telegram to the President stating that millions of dollars worth of spare parts were missing, and outlining how Tomcat and Phoenix parts had been stolen from US Navy carriers and sold to the USSR and Iran. The FBI traced stolen spares to the *Kitty Hawk*, *Vinson* and *Ranger*, and arrested seven members of the smuggling ring. Rumours suggest that in the early days of the black market sale of spares to Iran, Subic Bay was the major source of F-14 components. It was unclear how much equipment reached Iran before the arrests, but the shipment which was successfully halted was to have included AIM-54, AIM-9, AIM-7F and AIM-7M AAMs, Harpoon anti-ship missiles, TOW ATGMs, F-14 and F-4 spares, and 10 J79 engines. The TOW missiles alone represented $9.12 million, a staggering 1,140 rounds. This was the largest of eight

smuggling operations discovered during 1985 alone. The clandestine 'Irangate' arms-for-hostages deal almost certainly resulted in the delivery of more critical F-14 spares. When a defence exhibition was held in Tehran in 1996, two F-14s were displayed, and it was said that several squadrons were still in use.

When the Shah fell, the magazine *Aviation Week and Space Technology* reported that Saudi Arabia wanted to buy F-14s in order to replace the Iranian Tomcat long-range interception buffer between them and the USSR. The Saudis subsequently came under great pressure from the USAF to reconsider and to stick with their planned purchase of the shorter-range F-15. The F-14 was almost certainly too difficult to maintain, and the Saudis eventually received British Tornados to augment their F-15 Eagles.

There have been rumours that the F-14 was evaluated by the IDF/AF inside Israel, and even that a handful of aircraft saw service with an Israeli unit based in the Negev. This cannot be confirmed. In July 1984, Britain's *Sunday Times* reported that the delivery of 15 surplus ex-USN F-14As to Greece had been suspended, although this was subsequently strongly denied, and it seems that the F-14 was never even a contender to meet Greek requirements for a new fighter. It seems likely that Iran has been the only overseas operator of the F-14.

With its wings swept fully aft, an F-14A makes a low-level high-speed run past the carrier and its escort ships. The importance of the Tomcat to the protection of the carrier task force remains unparalleled to this day, despite the shrinking number of aircraft assigned to each carrier.

Fleet service

At the time when Iran started flying Tomcats, the F-14 was also becoming numerous in the US Navy fleet. CVW-15 (with VF-51 and VF-111) converted in 1979, followed by CVW-3 (VF-11 and VF-31) and CVW-1 (VF-102 and VF-33) in 1982, then by CVW-17 (VF-74 and VF-103) and CVW-14 (VF-21 and VF-154) in 1983. Eventually, each carrier in the US Navy, with the exception of *Midway* and *Coral Sea* (whose elevators were too small), had Tomcats aboard.

Although much of its equipment was no longer at the leading edge of technology, the Tomcat, with its AWG-9 weapon system and Phoenix missile, was considered more advanced than anything in Soviet hands. This much was clear from the West's then-recent examination of Belenko's windfall defecting MiG-25. With the Cold War still under-way – and several years before any Iranian Tomcat could become a targhet of Soviet intelligence – an F-14A of VF-32 rolled off the deck of *John F. Kennedy* (CV-67) on 14 September 1976, 75 miles (120 km) from Scapa Flow, Scotland. The Tomcat sank intact in international waters, provoking a major salvage operation by US Navy vessels to prevent the Soviet navy retrieving the aircraft and learning its secrets.

Continuing dissatisfaction with the TF30-engined Tomcat kept alive hopes that a re-engined variant would

eventually be produced, even though the original F-14B and F-14C had been cancelled years before. Funding for the development of a new F-14 engine was not included in the FY77 budget, due to bureaucratic delays, but was finally added to the FY79 budget, beginning the long process that eventually led to the F-14D.

It was in 1979 that the eventual successor engine began to be developed. In an effort to build up General Electric (which was thought to be lagging behind Pratt & Whitney in advanced fighter turbofan development), the company was given a development contract to produce a common USAF/US Navy fighter engine for possible application in the F-15, F-16 and F-14. The resulting F101-DFE (Derivative Fighter Engine) was developed from the F101 designed for the B-1 bomber, with a new fan and afterburner scaled up from that used by the F/A-18's highly successful F404.

Fix the engines – at all costs!

Paul Gillcrist expressed no doubt about the motivation for the F-14D programme. "Although the programme was advertised as a threefold improvement in engines, avionics and radar, the hidden agenda was really to fix the engines as all costs." By 1982, the Tomcat was exhibiting four major weaknesses. First and foremost, the F-14A had entered service with an engine originally intended for only the first 36 aircraft, an engine meant to power test, development and training aircraft, and never contemplated to get to the front line. The engine had never been adequately fixed, let alone improved. Reliability and maintainability of the aircraft and its systems remained poor, particularly in the valve-driven fire control system. Radar and missile perfor-mance in the face of modern electronic warfare needed to be upgraded. Finally, the aircraft was obviously ready to benefit from high-speed multiplex digital databuses, modern 'glass cockpit' multi-function cockpit displays, new high-speed high-capacity computers, and other improvements including a fly-by-wire control system,

At the height of the Cold War, the US Navy deployed 22 front-line fleet Tomcat units, whose skills were honed through use of an adversary force of several squadrons, plus the Navy Fighter Weapons School. This taught Tomcat pilots how to deal with small and nimble opponents like the MiG-17, using A-4s and F-5Es as 'replicants'.

Already well inside minimum gun range, an F-14 closes in on an F/A-18 for a flypast. The photo serves to highlight the relative size of the two aircraft, and the more modern aerodynamic ideas incorporated in the F/A-18. The Hornet is a particularly difficult opponent for the F-14 in dissimilar air combat training, for it has similar excess thrust available but with low-speed handling.

a sidestick, and a modern HUD. Most of these improvements became the core of the F-14D project.

The same Tomcat which had been the F-14B test ship, BuNo. 157986, was picked to evaluate the F101-DFE. The so-called 'Super Tomcat' made its first flight at Calverton on 14 July 1981, with the new engines installed, with Joe Burke and Roger Ferguson at the controls. This aircraft was described by Gillcrist as being a "fighter pilot's dream" – an exaggeration, but one which did reflect how much of an improvement it marked over the TF30-powered F-14A. Tests with the F101-DFE were completed in the autumn of 1981.

One of the most unusual incidents to befall a Tomcat crew occurred on 11 September 1980. Lieutenants Blake Stichter and Chris Berg of VF-24 had the ride of their lives when they lost flight control system power. The aircraft dived steeply, negative *g* pinning the crew to the canopy. Stichter broke the top off his control column when he tried to prevent the ensuing inverted bunt to -7 or -8 *g*, though he regained control as the aircraft completed half of the outside loop back to inverted level flight, when the shaken pilot disengaged the stability augmentation system. He then rolled the aircraft erect and recovered aboard the *Constellation*, using the remaining stub of control column.

Tomcat as movie star

For many years the F-14 has been the most 'visible' aircraft in naval aviation, and the most glamorous, thanks to its fighter role and to the colourful unit markings which were *de rigeur* until the early 1980s, and which have re-emerged repeatedly despite attempts to impose a more tactical low-visibility grey. Part of the aircraft's popular appeal can also be traced to its use (over the years) in a number of major Hollywood motion pictures. The first such blockbuster movie was *The Final Countdown*, in which the USS *Nimitz* time-warped back to 1941 to be placed in a dilemma – what to do about the Japanese invasion of Pearl Harbor. The flying sequences included Tomcat-

versus-Zero dogfights, and VF-84 (with its skull-and-crossbones tail badge) hogged much of the limelight.

By 1981 the F-14 was becoming firmly established within the fleet. During that year the CO of VF-114, Commander Jay Yakeley, became the first Tomcat pilot to log 2,000 hours on type, and with VF-24 Lieutenant Chris Berg and Commander Bill Bertsch logged their 1,000th Tomcat hour in the same aircraft, at the same time. The US Navy's leading active-duty tailhooker, Captain John Waples of VF-2, was inevitably flying an F-14A when he logged his 1,505th arrested landing (a major achievement, when 100 traps qualifies a pilot as a 'centurion'). The same year

A VF-2 Tomcat (decorated in temporary blue-grey camouflage) leads a pair of VF-126 F-16N Fighting Falcons prior to a two-vs-one ACM sortie over the Fallon ranges.

Grumman F-14A Tomcat
VF-143 'Pukin' Dogs'
Air Wing Seven
US Navy
USS *Eisenhower*, 1984

This F-14 wears the toned-down markings eventually settled upon by VF-143. Earlier colour schemes had reduced-size, toned-down 'stars and bars', and a considerably smaller 'dog' (really a griffin) on the tail. During 1981 and 1982, several of the squadron's aircraft trialled the blue-grey colour scheme, with markings applied in lighter shades of grey, but this 'negative' camouflage was not adopted for the long term. During 'Ike's' 1984 Mediterranean cruise, much of VF-143's efforts went on monitoring the worsening situation in the Lebanon, from where the US Marines had finally been withdrawn in February 1984.

Keith Fretwell.

Above: Two sections of F-14As from VF-213 'Black Lions' queue to take on fuel from a KA-6D tanker. Interestingly, only one of the Tomcats is in low-visibility colours, foreshadowing the shape (or at least the shade) of things to come.

Top right: There is an old joke that runs 'It takes no great fitness, strength, or skill to clamber up the ladder into the Tomcat's cockpit, but it takes plenty of all three to simply sit still in it, once you're in the dogfight'. It is true that after a typical sortie it seems harder to climb down the ladder than it was to climb up it. F-14 pilots are well prepared to meet the challenge.

(1981) saw the first deployment of the new TARPS reconnaissance pod. The first squadrons to be TARPS-equipped were VF-84 aboard the *Nimitz* on the East Coast, and VF-211 aboard the *Constellation* on the West Coast. Four crews from each squadron received formal TARPS training, and they then trained the rest of their squadron aircrew, allowing any squadron crew to fly reconnaissance missions.

TARPS units

Eventually, half of the F-14A squadrons (one per carrier) received a secondary reconnaissance tasking and about three TARPS-capable aircraft. The original TARPS squadrons were VF-2, VF-21, VF-31, VF-32, VF-33, VF-84, VF-102, VF-111, VF-202, VF-211, VF-213 and VF-302. The deployment of TARPS Tomcats allowed the retirement of the RF-8G in 1982. As the TARPS Tomcat entered service its operators were aware that theirs was a strictly interim solution to the Navy's reconnaissance requirement, and that the RF-18 would take over in about 1989. In 1983, joint exercises with British and Egyptian forces saw the F-14 pitted against a variety of Soviet-built fighter types. The F-14 proved superior most of the time, although the Egyptians were cock-a-hoop that some

encounters had been less one-sided, with at least one MiG-19 getting the better of an F-14. Egypt's Air Marshal Hilmi attributed his pilot's success to the lessons passed to them by combat-experienced Royal Navy pilots who had fought in the Falklands the previous year.

By the end of March 1985 the US Navy had taken delivery of 509 F-14As from its planned total of 899 aircraft. Two landmark aircraft (the 400th and the 500th) were delivered less than one year apart, both going to the prestigious VF-1.

In April 1985, F-14 deliveries were suspended as a result of the discovery of bulkhead cracks in the area of the wing mount and landing gear stays. An interim fix was designed very quickly, and no aircraft needed to be grounded, though a backlog of about 12 undelivered Tomcats gathered on Calverton's ramp before deliveries recommenced.

Tomcats in the Reserve

As front-line Navy squadrons went to sea, the Tomcat was even cleared for use by the Naval Air Reserve. The allocation of F-14s to the Reserve was a controversial step, since many felt that the aircraft was too complex, too maintenance-intensive and too expensive for the reservists to operate. Furthermore, the Navy had hardly enough money to buy sufficient F-14s to re-equip all of its front-line units, let alone to equip the two new air wings it was then planning. The then-Secretary of the Navy was himself a Reserve A-6 bombardier navigator, and under him re-equipment of the Reserve was accorded a high priority. Reservists with VF-301 and VF-302 began their F-14 era in 1984, and VF-201 and VF-202 received the first of 25 reworked early F-14s in December 1986. The aircraft were withdrawn from storage (or from test units) and were rewired and brought up to the latest production standards, with new avionics and reworked engines.

This pair of F-14As is from VF-41, the unit which scored the Tomcat's first air combat victories by splashing two Libyan 'Fitters' over the Gulf of Sidra.

Following the successful trials with the F101-DFE-powered 'Super Tomcat', the new engine was selected for the USAF's F-16C as the F110-GE-100 in February 1984, and later in the same year the Navy announced plans for an F-14D to be powered by the closely related General Electric F110-GE-400. This engine was closely related to the original F101-DFE, but introduced a 50-in (127-cm) plug in the afterburner section. The new engine's nozzle design made it necessary (for drag reasons) to position the new engine 11 in (28 cm) farther aft, and the extended section brought the fan and compressor section 39 in (99 cm) farther forward than the F101-DFE mounting. This helped maintain centre of gravity limits and minimised structural changes to the airframe.

Grumman's hard-working test ship, the former F-14B BuNo. 157986, made another landmark first flight on 29 September 1986 with the F110-GE-400 engine. Piloted by Joe Burke at Grumman's Calverton facility, 157986 reached 762 mph (1226 km/h) and 35,000 ft (10670 m) during this 54-minute trial run. Success with tests of the F110 powerplant led to a $235-million contract on 15 February 1987, the first of several for production of the GE powerplant. The Navy took delivery of its first production GE F110-GE-400 engine on 30 June 1987. It was to become the power source for the better-performing F-14A (Plus) and for the F-14D, which are now serving in some fleet fighter squadrons. These variants, production of which has been drastically restricted by budgetary constraints, are very much the aircraft the F-14 should always have been, and were a welcome addition to fleet squadrons.

A new engine, at last

The new F110 engine was the single most vital part of the F-14A (Plus) and D upgrades, and was fought for with vigour and determination by a group of senior Navy officers in the Pentagon. None was more influential or hard-working than Rear Admiral Paul Gillcrist, whose own book offers a fascinating insight into the political machinations that accompanied the programme. The original plan called for 304 new F-14Ds, with the remanufacture of 200 F-14As to the same configuration; these figures soon changed to 127 new aircraft, with 400 more conversions to full D standards. More F-14As would be re-engined to fill the inventory gap, but without the other F-14D improvements. They would be interim aircraft only, designated as F-14A (Plus). Although the unit price of the basic F-14A had already reached $36 million, the specified 'not to exceed' price of the F-14D was set at $30 million (in 1983 dollars). It quickly became apparent that this could not be met, nor could the stipulated

$750 million fixed-price development programme.

The new engines were robust and reliable enough for pilots to handle their throttles with much more abandon, and the strict throttle-handling limitations of the TF30 were gone forever. Other improvements were less important. The engines nominally produced 30 per cent greater thrust, but they proved to have increased specific fuel consumption. Thus, although the Plus could get off the catapult with 600 lb (270 kg) more fuel because it did not need to use afterburner on take-off, and could reach altitude more quickly and with more fuel, it burned about 100 lb (45 kg) of fuel more, per engine, in cruising flight. The increase in combat radius was therefore negligible, although the F-14A (Plus) can extend the limits of the outer air battle by making an operational sortie 150 miles (240 km) from the carrier, loitering for two hours, and retaining sufficient fuel reserve for several passes on its return to the flight deck.

Although he never flew a re-engined F-14, Gillcrist did fly an F-16XL with the same F110-GE engine. During his flight he semi-stalled the aircraft and, nose-high and descending, put the engine in full reheat and simultaneously put in full left stick. "Throughout the roll the engine spooled up from idle power all the way to full military thrust, into afterburner and all the way to full afterburner without so much as a tiny burp. This was truly a fighter pilot's dream come true."

The definitive Tomcat

The definitive new F-14D variant was also to be equipped with a more sophisticated Hughes AN/APG-71 radar system, an onboard oxygen-generation system, revised cockpit displays with night vision goggle (NVG) capability, infra-red search and track set, ALR-67 radar-warning receiver, NACES ejection seats and all-digital avionics. The last were the most vital element of the F-14D upgrade,

Above: Afterburners blazing, an F-14A of VF-24 thunders along the catapult aboard the USS Constellation. Before the decision was taken to concentrate the F-14Bs with the Atlantic Fleet, VF-24 actually traded its F-14As for new F-14A+s in 1989, prior to transitioning back to the A-model. The 'Fighting Renegades' disbanded in August 1996, a casualty of the drawdown of the F-14 fleet.

Top: The CO of the East Coast training unit, VF-101, has the most appropriate Modex in the Tomcat fleet. This aircraft is an F-14B, reflecting the division of the F-14 fleet between East and West Coasts. Both communities used the baseline F-14A, but all F-14Bs were assigned to the Atlantic Fleet, and all F-14Ds to the Pacific Fleet. All that has changed now, with all F-14s, of all variants, based at Oceana, and with VF-101 as the sole training unit.

Deployment & Further Development

Right: When VF-84 disbanded in 1995, the squadron's skull-and-crossbones insignia and 'Jolly Rogers' name and traditions were taken over by VF-103. This tail belongs to a VF-84 aircraft, and incorporates the badge of Air Wing Eight.

Right, below: These fins bear the markings of VF-21 and VF-54, which served together with Air Wing Fourteen aboard the Constellation and the Independence, before VF-21 disbanded in January 1996.

Below: This underside view of a clean F-14B shows off the aircraft's underfuselage Sparrow recesses, the underwing pylons for external fuel tanks, and the wing glove pylons. Also apparent is the length of the sharply raked intakes.

giving digital databuses, ASPJ, IRST, JTIDS and new RWR gear. The APG-71 is a digital processing system that replaces the AWG-9 and gives the F-14D improved detection and tracking range. This enables the F-14D to fire its Phoenix missiles at slightly longer range than with the older analog radar. The system is also able to operate in more severe electronic countermeasures environments. The APG-71 is a development of the APG-70 used in the F-15E Strike Eagle and has about 60 per cent commonality with the APG-70. The new avionics included a new software package for air-to-air gunnery, almost left off the F-14D because (in the words of the then-head of Naval Air Systems Command), "the F-14 isn't really a fighter plane anyway." It was accompanied by the multi-mode gun sight as a pre-deployment upgrade. This equipment was similar to the F/A-18's director gun sight, with a wider field of view (30°) than the standard F-14 gunsight (10°). While the full F-14D equipment suite was being developed, the interim F-14A (Plus) would introduce the F110 engines as rapidly as possible.

A (Plus) production and D development

By the time Navy test crew Lieutenants Joe Edwards and Scott Stewart flew the first F-14A (Plus), the familiar Grumman test ship, on its 200th flight on 16 September 1987, the type was well on its way toward acceptance. Conversion of existing F-14As to A (Plus) standard followed production of the first aircraft to A (Plus) standard. The final F-14A for the Navy was 'fab' (fabrication) number 557 (BuNo. 162711). The first F-14A (Plus), 'fab' number 558 (BuNo. 162910), made its maiden flight in the hands of Kurt Schroeder and Tony Springs, and was accepted by the Navy on 16 November 1987.

Development of the definitive F-14D was conducted

concurrently with the A (Plus) programme. On 23 November 1987 flight testing began on the F-14D avionics development aircraft, with David Kratz at the controls, and with Tony Springs in the backseat. A second aircraft joined the F-14D development flight test programme on 21 April 1987, when Tom Cavanaugh went aloft in aircraft 161867 (often identified by its Grumman 'fab' number 503), which was fitted with F110 engines and subsequently brought to partial F-14D configuration with the D model's avionics and radar. The first flight of the aircraft considered to be the F-14D Tomcat prototype, 'fab' number 501 (161865), was made on 8 December 1987 at Calverton by Edwards and Stewart.

Externally, the new F-14A (Plus) is readily distinguishable by its larger engine exhaust nozzles, deletion of wing glove vanes, a modified door near the gun port, and radar warning antennas under the glove area.

The re-engined F-14A (Plus) entered fleet service in April 1988, when the first aircraft was delivered to VF-101 at NAS Oceana. Progress was rapid, and the F-14A (Plus) quickly began to pass the milestones which marked the route to front-line service. The first F-14A (Plus) carrier landing was made aboard USS *Independence* (CV-62) on 15 April 1988, and VF-24 and VF-211 converted to the F-14A (Plus) in the spring of 1989, being followed by VF-142 and VF-143 in the late spring of 1990 and by VF-74 and VF-103 in the summer of that same year. The US Navy subsequently decided to redesignate the F-14A (Plus) using the now-redundant F-14B designation, the change taking place in 1991. VF-24 and VF-211 subsequently transitioned back to the F-14A to allow the F-14B to be an Atlantic Fleet type, while the new F-14D was limited to the Pacific Fleet.

Cancelling ASPJ

The first production F-14D was first flown on 9 February 1990 and was displayed in a 23 March 1990 ceremony at Calverton. F-14D aircraft are distinguishable

by a dual chin pod under the nose containing both TCS and infra-red search and track set. By the time it entered service, the F-14D had lost its ASPJ, because the equipment (also intended for applications in the F/A-18 and other front-line types) was cancelled after it failed to meet its performance specifications. Despite this, the ASPJ marked a considerable improvement over older EW equipment, and was selected on merit by a number of Hornet export customers. Fortunately, some ASPJ sets were delivered to the US Navy, and were later fitted to Hornets and Tomcats operating over Iraq, Bosnia and other trouble spots. Whereas the F-14D was just too late to see action over Iraq in 1991 – entering fleet service in July 1992 – the F-14A (Plus) was in front-line service in plenty of time to participate in the Gulf War.

Desert Shield show of force

Saddam Hussein launched his invasion of Kuwait on 2 August 1990. When President Bush announced Operation Desert Shield on 6 August, the nearest American air power belonged to USS *Independence*, then cruising in the Indian Ocean. The carrier's paired F-14A Tomcat squadrons were VF-21 and VF-154, the first of many Tomcats to be brought to the Persian Gulf. Soon afterward came USS *Dwight D. Eisenhower* with two squadrons of F-14A (Plus) Tomcats, VF-142 and VF-143. In September, *Independence* operated in the shallow, confined Persian Gulf. By the time 'Indy' and 'Ike' headed home, a show of force had been made that was almost unparalleled in history.

It was not enough to dislodge Iraq from Kuwait, however, so on 17 January 1991 coalition forces launched Operation Desert Storm. With carrier battle groups under threat (though, in the end, they were never attacked), F-14 Tomcats flew combat air patrols and waited for an outer air battle that never came. Tomcats flying TARPS reconnaissance sorties saw more action that those on fighter missions. The squadrons aboard USS *Saratoga*, which returned to the cramped Persian Gulf, saw more action than anybody else.

The 40-day air war and 100-hour ground war against

Above: A Tomcat from VF-102 'Diamondbacks' banks away after taking off from USS America, *the squadron's long-term home. The squadron now flies F-14Bs from the USS John Stennis.*

Top left: This unique night photograph shows aircraft about to launch for Operation El Dorado Canyon, the 1986 strikes against Libyan targets. Nearest the camera is an F-14A of VF-102, waiting to launch behind a HARM-carrying A-7 Corsair.

Left: Using the callsign 'Vandy One', this VX-9 F-14A inherited its callsign and all-black colour scheme from an F-4S previously used by VX-4. The squadron has used a succession of all-black F-14 Tomcats, though in recent years, in the new politically correct navy, the Playboy Bunny insignia has disappeared.

Deployment & Further Development

Right: An F-14A viewed on final approach. The fact that the tailhook is not extended indicates that this aircraft is landing at a shore base, a rather more gentle procedure than the 'controlled crash' of a carrier 'arrival'.

Bottom: Deck crew swarm over an F-14A of VF-142 'Ghostriders', preparing the aircraft for its next sortie. Despite primitive conditions, engineers manage to achieve a high rate of serviceability and availability, even onboard ship. The F-14's four-section spoilers are shown to advantage.

Below: This F-14A was especially painted for participation in the motion picture Top Gun. *It wears the spurious markings of a fictionalised 'VF-213', and the name of the film's 'bad guy', 'Iceman', played by Val Kilmer. The film's hero Pete 'Maverick' Mitchell (played by Tom Cruise), flew an aircraft marked up with equally spurious 'VF-1' markings, actually drawn from VF-114 'Fighting Aardvarks'.*

Iraq ended with what seemed a clear-cut victory, but details were still sparse after it was over. Despite their importance to seven carrier battle groups operating in dangerous waters, Tomcats apparently had few actual chances to fight. Although the *Washington Times* reported on 13 February 1991 that Tomcats had scored four aerial victories in all, the sole F-14 kill came on 6 February when an F-14A of VF-1 shot down a Mil Mi-8 'Hip' helicopter. The Gulf War did provide an opportunity to revise some old lessons, however, with several Red Sea-based F-14s experiencing compressor stalls while undertaking aerial refuelling. The TF30-engined F-14As proved unable to refuel above 23,000 ft (7010 m) in the hot air, especially when heavily laden, needing to use afterburner above that height.

F-14D into service

The F-14D was originally intended to have entered service with VF-51 and VF-111, with VF-191 and VF-194 reactivating to become the third and fourth squadrons. Some sources suggest that the first two squadrons did receive a handful of F-14Ds, but, whatever the truth, their conversion to the new model was abandoned when the two squadrons of CVW-6 (VF-11 and VF-31) moved to Miramar from Oceana. They then converted to the F-14D in July 1992, and VF-2 became the third F-14D unit in early 1993. VF-51 and VF-111 reverted to the F-14A. The conversion of VF-1 to the F-14D was abandoned when half complete. The squadron was to have joined the *Constellation* when fully converted, but instead disbanded in late 1993.

As recently as 1988, Grumman had hoped to continue delivering the modest number of 12 'new-build' F-14Ds annually to the US Navy through 1998, and to be one of three sources for the remanufacture of existing F-14As. The following year, Defense Secretary Dick Cheney cut back

further developmental efforts, making it likely that production of the Tomcat would end with delivery of F-14D 'fab' number 614 (BuNo. 163904) in December 1991. Newspaper and TV ads floating the theme 'America needs the F-14' did nothing to persuade Cheney to change his mind, although 12 remanufactured F-14D(R)s were eventually reprieved along with 15 F-14A to F-14B conversions. The latter aircraft were drawn from Block 130 and Block 140 F-14As, and were converted to full F-14B standards at Grumman's St Augustine plant between February 1994 and December 1995.

They are referred to as Type KMs in engineering documents, but are identical to the 32 Block 115, 120, 125 and 130 F-14As converted as Type KBs during Fiscal Years 86, 87 and 88 alongside the new production F-14A (Plus) aircraft. Eleven of the KBs were TARPS-equipped. The F-14D(R)s were converted from Blocks 85 and 110 F-14As by Grumman (12 aircraft) and NADEP Norfolk (six aircraft). Five were TARPS-compatible, leaving seven without TARPS (the only non-TARPS capable F-14Ds).

At this juncture, it appeared that the final production figures for the Tomcat would be: 12 YF-14As and 545 F-14As for the US Navy; 80 F-14As for Iran (the last diverted to the US Navy before delivery); 70-90 F-14A (Plus) consisting of 32 remanufactured and 38 'new build' ships and 15 further conversions; 37 F-14Ds, all 'new build'; and 18 F-14D(R)s, giving a total of 762-782 aircraft.

Since then, there have been continuing skirmishes over the future of the F-14 Tomcat. In December 1990, a month before the Persian Gulf war, Secretary of the Navy H. Lawrence Garrett appealed unsuccessfully for new-build F-14D Tomcat production of 132 airframes from 1992 onwards. In March 1991, F-14D Tomcat production funds were yanked from the administration's budget request for FY 1992.

Jon Lake, Julian Lake, and Robert F. Dorr

Defence cuts accompanying the end of the Cold War saw the Tomcat community dramatically slimmed down, and production was prematurely halted after only 37 new-build F-14Ds had been produced. With squadrons disbanding, morale plummeted.

Chapter Three
Grumman F-14 Tomcat Technologies

Although overshadowed in the close-in manoeuvring arena by purpose-built air superiority fighters, it is worth remembering that the F-14 was never intended to destroy its targets in the aeronautical equivalent of a hands-on, down-and-dirty knife-fight. The Tomcat is an assassin, armed with weapons which enable it to pick off its victims at such extreme range that they often do not even know they are in danger. In that long-range intercept role it remains unbeatable. This is because the F-14 is the product of a unique combination of advanced technologies, which remain impressive even today, decades after the aircraft's troubled birth. To the original technologies have been added a number of new ones, so that the latest F-14D is very much a 1990s fighter.

The long, clear blown canopy of the F-14 gives its crew a superb all-round view, as seen in this 'over-the-shoulder' view of an F-14 RIO and his wingman. These F-14As are from VF-2.

Much of aircraft design is simply fashion, though there is nothing necessarily wrong with this, since fashion could be defined as the 'simplest solution engineers can produce with the technology of a given era'. A quarter of a century ago pivoted 'swing wings' were in fashion. No fighter designed today is likely to have them, despite their obvious advantages. They are especially essential for a multi-mission aircraft, as will be explained, and yet the 'swing-wing' F-14 was designed as a single-mission aircraft.

The late Captain L. S. 'Scotty' Lamoreaux, project co-ordinator on the F-14 programme, said in 1969: "The time has come to provide our air wings with a fighter designed from scratch for air superiority. The F-14 is all fighter. Multi-mission capability has not been permitted to dilute the original concept, or degrade the performance required to out-fly and out-fight any aircraft encountered. Comparable in size to the F-4, it is a twin-tailed, swing-wing, twin-engined airplane carrying a mix of weapons and a two-man crew: pilot and missile control officer."

Configuration

The F-14's characteristics and capabilities are a direct result of the aircraft's configuration, aerodynamic design, powerplant and internal equipment, which were in turn determined by the Navy's VFX requirement. The Navy VFX Specification of July 1968 required a crew of two seated in tandem, an internal M61A gun, an advanced radar/missile system and twin

The F-14 was the last in a long line of US Navy carrier-based fighters to be produced by the famous 'Ironworks', as the Bethpage-based company became informally known. Most bore cat names, from the piston-engined Wildcat, Hellcat, Tigercat and Bearcat through the jet-powered Panther, Cougar, Jaguar and Tiger to the Tomcat. Here an F-14 from VF-31 (appropriately known as the 'Tomcatters') is led by a Grumman F8F Bearcat.

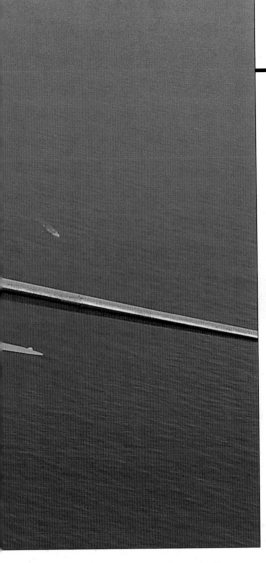

This beautifully clean F-14A belongs to the Pacific Missile Test Center based at Point Mugu (now the Weapons Division of the Naval Air Warfare Center). It has fuel tanks under the engine nacelles, and an AIM-54C Phoenix and an AIM-9 Sidewinder on the port underwing pylon.

engines. It was expected that the engines and radar/missile system would be those used in the unsuccessful F-111B, for which Grumman had been principal sub-contractor. By 1965 impending failure of the F-111B had spurred Grumman to try out 6,000 shapes under Project 303; via many convolutions, they led to the F-14, flown on 21 December 1970.

When it first appeared the Tomcat looked incredibly radical, although in fact few of its features had not been seen previously, on other aircraft. Variable geometry, for example, was hardly new, but the Tomcat was the first operational warplane with automatic, rather than manual, wing sweep. Automatic wing sweep is still not a feature of in-service Tornados, for example. The basic shape of the F-14 is a classic, although perhaps the original pioneer was the North American A-5 Vigilante, which established the use of two engines wide apart, leaving room between the inlets for a forward fuselage growing out of a broad flat area further aft. In the original Vigilante, this housed the aircraft's unique package of jettisonable fuel tanks and nuclear bomb. In the F-14 the two engines were separated by a shallow flat area that its designers called the 'pancake'. Precisely the same arrangement is seen in the MiG-29 and Su-27, which were designed later. This leaves a deep tunnel between the engines and, although this imposes a drag penalty, it generates a great deal of lift, and allows lower-drag weapons carriage. It also has the disadvantage of putting the thrust-line of each engine 54 in (138 cm) from the centreline of the aircraft. If the engines were a few inches further apart, F-14 pilots would qualify as 'non-centreline' rated. This, in turn, means that engine failure, and especially sudden asymmetric thrust in afterburner, causes a nose slice (rotation in yaw) so violent that spin departure and loss of the aircraft have frequently resulted.

Outboard of the engines the Russian fighters have rather stumpy fixed wings, but those of the F-14 are pivoted, and this profoundly affects the wings' geometry. Wings of supersonic fighters

An early F-14A (still without the nose-mounted pitot probe) of VF-31 'Swordsmen' launches from the USS John F. Kennedy, laden with Phoenix, Sparrow and Sidewinder AAMs.

The F-14A's wing is optimised to allow the lowest possible landing speed with comprehensive high lift devices on the leading and trailing edges. Here an F-14A of VF-41 lands aboard the John C. Stennis during shakedown trials of the new carrier. The undercarriage is seen at full extension.

have to be very thin, the ratio of thickness to chord (distance from leading to trailing edges) typically being about 3 per cent. Thin wings obviously have to be extremely heavy if they are not to break, and even with complex high-lift devices they are inefficient at low speeds. By being able to sweep the wing in flight the designers produced a wing which can mimic a short-span, long-chord low aspect-ratio wing for the best possible acceleration, but which can also be a high aspect-ratio wing, with good sustained turn capability, good low-speed handling, and lower thrust requirements. Unlike more conventional supersonic wings, the F-14's wings more nearly resemble those of traditional subsonic aircraft, with a thickness/chord ratio at the pivot of no less than 10.2 per cent. The wing is of NACA 64A2 profile, with a thickness chord ratio tapering to 7 per cent at the tip.

This means the wing can have thinner skins and thus weigh less, and be fitted with efficient high-lift movable surfaces. Moreover, the aspect ratio (the ratio between chord and span, or the 'slenderness' in plan) can be much higher, again increasing aerodynamic efficiency.

The 'Black Knights' of VF-154 are home-ported in Japan. Here one of the squadron's aircraft is seen flying past Mount Fuji. Poor weather is no real handicap to the F-14, which can launch, find and engage its target and recover in weather which would keep many naval fighters on the carrier deck.

Gruman F-14A Tomcat VF-111 'Sundowners'

This F-14A wears the now-vanished markings of VF-111, the 'Sundowners', one of the famous and historic fighter squadrons which disbanded during the early 1990s. The aircraft is seen with four AIM-54 Phoenix missiles under the belly, and is firing an AIM-7 Sparrow from one of the wing glove pylons. The wing stations also carry AIM-9 Sidewinders on their stub pylons. Auxiliary fuel tanks (decorated with the squadron's famous sharkmouth) are carried under the intake trunks. This stores configuration was broadly representative of those carried by F-14As operating in the air defence role, although it was never usual to carry four AIM-54s, because of the limits they imposed on landing back on the carrier, and because the missiles have always been extremely costly. Today, the F-14 is much more of a multi-role aircraft, and mixed air-to-air and air-to-ground loadouts have become more common in front-line units.

Cockpits

The F-14's two crew members sit in separate tandem cockpits, giving a lower-drag fuselage than would have been possible had they sat side-by-side, at the cost of some ease of communication. The cockpits are covered by a huge, blown canopy, giving an excellent all-round view.

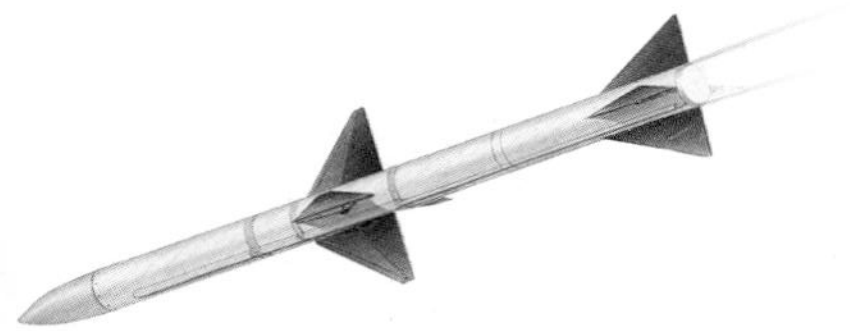

Variable-geometry wing

The F-14 was designed around a sophisticated variable-sweep wing, which could be swept forward to provide a virtually unswept, high aspect ratio wing of massive span (64 ft 1.5 in) for take-off, landing and low-speed manoeuvring, or swept aft to transform the wing and tailplanes into what was virtually a very low aspect ratio delta wing, optimised for supersonic performance and very low drag. Wing sweep angles are normally controlled automatically by a 'Mach Sweep Programmer'.

High lift devices

The moving outer wing panels are provided with devices to alter the wing's camber and chord to generate extra lift (and drag) for enhanced manoeuvrability and slow-speed handling, and also to give a lower nose attitude on approach. On the leading edge are full-span two-section slats, deployable to 7° for manoeuvring, or 17° for landing. On the trailing edge are two-section flaps, deployable to 10° for manoeuvring, or 35° for landing.

Materials

Whereas today's fighters use a high proportion of advanced carbon-based composites, most of the F-14's airframe is of aluminium alloys, albeit with a high proportion of strong, light and corrosion-resistant titanium. The extensive use of titanium was made possible by Grumman's adoption of many new manufacturing processes. The structural heart of the aircraft is a massive electron beam-welded 6A1/4V titanium alloy wing box, sealed to form a fuel tank, and incorporating steel rings in which the titanium/teflon/rhenium/silver wing bearings are carried. For an aircraft of its vintage, the F-14 makes surprisingly heavy use of composites, with composite taileron skins, and boron-epoxy taileron cores and titanium multi-spar sub-structure.

Powerplant

The F-14A was designed to use the same Pratt & Whitney TF30 engine as was used by the F-111. This was to prove a costly mistake. The F-14A has never had the engine performance, reliability or handling characteristics its pilots should have been able to take for granted, and the aircraft did not gain an operationally acceptable engine until the advent of the F110-powered F-14B and F-14D. Modifications were made to the TF30 engine in service, but none fully solved the problems.

Engine intakes

The F-14 has widely-separated engines, with straight-through intake ducts. The intakes themselves are sharp-lipped and of rectangular cross-section with considerable rake-back between the upper and lower lips, and are canted outwards because they were attached to the undersides of the wing gloves, which themselves incorporate considerable dihedral. Their design and location obviated the need for complex boundary layer removal systems. Each intake incorporates twin ramps driven by three powerful hydraulic jacks. These keep airflow at the optimum speed and mass flow for any given airspeed.

Semi-conformal weapons carriage

When the F-14 carries AIM-7s under the fuselage, the missiles are semi-recessed. Other stores (including the AIM-54) are carried on streamlined low-drag pallets, as shown here. Because the weapons are carried between the engine nacelles, they are fairly stealthy from side-on aspects.

Tomcat Technologies

Left: The most expensive warload in the world: an F-14A of VF-32 carries the type's theoretical maximum of six AIM-54 Phoenix missiles. The drag of such a load is tremendous, and the missiles put the aircraft above its maximum carrier landing weight, even with zero fuel; to land, several of the multi-million dollar missiles would actually have to be jettisoned or fired, whether or not 'trade' had been found.

Opposite page: This F-14B is from VF-101 (the 'Grim Reapers'), the Atlantic Coast Tomcat Fleet Replenishment Squadron. The aircraft carries four Mk 83 1,000-lb bombs, with high-drag Blute tailfins. The 'Bombcat' modifications have not been enough to save the F-14 community from several squadron disestablishments, as some F-14 units give way to Hornet squadrons on the decks of the US Navy's supercarriers.

the maximum lift coefficient needed on landing. The wing actually varies in area as it sweeps, but more important is the contribution to overall lift from the fuselage, which becomes significant at higher speeds and higher sweep angles. With the wing swept fully forward at 20°, the area is 595 sq ft (55.3 m²), giving even the heavy-weight D model a wing loading of 95 lb/sq ft. With the wing at 68° the fuselage contributes 443 sq ft (41.2 m²) more lift, raising total area to 1,038 sq ft (96.5 m²) and reducing wing loading to 53 lb/sq ft. The extra area means extra drag, and the F-14 pilot must unload in order to accelerate.

For take-off, landing and low-speed loiter the wings are set to a minimum sweep of 20°. This gives the remarkable span (for a fighter) of 64 ft 1.5 in (19.55 m), far more than would have been possible with a fixed-sweep wing that would have been unable to meet the carrier wave-off requirement. For supersonic dash the wings hinge back to 68°, and to reduce deck spotting area they can be 'overswept' to 75° with weight on the wheels, on the ground. This is possible because, unlike the F-111B, the wings are higher than the horizontal tails. This makes it unnecessary for the Tomcat to have a

Below: The AIM-7 Sparrow is a beyond-visual-range air-to-air missile which uses semi-active radar homing, which is to say that it homes in on radar reflections from the target, which were originally transmitted by the launch aircraft. This means that the launch aircraft has to continue illuminating the target throughout the missile's flight time.

The final arrangement was the best compromise between many variables. A fixed wing would have had to be larger (745 sq ft/ 70 m²), and would have weighed 4,920 lb (2230 kg) more. Even the swing wings were made large (565 sq ft/53 m²) which, together with powerful lift from the huge 'pancake', reduces

Below: An F-14A of VF-114 'Aardvarks' lets fly with an AIM-54 Phoenix. Tomcat aircrew call the AIM-54 the 'Buffalo', because this is apparently what the missile looks like as it stampedes away from the launch aircraft.

An F-14A of VF-124 'Gunslingers', the West Coast training unit, streams vapour as its reefs round in a fast hard turn. The F-14 is an extremely agile aircraft, particularly with its wings swept fully forward, and especially by comparison with the fighters which it replaced, although it is not as agile as the latest lightweight superfighters.

folding wing, to reduce still further the area it occupies during carrier stowage. Parked Tomcats already occupy so little deck space that a wing fold would merely add unnecessary weight. At the normal inflight sweep limit of 68°, the wing trailing edges are aligned with the leading edges of the horizontal tails.

Swing wing

The Tomcat's variable-geometry wing is fitted with a highly capable Mach-sweep programmer which automatically sweeps the wing between 20° and 68° according to Mach number and altitude. Like the engine intake control mechanism, the Mach-sweep programmer relies on data from pitot, static, temperature and Alpha sensors, which were analysed by the AiResearch CP-1166B/A Central Air Data Computer. Block 90 aircraft introduced a new Garrett AiResearch single-channel central air data computer, which brought much improved reliability and maintainability. The Mach-sweep programmer moves the wings from 20° to 25° as speed builds to Mach 0.7, to 50° at Mach 0.8 and then pivots them all the way to 68° as Mach number increases to 0.9. As the angle goes through 62° the spoilers are cut out. Thereafter roll control is effected solely by the tailerons (stabilators), which are more than powerful enough at high airspeeds and with the much-reduced roll inertia that results from the wings being folded back.

The wing-sweep mechanism was rescheduled early in the test programme, when it was found that the wing might bend too much at the aircraft's limiting load factor. The solution was to sweep the wing slightly farther aft at a given Mach number, increasing buffet-free manoeuvring ability and reducing the wing-bending moment. Remarkably, wing loading is actually relieved by increasing body lift as the aircraft reaches its maximum lift coefficient, making wing-loading effectively self-limiting. When swept forward, the fuselage slot into which the wing retracts is sealed by inflatable bags filled with bleed air from the 12th stage of the TF30. The undersides of the wingroot are coated in Teflon to reduce abrasion.

The pilot can override the auto wing sweep, and is also provided with an emergency sweep control, but minimum angle is always automatically limited. This means that the pilot cannot undersweep the wings. A ground attack mode locked the wings at the 55° sweep position (or further aft if speed required it) for bombing, rocketry or gunnery. This removed one variable, thereby simplifying the task of the weapons delivery computer. This is also said by some to be the optimum position for low-level manoeuvres with heavy ordnance loads. Should the wing lock fully aft, it has been claimed that the F-14 can still land safely at 175 kt (200 mph; 323 km/h) with 4,000 lb (1815 kg) of fuel, or 145 kt (166 mph; 268 km/h) with 2,000 lb (907 kg) of fuel, despite the flaps being inoperative when the wing is swept. Current Tomcat aircrew reject these speeds, claiming that even with only 2,000 lb of fuel you are closer to 190 kt (218 mph; 351 km/h) with no flaps, no spoilers, and thus no DLC (direct lift control) – "not a fun place to be."

Going supersonic

As Mach number increases from subsonic to supersonic, the centre of lift moves aft, making the aircraft seem very nose-heavy. With a swing-wing aircraft the effect is obviously even more pronounced. The pilot could trim the aircraft to maintain level flight, but this would reduce tailplane effectiveness and inhibit manoeuvrability. A better solution is to generate extra lift forward of the centre of gravity. In the F-14A this was provided by glove vanes pivoting out from the front of the fixed inboard part of the wing (called the wing glove). The vanes were triangular flat plates, not lift-generating surfaces per se, but intended purely to decrease excessive longitudinal stability caused by the 'pancake'. At Mach 1.4 they were automatically swung out hydraulically through an angle of 15° to increase lift ahead of the centre of lift, and to unload the tailplanes, leaving the latter with enough authority to pull 7.5 g at Mach 2. The vanes compensated for nose-down pitching and reduced stress on the rear fuselage by generating lift and absorbing the load which would otherwise have gone to the horizontal stabiliser. The vanes could be manually extended between Mach 1 and Mach 1.4, but would not operate at wing sweep settings of below 35° at subsonic speeds because they would have destabilised the aircraft in pitch to an unacceptable degree. If the pilot selected the ground-attack mode (constant wing sweep), the glove vanes locked fully out, even down to Mach 0.35. The benefits of the vanes proved marginal except at speeds above Mach 2.25 and, since they added to weight and complexity, they were locked shut, and their actuators were removed. In retrospect, some Grumman designers considered that a fixed canard surface

Opposite page: A pair of F-14As from VF-24 overflies the rugged Nevada desert. Carrying air-to-ground ordnance under the belly, the nearer aircraft also carries an AIM-54 Phoenix, an AIM-7 Sparrow and an AIM-9 Sidewinder, as well as its internal gun.

Left: Obviously no-one told this F-14 pilot that he was flying a heavyweight interceptor, and that his best tactics against a more agile lightweight opponent would be to 'smack him in the teeth with a Phoenix or a Sparrow' from maximum range. Maturity, cunning and luck can allow the experienced F-14 hand to get the better of even an adversary F-16.

The modifications which have earned fleet F-14s (like these VF-24 F-14As) the 'Bombcat' nickname allow the aircraft to drop only a narrow range of 'dumb' air-to-ground weapons, including Mk 80 series freefall bombs (slick and retarded) weighing up to 2,000 lb, and various CBUs. The aircraft is not compatible with any air-to-surface missiles, laser- or electro-optical-guided bombs.

(working with vortices) would have been a more elegant solution. On today's new or rebuilt aircraft – the B and D versions – the pivoted vanes are eliminated altogether, longitudinal control being adequate without them even at supersonic speed and with the centre of gravity at its aft limit. The gloves themselves (i.e., the whole outer parts of the 'pancake') have sharp dihedral, to reduce cross-section and also to minimise supersonic wave drag. The glove vanes also reduced supersonic trim drag. At rest, the outer wings are horizontal. Under vertical accelerative loads they naturally bend upwards, especially at minimum sweep. The wing-sweep mechanism is designed to function reliably even under the limit design load factor of 7.5 g, although rate of change of sweep is reduced from 7.5°/sec to 4.0°/sec.

Although it used a variable-geometry wing, and although it needs sophisticated systems and aerodynamic devices for carrier landings and high supersonic speeds, the Tomcat employs a remarkably conventional flight control system. The F-14 is the last of the pre-FBW fighters, and makes no use of artificial stability or fly-by-wire. Instead the Tomcat's aerodynamic flight control surfaces use a conventional mix of rods and cables, springs and weights, servos and boosters. The wing sweep mechanism, the slats, flaps, tailerons and rudders all have direct mechanical linkages, and only the spoilers are indirectly electrically driven. The aircraft is a basically stable machine, quite flyable throughout most of the envelope even without stability augmentation.

One historical problem with the F-14 was caused by the close proximity of the ECS ducting and the control rods aft of the cockpit, in the 'turtleback'. Over the service life of the aircraft there have been a number of control rod burn-throughs caused by ECS failures, making the benign-sounding ECS failure one of the F-14's scariest emergencies. On one occasion, the pitch control rod burned through while an aircraft was supersonic, driving the stabilators to their full deflection and literally vaporising the aircraft and crew by generating a sudden 'spike' to an estimated load of 33.

High lift devices

The 'movables' on the outer wings comprise leading-edge slats and trailing-edge flaps. The slats are conventional constant-profile surfaces in two sections extending over the whole span of the movable wing, power-driven together to 7° for air combat manoeuvres and to 17° for landing. The leading-edge slats were initially available only for landing (when they deployed to 17°) but were eventually modified to allow their use as manoeuvre devices at slow airspeeds, deploying to 8.5°. The trailing-edge flaps are simple-hinged, single-slotted surfaces, again in

The skull and crossbones insignia on the fin of this F-14A identifies it as belonging to VF-84 'Jolly Rogers'. Taking off from a carrier deck in daylight is difficult, landing back aboard is even more challenging, and trying to land at night is harder yet. Only the pick of the US Navy's elite fighter pilots get to fly the F-14, where such operations have to be routine.

Above: A flight of four 'Diamondback' F-14s breaks for the camera. As the long-range defender of the carrier battle group, the F-14 usually mounts a lonely combat air patrol (often in conjunction with one more F-14, to allow constant radar coverage of the most likely threat axes) miles out from the ship, often with tanker support from a KA-6D Intruder, and perhaps under the control of an E-2C Hawkeye.

This F-14A of VF-21 'Freelancers' is seen 'popping' IR decoy flares during a high-speed low-level run. The F-14 has a comprehensive defensive EW suite, although it is only now receiving the much-needed ASPJ jammer.

Right: Steam streams from the catapult shuttle and the deck crew rush forward to prepare to launch another aircraft as an F-14D of VF-2 (the 'Bounty Hunters') blasts off from one of the two bow catapults of the USS Constellation. The new engines of the F-14D (and F-14B) allow it to make zero-wind take-offs or to take off at higher weights, or merely give a greater safety margin. The Tomcat's full-span flaps are clearly visible in this view.

On final approach to the carrier, this F-14A has hook, flaps and gear down and airbrakes deployed. The orange 'meatball' and line of green horizontal lights which the pilot uses to maintain the correct approach path can just be seen on the port side of the deck, beyond the parked A-6s.

two sections extending to the tip. Auxiliary flaps are located even farther inboard, on the trailing edge of that part of the wing which retracts into the fuselage, and can thus only be used when the wing is swept fully forward. The normal two-section flaps can be extended to 35° for landing, or to 10° when used as fast-acting manoeuvre devices, controlled via the air data computer, and can be used at wing sweep angles of up to 50°. They were originally manually actuated by use of a thumbwheel on the control column, generating lift, and permitting higher *g* during a turn. The fact that the pilot had to assess when to use them increased workload and, as often as not, they were simply not used. The manoeuvre flaps were automated in Block 90 aircraft, scheduling automatically as a function of Mach number, wing sweep angle and angle of attack. The automated manoeuvre flaps allowed modified aircraft to pull between 0.5 and 1 *g* more in a sustained turn than

For close-in engagements, for extra combat persistence or for destroying low-value targets, the F-14 uses the IR-homing AIM-9 Sidewinder AAM.

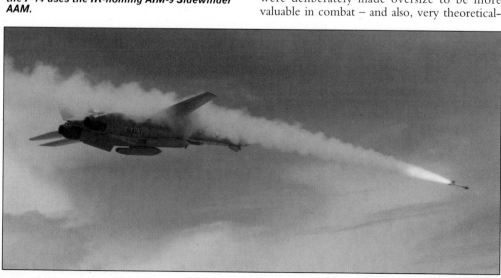

unmodified aircraft. In Block 90 aircraft the flap drive actuators (which had proved prone to failure) gained slip clutches and driveshaft couplers. The provision of full-span flaps is possible because, instead of ailerons, control in roll is provided by tailerons (differential tailplanes) and spoilers.

The F-14 has four-section spoilers on the upper surfaces of its wings, and uses them to augment the differential use of the tailplanes at wingsweep angles of 57° or less. The spoilers can be pre-armed to actuate to 55° on touchdown, to reduce the landing roll by acting as lift-dumpers. The inboard spoiler sections are actuated hydraulically, while the outboard sections operate electro-hydraulically, using their own independent hydraulic system, and are not connected to the back-up flight control system which can actuate the rudders and tailplanes electro-hydraulically.

Quick-opening speedbrakes

The rear part of the broad fuselage 'pancake' is reflexed (gently curved upwards), which reduces both supersonic trim drag and the negative zero-lift supersonic pitching moment. Above and below this region are door-type speed brakes, the lower one split by the hook. Opening quickly above and below to 60°, they were deliberately made oversize to be more valuable in combat – and also, very theoretical-

ly, to stabilise speed in dive-bombing attacks, should an F-14 ever be called upon to do this. (Upon reading an early draft of this chapter, one Tomcat RIO was moved to comment that, "If my pilot EVER uses speedbrakes to slow us down in a bomb run over enemy territory, I'll shoot him myself.") The upper brake has an area of 8.6 sq ft (0.8 m²), while the lower brake is only 7.4 sq ft (0.69 m²). The use of brakes above and below the fuselage minimises trim changes on actuation. The smaller lower brake is nevertheless long enough to run the risk of scraping the runway on landing, so is interlinked to the landing gear, restricting its deflection to 18° with the gear lowered.

The flying controls are actuated using three systems: hydraulic and electro-hydraulic, with a back-up electro-hydraulic system available for pitch and yaw control. The four-section spoilers are usable at wing sweep angles below 57°. The inboard segments are actuated via the main hydraulic system, the outboard segments using the electro-hydraulic system, like the rudders and tailerons.

The final winning F-14 design had a single fin with two large ventral fins that hinged sideways to clear the deck on landing. The Navy (perhaps shortsightedly) objected to the ventrals on the grounds of weight, complexity and engine access, so the F-14 had to have two large fins, canted outwards by 5°. This countered the powerful vortices which streamed back from the body, inlets and gloves at the (previously impossible) angles of attack which

An F-14D taxis on the deck of the Constellation. The aircraft is externally distinguishable from the similarly-powered F-14B by the small RHAWS antennas on the wing glove leading edge, and by the dual sensor pods below the nose.

the F-14 can reach, in the region beyond 50°. Above all, twin fins provided adequate directional stability and control in the event of a single engine failure. Duplication in the event of battle damage was once said to have also been a factor, though if battle damage was ever bad enough to take out one fin, the crew would be in very deep trouble indeed. The port fin houses the VHF antenna, and a TACAN antenna is housed in the starboard fin. The twin fins also provided the added advantage of reducing overall height for below-decks carrier stowage. To enhance directional stability the Navy did allow shallow fixed ventrals to be retained, and these also act as heat exchangers. They are canted outwards and exert lateral forces greater than their area might suggest. They not only enhance yaw stability but also oppose the twisting effect of the main fins on the rear fuselage, and thus enable structure weight to be reduced.

Intakes and construction

Utterly unlike the F-111B, the engine air inlets are two-dimensional sharp-lipped rectangles with the sides very acutely swept back. Due to the glove dihedral the inlets are tilted, and even at the top the inner wall is at least 8 in (20 cm) from the side of the fuselage upstream. Thus, the sluggish boundary layer from the forward fuselage can be ignored, no complex diverter system being needed. The upper wall of the duct is made up of front and rear hinged panels, driven by three hydraulic jacks controlled by a system that senses flight Mach number, duct-exit Mach number and angle of attack to feed the engine with the correct airflow. The hinged panels, or ramps, vary the diffusion in the inlet and at supersonic speeds close down the throat area while diverting a large excess airflow out through a door in the top of the 'pancake'. At Mach 0.5 there is no flow through this aft-facing door, but at low speeds (especially on take-off) the flow is in the reverse direction, extra air being sucked in. The nacelle installation gives quick access for pre-flight inspection and engine oil replacement. Grumman claims that 80 per cent of on-aircraft engine accessory corrective maintenance can be performed with the aircraft in an operational mode and its clamshell access doors open.

In a fighter designed today, most of the airframe would be of advanced composites, but 96 per cent of each F-14 is plain metal. The

Although the US Navy F-14 fleet has seen some unit disestablishments recently, the type's future is not in doubt, and it continues to play a vital role in defending the US Navy's carrier battle groups, still the tip of America's foreign policy spear.

This NATC F-14D is covered with tiny camera calibration markings, indicating that it has been much-photographed during separation and firing trials of external stores. It is seen here coming aboard the Stennis.

fuselage is a conventional semi-monocoque, with machined main frames and titanium longerons. In very few places the metal is used unconventionally, notably the tailerons whose skins are panels of boron-filament composite bonded with epoxy adhesive.

Low aluminium content

On the other hand, only 36 per cent is aluminium alloy, whereas 20 years earlier the percentage would have exceeded 95. The brutal strength requirements of catapult shots, arrested landings and hitting the deck at a vertical velocity of 24.7 ft (7.5 m) per second results in no less than 15 per cent of the F-14 being steel (opposed to 5.5 per cent in the F-15). A total of 25 per cent is titanium, a remarkable figure for the 1960s, though this was very similar to the contemporary F-15. The extensive use of titanium instead of steel results in a weight saving of some 40 per cent (900 lb/410 kg in the case of the wing box alone). The use of titanium (actually an alloy comprised of six parts titanium to four parts of vanadium in the F-14) was also significant in that its corrosion resistance makes it particularly suited to maritime aircraft applications, but it is a very difficult material to work with, requiring expensive hot- and creep-forming processes which make manufacture expensive and time-consuming. Grumman broke much new ground in titanium working, developing new hot-forming processes, refining chemical etching methods and perfecting the moulding of components from heated titanium powder. These processes have since been exploited in many newer aircraft. In addition to the fuselage longerons, the inlet support frame and engine support beams are of titanium construction,

while the main gear support frame and the engine mounts and taileron connections are steel.

Grumman actually built the forward and mid-fuselage section of the F-14, including the vital wing box, at Bethpage, and then sent the entire unit (with engine nacelles, wing gloves and intakes attached) by road the 45 miles (72 km) to Calverton for final assembly. Large parts of the F-14 were not actually built by Grumman, with fully 60 per cent of Tomcat sub-assembly production being undertaken by a total of 150 sub-contractors. Bendix built all the landing gear struts and traces, with B. F. Goodrich supplying the wheels, tyres and the original brakes. (Goodyear supplied the later carbon brakes.) Fairchild Republic built the aft fuselage at its Farmingdale plant (on Long Island, quite close to Bethpage) and produced the tailfins and rudders at Hagerstown. Aeronca built the speed brakes and access doors for the tail section, while engine inlet ducts and nacelles were built by Rohr Industries. Kaman Aerospace was another major sub-contractor, producing wing skins, leading-edge slats, trailing-edge flaps and spoilers, while Hamilton Standard took responsibility for the wing-sweep actuator and Sargent the titanium wing pivot bearings. The Tomcat's canopy and windshield was produced by Swedlow, and Brunswick made the upward-hinging radome.

Sub-contractors

Internally, even more of the F-14 comes from outside sources. Sundstrand supplied the emergency generator and integrated drive generator. Garrett AiResearch built the ATS200-500 engine starter, the central air data computer, the temperature control system and the environmental control system refrigeration unit. Control actuators for the stabilators and rudders come from Bendix, Marquadt supplies the inlet control servos, and Plaseau the ram air door actuators. Pneumo's National Water Lift

Division supplied spoiler servos and other flight control system components. Gull Airborne Instruments was responsible for fuel measuring equipment, and for engine instruments, flap position indicators and an AoA indicator. The various components and sub-assemblies of the F-14 were assembled at Grumman's Calverton Plant 6, taking about 65-70 days per aircraft.

The aircraft's structural heart is the 22-ft (6.7-m) wing carry-through box, which joins the pivots for the wings. It is entirely made of 6Ti/4V titanium alloy, and was the largest electron beam-welded titanium structure fabricated up to that time; it saved 900 lb (410 kg) by comparison with a similar steel structure. The box was built with 70 welds created by a focused electron beam, giving a very narrow, strong and distortion-free join. The use of bolts was studiously avoided in the vital and highly-stressed wing box in order to avoid any of the fatigue problems which such fasteners can produce. It formed a fuel-tight integral tank, part of a group of tanks which occupied most of the fuselage behind the cockpit, along with integral tanks in the movable outer wing panels. They used no sealant, instead employing oversized rivets punched into holes in the titanium alloy skins with such force and accuracy that they fused into the metal to produce a fuel-tight joint. The Tomcat's need for a long endurance and extended range meant that internal fuel tankage was maximised and, as a result, some F-14 missions could theoretically be flown on internal fuel alone. This is hardly ever practised, though, since to discard the external tanks is to lose about one hour of flight time.

The RAG (Replacement Air Group) sometimes flies without external fuel to make the aircraft less heavy and cumbersome to handle, and to make conversion training easier for nugget pilots. Grumman therefore designed supersonic external tanks for carriage below the intake ducts, which are now carried almost as a matter of routine. These 267-US gal (1010-litre) drop tanks can be flown at speeds of up to 660 kt (760 mph; 1225 km/h) or Mach 1.8, and have no *g* or altitude restrictions. They can theoretically be jettisoned full at all altitudes, from VMin to 600 kt (690 mph; 1110 km/h) or Mach 1.2, and at 0 to 7.5 *g*. Empty tanks can theoretically be jettisoned only up to 350 kt (400 mph; 645 km/h), and when pulling 3 *g* or less. Part-full tanks have to be jettisoned at 1 *g*, with the same speed restrictions as empty tanks. In service, jettisoning is restricted to speeds below Mach 0.9 at all altitudes, from 1 to 3 *g*, whether full, empty or part-full. The F-14 cannot trap with partial tanks, due to the danger of overstressing the connections.

At the ends of the centre-section box are the pivots which, instead of being massive steel rings enclosing a giant cylinder as in other 'swing-wing' aircraft, are titanium annular rings with a part-spherical surface coated with Teflon and rhenium/silver. Either the upper or lower bearing can fail without danger to the aircraft. Each wing is swept by a ball-screw actuator behind the carry-through box, the left and right drives being synchronised to ensure that sweep is always the same on both sides. The tight sliding joint between the glove and the front of the wingroot is designed to 'breathe' as the sweep changes, while the rear seal is maintained by a curved row of flexible plates. The rotary flap and slat drives are telescopic to allow for wing sweep changes. The wing box is so strong that the component from the crashed first prototype was actually recovered intact from the wreckage and used for ground testing.

Fuselage structure is mainly conventional, although many frames are machined forgings. Almost the whole centre-fuselage structure is titanium alloy, although the flush-riveted skins are aluminium alloy. The nose is an enormous radome of epoxy-glassfibre that can be hinged upwards for access to the radar. Equally impressive for its size, the canopy is moulded from a single sheet of Plexiglas, bulged for minimal optical distortion yet giving both crew a superb all-round view. The propulsion pods, including the ducts, are composed primarily of bonded aluminium-alloy honeycomb. The fins and rudders are likewise of bonded aluminium honeycomb structure, whereas the tailerons are boron/epoxy composite laid on a titanium multi-spar substructure, but with honeycomb leading and trailing edges. The taileron skins were the first major structural production components on any aircraft, civil or military, to be manufactured of composites.

Landing gear

Among the most highly stressed parts are the landing gears, which in consequence use shock-absorbing legs made largely of high-tensile vacuum-melted steel. The main legs are single tubes, nearly vertical when extended, and are hydraulically retracted forwards as the single wheel rotates through 90° to lie flat above the leg in the wing glove. The tyre has high pressure (there is little chance of deployment to a soft airstrip) and the brakes are

An early F-14A (modernised and brought up to the latest standards) lands at the Dallas home of VF-201, the sole remaining Reserve Tomcat unit. VF-201 has long been based in the Lone Star State, a fact reflected in the unit's flying suit patch.

multi-disc carbon units, replacing beryllium brakes from 1981. The nose gear has twin steerable wheels and retracts forward under the front cockpit. Once aligned over the carrier catapult the nose gear is compressed, shortening by about 14 in (36 cm). The steel towbar, or strop link, is then released to fall downwards and be positioned over the catapult shuttle. The brutal pull of the shuttle would fling the F-14 off the bows at flying speed even with engines off and the park brake on. Shortening the leg reduces the severe bending strain and, by making the fighter 'kneel', prevents the wings from trying to lift until rotation as the aircraft leaves the ship. On return, as the hook is lowered, the nosewheels are automatically centred. This avoids problems on hitting the deck, and especially prevents the gear from castoring as the fighter rolls back under wire tension after coming to rest. Tyre pressures are adjusted between ship and shore operations, with higher pressures aboard ship. Aboard ship, main and nose tyres are inflated to 350 psi, whereas for airfield operations, the nose gear tyres are at 105 psi, with the main gear tyres at 245 psi. Goodyear is the sole supplier of Navy aircraft tyres, and is paid according to the amount of wear the tyres endure before failure.

The crew boards via a retractable ladder on the left side, from the top of which outward-folding steps give access to the front and rear cockpit. The seats are Martin-Baker GRU.7A or, in the F-14D, NACES (Mk 14) units. The arrester hook is a single 'sting' of high-tensile steel, normally housed in a small fairing under the extreme tail on the centreline. No braking parachute is provided.

Powerplant

The obvious engine to choose for the F-14A was the Pratt & Whitney TF30, as qualified for the F-111B. This truly revolutionary bypass jet engine, or low-bypass-ratio turbofan, had been the world's first augmented axial-flow turbofan and was derived from the JTF10A. It was marginally adequate in thrust but had a bad history of compressor stalls in its only previous application, the F-111. It was expected that the much better inlet and longer duct of the F-14 would avoid this problem – and in any case, a much later and more powerful engine, the F401, was planned for all but the first few F-14s. The TF30-P-412 (derived from the F-111D's TF30-P-12, and broadly equivalent to the F-111F's TF30-P-100) became the standard powerplant in early production aircraft. It was

the cause of more than a few headaches to the Navy, at one stage having to be removed, stripped down and inspected every 100 flying hours. In one early example of the tribulations the Navy was to endure for years, an F-14A powered by the -412 had to make an emergency landing at San Clemente, California, due to fan blade failure. Embarrassingly, San Clemente was the home of soon-to-resign President Richard M. Nixon, thereby assuring close media attention. The actual F-14A engine, today the TF30-P-414A, at least features an excellent variable nozzle with movable leaves or petals which, instead of merely being hinged, are mounted on rollers and slide on curved tracks to preserve the optimum profile, closed down to minimum area in subsonic flight (except for afterburner take-off) and fully opened to a convergent and then divergent profile at supersonic speed in afterburner.

The engine in detail

The TF30 has a three-stage fan with a titanium rotor and stator, with a titanium six-stage low-pressure compressor (with steel stator blades) and a nickel alloy seven-stage high-pressure compressor. The annular combustion chamber consists of eight Hastelloy X flame cans, each with four dual orifice burners. The single-stage high-pressure turbine, built to withstand temperatures exceeding 1,832°F (1000°C) is made of cobalt-based alloy, while the three-stage low-pressure turbine is of nickel-based alloy construction. The augmentor consists of a five-zone afterburner within the inner liner of the double-walled outer duct.

The TF30, like all similar fighter turbofans, delivers very low fuel consumption in cruise power (less than 2,000 lb/907 kg per hour, per engine, and typically about 1,800 lb/820 kg per hour per engine), but consumption shoots up in afterburner. During a zone one afterburner climb, consumption typically rises to 11,000 lb (5000 kg) per hour, per engine, and in zone five afterburner fuel consumption can rise as high as 41,000 lb (18635 kg) per hour per engine. To put this in perspective, the F-14's internal fuel capacity is 16,000 lb (7270 kg) (16,500 lb/ 7500 kg according to some sources). This was intentionally greater than was strictly necessary to meet the aircraft's stated air superiority mission combat radius, the extra tankage anticipating the higher fuel consumption of the advanced technology F401 engine planned for the original F-14B and F-14C. Interestingly,

An astonishingly clean F-14B of VF-24 makes a high-speed run, shock diamonds streaming from its F110 engine's augmentors. The F110 brought about a revolution in F-14 performance and operating procedures.

best cruise and best loiter speeds are very similar (about 500 kt/575 mph/925 km/h), significantly slower than the F-4's cruise speed (by about 100 kt/115 mph/185 km/h) but burning only half the fuel.

The planned F401 was cancelled, however, and for 20 years the TF30 was the worst feature of the F-14. Only over many years has the problem of compressor stall, and the usually associated one of blade containment, been progressively solved. In fact, it took a decade just for an improved TF30 to become reality: the -414 version arrived in 1977 with the 252nd Tomcat. As an interim measure, some improvements were made to produce the TF30-P-412A. The fan blades themselves were redesigned and constructed of a different composition of titanium, less susceptible to stress corrosion cracking. Thin steel sheets, lined with an ablative surface, were added to protect control rods from fires in the engine nacelles, while titanium sheets were added above the engines themselves in a further effort to contain fires. Two fire extinguishers were also added, one in the nacelle and one in the accessory area intended to protect the flight control rods in the centreline duct. The most notable change on the definitive -414 was the fitting of steel containment cases around the first three fan stages as a precaution in the event of blades being thrown by the rapidly revolving turbine. This hardly solved the engine's problem, but it did protect the aircraft from its engine. These alterations increased aircraft weight quite dramatically, and slightly reduced thrust. Until these changes were made, most aircraft which suffered a fan-blade separation were lost in the ensuing uncontrollable fire.

Re-engining with new TF30s

Existing Tomcats were retrofitted with the -414, so that the final TF30-P-412 engine was out of service by the summer of 1979. Development work on the -414 engine did not go without mishap. On 2 February 1977, an F-14A of the Strike Test Directorate, Naval Air Test Center, NAS Patuxent River, Maryland, crashed after entering a spin during engine stall tests of the -414. The two crew members were killed.

Once this engine became standard, a further improved version came along. The first production Pratt & Whitney TF30-P-414A was delivered in early 1981 and began to replace existing TF30-P-414s. The -414A involves 31 minor changes for improved reliability and durability and was adopted after a development programme instituted from October 1978, which included 3,300 hours of engine testing. This extended the hot cycle inspection period from 550 to 1,000 hours, and doubled the TBO from 1,200 to 2,400 hours. Some 1,007 kits were issued to the Navy, and the engines were modified as the aircraft came in for their 30-month overhauls. Improvements to the TF30 have been little more than band-aids, however, and have still cost more than a quarter of a billion dollars. The containment case and other engine modifications were accompanied by some fixes that were cheaper to accomplish, but which caused greater resentment. They led to additions to the flight handbook which forbade fast throttle movements in huge swathes of the flight envelope, "preventing the pilot from using the throttle chops and jams to full afterburner that are necessary to win the fight," as Gillcrist put it.

Dogfight

In any dogfight situation the pilot has always had to handle the engine carefully to avoid a stall. With or without a stall, afterburner ignition failure posed a further problem and is still a hazard with the F-14A, since it inevitably results in the severe asymmetric thrust that can all too easily lead to control loss and entry to a spin, from which the only answer is to eject. This is a problem in all flight regimes, but particularly at take-off when, because of basic lack of thrust, use of afterburner is mandatory. Pratt & Whitney has striven over the years to improve matters, but it has been an uphill struggle.

The engines' handling limitations also imposed constraints on the F-14 pilot's exuberance in a close-in turning fight. In his excellent book *Tomcat, the F-14 Story*, Rear Admiral Gillcrist wrote, "I had ample opportunity to rage at 'those idiots in the Pentagon' for what was abominable engine performance in the F-14A. I had plenty of reason to complain, for, despite extremely restrictive throttle movement limitations imposed on the aircrews, we were experiencing a little over one compressor stall per week in the fleet squadrons." The compressor-stall problem remains particularly serious, especially at high angles of attack, and engine problems have accounted for an unacceptably high proportion of Tomcat attrition. This was underlined by outspoken Navy Secretary (and Naval Reserve aviator) John F. Lehman, Jr, who told Congress in 1984 that the F-14/TF30 combination was, "probably the worst engine/airframe mismatch we have had in many years. The TF30 is just a terrible engine and has accounted for 28.2 per cent of all F-14 crashes. The F-14 can perform its mission, but has to be flown very carefully. You have to fly the engine, and cannot fly it in certain parts of the upper left hand corner of the envelope without high risk."

Arguably more serious still, until the introduction of the re-engined F-14B and F-14D, was the Tomcat's lack of thrust. The low-drag airframe meant that performance was impressive, but the lack of specific excess power from the TF30 was a major limitation in sustained manoeuvring, reducing the benefits of the variable-sweep wing. Even with all the improvements, the engine's power has never been more than marginal, the combined thrust at sea level in full afterburner being 41,800 lb (185.9 kN), compared with the maximum weight of 74,349 lb (33725 kg), which makes it harder to dogfight with later aircraft whose thrust/weight ratios are well above unity.

A total of 557 F-14As was built and they still comprise the majority of F-14s. Few are now likely to be rebuilt into the F-14D(R) version. Their engine will remain the TF30-P-414A, still rated at 20,900 lb (92.97 kN) but producing much less visible smoke than earlier TF30 engines. Compressor stalls and even blade shedding are still a problem, although a much reduced one, and containment of shed blades is now considered to be certain.

An all-new engine

The final answer to the engine problem was, of course, to use a different engine, and Grumman kept evaluating possible replacements. It eventually found a suitable new powerplant in the shape of the General Electric Derivative Fighter Engine (DFE). The DFE programme was launched in an effort to bring General Electric back to technological parity with Pratt & Whitney, whose predominance promised to make future engine competitions somewhat one-sided. Pratt & Whitney engines powered the F-14, F-15 and F-16, with General Electric's only modern fighter engine being the F/A-18's F404. The DFE resulting from the programme might never actually have entered production, although continuing problems with the F100 in the F-15 and F-16, and with the TF30 in the F-14, led some to regard the new engine as a potential replacement or fall-back. On 5 November 1978, the USAF's Systems Command finished definition of a limited development programme, outlining the combination of the core of the B-1's F101 engine with a scaled-up fan and afterburner derived from that fitted to the F/A-18's F404. General Electric was awarded a 30-month development contract in March 1979, producing three full-standard prototype F101DFE engines and two 'boilerplate' F101-X engines purely for ground testing. Engine no. 003 (the first F101DFE) underwent general systems and operability trials, while 004 'flew' two blocks of 1,000 flying hours, each simulating the respective flight profiles of the F-16 and the F-14. One of the F101DFE engines was then fitted to the F-16/101 testbed (the first FSD F-16A 75-0745), which flew for the first time with its new powerplant on 19 December 1980.

'Super Tomcat'

The first F-14 with the two remaining F101DFE engines made its initial flight on 14 July 1981. Dubbed 'Super Tomcat', it was actually the original F-14B prototype, retrofitted with a pair of F101DFEs. The F101-X-engined Super Tomcat flew an initial block of 24 flight tests lasting until September 1981, then flew another 20 test flights until March 1982.

The new engines proved a great success, increasing CAP endurance by 34 per cent, improving DLI radius by 62 per cent and allowing catapult launches to be made in dry power. The engine also showed none of the TF30's tendencies to stall. The only drawbacks were slow 'burner light-ups and a difficulty in air-starting the engines, which required an IAS of 450 kt (515 mph; 830 km/h), far too high to be safe or practical. The Navy was extremely impressed, however, and began to think seriously about re-engining the F-14. Although the F101DFE had demonstrated the advantages of a new engine, it was not the only contender; Pratt & Whitney offered a derivative of its F100, the PW1130, which was slightly lighter.

General Electric pulled ahead, receiving a Full Scale Development contract for the engine in October 1982. On 3 February 1984 the company received an order for 120 of the engines (under the designation F110-GE-100) for the F-16, with proposed follow-on orders for 3,000 more engines. With the engine already in large-scale production (and with the USAF order having paid the R&D costs), the Navy ordered the F101DFE as the F110-GE-400, to be fitted to all the latest Tomcats. They comprise the F-14B, the F-14D Super Tomcat, and the F-14D(R) rebuild. The F110-GE-400 had 82 per cent parts commonality with the USAF's F110-GE-100.

The new F110-GE-400 features an annular intake with a bullet-like spinner, and with 20 fixed radial vanes, each with a variable trailing-edge flap. The intake featured hot bleed air anti-icing. The three-stage fan (the original F101-X had made do with two stages) has a pressure ratio raised from 2.3:1 to more than 3:1. Mass flow is increased from 250 lb/sec to 270 lb/sec. The first three compressor stages are titanium, with the remaining six of steel. The first six stages have a sprayed-on aluminium, bronze and nickel graphite shroud, with Metco 442 nickel graphite on the last three stages. The annular combustion chamber is machined from Hastelloy X and incorporated 20 dual-cone fuel injection and swirl cup vaporisers. The F110-GE-400 has a single-stage high-pressure turbine, and an uncooled two-stage low-pressure turbine. The fully modulated afterburner is scaled up directly from that fitted to the F404. The hot end inspection period rises to 1,500 hours (compared to 880 hours for the TF30-P-414A).

Structural changes

The F110 is almost completely installationally interchangeable with the TF30, requiring a minimum of structural changes and none to the aircraft's primary structure. The production engine for the Tomcat needed just an extra 50-in (127-cm) section downstream of the turbine (because the newer engine is much shorter, basically 182 in/462 cm compared with 236 in/600 cm). This moved the intake face forward by 39 in (99 cm) and moved the nozzle 11 in (28 cm) further aft. Almost the only other change was rearrangement of the engine accessories and their drive gearbox, plus minor modification to the surrounding F-14 secondary structure. The costs involved were modest. Diameter of the GE engine is actually less, at 46.5 in (118 cm), yet airflow at take-off is increased from about 242 lb/sec to 270 lb/sec. Power is increased in a similar ratio, nominally to 29,000 lb (129 kN), although the Navy -400 engine is matched to F-14 requirements at 27,000 lb (120.11 kN). All-round combat performance has dramatically improved, and

catapult take-offs can be made in MIL power (without afterburner).

This backs up the great increase in power by a significant reduction in fuel consumption, because fuel burn in afterburner is multiplied by about four. Thus, at a round figure, the mission radius is increased by the new engine by no less than 62 per cent. Time to high altitude is reduced by about 61 per cent. Not least, the F110 allows the pilot to forget about the engines during air combat and slam the throttle shut or wide open no matter what the angle of attack or airspeed.

The TF30 was an advanced engine for the 1960s, but the F110 illustrates the progress made in the subsequent 20 years. The TF30 has a total of 16 stages of compression, the three-stage fan rotating on the same shaft as the six-stage low-pressure compressor. The F110, in contrast, has only 12 stages in total, comprising a three-stage fan and a nine-stage high-pressure compressor, yet, with hundreds of blades fewer, the overall pressure ratio of 31 is much higher than that of the older engine, which equates to better fuel economy. A further index of progress is overall length. The comparative figures given previously show how modern engines can burn fuel in a shorter distance, and this is particularly true of the afterburner. The distance from the augmentation fuel nozzle rings to the end of the exhaust nozzle of the F110 is not much over half that of the TF30, but it was cheaper to add an unnecessary extra section to the F110 than to shorten the F-14. Aircraft fitted with the F110-GE-400 have a ram-air turbine to provide power in the event of a dual engine failure, and are also fitted with a new air turbine starter, generator, heat exchangers and approach power compensator.

Bill Gunston, Jon Lake and Robert F. Dorr

Development of the Tomcat continues at a steady pace, with much of the work being undertaken by the Naval Air Warfare Center – Aircraft Divsion at Patuxent River. This F-14D, complete with four AIM-54s, two AIM-7s and two AIM-9s, was the testbed for the DFCS (Digital Flight Control System).

Northrop Grumman F-14D Tomcat cutaway

1 Pitot head
2 Radar target horn
3 Upward-hinging glass-fibre radome
4 Radome hinge point
5 AN/APG-71 radar scanner
6 Articulated scanner mounting
7 Undernose IRST/TCS sensor pod
8 Infra-Red Search and Track (IRST)

38 Steerable twin nosewheels, forward retracting
39 Nosewheel undercarriage leg strut
40 Hydraulic retraction jack
41 Ammunition magazine, 675 rounds
42 Ammunition feed and cartridge case return chutes
43 Tactical information display hand controller
44 Radar Intercept Officer's display console

70 Telescopic flap/slat drive shaft
71 Port wing pivot bearing
72 Electron beam welded titanium wing pivot box
73 Intake bypass air spill duct
74 Emergency hydraulic generator
75 Central flap/slat drive motor
76 UHF datalink /IFF antenna

77 Fuselage upper longeron/ pivot box attachment links
78 Wing pivot box integral fuel tank
79 Telescopic fuel feed pipes
80 Variable wing sweep control screw jacks
81 Centre-section fuel tankage
82 Intake ducting
83 Honeycomb skin panels
84 Starboard mainwheel, stowed position
85 Starboard wing pivot bearing

86 Flap/slat interconnecting drive shaft
87 Starboard wing integral fuel tank
88 Starboard two-segment leading-edge slats
89 Wing forward (20° sweep) position
90 Starboard navigation/strobe light
91 Wingtip formation lighting panels
92 Two-segment slotted flaps, down position
93 Starboard spoiler panels
94 Inboard auxiliary flap
95 Wing glove flexible sealing plates
96 External glove stiffeners/dorsal fences
97 Forward/rear fuselage longeron joint
98 Flight control system artificial feel units
99 Control rods and linkages

100 Rear fuselage fuel tank bays
101 Starboard engine bay
102 Finroot fairing
103 Pneumatic wingroot glove seat
104 Starboard wing fully swept (68°) position, may be 'overswept' to 72° for carrier deck stowage
105 Starboard fin
106 Fin honeycomb core skin panels
107 Fintip antenna fairing
108 Tail navigation light
109 Starboard rudder, honeycomb core structure
110 Port fintip antenna fairing
111 Anti-collision light
112 Formation lighting strip
113 ECM antenna
114 Starboard all-moving tailplane
115 Variable-area afterburner nozzle
116 Carbon-fibre composite nozzle shroud

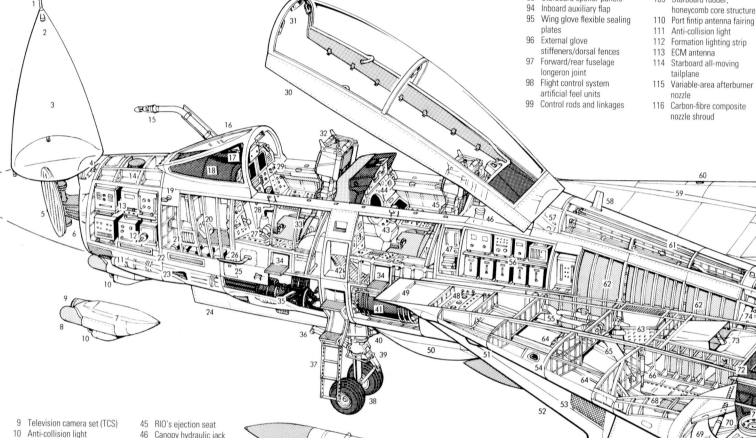

9 Television camera set (TCS)
10 Anti-collision light
11 Cannon barrel aperture
12 Incidence transmitter
13 Weapons system avionics equipment
14 ADF antenna
15 Retractable inflight-refuelling probe
16 Windscreen panels
17 Pilot's head-up display
18 Instument panel shroud
19 Temperature probe
20 Rudder pedals
21 Avionics cooling air exhaust
22 Electro-luminescent formation lighting strips
23 Gun gas purging intake
24 Nosewheel doors
25 Canopy emergency releaser
26 Dynamic pressure probe
27 Engine throttle levers
28 Control column
29 Pilot's instrument panel with dual multi-function displays
30 Cockpit canopy, open position
31 Rear view mirrors
32 Ejection seat headrest with canopy breakers.
33 Martin-Baker Mk 14 NACES ejection seat
34 Boarding step
35 M61 Vulcan six-barrelled rotary cannon
36 Catapult strop link
37 Fold-out boarding ladder

45 RIO's ejection seat
46 Canopy hydraulic jack
47 Electrical system controller
48 Electrical relays
49 Engine intake lip
50 Ventral missile pallet
51 EW antenna
52 Port engine air intake
53 Intake sidewall honeycomb core structure
54 Port navigation light
55 Conditioned air ducting
56 Rear avionics equipment bay
57 Canopy hinge point
58 UHF/TACAN antenna
59 Starboard wing glove fairing
60 Starboard navigation light
61 Dorsal control and cable ducting
62 Forward fuselage fuel tank bays, total internal fuel capacity 9029 litres (1,986 Imp gal)
63 Air conditioning system heat exchanger, port and starboard dual system for crew and avionics
64 Variable-area intake ramp doors
65 Intake ramp hydraulic actuators
66 Main undercarriage wheel bay
67 Mainwheel door
68 Rear intake ramp
69 Wing glove sealing horn fairing

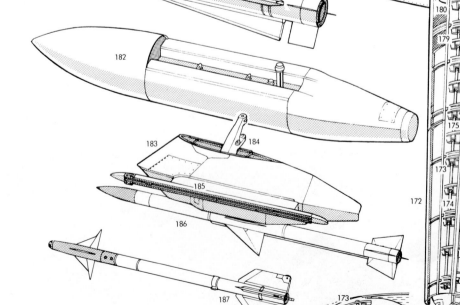

117 Flexible sealing plates
118 Flight control system back-up hydraulic module
119 Dorsal airbrake panel, split lower surfaces
120 Airbrake hydraulic jacks
121 Airbrake housing
122 Ventral AN/ALE-29 chaff/flare launchers
123 Fuel jettison
124 ECM antenna
125 Deck arrester hook, stowed
126 Port engine exhaust nozzle
127 Afterburner duct outer sealing plate
128 Variable-area nozzle actuator
129 Afterburner duct
130 Rudder hydraulic actuator
131 Fin/tailplane main mounting frame
132 Tailplane pivot bearing
133 Multi-spar tailplane structure

134 Arrester hook, down position
135 Honeycomb trailing-edge panel
136 AN/ALR-45 (V) radar warning antenna
137 Boron fibre tailplane skin panels
138 Wing rib (typical), machined on inner face
139 Port wing, fully swept position
140 Ventral fin
141 Afterburner duct cooling air intake

142 Tailplane hydraulic actuator
143 Rear fuselage sponson fairing structure
144 Port General Electric F110-GE-400 afterburning turbofan
145 Hydraulic system filters
146 Formation lighting strip
147 Hydraulic reservoir, port and starboard

148 Engine bay access panel
149 Engine accessory equipment bay
150 Port auxiliary flap
151 Main undercarriage hydraulic retraction jack
152 Auxiliary flap hydraulic jack
153 Main undercarriage leg pivot mounting

154 Retraction breaker/drag strut
155 Shock absorber leg strut
156 Torque scissor links
157 Port mainwheel
158 Trailing-edge flap section, cruise condition
159 Flap eyebrow fairing
160 Flap 10° down, manoeuvre position
161 Flap slotted, 35° down landing position
162 Port outboard flap segments
163 Flap honeycomb core structure
164 Port spoiler panels
165 Flap drive torque shaft
166 Spoiler hydraulic actuators
167 Fuel system piping
168 Machined wing ribs
169 Bottom wing skin/stringer panel
170 Wingtip formation light
171 Port navigation/strobe light
172 Two-segment leading-edge slat, extended

173 Slat guide rails
174 Slat drive torque shaft
175 Leading-edge ribs
176 Two-spar wing torsion box structure
177 Port wing integral fuel tank
178 Slat guide rail fuel sealing cans
179 Leading-edge slat honeycomb core construction
180 Tank pylon beneath intake trunk
181 AIM-54A Phoenix long-range air-to-air missile
182 1011-litre (267-US gal) external fuel tank
183 Glove pylon
184 Pylon attachment link
185 Shoulder-mounted Sidewinder launch rail
186 AIM-120 AMRAAM medium-range air-to-air missile
187 AIM-9L Sidewinder short range air-to-air missile

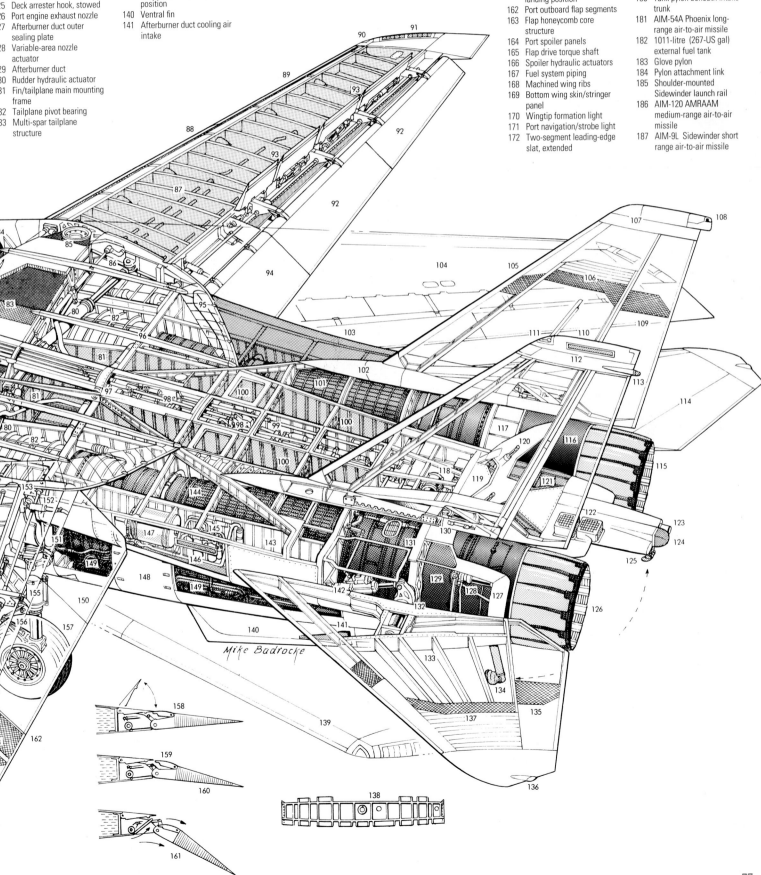

Mike Badrocke

Chapter Four

Systems, Primary Mission Equipment and Weapons

Lt Dave Chandler of VF-211 poses 'his' F-14A Tomcat high over the Indian Ocean during a 1989 Westpac cruise.

modern agile fighters. 'Difficult' opponents are usually listed as including aircraft like the F-15, F-16, F/A-18, MiG-29 or Su-27. Even the baseline F-14A Tomcat's agility is hardly 'old hat' today, in an era dominated by fighters which take the ability to sustain a 9 *g* turn for granted.

9 *g* turning

In the early 1970s, the ability to briefly attain 9 *g* was extraordinary, and the TF30-powered F-14A demonstrated the ability to do so at Mach 1.2 at 20,000 ft (6095 m). The aircraft could attain 8 *g* at Mach 0.9 at the same altitude even with six Phoenix missiles and two Sidewinders, and with two fuel tanks, and 7 *g* at Mach 2.04 at 50,000 ft (15243 m). It could then sustain maximum *g* as the speed bled off down to Mach 0.8. The aircraft could sustain 6.5 *g* at Mach 2.2 using manoeuvre flap and slats, or could hold its entry speed through a 1,800-ft (550-m) radius 6.5 *g* level 180° turn. A *g* limit of 7.5 was available at very high gross weights, even with full internal fuel, and four AIM-7s, giving the pilot a 7.5 *g* envelope from take-off on some missions. At the other end of the spectrum, the aircraft was flown to -5.5 *g*.

Although it is no F-16, it can be seen that the Tomcat is no slouch in the dogfight arena. Today, though, and for as long as most current Tomcat aircrew can remember, the F-14's *g* limits are lower, from -2.4 to +6.5, with a temporary 5 *g* restriction in 1994-95 due to a wing pin problem.

Any lack in dogfighting agility is not a major problem, however, since the Tomcat's BVR (Beyond Visual Range) kill capability remains unmatched, and, if Rules of Engagement permit, the F-14 pilot will always want to destroy his opponent at the maximum possible range. Today, the Tomcat may be overshadowed by purpose-built air superiority fighters in the close-in manoeuvring arena. The F-14 was once intended to destroy its targets in the aeronautical equivalent of a down-and-dirty knife-fight, but it is now accepted that the Tomcat is an assassin, armed with weapons which enable it to pick off its victims at such extreme range that they often do not even know they are in danger.

Departure characteristics

More of a problem are the F-14's spinning and departure characteristics, which would be regarded as completely unacceptable if found in a new fighter today. Excessive yaw can blank off the inboard engine intake, leading to a flame-out. At some airspeed/power setting combinations this can lead to a very violent departure, which can, in turn, become a self-sustaining irrecoverable flat spin if the appropriate recovery actions are not taken within a couple of seconds. At the very high levels of negative *g* encountered in such a spin, it rapidly becomes impossible for the crew members to reach their ejection seat handles. The problem is that if the yaw rate is allowed to build up, the spin will flatten. The yaw rate actually increases to 180° per second, nose slightly low, with zero AoA and zero airspeed. The pilot then begins to experience a debilitating level of centrifugal

The Tomcat remains the king of the so-called 'outer air battle', capable of detecting, locating and engaging its targets at enormous distances and of sanitising huge blocks of airspace around the carrier battle group. The F-14 achieves its extraordinary capabilities through what remains one of the most impressive weapons control systems in the business, cleverly blending sensors and advanced weapons to fulfil its role.

The Tomcat is at the sharp edge of the 'maritime strategy' set forth by (then) Secretary of the Navy John Lehman in the mid-1980s. The strategy is to project power from forward-deployed locations against the home territory of any likely adversary, using the US Navy's capital ship, the aircraft-carrier, as the king of a surface battle group. A Pentagon insider puts it this way: "We have carrier battle groups to project power. Like it or not, the biggest purpose is to go out where we don't have a 15,000-ft (4644-m) concrete runway and project a tactical wing in that place." This battle group is composed of many elements – in addition to the carrier, you have cruisers, destroyers, frigates and submarines, which form a defensive screen around the carrier. The F-14 provides a long-distance shield for that defensive screen. If someone tries to attack the battle group, the F-14 is the primary defender of what is called the 'outer air zone'. This is

where the term the 'outer air battle' comes in.

The outer air battle starts, literally, hundreds of miles from the carrier itself. In conjunction with E-2C Hawkeye surveillance aircraft, the F-14 will begin engaging incoming enemy aircraft sometimes 300 to 400 miles (483 to 643 km) away, plus another 100 miles (160 km) from the enemy aircraft. Though the Tomcat is often billed as a fleet defence interceptor, its mission being to defend carrier battle groups from bombers and cruise missiles, the aircraft was originally intended to fight and defeat enemy fighters. To quote Captain L. S. (Scotty) Lamoreaux, the first F-14 project co-ordinator: "The F-14 is all fighter. [Interceptor] capability has not been permitted to dilute the original concept or [to] degrade the performance required to out-fly and out-fight any aircraft encountered." Even today, there are those who claim that the F-14, particu-

larly in its D-model form, remains a viable air-to-air aircraft. Rear Admiral Julian Lake opined that today's F-14 does not have a poor capability against new generation fighters. With the new engines, the F-14D would not have trouble with any one of the new fighters. The advantage of the variable-sweep wing makes the F-14D a formidable opponent in the hands of a trained pilot, and more so with a competent RIO in the back seat. The F-14 was intended from the initial design to dogfight, down and dirty, and it can do so, with the new engine, although the TF30 could be a decided handicap.

Others maintain that the F-14's fighter-versus-fighter capability is less respectable. Against older aircraft like the F-4 (or the MiG-23 'Flogger'), the baseline Tomcat has few problems, but its rate and radius of turn, thrust-to-weight ratio and high-Alpha capability are such that its critics insist that it would perform poorly against force. If positive recovery actions are not taken, the crew will eventually become disorientated and finally incapacitated. The pilot has about 15 to 20 seconds of consciousness at the 5.5 to 6.5 *g* he encounters, and the RIO behind, suffering 3.5 to 4.5 *g*, has longer. Crews have recovered from flat spins, but not consistently, and if full anti-spin controls can be held until the aircraft is below 10,000 ft (3050 m), recovery is likely if the pilot is not incapacitated. Even if the crew does eject, the low airspeeds encountered in a flat spin mean that the canopy separates slowly, and there have been incidents of ejecting crew members actually hitting the canopy (such a seat/canopy collision killed the character 'Goose' in the film *Top Gun*).

High-rotational spinning departures are said by many to have resulted in a steady stream of accidents and losses during ACM training, and have resulted in the imposition of severe handling limitations. They in turn limited turn performance and high-Alpha capability. The violence of these departures was blamed on the wide distance between the engines and their intakes. Some former F-14 pilots refute this problem, claiming that the F-14's engines were no more widely spaced than those of the F-4, conveniently ignoring the fact that the F-4's engine intakes were separated by an inertia-inducing fuselage rather than by a lift-generating pancake, and that the engines themselves were adjacent. Others are typified by Rear Admiral Paul Gillcrist, who wrote: "The engines are mounted in nacelles 9 ft [2.74 m] apart. The 9-ft dimension represents a large yawing moment whenever there is unbalanced thrust. The most out-of-balance thrust circumstance would be with one engine in maximum afterburner and the other flamed out. This is the situation which could develop in a slow-speed, high angle-of-attack manoeuvre in which the engine has a tendency to stall and flame out. Even with the engine alarm signalling a stalled condition, the large yawing motion is not always recognised as such since it generates a rolling motion, and it all happens fast. If the pilot recognises the rolling motion and tries to correct for it with opposite aileron, it aggravates the yaw and puts the airplane into a flat spin."

Although the F-14's flat, high-rotational spin is lethal, it is not easy to enter, and the aircraft does not depart from straight and level flight except with severe asymmetric thrust. When the aircraft was flown with full pro-spin controls (opposite rudder and aileron) at 45° AoA, and with full lateral stick displacement at angles of attack up to 60°, the pilots were unable to induce the aircraft to spin by using aerodynamic control surfaces alone. Following the first losses of F-14s in spinning accidents, the 1X prototype was used to examine the aircraft's yaw characteristics with severe asymmetric thrust. The trial was flown by Chuck Sewell who flew the aircraft at 150 kt (172 mph; 277 km/h) and 41° Alpha, then deliberately stalled the right engine. The aircraft pitched up to 72° Alpha and developed a yawing moment of 47°/sec. The airspeed dropped to 25 kt (28 mph; 46 km/h) and recovery was initiated, recovering positively within 10 seconds. The F-14 has demonstrated sustained controlled flight, without buffet, yaw, or wing-drop even at up to 55° AoA, or at

sink rates of up to 9,000 ft (2745 m) per minute. The aircraft has briefly attained 90 AoA, though not as predictably and controllably as aircraft like the MiG-29 and Su-27, and from a vertical entry (i.e. attaining 90 units AoA falling out of a tail-slide). It was even demonstrated at -50° AoA and -3.8 *g*. The aircraft cannot be compared to the latest Soviet fighters, which can demonstrate their high Alpha capability at air show altitude. Recovery from a tailslide takes 10,000 ft (3050 m), with a pullout at 200 kt (230 mph; 370 km/h).

Unlike many single-role interceptor aircraft, the Tomcat was not completely optimised for high-speed, high-altitude flight, its variable-geometry wing endowing the aircraft with relatively benign low-speed handling characteristics.

Landing back

Not that the Tomcat is the easiest aircraft to land. Compared to the F-4, the Tomcat is neither stable nor smooth on the glideslope. It is not as good at holding an accurate approach speed, or glideslope angle, and also tends to veer away from the heading. It has high pitch inertia and tends to float. Its high residual thrust enforces the use of low throttle settings, giving poor engine response. The poor lateral control makes precise heading control difficult. One distinguished pilot said, "The F-14 can be a bit of a handful in the pattern. You've got a very big airplane which is also very manoeuvrable and very dynamic. You've got a lot of things happening at once when it's coming in to land. Which is why they call it 'the Turkey', because you've got multiple surfaces flapping in all directions." Another pilot commented, "Landing the F-14 aboard is like shepherding an elephant. It goes pretty much where it wants to go, and when it wants to sit down, it SITS!"

Despite criticism of the F-14's approach handling, the aircraft demonstrated the ability to land successfully and go-around (bolter) even in a number of simulated emergency configurations. These included having the wings locked at 60°, with one engine at idle, and even in the nightmare

Above: Dayglo tailfins and wingtips mark this NAWC F-14A as a test aircraft. It is seen here flying with a full operational warload of four AIM-54s, two AIM-7s, two AIM-9s and a pair of auxiliary fuel tanks. Unusually, the aircraft still has operable wing glove vanes.

Below: An early US Navy F-14A has its radome hinged up to show the aircraft's AN/AWG-9 radar antenna. Below the radome is the covered sensor of the AN/ALR-23 infra-red search and acquisition set. The six dipole antennas on the planar array serve the IFF system.

cleared for a sink rate in excess of 25 ft/sec (7.62 m/sec).

The F-14's ability to land successfully and safely aboard ship is largely due to a simple direct lift control system, which uses partial spoiler deployment to force the pilot to use higher throttle settings, giving the aircraft better controllability and a better view of the deck in the approach configuration. It has been stated that the system improved directional and lateral stability, but current aircrew dispute this. "Directional and lateral stability is the same with or without DLC," said one, "i.e. in the F-14 it sucks, and even DFCS will not change a lot of that for us."

One of the great problems with landing on an aircraft-carrier is that normally every change in approach path requires a change of attitude, and a compensating change of throttle setting to maintain the desired airspeed, before reselecting the correct attitude. The F-14 employs a system called Direct Lift Control (DLC) to make this unnecessary, using the spoilers to give approach path adjustments by adjusting lift without altering aircraft attitude. When DLC was engaged the four spoilers on the upper surface of the wing popped up to what became the new 'neutral' position (actually about +7°). Because the neutral position killed some lift, it demanded an increase in approach speed of about 8 kt (9 mph; 15 km/h). Using a small thumb-wheel on the control column they could be commanded DLC down, or full (spoilers full-up , or +15°) or DLC up (spoilers in, flush with the wing skin). When lowered they generated instant lift, with no need for an attitude change. At one time it was hoped that the aircraft would be able to fly a constant 10.8° AoA approach, giving the pilot a view of the waterline at the carrier's stern, since the F-14 offers a 15.5° view down, over the nose. When DLC was first tested it was found that the specified 128-kt (147-mph; 237-km/h) approach speed could not be achieved at the maximum arrested landing weight. Grumman proposed that the approach should be flown at 17 units of Alpha instead of 15, but this was opposed by pilots, who felt that the aircraft flew better at 15 and with DLC engaged, because it gave better engine response and flying qualities. At 17 units it was also difficult to see ahead over the nose. They believed that the extra 6 kt (7 mph; 11 km/h) at maximum weight was a worthwhile sacrifice. Pilots therefore proposed retaining DLC with a 15-Alpha approach, making use of the system mandatory at night. They were prepared to accept the slightly higher approach speeds needed for the benefit of better vertical response without altering attitude. In fact, the Navy adopted a compromise solution of a lower authority DLC system, using only the outboard spoilers. This proved inadequate for large corrections, and on the F-14B and F-14D the inboard spoilers are used at higher deflection, giving the perfect system, which has since been adopted fleet-wide. DLC neutral is now 17° up, with DLC full being 55°, and DLC 'up' being -4°, actually drooped below the 'flush' position. Ashore, as the wheels hit the runway, all the spoilers flick fully up and the flaperons deploy to 55°. Aboard ship, this system is disabled to make wave-offs or bolters easier.

Above: Final preparations are made to an F-14A of VF-103 aboard the Saratoga before a launch from the port bow catapult.

Left: Deck crew load an AIM-7 Sparrow into the port forward recess (station 3). The AIM-7 lacks the range and fire-and-forget capabilities of the AIM-54, but is considerably cheaper.

Below: A VF-211 Tomcat lets fly with an AIM-54 Phoenix. The AIM-54 is the most powerful weapon available to the F-14 crew.

scenario of having only one engine, with the outboard spoilers failed, the wings locked fully aft (thus with flaps unavailable), and with both hydraulic systems 'failed' and with the emergency backup system operating in its reduced capacity mode, providing 5° of stabilator motion per second instead of the usual 10°. With 1,800 lb (818 kg) of fuel aboard, the landing speed in this configuration was 147 kt (168 mph; 271 km/h), probably low enough to permit a barrier engagement, even if too fast for an arrested landing. This capability should be compared with the MiG-23, whose pilot is forced to eject if the wing sweep mechanism fails fully aft. With wings weep available, the F-14 approaches at the same angle even with one engine, giving the pilot the same approach picture. At the maximum arrested landing weight of 51,800 lb (23496 kg), the aircraft has an approach speed of 127 kt (145 mph; 234 km/h), and stores are

Without DLC the F-14 was described as having high pitch inertia, similar to the Vigilante, float characteristics like the A-6A, residual thrust from the fan engines which kept the throttles in the lower, less responsive zones, a sensitivity to sideslip, a lateral control system that diminishes precise heading control and an auto throttle that requires considerable anticipation. Without DLC, in short, the F-14 was a turkey on approach.

On 14 July 1995, an F-14D flew with a new digital flight control system jointly developed by Northrop Grumman, GEC-Marconi Avionics and the US Navy to replace the analog stability augmentation system. A budget request to retrofit the system to 251 aircraft (with an estimated cost of only $80 million) was rejected in 1994, but funds for flight testing were voted by Congress. The programme hopes to halt the landing mishaps and departures during high Alpha flight that have accounted for 20-25 F-14 losses. In power-approach configuration, with gear and flaps down, the F-14 is reckoned to be more difficult to land than other Navy types, with Dutch roll causing yaw in response to roll inputs. A new stick-rudder interconnect will improve handling characteristics and reduce pilot workload on approach. High energy departures can lead to excessive yaw rates, of up to 180°/second in fully developed flat spins. At low airspeed the new DFCS will reduce pilot control inputs, slowing aircraft responses and giving the crew time to recognise and prevent an impending spin. Front-line aircrew are keen to get the new DFCS, which will "expand the entire envelope, and also make the F-14 a MUCH more stable beast when landing on the boat. Plus, if it fails, we'll still have a manual backup, unlike the F/A-18 in which the plane craps itself if the computers die."

Handling perspective

The Tomcat's handling problems should be seen in perspective. Judging an aircraft designed in the 1960s by the standards of the 1990s is not entirely fair. Handling regarded as difficult today would have represented good handling in past years. Even handling on approach, recognised as being poor at the outset of the F-14's service career, marked an improvement over most of the F-14's predecessors, albeit with the exception of the rock-solid F-4. Not all aviators would accept that the F-14's approach handling is in any way wanting, especially older carrier aviators with experience of the older generation of naval aircraft. Julian Lake described the F-14 as being "very stable on the glide-slope. As a two-hop F-14 expert, with bags of traps in the F-4, I thought the F-14 was a sweetheart on the glideslope. You should talk about the F-8, the A-3 and the A-5. I day and night carqualled in the first two, they were real handfuls on the approach. The F-8 was hot and touchy, the A-3 was just plain hard work. Both had the main gear well aft of the C of G and it just sounded like a crash when you flew the ball down to touchdown."

The Tomcat was heavily influenced by the F-4 Phantom, its immediate predecessor, and adopted the same two-seat concept with a pilot up front and the radar intercept officer (RIO) behind. The side-by-side seating layout of the F-111B had always been resented and opposed by the Navy, who took the opportunity of ditching it when the F-111B was scrapped. The job of the backseater was to engage 'hostiles' beyond visual range (BVR), exploiting the capabilities of radar, AWG-9 (Air Weapons Group) and missiles, while providing another pair of eyes in close combat. The tandem cockpit is enclosed by a blown canopy giving excellent visibility, if not quite so spectacular as that from an F-16D Fighting Falcon. The crew are provided with Martin-Baker GRU.7A rocket-propelled ejection seats which are effective at zero altitude and from zero airspeed to 450 kt (517 mph; 832 km/h).

Right: This VF-103 F-14A, seen on approach to USS Saratoga, carries four underfuselage AIM-7 Sparrows, and four AIM-9 Sidewinders on the wing gloves.

Below: An AIM-7 Sparrow streaks away from an F-14A of VF-84, the 'Black Aces'. The AIM-7 has gone through several incarnations, and is now in service in its AIM-7M form.

Wearing NAWC markings, this F-14 was used for tests with the AIM-7 in conjunction with the F-14D programme.

Two decades later, about 80 per cent of Tomcats are still equipped with the reliable 'grew-seven.' In 1988, the US Navy embarked on an ambitious programme to equip all F-14, F/A-18C/D and T-45 aircraft with the Martin-Baker SJU.17A/V NACES (Naval Aircrew Common Ejection Seat), partly to achieve a greater degree of commonality and partly because the newer seat (also with 'zero-zero' capability) reportedly offers higher velocity escape at speeds of 700 kt (805 mph; 1295 km/h) in level flight and 600 kt (690 mph; 1110 km/h) in any attitude, although the service limit is 600 kt. The new seat dispenses with the optional face blind

handle employed on its predecessor. Because production of the Tomcat was abruptly halted in February 1991, the Navy halted installation of the new ejection seat in the F-14 except in the new-build and converted F-14Ds.

Unlike many two-seat aircraft, the F-14 cockpit gives minimum duplication of controls and instruments for the pilot and radar intercept officer. The pilot has three multi-purpose displays for viewing flight, navigation and tactical data, including armament controls and flight instruments, while the aft cockpit is equipped with controls and displays for the AWG-9 weapon system. The RIO relied on two main displays, a 5-in (12.7-cm) diameter Detail Data Display giving basic raw radar data, and a 10-in (25.4-cm) Target Information Display presenting a synthetic,

processed picture of the tactical situation, with alphanumeric notation showing the altitude and bearing of radar contacts, whether they were friendly or hostile, and giving the computer's numerical order of firing priority. The display could be orientated with the direction of flight, with the F-14 at the bottom centre, or geo-stabilised with true north at the top, showing the F-14 and the various targets on the display. Eighteen additional contacts (from the ASW-27 datalink) can be displayed.

The F-14 was comprehensively equipped with advanced avionics and defensive systems. For navigation, the Tomcat was equipped with a Gould ARN-84 TACAN, which measured slant-range and bearing to TACAN beacons or VORTAC stations, operating between 932 and 1213 MHz. This relied on the pres-

ence of suitable ground stations, and was thus unsuitable as a stand-alone navaid. Autonomous navigation capability was made possible by the ASN-92(V) CAINS II, an inertial platform which could be linked by microwave datalink to the ship's own highly accurate INS for alignment before flight.

The Tomcat had to be able to recover aboard a carrier in all weathers, by day or night. To be able to achieve this, the aircraft was fitted with AACA (Aircraft Approach Control Apparatus) with an AN/ARA-63 receiver aboard the aircraft operating with the AN/SPN-41 and AN/TRN-28 transmitters aboard the carrier. They generated a left/right, above/below centreline picture in the form of cross hairs on a cockpit instrument. The AN/ARA-63 was replaced by the AN/ARN-128(V)2 multi-mode receiver.

Radios and RHAWS

For communications, the Tomcat relied primarily on an AN/ARC-51A UHF set, though this was subsequently replaced by an AN/ARC-159 V/UHF and then by an AN/ARC-182. The Collins Radio Group ARC-159 UHF radio incorporated state-of-the-art improvements and a head-up frequency display, while offering more than 10 times the reliability of the radio it replaced. All were operated in conjunction with a KY-58 cryptographic system, when secure communications were required.

A good radar warning receiver can be a beneficial sensor, giving the crew a useful idea of the range, bearing and nature of a potential threat, and whether its radar was in a search mode or a tracking mode, and even whether a missile was being fired. Unfortunately, the Tomcat's ECM suite

Left: An NATC F-14A fires an AIM-9 Sidewinder. Most of the Tomcat's real air-to-air victories have been scored using the IR-homing AIM-9.

Right: This F-14A wears the new markings of the Weapon Test Squadron at Point Mugu, which has taken over the role of the PMTC.

Above: This otherwise clean F-14A carries Expanded Chaff Adaptors in modified forward Phoenix pallets. The ECA is a common F-14 store.

Right: This NATC aircraft is seen during catapult trials at NAS Lakehurst. The same unit also tested the F-14 on a ski-jump.

was inadequate when the aircraft entered service, and upgrades came too slowly to give the aircraft the level of capability it required. After the first cruise by VF-1 and VF-2, Rear Admiral 'Swoose' Snead, Miramar's commander, said, "the ECM/DCM suite in the F-14 is totally inadequate. Known threat capabilities dictate that we be ready to fight in highly sophisticated environments. But we are not nearly ready to do so with our current ECM suite." The F-14A was originally equipped with AN/APR-25 and AN/APR-27 RHAWS, but they were subsequently replaced by the AN/ALR-45 and -50 and later by the AN/ALR-67. If attacked, the Tomcat could use chaff or flares to decoy a hostile missile, launching these from AN/ALE-29 (or later AN/ALE-39) chaff/flare dispensers. The aircraft was also fitted with an AN/ALQ-100 jammer, replaced by the AN/ALQ-126 on later aircraft. The latter formed part of the PRIDE defensive avionics suite, with ALR-45 and ALR-50 RHAWS. Plans to fit the AN/ALQ-165 Advanced Self-Protection Jammer (ASPJ) were cancelled when the equipment failed to pass its development tests, though F-14Ds later had the equipment reactivated, since it proved extremely effective and useful, even if not up to its originally specified absolute performance.

Datalinks

The Tomcat could be linked to other interceptors, or to an E-2C Hawkeye airborne control platform or the carrier's Naval Tactical Data System using the Harris ASW-27B digital datalink. This helped the Tomcat crew get a true idea of the 'big picture' and enhanced their situational awareness – perhaps the most crucial factor in modern air combat. It also allowed the aircraft to operate without using its own onboard sensors, remaining radar silent when tactically appropriate. Today, Link 4 has been replaced by Link 16 ("Eons ahead of Link 4, Wow!!!!!!, Great Stuff," scribbled one RIO on an early draft), or JTIDS. "Under some circumstances, the datalink is a more valuable tool than our own radar!" said one Tomcat RIO.

In addition to their onboard fire control systems, early Tomcats were also equipped with a gimbal-mounted AN/ALR-23 infra-red detection set. This could be slaved to the radar or used independently to scrutinise areas not being scanned by radar. The IRST used indium-antimonide detectors, cooled by a self-contained Stirling-cycle cryogenic system, and was particularly useful for detecting afterburning targets at higher altitude, and rocket-engined stand-off missiles, or for operation

Above: This badge is worn by aircraft of the NATC's Strike Test Directorate at Patuxent River.

Systems, Equipment and Weapons

when use of radar was tactically unsound or impeded by heavy ECM. Angular tracking was more accurate than with radar, providing better target elevation and azimuth data than radar. It was sufficiently accurate to allow it to be used for missile launch. This sensor was replaced by the Northrop AAX-1 TVSU (later TSU) Television Sight Unit, universally (but strictly inaccurately) referred to as the TCS. The TVSU can be likened to a high-resolution closed-circuit TV with telephoto lens, following a 1977 evaluation of F-14s equipped with the broadly similar AAX-1 TCS. The original TCS was based on the TISEO, then in use on USAF F-4E Phantoms, which had in turn been developed from equipment used in the Rivet Haste and Combat Tree programmes. The equipment was basically a video camera with a stabilised optical telescope, with a 30° field of view and up to 10 times magnification. This allowed the visual identification of targets at ranges in excess of 9.2 miles (14.8 km) rather than the 2-3 miles (3.2-4.8 km) possible with the naked eye. One RIO claimed to have routinely identified tankers and airliners at more than 40 nm (46 miles; 74 km) using TCS. The TISEO was ruggedised for carrier use. The success of this led to trials by VF-14, VF-32, VF- 24 and VF- 211 aboard *Kennedy* and *Constellation* with Northrop's TVSU, which was in turn developed to become

the TSU. The *Constellation* squadrons even used the equipment for BVR identification of surface ships.

An unclassified account of much of the ACEVAL/AIMVAL test can be found in *Arsenal of Democracy II* by Tom Gervasi (Grove Press, New York: 1981).

According to Rear Admiral Julian Lake, who was the Test Director the ACE-VAL/AIMVAL tests, "The TVSU played an important role in the 18-month joint USAF/USN ACEVAL/AIMVAL (Air Combat Evaluation/Air Intercept Missile Evaluation) tests in 1976-77. The purpose of these tests was to evaluate tactics and missile performance characteristics. The tests were flown on an instrumented (ACMI) range with computer simulations of several missiles under evaluation. A fly-out of each missile shot was performed to missile/target intercept and recorded for evaluation. The six brand-new Navy Block 90 F-14As (flown by crews from VF-1 and VF-2), and the six F-15As were flown against 12 F-Es flown by USAF/USN aggressor/adversary pilots, the latter acting as MiG-21 surrogates. The small F-5 was very hard to see visually and the large fighters were dependent on their radars to detect the F-5s. The F-14s and the F-15s were equipped with both AIM-9 heat-seeking missiles and AIM-7 semi-active radar missiles. (Both were all-aspect.) The AIM-7 is often under-rated by those who

don't fully understand it. It was a beyond-visual-range, all-aspect weapon, and long before its time. It lacked an identification system, so could not use its best shot, down the throat. A co-speed tail shot was its very worst scenario and that is why it had such a miserable combat record in Vietnam. The F-5 was equipped only with all-aspect AIM-9 type missiles.

AIMVAL results

"This was a first test of weapons with these capabilities and an unexpected development took place. The first aircraft that identified a target (usually an F-14 or F-15) would launch a missile but it would then be detected by the F-5, which would launch a missile at the first fighter in return before it could be shot down, figuratively, by the first fighter's missile (or at least by that missile's simulated computer fly-out). In the meantime, the F-5's missile computer fly-out would figuratively shoot down the F-14 or F-15. In actual combat both aircraft would be destroyed. This was a deadly result. In the absence of counter-measures or other compensating factors, a 1:1 exchange ratio was obtained! Such a ratio was not remotely acceptable, particularly in view of the cost ratio disparity between the F-14/-15 and the F-5!

"The use of countermeasures was not part of the test plan, but the TVSU in the F-14 did provide some compensation and

enabled the F-14 to identify the F-5 at 10 miles without the radar. Using the BVR AIM-7 (Sparrow) and the AWG-9 the F-14 could engage the target many miles sooner than the F-15, a decided advantage. This was partially offset by the necessity to continue to provide illumination for the semi-active AIM-7, and forced the F-14 to continue to close the target (although at an angle governed by the radar antenna gimbal limits). Even so, the F-5 would often visually detect the F-14 and get off a shot before the AIM-7 got him. Although the F-14 achieved a better exchange ratio it still hovered in the 1.4:1 to 2:1 range – unacceptable with $8 to $10 million fighters.

"The F-5 had an additional tactic against the radar in the F-14 and F-15. This involved a radar warning receiver that could detect the radar before the radar could detect the F-5 (simulated in the AIMVAL/ACEVAL test). This is a normal expectation with radar warning receivers. The F-5 could then take advantage of the pulse-Doppler radar by turning to keep the radar on its beam, which placed the F-5 in the own speed Doppler blind zone. This would prevent or delay radar detection until the range was very short. Generally the F-5 would then visually sight the F-14 or F-15 first and get off the first shot, frequently killing the F-14/F-15 before radar detection or a return shot. In these

Right, far right and below: Among the F-14s flown by VX-4 at Point Mugu have been a series of black aircraft, usually with the famous 'Playboy' bunny prominently displayed on the tailfins. This has sometimes appeared on grey Tomcats, too. In today's politically correct Navy, the insignia is anathema, and has disappeared, although VX-4's successor, VX-9, continues to operate occasional black-painted F-14 Tomcats.

engagements the F-5 achieved the favourable exchange ratio.

"The counter to the all-aspect missile requires several if not all of the following: 1. low probability of detection radar; 2. a fire and forget, medium range missile; 3. an integrated TVSU/IRST; 4. countermeasures.

"Surprisingly, both the F-14 and the F-15 proved able to outmanoeuvre the F-5Es when engagements became close-in gun fights, and their superiority in this phase helped maintain the overall two-to-one advantage enjoyed by the F-14 and F-15 over the F-5. Good camouflage also helped negate the F-5E's small size, the six participating aircraft being painted in the dark-grey on light grey camouflage designed by noted aviation artist Keith Ferris. The tests resulted in the development of most of the F-14's current dogfight radar modes, and the VTAS (Visual Tactical Aircraft System) proved crucial in obtaining a large proportion of lock-ons.

"It took the Navy a decade to augment the TVSU with IRST and to integrate the two into the weapons system, to improve the radar warning system and to improve the electronic and infra-red countermeasures. This time was so long that it is now time for the next generation of improvements."

TSU is a passive electro-optical sensor which gives the pilot an ultra long-range telescope able to spot an enemy visually and identify him early. TSU is operated via a stabilised, gimbal-mounted closed-circuit television system. Two separate cameras are used for the two modes: wide angle for

target acquisition, and close-up for target identification. The TSU is normally slaved to the radar, and automatically locks on to the first target acquired. The NFO can also manually control the unit in the target identification mode, steering the lens with a joystick. The picture can be projected onto the radar display. A target can thus be visually identified while still far enough away to be engaged by a radar missile.

Under a $12.5-million contract, Northrop began deliveries of the first 36 TSU systems in late 1983, the first examples being operated by VX-4 at NAS Point Mugu, California. Subsequent orders went to 133. Some credit the TSU with enough definition to allow the F-14 crew to identify the weapons being carried by an enemy aircraft, which would be of great tactical value, if true. On a hazy day, however, natural conditions apply. Interestingly, an IRST has been refitted on the top-of-the-line F-14D, giving this variant 'spectrally distributed sensors' which increase firing opportunities by providing complementary methods of target search, which work better under different conditions.

Weapons

The Tomcat's comprehensive and sophisticated array of sensors is backed up by a range of weapons which allow the aircraft to engage multiple targets over a considerable range, from close-in within-visual-range (WVR) to far beyond the horizon, well beyond the reach of any other interceptor fighter.

Perhaps the most remarkable feature of the F-14 remains its primary weapon. The

Tomcat can theoretically carry six AIM-54C Phoenix long-range radar-guided missiles, four in side-by-side pairs in the 'tunnel' between the widely-separated engines and two on underwing pylons which can also accommodate AIM-9 Sidewinders. These two extra AIM-54s were originally to have been carried under the nacelles, but those hardpoints have less clearance and are better used by tanks. The missiles in the tunnel are slung on removable pallets which contain the necessary wiring, frequency decoders and cooling lines, and which also minimise the drag generated by these huge weapons. An internal hoist system simplifies loading of the missiles and their pallets. The front left-hand pallet contains the environmental control system for the missiles, while the right-hand pallet contains the tactical telemetry equipment for the missiles. These pallets are not carried in non-Phoenix missions, except in the air-to-ground role, thereby saving weight and internal space, and reducing the overall size of the aircraft. The pallets were designed from the start to be able to carry a variety of bombs. The AIM-54s are nicknamed 'Buffaloes' by air crew because of their size, and their appearance when they come off the racks. A less reverential Tomcat RIO explained more succinctly: "We call 'em Buffaloes because they're so goddamn heavy – 1,000 lb of weight that's not doing anything for you unless you kill somebody!"

The AIM-54A as originally deployed in 1974 was a revised version of a missile that had been in test for almost 10 years, and whose conception had occurred the decade before that, originating with the Missileer's

Bendix Eagle and the IR-homing Hughes GAR-9 or AIM-47. Remarkably, the Phoenix missile was actually ready in time for the F-14. Admiral Moorer describes the early stages of the programme: "The programme had begun with a letter contract to Hughes in December 1962. The proposed programme was keyed to the first F-111B fleet squadron delivery scheduled for February 1969. In the spring of 1964 the Navy learned of technical difficulties being encountered by two major sub-contractors: Litton (computer, controls and displays) and Rocketdyne (missile rocket motor). These technical problems, together with the attendant cost increases, resulted in a corrective plan which essentially would have slipped Phoenix development by one year. Subsequent to these events, further F-111B funds were denied by Congress in FY 1969 and the Phoenix was reorientated to the F-14A requirements and schedule, which then deferred fleet introduction to April 1973."

The Phoenix was the first air-to-air missile specifically designed for the simultaneous destruction of multiple incoming targets, including bombers, fighters and even missiles. Design of the missile, of course, predated the Tomcat itself, as did its associated fire-control system, the AWG-9. The Phoenix had been repackaged, re-engineered, and had gone through minor block improvements to produce what was very much a weapon for the future. In May 1970, it was revealed that $129 million of the $414 million spent on development had been for adapting the missile to the F-14. Although the size of the production run had not then been

Some 2,500 AIM-54As were delivered from December 1970 (though trials were not completed until 1972), and deliveries from Hughes's Tucson facility concluded in 1981. The AIM-54A remained unchanged for several years although there were minor block improvements through the late 1970s. The missile continued to be one of the most tightly-guarded secrets in the US arsenal. Work on a follow-on version began in the late 1970s.

The AIM-54B was an interim Phoenix improvement. It was an oddly timed, intermediate version whose roots lay in a stark fear that the Soviets were acquiring Western technology rapidly, so the missile had to be improved faster than original plans (which eventually resulted in the AIM-54C) would allow. The AIM-54B had improved resistance to jamming and re-engineered software modules, and was rushed into service to keep a technological edge over the Soviets. Getting the AIM-54B in service by 1983 was a genuine achievement. Said Moorer: "Hughes Aircraft, which produced the missiles at Mesa, did not even run [existing] missiles back through the factory as they normally would have done. Instead they produced kits which were taken out to Concord and Yorktown where conversions were done at depot level. The conversion was a matter of changing over software tapes and yanking circuit boards. This was in no way a factory remanufacture of the kind which occurred later when we upgraded some AIM-54A models to C models."

The ultimate Phoenix

Production AIM-54Bs featured many simplified engineering features, including simple sheet metal control fins in place of the honeycomb structure fins of the AIM-54A, and were fitted with non-liquid hydraulic and air conditioning systems. The improved AIM-54C Phoenix, though it has had development problems, was viewed as "the model that had everything they'd ever wanted in it" – a higher-thrust motor, an improved warhead and an improved fuse. Development of the AIM-54C actually began in October 1976, though prototypes were not delivered to the US Navy until December 1980. A pilot production batch of 30 missiles was delivered for evaluation in October 1981, and full production began in 1983. The AIM-54C suffered a setback on 22 July 1984, when deliveries were suspended following the discovery of poor workmanship in one missile. The Navy subsequently made an 'unconnected' announcement that there would be an attempt to find a second manufacturing source.

The new version of the missile was given a new solid state transmitter/receiver for the seeker head, a programmable digital signal processor, a digital autopilot, and a strapdown inertial reference unit. The new Motorola DSU-28C/B fuse was more capable of detonating at various altitudes, "so that it can take down targets such as high-diving air-to-surface missiles launched by 'Badgers', 'Bears' and 'Backfires'. Until the C-model fuse came along, we had the problem that they cruised at very high altitude at Mach 2.0 to 3.0 and when they tipped over into a steep high-angle, high-velocity dive it was impossible to intercept them with Phoenix. The AIM-54C model changes that."

Above: An F-14B of VF-211 banks away to reveal the maximum loadout of six Phoenix missiles. Even without external fuel tanks, this load would be too heavy for the aircraft to land back on a carrier.

more test points being cancelled because all launches and jettisons so closely conformed to wind tunnel behaviour and computer predictions.

In a typical long-range engagement, the missile initially follows a pre-programmed course, controlled by its autopilot. The missile is lobbed into a high trajectory, using altitudes at which the rocket motor is most efficient, and where drag is minimised. The predictable initial course minimises energy losses and also makes minimum use of the limited duration of available missile control surface power. The high trajectory reduces interference between the AWG-9's transmitter and the missile's receiver antenna. In a simulated engagement against a Mach-1.5, 50,000-ft target (aping a Tu-22M), a Phoenix fired from a Tomcat flying at Mach 1.5 and 44,000 ft (13415 m) reached an apogee of 103,500 ft, (31545 m). The missile then goes into a semi-active radar homing mode, using samples of radar data transmitted by the Tomcat's AWG-9 in its track-while-scan mode, during which the target is not constantly illuminated. During a multiple missile launch even this radar data is 'time-shared' between the missiles in flight. Finally, for the last 9-11 miles (5.5-6.8 km) of its flightpath, the missile's own active radar seeker (with its DSQ-26 planar array antenna) takes over, and it is fully autonomous. The Phoenix is thus only truly fire-and-forget capable if fired within 11 miles!

A PMTC Tomcat carried (left) and fired (above) an AIM-120 AMRAAM during the very early days of the advanced missile programme. The weapon has not yet been adopted for service aircraft.

Downey Mk 334 proximity fuse, or a Bendix IR fuse. Powerplant is the Rocketdyne Mk 47 or Aerojet Mk 60 long-burning rocket motor. This steel-cased monster engine, combined with the low-drag tail-mounted control surfaces, gave a claimed performance approaching Mach 5 at very high altitude. The missile was also surprisingly manoeuvrable, recording 17 *g* in trials, while the wide antenna gimbal limits allowed the engagement of targets offset widely from the launch aircraft.

As a result, the Phoenix has an extraordinary reach. During the initial development programme 26 R&D missiles were fired, one hitting a target at 78 miles (48 km) range, and others simultaneously hitting targets separated laterally by 10 miles (16 km). The Phoenix can be launched from all stations from VMin to Mach 1.6, up to 50,000 ft (15240 m) and from 0-6.5 *g*. Ten were launched or jettisoned during separation/release trials, four

determined, the unit cost of the Phoenix was estimated at less than $250,000. This was a considerable price for a single weapon, in 1970. All variants of the missile used semi-active radar homing and mid-course guidance, and therefore required that the target be 'painted' by the fighter's onboard AWG-9 weapon system. Once it gets within about 14 miles (23 km), the Phoenix missile's own DSQ-26 active radar takes over for the final thrust to target. A home-on-jam facility ensures that ECM will not usually defeat the missile in its terminal phase.

The Phoenix is fitted with a 132-lb (60-kg) annular blast fragmentation warhead and can be fitted with an impact fuse, a

Importantly, AIM-54C electronics were re-engineered to not generate the internal heat, when powered up on pallet, that had been a characteristic of A and B models. Left uncooled on their rack, A and B models would catch fire or melt down: these Phoenixes, when powered up on the launch pallet on the belly of the aircraft, generated so much heat in their electronics that they required a liquid cooling loop, which was fed from the F-14 – so part of the missile launch sequence was the cumbersome cut-off and sealing this liquid cooling loop. Despite their complexity, six AIM-54Cs can still be loaded onto an F-14 in under 18 minutes. The A- and B-model electronics were a hybrid between the tube technology of the late 1960s and the discrete solid-state of the 1970s, whereas the C model was entirely solid-state and could take on targets, including cruise missiles, at greater range and higher altitudes than its predecessors. The missile also has improved target discrimination, and is better able to make beam attacks. It features improved ECCM capability.

Hughes manufactured more than 2,500 of the initial production model of the Phoenix, the AIM-54A, for the US Navy and Iran before proceeding in 1981 to later versions.

Fire-control system

The Phoenix missile would be nothing without the Tomcat's AWG-9 weapons control system.

Almost ancient by today's standards, the AWG-9 was derived from the AN/ASG-18 radar and fire control system developed for the F-108, and then further developed for the Douglas Missileer and the F-111B. Power output was increased steadily during development. The system still has an impressive air intercept capability. At the heart of the system is a lightweight (60-lb/27-kg), 24-bit 5400B digital computer, capable of 550,000 operations per second, and a powerful 10.2-kW, coherent pulse-Doppler radar. This power output compares with 5.2 kW for the AN/APG-63 of the F-15. The AWG-9 has a 36-in (91-cm) diameter slotted planar array antenna, one of the largest such antennas ever fitted to a fighter aircraft. This mounted the dipole antennas for the IFF. Planar array antennas inevitably have higher 'gain' than parabolic antennas of the same size. Since radar range is proportional to both power and antenna size, it is unsurprising that the AN/AWG-9 has an unparalleled long-range capability. The use of coherent pulse-Doppler and high PRFs (Pulse Repetition Frequencies) minimise the susceptibility to clutter (ground returns swamping the radar returns of airborne targets) when operating in a look-down mode. The AWG-9 can be employed to engage an oncoming enemy from distances as great as 110 nm (126 miles; 203 km). A fighter-sized target of around 54 sq ft (5 m²) cross-section can be detected across a 135-nm (155-mile; 250-km) horizon. Hughes claimed its antenna was less prone to jamming than other contemporary fighter radars, although, interestingly, the UK MoD considered the system "too vulnerable to hostile jamming" in a 1976 report to the British Parliament. This conclusion was privately shared by many within the infant F-14 community, and became even more of a factor after the fall

Above: With a little imagination, and without the benefit of a photograph freezing the action, the AIM-54 can be seen to resemble a buffalo as it comes off the rail. This early test firing was undertaken from an A-3 Skywarrior. Other tests were made from F-111Bs and early F-14As.

Right: Senior officers examine a Phoenix test-round on the pylon of a Skywarrior test aircraft. The missile has always been expensive, and its actual capabilities have never been demonstrated under true operational conditions. Six AIM-54s have been launched simultaneously only once.

Below: A Hughes technician works on the AWG-9 fire control system of one of the earliest Tomcats. The radar's planar array antenna is deceptively simple looking, though its large size is evident in this view. Radar range is a function of antenna size and transmitter power.

Above: An early F-14A manoeuvres onto the tail of a target F-4J. In trials, the F-4 proved unable to escape the F-14, no matter what its pilot tried.

Below: The name of the F-14's game was fleet air defence, particularly against Soviet maritime patrol aircraft and missile carriers. Here a VF-84 Tomcat sees off a Tu-95RT.

of the Shah of Iran in 1979, when it became increasingly clear that the Tomcat and its equipment had been compromised to the USSR.

The AWG-9's radar offers more than crude power output. The system can operate in a number of useful modes, designed to make the best possible use of the antenna and output characteristics. This is made possible by simple good design and good processing capability, making the radar an extremely powerful tool.

In Pulse Doppler Search the radar has a range of 125 miles (200 km) or more, and can scan 'slices' of sky 10°, 20°, 40° or 65° on each side of the centreline (azimuth), with 1, 2, 4, or 8 bar elevation searches. Using a track-while-scan (TWS) mode for multiple target-tracking, the AWG-9 can carry out near-simultaneous long-range missile launches against up to six targets while tracking 24 more. In a multi-shot Phoenix engagement, or when tracking

multiple targets, the radar is limited either to an 80° azimuth, 2-bar search ("40 degree 2 bar"), or to a 40° azimuth, 4 bar search ("20 degree 4 bar"). Threats are automatically prioritised according to their range, closing velocity and direction, and are allocated an attack priority, which can be overridden if required. Missile range in a multi-shot engagement is limited to 55 miles (90 km).

In Track-While-Scan mode, any enemy aircraft's radar warning receiver would only detect what appeared to be a radar searching for him, and not one that was locked on. Warning of an incoming AIM-54 is therefore minimal. The AN/AWG-9 has 19 transmission channels, six of which are used for the guidance of AIM-54s, and five constant wave channels for illuminating targets for semi-active radar homing Sparrow missiles.

In Pulse Doppler Single Target Track (PDSTT) mode, target tracking is possible

out to 70 nm (80 miles; 130 km), and a missile can be launched from 54 nm (62 miles; 100 km). The AWG-9 incorporates a number of useful close combat modes, giving automatic lock-on at ranges of up to 5 nm (5.75 miles; 9.2 km) using a 2.3° diameter boresighted cone, or a narrow (4.8° azimuth) vertical beam positioned either from 15° above the nose to 55° above, or from 15° below the nose to 25° above. The higher beam position allowed the radar to be locked on to a turning target before the F-14 pilot had to bring his own nose to bear on the enemy aircraft.

New system for the D

The AWG-9 remains in service today virtually unchanged from its original application in the first F-14As, though the F-14D uses a radar and fire-control system so radically updated as to warrant the new APG-71 designation. In 1983, 23 AWG-9 sets were delivered with a new programmable signal processor which used target skin shape and engine fan/compressor characteristics to provide aircraft type identification capability at beyond visual range. The programme was abandoned, presumably as a result of cost or development problems, and F-14s lacked this capability until the introduction of the F-14D.

The F-14D does not actually have a new fire-control system, although the existing AWG-9 is very heavily modified. Only four of the original AWG-9 WRAs were retained unmodified, with four more being retained in modified form. Fourteen more were deleted altogether, and were replaced by nine entirely new units, some from the F-15E's APG-70 radar. The F-14D fire control system was originally known as the APG-XX, before the APG-71 designation was adopted. The aircraft also has two AYK-14 computers as controllers for its dual digital databuses.

Although the AWG-9 theoretically permits the F-14 crew to loose off as many

as six AIM-54s in a single near-simultaneous salvo, six missiles are seldom carried. In actual operations, a possible Tomcat load would be four Phoenixes, two Sparrow radar-guided missiles, and two Sidewinders. They, with the gun, give the F-14 considerable flexibility in engaging an enemy. More typically, the F-14 would be limited to only two Phoenix by bringback weight considerations, and today, with LANTIRN pods and/or bombs, carriage of a single Sparrow, a single Phoenix and two AIM-9s is routine.

Why one, two or four Phoenix and not six? According to Hughes's F. B. Newman, "The original specification for the F-14, written in the late 1960s at Navair [US Naval Air Systems Command, known as BuAer or the US Navy Bureau of Aeronautics until 1 December 1959, and as BuWeps or the US Navy Bureau of Weapons until 1 May 1966], specified the ability to take off, engage, and land with six AIM-54A Phoenix missiles, and throughout the development period this remained a primary goal. But during tests at Patuxent River, it was found for a variety of reasons that it was desirable to have the F-14 land at a higher sink rate and trap speed than had been originally specified by Navair."

This led to a major problem – the decks on the carriers were not stressed to take this impact, with the result that the aircraft were limited to four Phoenix, two Sparrows and two Sidewinders, plus the necessary fuel to go around several times in the pattern.

Continues Newman, "The F-14 can in fact land with six Phoenix on a land base because an airfield runway does not have the weight restrictions of a carrier deck, on which the arrester gear can be damaged by overweight landings. Moreover, a land-based F-14's undercarriage does not have to withstand as high a sink rate (from the landing aircraft) because it can have a longer roll-out." Some sources strongly refute this 'fact'. According to Lamoreaux, for example, the "missile configuration was a function of other considerations, primarily the missile mix and tactical options. The normal fleet operation was to use two of each, we know of no restriction that would limit the number of AIM-54s because of their weight. The CNO letter covers as a requirement that the airplane should be able to return aboard with a full load of missiles. There has, according to my knowledge, been nothing said about this design point having been missed."

In any event, production of Phoenix has been hampered by frequent delays, so there are probably not enough Phoenix in the fleet for sustained operations relying on missions which involve multiple aircraft carrying six at a time. Although reducing the number of Phoenix on an aircraft may limit the number of engagements which can be fought, a radar intercept officer commented, "While it is a very powerful, very high-yield missile – in terms of what it generates – in the end-game it is a very high-drag missile. If you have them out on the glove pylons, they are generating a lot of drag and you are paying for it in terms of reduced time on loiter out at your CAP station. Frequently, for the guys who are going to be out there during the outer air battle – who are going to be the tripwires, the first guys engaged – loiter time is more important than payload."

Although we have learned that the Tomcat rarely flies from carrier decks with a full load of six Phoenixes, the full 'six-shooting' capability of the weapon system has been demonstrated once (and only once!), on 21 November 1973 when a single Tomcat, piloted by Commander John R. 'Smoke' Wilson, fired six Phoenixes in 38 seconds while flying at Mach 0.78 at 24,800 ft (7560 m) over Point Mugu, California – its six drone targets operating at speeds between Mach 0.6 and 1.1. Wilson was a highly experienced carrier and test aviator. The key individual in the Phoenix test has hardly ever rated a mention in the history books. He was Lieutenant Commander Jack H. Hawver, who worked his magic in the backseat actually to get the missiles away and onto their targets. Though one missile failed when a flaw arose in its antenna control loop and a second was released against a drone which lost augmentation, causing the AWG-9 to break lock, the four remaining missiles scored direct hits, or passed within 'lethal distance'.

The validity of the tests was undermined by the fact that the test crew were able to carry out an extensive dress rehearsal, using F-8s, A-4s and T-33s flying exactly the same tracks as the drones. This was carried out to allow the F-14 crew to work out and practise the best way of launching their six missiles. In other tests, smaller numbers of AIM-54s have succeeded against Bomarc missiles simulating the MiG-25 'Foxbat' (flat out at Mach 2.8 and 72,000 ft/21945 m), drones simulating the Tu-26 'Backfire', and drones simulating sea-skimming missiles. In the latter test, a BQM-34 flying at 50 ft (15 m) was engaged by a Tomcat 22 nm (25 miles; 40 km) away, flying at Mach 0.72 and 10,000 ft (3050 m). The missile was even tested against drones simulating hard-turning fighter targets. In one test, a 'Backfire' was simulated by a BQM-34E flying at 50,000 ft (15240 m) at Mach 1.5, using intermittent noise jamming. The F-14 detected the target at very long range and accelerated to Mach 1.5, launching a single Phoenix at a range of 110 nm (126 miles; 204 km). This then climbed to 103,500 ft (31554 m) before swooping to destroy the target, having covered 72.5 nm (83 miles; 134 km) in just under three minutes.

Doubt has been cast on the validity of some of the much-hyped tests, however. In the six-missile test, for example, some felt that the scenario was too difficult and 'unfair'. Others asked awkward questions: Why were all six targets so conveniently positioned within a 15-mile (9.3-km) front and separated by less than 2,000 ft (610 m) vertically, and flying at 'easy speeds' of between Mach 0.6 and Mach 1.1, with the enemy fighter formation hardly manoeuvring, and with no evasion, jamming, or chaff? Others questioned how one of the AIM-54s could have missed a QT-33 flying along straight and level at Mach 0.6, and how another needed a larger radar signature than was provided by a BQM-34A cruising along at Mach 0.8. A former AV-MF Tu-16 'Badger' pilot questioned how anyone could expect a formation of inbound bombers to behave so co-operatively, and expressed relief that his AS-6 'Kingfish' missiles would obviously have been safe as long as the ground crew

had forgotten to strap on bagfuls of radar reflectors. On a more serious note he averred that the formation would be inbound at faster speed, with fighter and EW support, and spread out over a wider, deeper front. Since the F-14's LAR (Launch Acceptable Region), a cone emanating from the nose, narrows with increased target speed, a faster inbound formation would have made even the 15-mile, 2,000-ft front harder to defend.

However realistic or unrealistic the test may have been, and whether or not it proved the AIM-54, the test was undeniably expensive. Pilot Wilson recalled that the firing sequence lasted 38 seconds and cost $154,000 per second. "It was like setting fire to a 10-storey car park filled with new Cadillacs." Regardless of the expense, the test was considered to be essential, and had to be seen to be successful. Some even felt that failure would have led to cancellation of the entire project. Fortunately, Grumman, Hughes and the Navy were able to present the test results as a great success, although the achievement has never been repeated, and the AIM-54 survived. Cynicism about the much-hyped six-Phoenix capability remains, however, one distinguished analyst commenting, "This attribute has never been used, and at best remains a manufacturer's advertising ploy."

Phoenix conclusions

Concentrating on whether or not six Phoenix was possible, operationally relevant or whatever tends to obscure the real importance of the Tomcat's capability. The importance of the Phoenix/AWG-9 combination was that it allowed missiles to be fired without being locked on to a specific target (a first), allowing the crew to still see what was happening elsewhere. Moreover, any kind of multiple BVR missile shot capability marked a major advance, and a capability unavailable to USAF fighters until the introduction of

Below: A service test Phoenix (a YAIM-54A) waits to be loaded aboard one of the early F-14A development hacks, to form part of the aircraft's six-missile loadout.

Above: The AIM-54C introduced a digital guidance section and solid-state active radar, with improved range, reliability and ECCM capabilities.

AMRAAM many years later.

At medium range, the Tomcat uses the AIM-7 Sparrow semi-active radar homing missile, which has had a no less controversial background. The Sparrow requires a target to be illuminated constantly by the continuous wave travelling wave tube transmitter within the AWG-9 in order to home onto its target. Only one AIM-7 can be guided at a time, so only one target can be engaged at once. This is a stark contrast to the simultaneous six-target engagement capability using the AIM-54 Phoenix. The AWG-9 CW illuminator has twice the power output of the illuminator in the Phantom's AWG-10 radar, and this gives

the missile more 'reach' when fired by an F-14 than it has from any other launch platform. The AWG-9's 65° cone is also wider than that produced by the radars of some Sparrow launch platforms.

The Sparrow missile began life as the Sperry XAAM-N-2 Sparrow I which attained IOC (Initial Operating Capability) in July 1956. The fully active Sparrow II, later proposed for the Douglas F5D-I Skylancer and Avro Canada CF-105 Arrow, was never built. The current, semi-active radar homing (SARH) Sparrow III reached IOC aboard the McDonnell F3H-2M Demon in January 1958, was redesignated AIM-7A in 1962 and is now produced by Raytheon. The Sparrow gained a poor reputation in Vietnam, though this was as much due to the unhelpful rules of engagement as it was to the missile's inadequacies. During 1967, for example, the 366th TFW fired 21 Sparrows at MiGs below 8,000 ft (2440 m), and all missed their targets. The first Sparrow variant used on the Tomcat was the AIM-7E-2, which was considered to have 'fixed' problems of reliability encountered by early Sparrows. It also had clipped wings, an improved autopilot, better fusing and a lower-thrust sustainer motor with a longer burn time. The AIM-7E-4 was designed specifically to be used by aircraft with higher-powered radars, like the F-14 and F-15.

"AIM-7 acquired a real mixed reputation during the war in Vietnam," said Tomcat RIO Lieutenant Joseph Ulshafer. "But if you could ever get the thing locked-up and off the rail, it was a magic bullet with extremely good manoeuvrability and it would just blow the crap out of anybody."

After Vietnam, Raytheon shifted to production of the AIM-7F variant. This had vacuum tubes replaced by compact solid state electronics. The warhead was moved forward of the wings, leaving space behind for a bigger, longer-range dual thrust booster/sustainer motor. This version had a 28 to 30-mile (45 to 48-km) range head-on, almost double the range of the -7E.

The next major version was the AIM-7F POP (Project Optimization Program) of 1981-82, with more solid-state features. They have now been overtaken by the current version, the AIM-7M, which gained IOC in 1987. The M model introduced a monopulse seeker which is much tougher to detect and to jam, and is thus more effective in an electronic warfare environment. It also introduced digital signal processing. Many AIM-7Fs were subsequently rebuilt as AIM-7Ms.

Ulshafer: "The Sparrow's biggest problem is that just getting the doggoned thing off the rack is an incredible labour of love. You've got over 90 pneumatic, electronic, hydraulic and other actuator steps between the time the guy squeezes the trigger and, three seconds later, the thing pops off the bottom. There's explosive cartridges firing it off the bottom of the aircraft. There's umbilicals being cut. You're powering up things inside the missile. There's a gas generator working … It's incredible."

In fact, new Sparrows are much quicker to launch, with an LTE of only 1.5 seconds. Sparrow can be fired (or jettisoned) from the Tomcat's wing pylons at all speeds from VMin to Mach 1.6, and from sea level to 50,000 ft (15240 m). From the fuselage stations, 1 g jettisons only are possible, from VMin to Mach 0.7, and firings were restricted following a collision between an aircraft and its AIM-7 when the latter was fired from the no. 4 (rearmost centreline) station at 0 g.

Tomcat crewmen once looked to the day when Navy Sparrows would be replaced by the AIM-120 AMRAAM (Advanced Medium-Range Air-to-Air Missile). AMRAAM has active terminal homing, and does not require constant wave illumination from the launch aircraft (since it can fly towards the target responding to datalinked commands), so is not easily detected by the target's RHAWS. All

the launch aircraft has to do is to keep the target within its radar scan. The AIM-120 is still not a true fire-and-forget weapon, however. Aircrew once thought service entry might be as late as 1996 – though this prediction, once thought pessimistic, has proved wildly optimistic! Recent plans had the F-14 as the last fighter in the inventory to be equipped with AMRAAM, but under current Department of Defense plans the F-14 will not get AMRAAM at all.

From Agile back to AIM-9

For closer-range combat, the F-14 uses the IR-homing AIM-9 Sidewinder manufactured by Ford Aerospace. The Tomcat can carry up to four Sidewinders, two being the usual load. Early in the programme, the Tomcat's close-range missile seemed likely to be the AIM-X (later AIM-95) Agile missile designed by the NWC at China Lake, or the USAF's proposed AIM-82A, or a Navy-sponsored Super Sidewinder. Agile was 7 ft (2.13 m) long and had the same diameter as the Sparrow, allowing it to be carried in existing Sparrow wells or on existing Sparrow-capable hardpoints. It was heat-seeking and wingless, using thrust vectoring for control. Development of Agile began in 1971, but was abandoned in 1975. In the event, the Tomcat used a series of less ambitious developments of the basic AIM-9, and these proved more than acceptable. The heat-seeking Sidewinder missile (originally designated XAAM-N-7 and dating to the early 1950s) has been so successful, especially in current versions, that carrier air crews call it the 'silver bullet'. To quote Lieutenant Ulshafer, "In multiple wars, in multiple scenarios, ranging from the Falklands to the Middle East, the Sidewinder has been the determining factor in more air combats than any other thing out there. If you are in the envelope, the Sidewinder is almost impossible to beat. It has never lost a fight, period."

Early F-14 Tomcats carried the AIM-9J model, which had an expanded target-engagement cone enabling it to be launched at any spot in the rear hemisphere of a target aircraft rather than merely straight up its exhaust. Compared with Vietnam-era AIM-9G, the AIM-9J version also had a higher impulse motor and improved warhead. To compensate for the plain handicap that no air-to-air missile in the inventory had been designed for fighter-versus-fighter combat, the AIM-9J introduced the SEAM (Sidewinder Expanded Acquisition Mode) which slaved the seeker head of the missile to the radar when in 'dogfight mode'. The purpose was to avoid accidental acquisition in a dogfight and prevent those Vietnam mishaps where US fighters were blown out of the sky by US Sidewinders. Rather than employing a 'dumb' search mode, the AIM-9J seeker head could be uncaged, slewed toward a specific target by the aircraft's radar, and made to track the proper target only.

Early Tomcats also employed the AIM-9H, which came after the AIM-9J and introduced minor improvements. It was followed by the AIM-9L which attained IOC in 1979. Most importantly, the AIM-9L – later employed by Tomcats against Libya in 1981, and by British Sea Harriers in the Falklands – was 'all aspect', able to engage a head-on target, freeing the launch aircraft from the need to manoeu-

vre into his opponent's 'six'. This was because the L model seeker head had a seeker element of more sensitive material, able to pick up heat from the friction off the leading edge of an aircraft wing (even at subsonic speeds) and to differentiate between aircraft and decoy flares. The L was completely re-engineered, retaining the airframe and mid-course guidance unit but introducing a higher-impulse rocket motor, warhead and proximity fuse (a DBFF or 'directional blast fragged fuse', rigged to detonate to blow outward toward the target, also introduced on late Phoenix and Sparrow missiles).

The AIM-9M entered production in 1982, with a closed-cycle cooling system for the IR detector offering better capability to discriminate between a target and IR decoy flares, and with a low-smoke rocket motor. Reliability was improved by reducing further the number of delicate vacuum tubes in the missile (leaving three) pending the introduction of the first fully solid state 'Winder, the AIM-9R, which has a new electro-optical seeker operating in the visual and IR wavelengths, and a longer-range rocket motor. The AIM-9R is, in fact, a rather ambitious effort by Ford Aerospace and Raytheon to fill a gap left by delays to and cancellation of the AIM-132 ASRAAM (Advanced Short-Range Air-to-Air Missile) and may be replaced by a new AIM-9X. The AIM-9 can be fired over a wide envelope, from VMin to Mach 2, without altitude restrictions, between 1 g and 7 g. Trials showed some danger of gas ingestion at Mach 0.55 (160 kt) at 40,000 ft (12190 m). Fortunately, there was no excessive airframe heating from the missile's exhaust plume.

'Fox Three'

The final air-to-air weapon fielded by the F-14 is the 20-mm General Electric M61A1 Vulcan cannon (frequently called the 'Gatling gun'). The cannon is 74 in (1.975 m) long and weighs 265 lb (120 kg), and is installed on the lower left of the aircraft below the front cockpit. It has 678 rounds of ammunition, and is capable of firing up to 6,000 rounds per minute, using a linkless feed system. The gun is a 'closed' system, with spent cases being retained in the belt, which forms a helical coil, returning the used rounds to the ammunition drum. This stows the rounds very efficiently, and also minimises any shift in centre of gravity. "We also keep the rounds because if we ejected them they'd go straight down our own intakes. Not quite the guns kill we're looking for," explained one RIO. The six rifled barrels rotate anti-clockwise. Having six barrels reduces wear and helps dissipate heat, thereby making possible a higher rate of fire. Boresighting the gun is

achieved using an ingenious built-in laser device and a collimating lens attached to the gun barrel, which eliminates the need for live firing in the butts to align the cannon. The cannon bay is cooled using ram air, with the intake opening automatically when the trigger is actuated, closing 10 seconds after the trigger is released. At one time, thought had been given to retro-fitting the 25-mm GAU-6 cannon which was under development for the US Air Force's F-15 Eagle, but residue problems with this gun's caseless ammunition prevented it from reaching service.

The F-14 Tomcat has always had the latent capability to carry up to 14,500 lb (6580 kg) of dumb air-to-ground ordnance. "Structurally, the air-to-ground mission was designed into the F-14 from the beginning. The delay was because of a lack of commitment to install the proper avionics to enable the latent capability to be used," observed Rear Admiral Julian Lake, whose long career frequently brought him into contact with the F-14 programme. Though the Tomcat was not assigned a bombing mission during the first two decades of its career, software for a ground delivery mission is now fitted on all F-14B and F-14D models, and has been added to some F-14As. They are now being tasked for dual-role air-to-air and air-to-ground operations. VF-211, equipped with the A(Plus), got a no-drop, minutes before VF-24 clocked up the first live bombs dropped from a fleet Tomcat on 8 August 1990 on targets near Yuma, Arizona. On 'Bombcat' practice with inert 1,000-lb (454-kg) Mk 83 bombs, VF-211 was soon joined by sister squadron VF-24 as the two squadrons prepared for the Tomcat's first dual-role deployment aboard USS *Nimitz* in early 1991. Fleet Replenishment Squadron VF-101 at NAS Oceana manages the Tomcat strike fighter programme, developed an air-to-ground syllabus for the F-14, and trains replacement air crews in strike warfare.

Some analysts believe that an advanced, bomb-equipped F-14 Tomcat could take over the all-weather, day/night, deep-strike interdiction mission which the Navy once planned for the General Dynamics A-12, cancelled in December 1990. This would theoretically enable the Navy to eliminate light strike aircraft (F/A-18C Hornets) from its air wings. The concept was tested in the 1980s aboard USS *John F. Kennedy* with the so-called 'all Grumman air wing', wherein two squadrons of A-7Es were deleted and an extra squadron of medium-attack A-6E Intruders was added. Opponents of this idea cite the greater success of the all-Hornet air wings also trialled during the 1980s, and see a brighter future for the planned F/A-18E/F Hornet

aircraft, especially in an era where the threat from ultra-long-range bombers carrying ultra-long-range stand-off missiles (the traditional Soviet 'Bear'/'Backfire' threat) has vanished, to be replaced by a threat from smaller nations, primarily equipped with short-range fighter-bombers carrying nothing with greater range than an Exocet. This, it is argued, will allow US carriers to move closer to an enemy coast before launching strike aircraft.

This is controversial stuff, however, and air wings deploying with all Hornets and no A-6s and F-14s have to spend a great deal of time and effort just inflight refuelling. Moreover, putting the carrier closer to 'bad guy' territory (with shorter range but often more lethal weapons) is regarded by many as a very bad idea. Tomcat supporters want a return to the traditional, heavy air wing in which every aircraft is an all-weather, day/night warplane. Grumman has proposed a host of suitable F-14 derivatives, including the 'Tomcat 21' which also has limited stealth technology.

TARPS

A late addition to the Tomcat's capabilities came in 1980 when TARPS (Tactical Air Reconnaissance Pod System) was introduced for the reconnaissance role. The Navy had previously relied upon aircraft developed specifically for the reconnaissance role, primarily the RF-8G Crusader and the RA-5C Vigilante. Their eventual replacement was to be a dedicated derivative of the F/A-18, but it was recognised that this would not begin to deploy until FY89. It was realised that the Crusader and Vigilante would not be able to serve that long and, in the interim, a pod-mounted system was developed for the proposed interim RA-7E Corsair. This dedicated aircraft was abandoned and its sensor suite was then adapted for carriage by the standard F-14 under the acronym TARPS. This was a very different aircraft from the briefly proposed and fully-dedicated RF-14C, an unbuilt F401-PW-400-engined version of the original F-14B, once known as the VRX and originally intended to enter service in 1975. This would have been equipped with photographic and IR sensors and an LLLTV camera. The RF-14C was originally sketched with a nose-mounted reconnaissance pack, and alternatively with a ventral canoe fairing, before it was decided that the role equipment would be podded. An aerodynamic model of the proposed variant's supersonic reconnaissance pod

Above: Armed with two Phoenix under the fuselage, and AIM-9Ps underwing, this Iranian F-14 looks little different to pre-revolutionary Tomcats, though it may incorporate stolen and Israeli spares.

Right: In recent years, some Iranian F-14s have received new air superiority colour schemes, and all have taken on a wider role, encompassing air-to-ground responsibilities, for which weapons like the AGM-65 Maverick may be carried.

(modified from a 267-US gal/1010-litre external fuel tank) was flown on the second prototype, intended for use at speeds of up to Mach 1.8.

Development of TARPS as we know it today began in April 1976, with flight testing commencing in September 1977. The pod was designed to impose the smallest possible performance penalty on the aircraft carrying it, and to be removed quickly, allowing host aircraft remodification to the fighter role within 30 minutes. TARPS can be fitted to the rear right Phoenix station of any Tomcat 'wired' for it. The original total number of TARPS-capable F-14As was about 50 aircraft, with one of the two F-14A squadrons on each carrier usually having three reconnaissance-configured ships. At one time, it was expected that the TARPS Tomcats would equip a single dedicated reconnaissance unit, which would then provide detachments for service aboard the Navy's carriers, in just the way that RF-8 Crusaders had been deployed. The delivery of TARPS-compatible aircraft to ordinary squadrons gave much greater flexibility, however. Any F-14 can be modified for TARPS carriage (though only through a return to

Grumman or NADEP), and attrition replacement is thus easy.

Today, with most carriers embarking only a single F-14 squadron, most Tomcat units are TARPS capable, and most thus have a number of TARPS-modified aircraft. Every F-14D can carry TARPS.

Designed for a low-to-medium altitude reconnaissance role, the pod contains a KS-87B frame camera (vertical or forward oblique) in station one, a KA-99 or KA-93 panoramic camera (or a KS-153A frame camera) giving horizon-to-horizon coverage in station two, and an AAD-5A (RS-720) infra-red line scanner in station three. The TARPS pod also includes an AN/ASQ-172 data display system for putting event marks on the sensors' film output to aid later interpretation. TARPS Tomcats accommodate pod controls in the rear cockpit (on the RIO's left-hand console) and data from the pod is displayed on the TID, with range- and time-to-target, range- and time-to-CAMERA OFF, pod status and even the AAD-5A image. A target marker, commanded ground track and steering cue can be projected in the pilot's HUD. The aircraft

provides power and air conditioning to the pod. TARPS became operational in 1981. A TARPS upgrade provided for the optional carriage of a KS-153T camera or an LLLTV system in station one, and for the further station two options of a KS-153T or KS-153L. Original trials TARPS pods were converted from early-model F-14 external fuel tanks, which are a commonly carried Tomcat store, and can be carried either underwing, or on dedicated hardpoints below the engine nacelle/ducts. The original F-14 tank was finless, and contained 270 US gal (1022 litres), while the later style has small fins, and contains 3 US gal (11 litres) less.

Jon Lake, Julian Lake and Robert F. Dorr

Below: This HAWK SAM is carried on a modified Phoenix pylon under the starboard wing glove of one of two Iranian F-14s (3-6034, 3-6073) confirmed as having carried this weapon. Integration of HAWK on Iran's F-14s may mark an attempt to circumvent a shortage of AIM-54s by producing a new BVR air-to-air missile. The operational status of the weapon is uncertain.

Below: Accompanied by an F-4E, this Iranian F-14A carries a HAWK SAM under its glove pylon. Two underwing HAWKs seems to be the standard loadout for the F-14. The aircraft appears to be from a front-line unit, wearing the 'circle 8' badge of Tactical Air Base 8 at Isfahan.

Weapon loadouts

Fleet Air Defence (multi bogey)

In the Fleet Air Defence role, the aim is to maximise long-range missile armament, within the constraints imposed by maximum weight considerations.

Although the F-14 can carry a theoretical maximum of six AIM-54s, it can only land on a ground runway. The F-14's maximum carrier arrestment weight (max trap) of 54,000 lb even limits the occasions on which four AIM-54s can be carried.

When four Phoenix are carried, stations 1B and 8B (main glove pylons) are usually used for the carriage of a pair of AIM-7 Sparrows, giving extra BVR capability. When a maximum load of AIM-54s is carried, the extra two are carried on these stations.

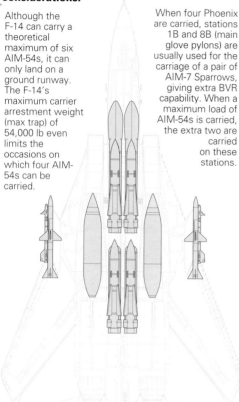

Fleet Air Defence (DLI)

Each Phoenix carried imposes a 1,500-lb weight penalty, including 500 lb per pallet. Reducing the number thus improves radius and performance.

In this configuration an AIM-7 replaces the rear pair of AIM-54s, reducing weight and drag. The forward centreline Sparrow recess cannot be used when two AIM-54 pallets are fitted. The aircraft still carries five BVR missiles and two AIM-9s.

The basic weight of the F-14A is about 44,000 lb, including launch rails for AIM-7 and AIM-9. Fuel, AIM-54 pallets and ordnance account for another 20,000 lb. The max trap weight must include 4,000 lb of fuel. Thus the F-14 can land with only 6,000 lb of ordnance.

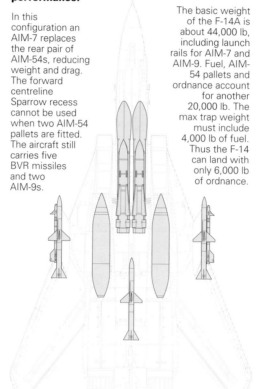

Fleet Air Defence (max loiter)

If the F-14 is not likely to have to simultaneously intercept multiple targets at maximum range, it can take off with this lower drag loadout.

The replacement of all four AIM-54s by four AIM-7s reduces the F-14's reach, but also reduces fuel burn. If ROE dictate visual identification, a mix of four AIM-7s and four AIM-9s gives increased flexibility.

The carriage of Phoenix imposes limitations on the Tomcat's manoeuvrability, as well as on range and endurance. If fighter-versus-fighter combat is anticipated, AIM-9s may represent a better choice than a load including the Phoenix, depending on ROE.

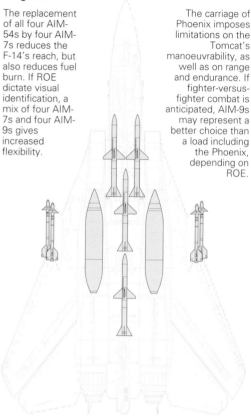

TARPS

The carriage of TARPs on station 5 (alternate) prevented carriage of underfuselage AIM-54s, although centre of gravity considerations necessitated the carriage of (empty) forward Phoenix pallets or inert AIM-7s for ballast.

In the TARPS role, the F-14's defensive armament is usually limited to pairs of AIM-7 Sparrows and AIM-9 Sidewinders.

It would be theoretically possible for a TARPS-configured aircraft to carry live Sparrows as ballast, but if these were fired, the aircraft would have to make an aft C of G landing, which has not been cleared. On the F-14D, TARPS could be carried in conjunction with AIM-54s on the wing glove.

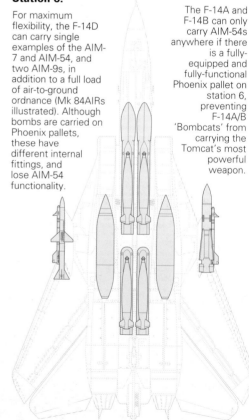

TARPS (Operation Desert Storm)

The TARPS-equipped Tomcats provided the US Navy with its only carrierborne tactical reconnaissance capability during the Gulf War.

During the Gulf War, TARPS Tomcats normally carried AN/ALQ-167 ('Bullwinkle') ECM pods on the starboard Phoenix pallet, with an Expanded Chaff Adaptor (ECA) in the starboard pallet. The TARPS pod then carried only wet-film based sensors.

The F-14D would not need to carry the 'Bullwinkle' when operating in the TARPS role, since it would normally carry the AN/ALQ-165 ASPJ internally. The F-14D was too late to see service in Desert Storm.

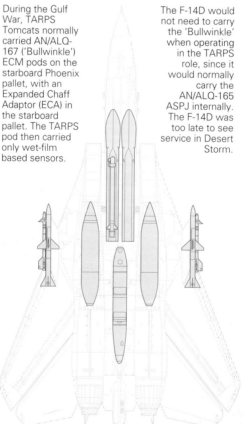

'Bombcat' multi-role (F-14D)

Subject to maximum carrier landing weight considerations, the F-14D can carry AIM-54s on its wing glove pylons without carrying a Phoenix pallet on Station 6.

For maximum flexibility, the F-14D can carry single examples of the AIM-7 and AIM-54, and two AIM-9s, in addition to a full load of air-to-ground ordnance (Mk 84AIRs illustrated). Although bombs are carried on Phoenix pallets, these have different internal fittings, and lose AIM-54 functionality.

The F-14A and F-14B can only carry AIM-54s anywhere if there is a fully-equipped and fully-functional Phoenix pallet on station 6, preventing F-14A/B 'Bombcats' from carrying the Tomcat's most powerful weapon.

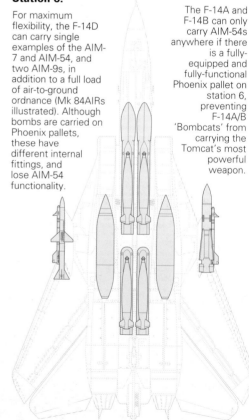

'Bombcat' I

The F-14 is cleared to carry a range of air-to-ground weapons, including the 1,000-lb Mk 83 seen here. These are carried on Phoenix-type pallets, which become BRU-42s when fitted with the appropriate interchangeable components.

The F-14 can carry external fuel, AIM-9s and AIM-7s in addition to four bombs, each of 500-lb, 1,000-lb or 2,000-lb weight, depending on weight considerations.

Only the F-14D could carry a mix of AIM-54s and bombs, since only the F-14D could carry the AIM-54 underwing without a Phoenix LAU-134 pallet on station 6. Mixed loads of AIM-54s and bombs underfuselage were not permitted.

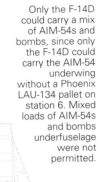

'Bombcat' II

The carriage of four Mk 82 bombs represented a lighter, lower-drag load than two AIM-54s, making the humble 500-lb bomb a useful Tomcat weapon.

With any 'Bombcat' loadout, the rear pair of Phoenix-type pallets could be removed to make way for a single AIM-7 on the centreline. Alternatively, there would seem to be no reason why a TARPS pod could not be carried on Station 5.

Remarkably, no effort has been made to clear the carriage of bombs under the wing gloves, though this would leave the belly clear for the carriage of four AIM-54s or up to four AIM-7s.

'Bombcat' (Max loadout)

The carriage of large numbers of relatively small bombs can be useful, if major damage is to be avoided. The carriage of side-by-side pairs of Mk 82 bombs on the BRU-42 launch rails is expected to be cleared soon.

This aircraft carries four Mk 82 bombs, yet can also carry a single underfuselage AIM-7 behind them, on the centreline. Alternatively, four more Mk 82s could be on two more pallets.

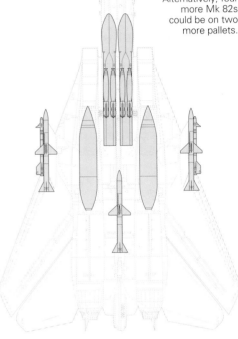

LANTIRN 'Bombcat'

The 'Bombcat' can carry the full range of Paveway II and Paveway III laser-guided bombs on the same BRU-42 launchers that are used for Mk 80-series bombs.

F-14s began carrying Paveway LGBs before they were capable of providing guidance to such weapons. Autonomous LGB delivery capability became possible with the integration of LANTIRN.

1,000-lb GBU-16 Paveway II LGBs were among the first precision-guided munitions carried by the F-14, together with the 2,000-lb GBU-10 and the 500-lb GBU-12. The GBU-16 was used operationally in Bosnia.

LANTIRN 'Bombcat' (F-14D)

Bomb-carrying F-14Ds can carry Phoenix missiles on the wing glove pylons without carrying a Phoenix pallet on Station 6.

The Paveway III offers better low-level and better stand-off capability than the original Paveway II. The F-14 carries the 2,000-lb GBU-24.

The carriage of a centreline Sparrow with LGBs forward was cleared in 1996. This allows LANTIRN-equipped aircraft to still carry two BVR missiles.

Rocket attack

Unguided rocket projectiles represent an excellent area weapon, as well as being highly effective against soft-skinned vehicles. The F-14 has been cleared to fire 5-in Zuni rockets.

The use of unguided rockets by the F-14 may become more common as the type takes on more of a Fast FAC role.

The F-14 will carry more modern 2.75-in rockets, as well as the 5-in Zuni, which is thought by many to be on the verge of obsolescence.

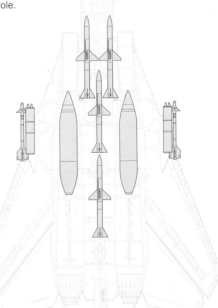

Chapter Five

The Tomcat in Action

Until Operation Desert Storm, the US Navy was not officially at war, yet the F-14 gained many opportunities to fly real combat missions. The Tomcat scored its first four air-to-air victories in two engagements during which the F-14 was faced by Libyan 'Fitters' and 'Floggers'. Those historic dogfights, and other combat missions, are described in detail in this chapter.

In the eary 1980s, Libya provided the F-14A Tomcat with an opportunity to show its stuff. In August 1981 USS *Forrestal* (CV-59) and USS *Nimitz* (CVN-68) conducted 'freedom of navigation' (FON) exercises in the Gulf of Sidra, aimed at showing Tripoli that Americans were serious about their right to project naval power in international waters. On 18 August, Libyan fighters, including the vaunted MiG-25 'Foxbat', challenged US Navy fighters and escorted them at close range. The Commander of Carrier Air Wing Eight aboard the USS *Nimitz*, Commander (later Rear Admiral) 'Bad Fred' Lewis, actually mixed it with a pair of Libyan Mirage F1s, ending up with him and his wingman sitting in trail with the two Libyans, in a perfect firing position. There exist both written and unwritten rules for this sort of thing, and on that day they were followed. There was plenty of aggressive manoeuvring, but no shots were fired, and the aircrews on both sides did no more than photograph each other. At the time, the Rules of Engagement (ROE) were exceedingly strict, enabling Tomcat crews to engage only if actually fired upon, and it was normal for a fighter jock to hope his chance would come. On 19 August 1981, it did.

In 1974 Libya's President, Colonel Khadaffi, had declared the waters below 32° 30' (the Gulf of Sidra) to be the territory of the Libyan Arab Republic, in clear violation of international conventions. The US response was an official protest, which was ignored. In 1980, a US reconnaissance aircraft was attacked in the area, and President Carter's response was to order the Sixth Fleet to avoid confrontation and stay out of the disputed area. When Ronald Reagan took office, the situation changed. Reagan ordered the Navy to conduct an exercise specifically intended to challenge the Libyans' claim. This was the highly provocative OOMEX (Open Ocean Missile Exercise) referred to above. The so-called Reagan Rules of Engagement provided for the on-scene commander to take any necessary action to defend his assets without clearing it through higher authority. For fighter pilots this translated into 'you may fire if fired upon'. The intensive naval and air operations generated concentrated activity in Libya, where the populace and armed forces were convinced that the Sixth Fleet was about to conduct a major strike. By the second day of the exercise, the Libyan air force had been placed at a higher state of readiness.

On that morning two Tomcats from VF-41 'Black Aces' using the callsigns 'Fast Eagle 102' and 'Fast Eagle 107', positioned themselves in a CAP station off the Libyan coast. At 07.15, near the end of their patrol, pilots Commander Henry ('Hank') Kleeman (the commander of VF-41) and Lieutenant Larry ('Music') Muczynski, with their respective RIOs, Lieutenants Dave Venlet and James Anderson, used their AWG-9 radars to detect a single contact heading straight at them after taking off from a Libyan air base. It was a pair of Sukhoi Su-22 'Fitter' fighters being

*USS **Nimitz** cruises in the Mediterranean during the 'freedom of navigation' exercises mounted to challenge Libyan claims to the **Gulf of Sidra**.*

*Less than a year after Evening Light, **Nimitz** (with VF-41 and VF-84) was back in the Mediterranean, off the coast of Libya.*

*Below: VF-41's 'Fast Eagle 107' is seen during **Operation Evening Light**, the 1980 support operation for the aborted Iranian hostage rescue attempt (Operation Eagle Claw), complete with red and black recognition stripes.*

vectored by GCI radar toward them. This time, however, the rules were being circumvented. As the Su-22s reached the 20,000-ft (6095-m) altitude of the Tomcats, attempts by the Americans to manoeuvre out of a head-to-head confrontation were fruitless. Every time they turned away from the Sukhois, intending to offset from them (in order to be able to turn onto their tails), the Sukhois turned to keep the F-14s on their noses. The Sukhois' actions could have been taken as demonstrating aggressive intent, or simply good defensive tactics. Muczynski climbed about 4,000 ft (1220 m), but remained about 10,000 ft (3050 m) off Kleeman's starboard wing, dropping back slightly despite climbing in zone five afterburner. The intention was for Kleeman to be the 'eyeball' passing close to identify the enemy visually, while Muczynski flew in behind them as the 'shooter'. In 'Fast Eagle 102', Kleeman made visual contact (or tally ho) at a distance of about 8 miles (13 km). At about 2 miles (3.2 km) he saw for the first time that the contact was a pair of Su-22s in a loose deuce formation with about 500 ft (150 m) separation, not quite as close as a typical 1970s Soviet 'welded wing' formation. It became clear that Kleeman and the Libyan lead would pass very close, left wingtip to left wingtip, and that the Libyan Sukhois would be about 500 ft below 'Fast Eagle 102'.

Missile firing

Kleeman banked left to enable him to keep sight of the Libyans as they passed and, while the formations were still about 1,000 ft (305 m) apart, he saw a flash under the lead Su-22's starboard wing and assumed that the Libyan flight lead had loosed off an AA-2 'Atoll' AAM. Although it was immediately evident that this missile had failed to track, a second missile could come at any instant. The die was cast. Muczynski in 'Fast Eagle 107' had just begun a turn hoping to 'skip' over the Libyan fighters, and saw the flash (he remembered it as coming from below the Libyan's left wing). "It was very obvious to me, with a tremendous orange flash and a smoke trail going off under Kleeman's Tomcat then doing a sort of a banana up towards my plane, but it was obvious that neither one of us was going to get hit by the missile." As soon as he saw the missile being fired at him by the lead Su-22, Kleeman reacted by breaking hard to the left, hoping to come out of the turn behind the Libyan fighters. (It remains open to argument even today whether the Americans saw a missile being deliberately fired, or whether it was merely an external fuel tank being punched off.)

Shoot him!

As the formations passed, the Libyans split, the leader going left, his wingman going right. "Take the one on the left!" Kleeman ordered. The Su-22s' turns were not hard enough to be classed as a break, and as the F-14s turned through about 180° they found themselves behind the Libyan 'Fitters'. Muczynski came out of his turn ahead of Kleeman, and behind the lead Sukhoi, which reversed the direction of its turn to pull right. Muczynski manoeuvred into position to have a clear 'six o'clock' tail shot at the Libyan flight leader. "Skipper, what should I do?" he

asked, only to be answered by an F-4 pilot (from *Forrestal*) who was simultaneously manoeuvring with Libyan MiG-25s, and who had followed the encounter. "Shoot him, shoot him, shoot him!" This was good advice, and echoed Kleeman's order. From about half a mile (800 m), Muczynski fired an AIM-9L from the port-glove station, just as the Su-22 began its break to the right. As the missile struck home, Muczynski pulled into the vertical at about 6 *g* to avoid the debris. The Sidewinder blew off the tailpipe of the lead Su-22, which immediately went into a vicious spin, and its pilot ejected – though the Libyan's parachute was not seen to deploy. Once Kleeman knew that Muczynski had this intruder 'locked up', he shifted his attention to manoeuvring to the tail of the second Libyan fighter, now passing in front of the sun in a continuing turn. "My 'Fitter' was approaching the sun; since I intended to use a Sidewinder heat-seeking missile, I realised that was not a good position from which to shoot." As the remaining Su-22 turned, Hank Kleeman calculated the point at which the sun would no longer distract the seeker head of his AIM-9L Sidewinder infra-red missile. "I waited until he cleared the sun, then fired my missile." He reached this point about 1,300 ft (410 m) from the Su-22, and fired the missile from the left-glove hardpoint. "The missile guided and struck him in his tailpipe area, causing him to lose control of the airplane, and he ejected within about five seconds." The Su-22 rolled and popped its drag chute, just as or perhaps just before Kleeman's Sidewinder exploded low on its fuselage, and the pilot ejected.

'Nimitz Two: Libya Nil'

On 19 August 1981 the F-14 achieved its first air-to-air kills when a pair of VF-41 Tomcats successfully engaged a pair of Libyan Su-22s over the Gulf of Sidra. This is a diagram of the engagement, showing how the Tomcats maintained a parallel offset track until the lead Su-22 fired a missile at them. At this point the Su-22s broke left and right, and the F-14s turned into them, rolling out behind for two easy Sidewinder shots.

Above: This is a Libyan Su-22 of the type downed on 19 August 1981. With no radar and no BVR missiles, the Su-22 was not much of an opponent.

Right: 'Hank' Kleeman demonstrates how he shot down 'his' Su-22 during a post-flight press conference, watched by the rest of his flight.

It had never been any sort of a match. The Su-22 was a dedicated attack aircraft and the Libyan pilots were, to quote Muczynski, "a couple of bush leaguers who

Flying high as the 'shooter', Muczynski and Anderson in the wing F-14 spot the missile fired by the Su-22s and begin to turn down and into the 'Fitters'. As they break, Muczynski takes the lead Su-22, which has broken left. The Libyan reverses, easily allowing Muczynski to get on its 'six'. After a request for instructions, Muczynski takes a tail shot at the Su-22, the missile guiding perfectly. After the missile is seen to guide, Muczynski pulls the Tomcat up to avoid any debris from the 'Fitter'.

Sun position

Su-22 wing

Su-22 lead

F-14 lead fires AIM-9

Altitude trace
F-14 wing
F-14 lead

Su-22 fires missile

F-14 wing fires AIM-9

F-14 lead (Kleeman/ Venlet)

F-14 wing (Muczynski/ Anderson)

After the Libyan missile has been seen not to track either Tomcat, Kleeman turns into the Su-22s and takes the right-hand (wing) 'Fitter'. This aircraft executes a lazy break, allowing Kleeman to reverse easily back on to its 'six'. He waits for the Su-22 to cross the sun before firing.

The Tomcat in Action

This VF-41 F-14A carries a typical weapon load for operations against Libya. It carries TCS undernose, which was not available in 1981.

couldn't even make the second-string team." US naval aviators receive training as intense as any fliers in the world - Kleeman, for example, had made over 1,000 carrier landings.

Although the Su-22s had been hopelessly outclassed from the start, the two air-to-air kills received far more media and public attention than they warranted, partly because Americans had not enjoyed a clear-cut 'win' since VJ-Day. Not all of the media coverage was helpful, or even friendly. In February 1982 Radio Moscow broadcast a documentary called 'The Atomic-Powered Pirate' about the *Nimitz* and its operations. Its listeners learned that, "American F-14 fighters attacked and shot down two Libyan patrol aircraft, and, having carried out this bandit raid, returned to their floating base!"

Although the two Su-22 kills was a far less important event than the media made

VF-33 flew in support of Operations Prairie Fire and El Dorado Canyon, the 1986 strikes against Libya.

them seem, they marked a turning point in another sense. 1981 was the first year of a decade in which American naval aviators were to see the distinction between peace and war merge into a blur. It was a time when you could be carrying out the most mundane tasks one day, and find yourself getting shot at the next. During the coming decade American forces would be committed in Lebanon, in Grenada, against Libya once more, and finally in Panama – all before a real war broke out against Iraq at the start of the 1990s. A record of sorts was attained by the two F-14 squadrons aboard USS *Independence* which found themselves in two clashes during a single aircraft-carrier cruise.

Air cover for an invasion

Independence's 18 October 1983-11 April 1984 deployment included combat operations in Grenada in October 1983 and in Lebanon two months later. US forces mounted their controversial invasion of Grenada (a former British colony and still a member of the Commonwealth) in

fear of the growing Cuban presence on the island, and in reaction to a *coup* on 19 October 1983. USS *Independence* (en route to the Mediterranean) was diverted to provide tactical air power to support the air-landed and parachute-dropped US Army invasion forces, and the Navy SEALs and USMC troops landed by sea. Within Air Wing Six VF-14 guarded *Independence*'s carrier battle group and flew CAP; VF-32 shared these missions and flew reconnaissance sorties using its TARPS-equipped aircraft. In Grenada, TARPS imagery provided intelligence on troop movements and gun emplacements to US Marines and Army Rangers, but with no enemy air opposition VF-14 had little to do, although the faint danger of Cuban intervention meant that the fleet air defence mission could not be ignored.

Tomcats over the Lebanon

Israeli over-reaction in its operations in the Lebanon (and particularly its heavy bombardment of Beirut) prompted the UN to back the despatch of a Multi-National Force to enforce and maintain a peace. British, French and American ground troops soon found themselves under attack by Lebanon's warring factions, and eventually withdrew to leave the various groups to slug it out. Before it did withdraw, the Multi-National Force was supported by RAF aircraft based on the island of Cyprus, and by French and American aircraft-carriers. America's contribution consisted of the two on-station carriers of the Sixth Fleet, together with a third carrier. Each vessel carried a full air wing, with two F-14A Tomcat squadrons. The USS *John F. Kennedy* hosted Air Wing Three with VF-11 and VF-33, while VF-142 and VF-143 equipped Air Wing Seven aboard USS *Dwight D. Eisenhower*. The *Independence* brought Air Wing Six and its two F-14 units direct from Grenada. Tomcats flew regular fighter sweeps and reconnaissance missions but were not, as the USSR claimed, "armed for striking against ground targets."

On 19 September it was claimed that

F-14s had pursued Syrian fighters over central Lebanon, but this was denied by the US Navy. On 10 November four Tomcats were forced to cut short a mission when they came under intensive fire from AAA and SAMs, for the first time. Tension increased following a terrorist truck bombing of the US Marines compound in Beirut, and Syria mobilised its forces. Tomcats flew reconnaissance and low-level flag-waving missions, which increasingly came under hostile fire. The reconnaissance missions were criticised by Admiral Stansfield Turner, director of the CIA, who felt that SR-71 missions could have achieved better results in complete safety. He felt that the missions were, "an empty threat, a demonstration, a political gesture. If we wanted photos of Lebanon we could have done it in total safety, instead we fly around up there and wait until they shoot at us!"

VF-32's TARPS-equipped Tomcats alone flew about 30 missions which came under hostile fire. These opposed missions included a TARPS sortie on 3 December 1983, during which a VF-32 aircraft had been fired upon by 10 Syrian SAMs, and the first bomb damage assessment mission mounted after the air strike flown in the Beka'a Valley on 4 December 1983. This was mounted as a retaliatory strike for the SAM firings on 3 December and was a unique event – poorly planned, hastily executed, and resulting in the loss of two aircraft of a 24-plane strike package. "We were just screwing around, running around in circles," remembered one VF-142 Tomcat pilot later. The strike aircraft were led by Commander Edward Andrews, *Independence* CAG, who flew an A-7 on the mission. Edwards had previously been an F-14 pilot, flying many of the sequences seen in the Hollywood motion picture, *The Final Countdown*. His A-7 was one of the aircraft shot down, though he ejected and was recovered safely. The strike aircraft were protected by a force of F-14s led by the *Kennedy* CAG, Commander J. J. Mazach, but the Syrian air force did not attempt to intervene. It was not the first military action of the decade which

produced such disappointing results, nor was it the last.

Tomcats returned to the Gulf of Sidra aboard the USS *Saratoga*. They overflew disputed territorial waters on 25 July 1984, provoking Libyan complaints of 'blatant aggression' and claims that the intrusions had involved '164 Tomcats', which had been driven off by Libyan fighters! Fortunately, the incident ended without weapons being fired.

Tomcats brought to ground the terrorists who, in October 1985, hijacked the Italian cruise liner *Achille Lauro* and murdered an elderly, wheelchair-bound American tourist, Leon Klinghoffer. Four Palestinians briefly heisted the vessel, murdered the elderly American and found refuge in Egypt, where plans were finalised for an Egyptair Boeing 737 to transport them to sanctuary in Libya.

A precision night ambush was set up, planned by the NSC's Lieutenant Colonel Oliver North, and performed by the F-14s of VF-74 and VF-103 aboard USS *Saratoga* in co-ordination with an RC-135 and an E-2C Hawkeye aircraft. Seven F-14 Tomcats launched from 'Sara', got into position, and pounced the airliner, forcing it to land at Sigonella, Italy. Not as part of the plan, Italian guards intervened, preventing American Delta Force commandos (who landed aboard a C-141B StarLifter behind the Boeing) from snatching the quartet away to stand trial on American soil – but the hijackers were prosecuted in Italy.

US naval and air power returned to Libya in March and April 1986 in response to Colonel Khadaffi's continuing support of terrorism. In a new version of the 'freedom of navigation' exercise, with newer and more liberal Rules of Engagement – even looser than the so-called Reagan ROE – USS *America* and USS *Coral Sea* launched Operation Prairie Fire in March, seeking to provoke Libya into reacting to US forces. Under the new rules of engagement such a reaction would have allowed US forces to return fire if threatened, and not just if actually fired upon. When Libyan SAM sites fired at several Navy aircraft and two MiG-25 'Foxbat-As' came out to challenge a pair of Tomcats, serious fighting got underway. Numerous strikes were flown against Libyan targets over 24-26 March, with Tomcats providing top cover.

Air strikes against Libya

On 2 April 1986, a bomb left by a terrorist in West Berlin blew up the La Belle disco, packed with off-duty US servicemen. Intercepts of Khadaffi's communications confirmed a Libyan role in the incident. Operation El Dorado Canyon – a joint air campaign against Libya – was launched on 15 April 1986. Tomcat crews are keen to point out that in this 'joint' operation, US Navy aircraft operated from off the Libyan coast, while the USAF participants had to fly all the way from England, bypassing France and Spain. USS *Saratoga* added a third carrier deck plus two more Tomcat squadrons to the off-shore force. Air Force F-111Fs attacked Tripoli while Navy strike aircraft

Soon after their successful 1989 cruise, VF-32's aircraft gained a 'Swordsmen' logo down the trailing edge of the rudder.

Above: In the winter of 1985/86 Saratoga was on station with the Sixth Fleet. Here a VF-74 F-14A traps, with a Shrike-armed A-7 in the background.

Right: Partnering VF-74 was VF-103, one of whose aircraft is seen here on patrol with an EA-6B. Both Tomcat squadrons were involved in the Achille Lauro airliner 'kidnap'.

went against Benghazi, the latter being 'CAPped' by F-14 Tomcats, although no enemy fighters were encountered. In any event, although Libya began to fall from its high priority on the American agenda, the F-14 Tomcat was not quite through with Khadaffi's forces.

On 4 January 1989, yet another exercise was under way to demonstrate 'freedom of navigation' in international waters off Libya, this time by USS *John F. Kennedy*'s battle group. The skipper of VF-32, Commander Joseph B. Connelly, using callsign 'Gypsy 207', was leading a section (a standard two-aircraft formation) of F-14As paralleling the Libyan coast; they had just 'topped off' with fuel from their KA-6D tanker. Each F-14 was laden with four Sparrows and two AIM-9 Sidewinders, having launched before the intended loadout of four AIM-7 and four AIM-9s was complete. Connelly's backseater was Commander Leo F. Enright, the CAG operations officer. The accompanying Tomcat was 'Gypsy 202', crewed by Lieutenant Hermon C. Cook III and Lieutenant Commander Steven P. Collins. The Tomcat crews were flying CAP when an E-2C Hawkeye, callsign 'Closeout', alerted them that two Libyan MiG-23 'Floggers' had taken off from the

Al Bumbah military airfield near Tripoli. The Tomcat crews almost immediately picked up the MiGs, 72 miles (116 km) away, coming straight at them. They locked up the Libyans, giving warning that they were being monitored by F-14s. This was sometimes enough to prompt Libyan fighters to turn tail, but this time the MiGs kept coming.

The Tomcats started the engagement at 20,000 ft (6095 m), while the MiGs were descending from 10,000 ft (3050 m) to 8,000 ft (2440 m). The Tomcats made a left turn, which could be interpreted as an avoidance manoeuvre or as a means of getting onto the tails of the Libyans, descending rapidly to get below the MiGs, as the two formations closed at around 1,000 mph (1610 km/h). They did this to try to force the MiG-23s into a lookdown engagement, in which they would be looking up at the MiGs (with no clutter) while the MiG-23's radar would be at a grave disadvantage looking down at the F-14s. The MiGs responded by turning towards the Tomcats, thereby preventing themselves being 'outflanked' – theoretically able to be taken as a defensive move, but equally indicative of hostile intent. The F-14s then descended to the

scattered cloud-deck at 3,000 ft (915 m) and made another left turn (officially interpreted as another avoidance manoeuvre), to which the Libyans responded by turning in once more. When the MiGs were 35 miles (56 km) at 7,000 ft (2135 m), they reacted the same way to a third, then a fourth, turn by the F-14s, and flew straight at the F-14s for the fourth time.

Cleared to fire

Some have averred that the Libyan pilots had still made no overtly hostile move, and were still reacting in a way which would simply prevent the F-14s from getting on their tails, though in the circumstances, their actions were certainly reckless, and probably aggressive. From *Kennedy* came the transmission: "Closeout ... ahh ... warning yellow, weapons hold. I repeat, warning yellow, weapons hold." The E-2C Hawkeye repeated the call: "Roger. Ah, Gypsies, [you are] directed, warning yellow, weapons hold."

The Tomcat crews were being ordered not to remain bound by the usual, strict, peacetime condition ('warning white, weapons tight') and taken halfway toward complete freedom for all-out war

This VF-32 'Swordsmen' F-14A carries a full load of six AIM-54s. Such a load would be used against mass raids by cruise missile-carrying bombers.

('warning red, weapons free'). 'Weapons hold' does not mean, simply, that 'you may employ your weapons if threatened'. It means that 'you must'.

This was the authority to Connelly to be ready to shoot. Libya was later to confuse things by asserting that the MiG-23s were unarmed reconnaissance aircraft which had been ambushed by 14 American warplanes. Fortunately, video footage recorded in the Tomcats' TCS clearly showed that the MiGs were armed with air-to-air missiles, although the imagery was not sufficiently clear to distinguish whether the missiles were close-range AA-2 'Atolls' or AA-8 'Aphids', or whether they were longer-range AA-7 'Apexes'. This was an important difference, since it had a direct impact on whether the Libyans were presenting a real threat, although, in the real world, the F-14 crews had to assume the worst case, and under the (classified) rules of engagement the enemy was demonstrably hostile. "A MiG-23 is a MiG-23 is a MiG-23. You just have to worst case that one. If you assume the enemy doesn't have his best weapon, you'll have a short career," observed one Tomcat RIO. In the pile of criticism laid on the Navy for the kills which followed, Congressman Les Aspin claimed that the Libyans' manoeuvring was too slight to be considered hostile. This was nonsense. Under the rules of engagement laid down the F-14 crews had to assume the worst: that these were MiG-23MLs armed with 'Apex', which they knew had a forward hemisphere range of about 12 miles (19 km). If the Libyans continued to close head-on, this was the range at which they would be 'taken out'. The MiGs reacted to a fifth turn by the Tomcats with a turn of their own, again preventing themselves from being outflanked.

"The bogies have jinked back at me for the fifth time. They're on my nose, now inside of 20 miles," reported the lead Tomcat's RIO at 12.00.53, directing the wingman to turn on his master armament switches. After an unanswered call by Connelly to the ship (he still hoped for last minute intelligence which he had been briefed to expect), a Sparrow was fired at 12.9 miles (20.7 km) by Enright, the RIO of the lead Tomcat, whose pilot muttered "Aw, Jesus!" Enright fired another Sparrow, calling "Fox One! Fox One!" Both of Enright's Sparrows failed to guide. The two Tomcats then made F-pole 30° turns, splitting left and right before turning back in to bracket the MiGs. The MiGs were still just outside visual range, but seconds later they turned left into the second Tomcat, and Cook called, "Tally Ho! Eleven o'clock high. They're turning into me."

First kill

Connelly noticed his wingman fire a third Sparrow at a range of seven miles (11 km), remarking to Enright, "They got one off!" and watching the missile guide into the right intake duct of the second MiG, which was engulfed in a huge fireball before entering a tightening right-hand turn. His RIO assumed he meant that the Libyans had fired a missile back, and frantically began firing off chaff cartridges. Connelly pulled into a hard right turn, yo-yoing high as the crippled MiG passed below, flying from left to right. The Libyan pilot ejected just as it passed by the second F-14, and he was seen in his chute.

Connelly came out of his turn behind the lead MiG, supported by his wingman, who had flown a similar manoeuvre. He followed it in a 4.5 *g* descending right turn, attempting to get a Sidewinder tone and failing. He selected an alternative Sidewinder station. Still no tone. He selected a Sparrow, but was too close. "Select Fox 2! Shoot 'em Fox 2! Fox 2, shoot a Fox 2!" shouted Enright, in frustration. Connelly shifted back to Sidewinder, and then noticed that the volume control was turned off; selecting a normal volume, he heard the tone and took the shot. The AIM-9 arced into the remaining MiG just behind the cockpit, its pilot ejecting after it hit. The time was 12.02.36. "Splash two 'Floggers', two good chutes in the air," reported Connelly as he dived to low level, accelerating away from the area at 700 ft (215 m) and 650 kt (745 mph; 1200 km/h), low on fuel.

The Navy and Pentagon rightly insisted that 'Gypsy 207' and 'Gypsy 202' had a 'righteous shoot'. Under the rules of engagement (to say nothing of simple common sense), Connelly and his fellow fliers would have been derelict not to shoot. Both MiG-23 pilots ejected safely and had good parachutes, but the Libyan air force was reportedly unable to mount a successful SAR (search and rescue) mission to save them. It had been another mismatch – although the MiG-23, at least, was a more serious air-to-air threat than the Su-22 had been.

Tomcat RIO Joseph Ulshafer recalled: "There were some Sidewinder firings by VF-21 'Freelancers' aboard USS *Independence* (CV-62) during the 1988-89 reflag tanker escort operations in the Persian Gulf. At one point, VF-21 had two Tomcats doing a head-on engagement with two Iranian F-4s, and an AIM-7F and an AIM-7L were both launched out of parameters, and didn't do anything." Other Tomcat aircrew remember this engagement as a multiple Sparrow firing at an Iranian C-130, by F-14s from the *Independence*. The missiles were reportedly fired in the wrong modes, and the aircraft then turned away, failing to illuminate their target. "Everyone knows who it was, but the names were classified to protect the incompetent!" recalled one former F-14 pilot. It was the supreme irony in an ambiguous era that Iran was the 'Bad Guy' in 1989, and Iraq would be the enemy only a year later, in 1990.

The Tomcat's part in the Gulf War is described in detail in a subsequent chapter, but it does not mark the end of the Tomcat's operational record – although the sole kill scored in the Gulf (against a helicopter) remains the aircraft's last air-to-air victory, at the time of writing.

Restoring hope in Somalia

The F-14s of VF-1 and VF-2 aboard the *Ranger* played their part in Operation Restore Hope, when the US Marines 'invaded' Somalia in December 1992, in an attempt to restore peace and stability to the war-ravaged country. Allied warplanes returned to Iraqi skies when they conducted airstrikes against Iraqi air defence command posts and SAM sites on 13 January 1993. They followed repeated Iraqi challenges to the 'No-Fly Zones' established by the USA and its allies over the north and south of the country, and were covered by a mixed force of fighters which included eight F-14As from VF-51 and VF-111 of CVW-15 aboard the *Kitty Hawk*.

The F-14 has long played a supporting role in the UN and NATO operations in the former Yugoslavia, as detailed in Chapter 10. As the situation worsened, Sixth Fleet carriers were often on station, and able to provide TARPS-equipped F-14s for reconnaissance duties, or missile-armed aircraft for (fruitless) CAPs. *Saratoga* gave way to *John F. Kennedy* in late 1992, neither seeing much action. The *Roosevelt* was deployed to the Adriatic during March 1993. The F-14As of VF-84 flew missions over Serb positions before the *Roosevelt* was replaced by USS *America* in early September 1993. When VF-102 flew TARPS missions along the Bosnian Serb border they found themselves shadowed by Serbian MiGs, but there was no combat. *Saratoga* was the next ship on station. Its cruise was eventful, particularly after the 9 February ultimatum to the Serbs to withdraw their heavy weapons from around Sarajevo. *Roosevelt* deployed to the Mediterranean again in March 1995, with the F-14As of VF-41, which dropped the Tomcat's first bombs in anger. *Roosevelt* was replaced by USS *America* with CVW-1 aboard in September 1995. The F-14As of VF-102 were not required to drop bombs in anger, but did conduct CAPs and flew more TARPS missions. More recently, the Adriatic saw the first deployment by the LANTIRN-equipped F-14Bs of VF-103, and although they had no opportunity to drop their weapons in anger, they were the theatre's 'primary strikers', being placed ahead of USAF F-15Es – to the delight of the F-14 community.

During late 1996, F-14Ds from VF-11 and VF-31 flew 90 per cent of the CAP missions for the battle groups and aircraft (ALCM-carrying B-52s) participating in Operation Desert Strike. In the unstable post-Cold War world, the F-14 is repeatedly proving its usefulness.

Robert F. Dorr and Jon Lake

Grumman F-14A Tomcat
VF-32 'Swordsmen'
Air Wing Three, USS *John F. Kennedy*
Mediterranean, 1989

On 4 January 1989, this F-14A was flown by Commander Joseph B. Connelly, CO of VF-32, with Lieutenant Commander Leo F. Enright as RIO. They downed the second of the two Libyan MiG-23s shot down on that day, the other falling to Lieutenant Hermon C. ('Munster') Cook and his RIO, Lieutenant Commander Steve Collins. All four men were decorated with the DFC in recognition of their success. 'Gypsy 207' (USN callsigns are based on the identity of the airframe, not the crew) is seen as it appeared a few days after the fateful mission, with a rather different loadout and with crew names removed, prior to those of Connelly and Enright being applied. Their regular aircraft was Modex 201, since Connelly was the squadron commander.

TCS
When VF-41 engaged a pair of Libyan Su-22s, they had no long-range identification device, but, in 1989, the VF-32 aircraft were each equipped with Northrop's TCS, giving them a magnified TV picture of the enemy aircraft, showing the crew that the enemy were 'armed and dangerous'.

Loadout
The aircraft is seen here with a fairly standard loadout of two AIM-54s, three AIM-7s and two AIM-9s. During operations off Libya, F-14s tended to carry a load more optimised for fighter-versus-fighter combat – four underfuselage AIM-7s, with four AIM-9s on the wing gloves. Rules of engagement and tactics precluded the use of the very long range AIM-54, which in any case imposed a heavy weight and drag penalty. On 4 January, the aircraft launched before they could be fully loaded, and each had only two AIM-9s, with four AIM-7s. The missiles were, of course, backed up by the Tomcat's internal 20-mm cannon.

Kills
To date, the F-14 has racked up five air-to-air combat victories in US Navy service. VF-41 splashed two Libyan Su-22s in 1981, VF-32 shot down two Libyan MiG-23s in 1989, and VF-1 shot down an Iraqi Mi-8 during Desert Storm. To this total may be added a number of victories claimed by Iranian F-14 pilots, though the exact number of such kills (and Iranian combat losses) remains unknown.

Insignia
VF-32 initially decorated its aircraft with a broad yellow band across the tailfins, flanked by narrower stripes. A sword was painted on the rudders. When markings were toned down, the sword remained, with only the uppermost of the narrow yellow bands. The narrow bands were soon reinstated (usually in grey, but in yellow on CAG- and Boss-birds), initially with the carrier code superimposed on a sword, and with 'Swordsmen' written on the top band, and the carrier name on the lower one. From 1983 the carrier code moved to the rudders and a piratical version of Grumman's cartoon Tomcat (leaning on a sword) was added between the bands. Subsequently, the narrow-broad-narrow bands were reapplied (albeit in grey), and the sword was moved from the rudder to the centre of the fin, with the carrier code superimposed..

Chapter Six
Tomcat at War

Although the F-14 scored only one air-to-air kill in the Gulf War, it did play a vital role in protecting the US Navy's carriers, and in escorting US Navy bombers to their targets. Few would have predicted that the Iraqi air force would be so unwilling to fight, or that the US Air Force would ensure that its F-15s grabbed the glory on the rare occasions that the enemy did make an appearance.

When Operation Desert Storm began, the F-14 Tomcat was the only in-service fighter in the US inventory to have scored an air-to-air kill 'in anger' in US service (although Israeli-operated F-15s and F-16s had scored many such victories). F-14 Tomcat squadrons were deployed to the Gulf

aboard all but one of the US Navy aircraft-carriers deployed to the region (the exception being USS *Midway*, which deployed with an attack-heavy air wing with three F/A-18 units and two A-6 squadrons). USS *Independence* and USS *Eisenhower* returned to the USA before Desert Storm began, but their squadrons (VF-21 aboard

Independence, and VF-142 and -143 aboard *Eisenhower*) played a part in Desert Shield. These two carriers were the closest to the area when the Iraqi invasion of Kuwait precipitated the crisis which became the Gulf War. *Independence* rushed in from the Indian Ocean, and was in a position to begin flying operations by 5 August, when

Above: *This patch was worn by aircrew aboard the USS* **Nimitz**, *though the carrier did not actually participate in Desert Storm!*

Top: *A VF-213 'Blacklions' F-14 tours Kuwait's burning oilfields at the end of the war. Putting Kuwait's oilfields to the torch was a desperate act.*

The '00' (Double Nuts) Modex indicates that the Kennedy CAG was allocated this colourfully marked VF-32 'Swordsmen' Tomcat, seen here during Desert Shield, the build-up to the war. The aircraft was almost certainly toned-down before Desert Storm began.

Left: A pilot from one of CVW-3's F-14 squadrons (VF-14 and VF-32) walks out to his aircraft for a Desert Storm mission.

A TARPS-equipped 'Swordsmen' Tomcat demonstrates low-level flying during Operation Desert Shield.

it was in the Gulf of Oman. *Eisenhower* steamed in from the eastern Mediterranean, and transited the Suez Canal to take up position in the Red Sea on 8 August. Carrier operations in the very tightly restricted and shallow waters of the Red Sea and Gulf would normally have been ruled out by the danger of attacks (which could not have been detected until too late), but this consideration was irrelevant in the light of the declared neutrality of Iran, and by the active co-operation of the other Arab states. Nevertheless, many carrier officers felt uncomfortable about not operating in their preferred 'blue water' environment, surrounded by 500 miles (800 km) of open sea.

Six carriers did serve in the region during Operation Desert Storm, five carrying F-14s. They were the *John F. Kennedy* (with VF-14 and VF-32 embarked) and the

Saratoga (VF-74 and VF-103, both with the F-14A+) in the Red Sea, for operations against targets in western Iraq. The *America* (with VF-33 and VF-102), the *Ranger* (VF-1 and VF-2), and the *Roosevelt* (VF-41 and VF-84) served in the Persian Gulf, for operations against targets in occupied Kuwait and eastern Iraq. *America* had moved from the Red Sea to the Persian Gulf in early February, before the start of the ground war. USS *Ranger* and USS *John F. Kennedy* each embarked the so-called 'all-Grumman air wing' dreamed up by former Navy Secretary John Lehman, with two F-14, two A-6 and no light strike squadrons.

The Tomcat squadrons mainly flew strike escort missions, although the TARPS-equipped aircraft on each carrier proved useful in the tactical reconnaissance role after it became apparent that the F-14

squadrons did not need to be fully committed to fighter duties, and after it became apparent that the F-14 units could not rely on USAF tactical reconnaissance assets to keep up with its need for bomb damage assessment photography. The TARPS aircraft played a particularly useful role in the coalition search for Iraq's mobile 'Scud' missiles, an operation whose importance is seldom realised, although by keeping Israel from intervening, it allowed the coalition to stick together, keeping the Arab members 'on-board'. There are unconfirmed reports that some F-14 TARPS missions were actually tasked by the Israelis, who told the F-14s where to look, and who then received the film soon after it had been downloaded and processed. This cannot be confirmed.

The F-14 community's hopes that their aircraft would add to its laurels in the air-to-air role were frustrated, however,

since the lack of enemy air activity provided few targets for the coalition air forces, and most of them were allotted to USAF F-15Cs, which were assigned CAP duties inside Iraq and over the borders.

Until the start of the ground offensive, when they received one CAP station over Iraq, the F-14s were tied to defensive CAPs for the fleets in the Red Sea and Persian Gulf, and routinely ventured over enemy territory only when escorting strike missions which the Iraqis chose not to challenge. A handful of offensive sweeps were flown, but the Iraqis refused to engage them. On 17 January, for example, VF-14 and VF-32 each sent a pair of F-14s on a sweep to H-2 and H-3 airfields, with

Tomcats of VF-14 and VF-32 ranged on the deck of the USS John F. Kennedy, which operated in the Red Sea during Operation Desert Storm.

no result. Among the most unusual missions flown by the Red Sea-based Tomcats were escort sorties covering cruise-missile carrying 'Secret Squirrel' B-52s.

There are some grounds for believing that Iraqi pilots consciously avoided the F-14s, fleeing whenever they picked up the tell-tale emissions of the AN/AWG-9 radar (which some came to refer to as the MiG-repeller). F-14 crews claim that the first two MiG-21s downed by F/A-18 Hornets from VFA-81 were actually fleeing from a Tomcat sweep, though this cannot be confirmed, while others claim that F-15s robbed them of two 'certain' MiG-29 kills on the first day. Many in the F-14 community have expressed the belief that USAF E-3 Sentries were partisan in allocating fighters (inevitably USAF F-15Cs) to deal with the few Iraqi aircraft which managed to get airborne. When CAP missions started, they were long and boring. Much of the Iraqi air force had been destroyed on the ground, or had fled to Iran, and what remained seldom ventured into the air. Missions could last between five and seven hours with inflight refuelling (with some exceptional missions of 11 hours being recorded), compared to the three-hour average strike escort hops.

The F-14 scored only a single confirmed air-to-air victory during the war, when Lieutenant Stuart Broce of VF-1, and his RIO and squadron commander, Commander Ron McElraft, downed an Mi-8 helicopter on 6 February 1991, using an AIM-9 Sidewinder. They were flying F-14A BuNo. 162603 (coded NE-103). Their success balanced the loss of another F-14, this time an F-14A+, which was downed by a SAM-2 derivative on 21 January. This aircraft (BuNo. 161430, AA-212) was from VF-103, and its crew ejected safely, pilot Lieutenant Devon Jones being rescued by helicopters, and RIO Lieutenant Lawrence Slade becoming a POW. The sole kill was almost an embarrassment, especially when compared to the multiple F-15 kills, the two fighter kills by bomb-laden F/A-18 Hornets, and two gun kills of helicopters by A-10s.

The F-14's standard load-out consisted of two AIM-54C Phoenix and two AIM-7F Sparrow missiles under the fuselage, with two more AIM-7s and two AIM-9s

underwing, and with external fuel tanks on the under-nacelle hardpoints. TARPS-configured aircraft flew with the reconnaissance pod replacing the underfuselage Sparrows, and usually with an Expanded Capability Chaff adaptor (with 120 chaff or

flare cartridges) in the port forward Phoenix rail, and an AN/ALQ-167 EW jamming pod carried under the starboard rail. All participating F-14s were equipped with the ASW-27C datalink, allowing the aircraft to co-operate closely with each

other and with USAF F-15s. Aircraft not equipped with this equipment (such as RAF Tornado F.Mk 3s) were not allowed over Iraq, in order to prevent blue-on-blue engagements.

The inclusion of two squadrons of F-14A (Plus) aircraft in the fleet of Tomcats involved in Desert Storm gave a useful opportunity to compare old and new under combat conditions. A number of TF30-engined F-14As experienced compressor stalls and even flame-outs when attempting to refuel in flight at high weights and at altitudes of above 23,000 ft (7010 m), when afterburner was required to stay 'plugged in'. Fuel flow into the F-14's tanks under these circumstances was almost balanced by the increased fuel consumption. The A (Plus), on the other hand, reportedly proved itself to be exceptionally reliable, and the extra increment in performance was judged invaluable.

Perhaps most crucially for the

Grumman F-14B (F-14A+) Tomcat VF-103 'Sluggers', CVW-17, USS *Saratoga* Red Sea, Operation Desert Storm

Flying controls
The F-14 has large slab tailerons which operate in unison to provide pitch control, or differentially to give roll control. At low speeds, the tailerons are augmented by four-section spoilers on the upper surface of each wing. The tailfins have conventional single-piece hydraulically actuated rudders for yaw control. There are no ailerons or separate elevators.

Spoilers
The four-section spoilers can be used at wing sweep angles of less than 57°, deploying differentially for roll control, or in unison on landing to function as lift dumpers.

Airbrakes
The F-14 has a pair of powerful hydraulically actuated speed brakes above and below the beaver tail. These open up to a maximum deflection of 60° in less than two seconds, actuated by a single button. The lower section incorporates a deep cut-out to prevent snagging the arrester hook when it is lowered, effectively being in separate left and right pieces, though both move together. The lower speed brake opens to only 18° when the hook is lowered. Each airbrake section is actuated by a pair of hydraulic rams. The interior of the airbrake bay, and the inner surface of the airbrake itself, are painted in a corrosion-resistant red paint.

Leading edge
The leading edge of each wing is occupied by a conventional constant-section two-segment slat. These deploy to 17° for landing, or to up to 7° when used as manoeuvre devices.

Trailing edge
The full span of the wing trailing edge is taken up by three-section, single-slotted flaps. The innermost section is usable only with the wing swept forward, but the other two sections can be used at wing sweep angles of up to 55°. These can be deployed to 35° for landing, or to up to 10° when used as manoeuvre devices.

VF-1 Tomcats launch from the USS Ranger during Desert Storm. VF-1 scored the Tomcat's only aerial victory of the war, downing an Mi-8 on 6 February 1991. This success was not enough to secure the long-term future of the squadron, which finally disestablished on 30 September 1993.

long-term future of the type, the F-14 was not used in the strike role. There was no shortage of air-to-ground aircraft in-theatre, but the F-14's participation could have been a useful and high-visibility demonstration of its versatility. Instead, the F/A-18 emerged from the war with an enhanced reputation for its multi-role capabilities, and this may have been a crucial factor in the final decision in favour of the new F/A-18E/F and in the termination of the F-14D and various Quick-strike-type air-to-ground 'Bombcat' variants.

Gulf veteran

Lieutenant Commander Dave Parsons was a RIO with the 'Swordsmen' of VF-32, and here describes his own view of the Tomcat at war. "Naturally, the Navy fighter crews wanted a piece of the diminishing air-to-air action. It was becoming obvious that the Iraqis were not going to use their large air force, and that dogfights would be few.

"Finally, as the Iraqi threat diminished, we paired off the fighters. It was obvious that the Iraqis didn't want to fight and were running from us, or we were shooting them out of the sky. They wouldn't go anywhere near an F-14. That's a big part of the reason why the F-14s didn't get any kills. Another reason was the way the Air Force set themselves up for on-station CAP. They were there all the time. If anything got airborne, the Air Force got vectors to it. We asked for those CAPs but they wouldn't give them to us.

"There was an F-15 squadron at Tabuk which was very close to Iraq, and it was easy to cycle them on and off those missions. We were anxious to show what the long-range Phoenix could do. But it didn't happen.

This Grumman F-14B wears the markings of VF-103 during the squadron's incarnation as the 'Sluggers'. Today, of course, Tomcats of VF-103 wear the markings and maintain the tradition of the 'Jolly Rogers', but at the time of Operation Desert Storm the colour scheme pictured was still firmly in vogue. For Desert Storm, the *Saratoga* embarked two squadrons of F110-engined F-14A+ fighters, VF-74 and VF-103. Two more squadrons (VF-142 and VF-143) participated in Desert Shield, flying from the USS *Eisenhower.* This aircraft wears the personal markings and '201' Modex of the 'Sluggers' executive officer (XO), Lt Cdr Fitzpatrick, and has the hard-won 'Safety S' low on the tailfin. This was the aircraft flown by Lt Devon Jones when he was shot down by an Iraqi SAM.

Avionics
The F-14A+ (F-14B) is equipped with the same analog avionics and systems as the baseline F-14A, although the type was once intended to represent an interim configuration, with an intention to convert most of the aircraft to F-14D standards. This never happened, and only 38 new F-14A+s were built, with 32 more produced through the conversion of F-14A airframes.

Powerplant
The F-14A+ was the first production version of the Tomcat to dispense with the troublesome TF30 engines, which had always been the aircraft's Achilles heel. The F110-GE-400 gave a useful increase in thrust, yet had lower specific fuel consumption. The new engine's 80 per cent commonality with certain USAF fighter engines eased logistics and support considerations. More importantly, the F110 proved reliable, dependable and rugged, and it was not prone to the compressor stalls and catastrophic failures suffered by the TF30. Moreover, the new engine was tolerant of throttle mishandling and of disturbed airflow in the intake. In short, the F110 was everything a fighter engine should be, while the TF30 was a case study of 'how not to do it'. Fitting the F110 to the Tomcat airframe was remarkably simple, requiring only a 4-ft 2-in (1.27-m) plug in the afterburner section of the engine, and changes to secondary airframe structure.

Armament
During the Gulf War, the US Navy's Tomcats were used only in the air-to-air role, armed with short-range AIM-9 Sidewinders, medium-range AIM-7 Sparrows and long-range AIM-54 Phoenix missiles. The F-14B's higher thrust engines make it particularly suitable for use in the 'Bombcat' role, and F-14B-equipped squadrons were among the first equipped with LANTIRN targeting pods and Paveway LGBs.

Above: An F-14 from VF-41 flies over the burning oilfield west of Kuwait City on 6 March 1991, six days after President Bush called a halt to the carnage.

Right: During Desert Shield the Tomcat squadrons routinely practised flying at very low level, as dramatically displayed in this shot from the RIO's cockpit.

"We were frustrated, but the attack guys loved what the AWG-9 did. They asked us, 'Is there a pod we can carry that will transmit the AWG-9's frequency?'

"The Iraqis were very familiar with F-14s, having fought them during the war with Iran. I don't know if they knew the F-15's radar frequency, but they wouldn't react when an F-15 got close. But when a Tomcat put his nose out there, they were gone.

"Our radar was so powerful that it could saturate their warning gear and would not give them a definite location of the F-14, only an indication that he was out there... somewhere. It must have been a weird, unsettling feeling knowing we were out there, stalking them.

"It was very frustrating for us not to get kills, but we were too disciplined to strip off and go after the MiGs. We were supposed to stay with our attack guys.

"They'd tell us they wanted us all around them. These were the guys who had told us during exercises, 'We don't need you. We're going to go this way without you.'

"So, we couldn't even have done TARPS if we'd wanted. Everyone wanted fighters. Early on, we were putting four F-14s on a fighter sweep. 'Shoot, they're running from us,' we said. 'We could probably put one F-14 out there.' Our basic unit is two, so we used two Tomcats on the sweep.

"As we headed for the target, the MiGs would run from us until we made our turn for home. Then they'd come after us. I was on the tail end of a strike and here come these MiG-23s running us down from behind. Our AWG-9s weren't pointing at them.

"We decided to let them come close enough that we could turn and point our radars at them. Then we could shoot them before they could run away. As we waited, some F-15s blew right by us. That was their job.

"Usually, regardless of when we approached or exited the target area, there'd be F-15s stationed all round us. There were even tankers in-country. They were serious about quickly winning air superiority. We'd see things on our radar

and then we'd discover they were friendly.

"There were a lot of aircraft out there, especially when 'Scuds' became such a priority. Whenever information on 'Scuds' came through, a strike package would go after the missiles. There'd be attack lanes ready to go. It was incredible what you'd run into. We even had an F-117A fly right by us at night, coming out of Baghdad. We ran into A-10As deep in western Iraq.

"The Marines were still calling for recce

assets. We were told to give a TARPS pod to VF-102 in *America*, so we gave them an extra pod. We now were down to two pods. We also got a new tasking: to look for 'Scuds' every day with our TARPS jets.

"We were working very long hours. We briefed for two to three hours, flew the long missions, debriefed for another two to three hours, then went back to planning the next mission, and in between

Right: VF-103 was one of two F-14A (Plus) squadrons to participate in Desert Storm. Here one of the unit's 'Super-Cats' is seen at low level over Saudi Arabia, during pre-war work-ups.

Below: Pre-war training was often at low level, whereas wartime flying was more normally conducted at higher altitude, over Iraq's more featureless desert.

The colourful tail markings of VF-32's CAG-bird disappear beneath a coat of washable distemper. Tomcat squadron groundcrew enjoy a remarkable *esprit de corps*.

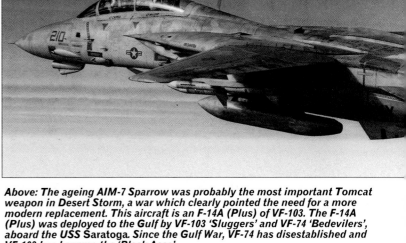

Above: *The ageing AIM-7 Sparrow was probably the most important Tomcat weapon in Desert Storm, a war which clearly pointed the need for a more modern replacement. This aircraft is an F-14A (Plus) of VF-103. The F-14A (Plus) was deployed to the Gulf by VF-103 'Sluggers' and VF-74 'Bedevilers', aboard the USS Saratoga. Since the Gulf War, VF-74 has disestablished and VF-103 has become the 'Black Aces'.*

tried to eat and grab some sleep."

Although the threat of Iraqi interceptors quickly retreated, the coalition aircrews still were concerned about the formidable AAA and SAM defences. The enemy had used this vast system to fairly good effect, and everyone treated the thickets of flak guns and SAM sites with respect. The 'Scud' campaign – a surprise to most of the coalition planners – also required immediate, intense attention.

"It was hard for intelligence to keep up because there was so much information coming in, such as where the enemy missile sites were. They were moving their SAMs around on us.

"Of course, we didn't want to fly in the SAM envelopes, but when the VF-103 F-14A(Plus) was bagged, everyone was electrified. If those guys got shot down with the better RHAW gear then we were certainly at risk in our regular F-14As.

"We plunged into 'Scud' TARPS. Requirements would come out every day on the ATO telling us where to look in the 'Scud Box'. These concentrations were usually along the main highways, like in the northwestern portion of Iraq that paralleled the border with Saudi Arabia. The Iraqis hid mobile 'Scud' launchers everywhere, under highway bridges and in trenches. Originally we thought they didn't have many mobile launchers, but it turned out that they had more than 300. They were like roaches and could easily hide in the underpasses. We had 'friendlies' on the ground looking for the launchers. There was just so much territory to cover. They dug trenches, drove the launchers into the trenches, then covered them over with tarpaulins.

"Every day a section of Tomcats from the 'Sara' or 'JFK' launched to look for 'Scuds'. That solved our BDA problem. I constantly visited the strike cell and looked at all the tasking we had for targets, which was usually posted two days ahead. I'd look

to see if we had already hit the targets with TARPS, or if it was within the big 550-mile (885-km) 'Scud' TARPS mission parameters. If the targets were anywhere in there, we'd just divert a little and try to get pre-strike BDA.

"If the strike were at night, we'd get the post-strike photography from previous missions. I kept a running database of what we had already hit and what we would hit so that we could provide strike leaders with current pictures.

Tanker support

"We had a dedicated USAF tanker, right up at the border. Those tankers would even cross the border. We'd always ask them to head north from the tanker track so we would be topped off as we crossed into Iraq.

"One day, I asked, 'Can you go north with us?', meaning north of his tanker track.

"'Stand by,' the tanker said. Then he came back, 'Yeah, how far in-country do you want to go?'

"'No,' I said, 'just to the border.'

"'We'll go in-country,' he replied enthusiastically. I just needed him to take us to the border, because we'd accelerate to 480 kt (550 mph; 885 km/h) when we crossed the border and be unable to tank. 'Well, we'd like to go in-country,' the -135 pilot said.

"'I'll tell you what,' I offered jokingly – we're doing this all on secure-comm channels – 'you can meet us on the way

out, and if we have gas we'll take you on a tour.'

"That was pretty funny, especially when my pilot, who thought we were serious, said, 'We're taking them on a tour?'

"We had seen tankers over the border. We joked that they were just looking for some excitement, or trying to accumulate points for an Air Medal. It was one point for a mission in-theatre, and two points if you crossed the border. Most of the tanker missions were as boring as all get-out. As we egressed, we'd join up on either side of a tanker's cockpit and wait until the crew had their cameras ready. Then we'd light the burners and climb or roll away. They loved it.

"The tanker guys were great. We really loved them. Everyone we worked with – Brits, USAF – came out to the ship during Desert Shield so we could meet them face-to-face. We resolved a lot of confusion. We kept telling them they were flying too fast. We couldn't refuel at higher weights and altitude without tapping burner.

"'We're just following what our book says,' they told us. They had some manual that told them the speed at which F-14s tanked. Of course, it was wrong. We tank at 250. They quickly understood, and were very accommodating.

"The TARPS missions geared up just after the F-14 got shot down on 21 January, near Al Asad, a very heavily fortified base, a megabase. One day, we were going to hit an airfield near there. A flag staffer – someone on the admiral's staff – came

down and told us, 'We want pictures of Al Asad.' That really got our attention.

"'Wait a minute, isn't that where the A(Plus) got bagged?'

"This was soon after we started using I-2000s on the bunkers – the laser-guided steel-nosed bunker-busters – that could penetrate the bunkers. The Iraqis were pulling their planes out of the bunkers, and hiding them all over the place. They had thought that their NATO-standard, Belgian-designed bunkers were impervious, but the I-2000 was one of the little surprises we had for them. That's when they started flying to Iran.

"With all this activity and information, intelligence thought they were hiding airplanes around the field and wanted pictures so we could hit them.

"'You're asking us to go into an SA-2 and SA-6 field,' we told them. 'Plus a lot of low-altitude stuff.'

"'They said F-14s would never go over the beach,' we said, 'then they told us we'd never go near the SAM envelope.'

"'Well, what do you need?'

"'We want a jammer (EA-6B) and a HARM shooter.'

"We tied into the main strike group so the Iraqis wouldn't know we were heading to Al Asad. The strike was going right by it. At the last second, the three F-14s and the EA-6B would split off. We had two F-14s from VF-32 – the TARPS bird (Lieutenant Jim Kuhn and me) and our escort – plus an F-14 from VF-14, our sister squadron, escorting the EA-6B

Burners blaze and steam gouts from the Kennedy's catapult as a VF-32 F-14A is launched on a mission during Operation Desert Storm. Underfuselage fuel tanks were carried routinely.

A VF-32 Tomcat thunders into the air during Operation Desert Storm. A lack of targets ensured that the squadron was unable to repeat its MiG-killing exploits off the Libyan coast several years earlier.

jammer/HARM shooter from VAQ-137.

"As we started approaching the time when we knew the SA-2 would fire – when we would be vulnerable – that's when the HARM would already be in the air. We planned for the pre-emptive HARM to be shot, followed by another if necessary.

"We raced up to the field, Mach 1.2. We went blowing through, and the Prowler shot the HARM just as he planned, broadcasting 'Downtown'. Then we heard it.

"'Damn!' we said, 'their radars are up!'

"Time really compressed as we looked out for SAMs. My biggest worry was to have a missile come unseen right up beneath us, so we kept jinking. My pilot wanted to keep jinking, even when we were over the target, but we had to hold it steady to take the pictures. It took a lot of discipline to fly straight and level over the target.

"We raced out of there. Nothing had been shot at us, although we knew they had tried. Later, the Prowler crew said that the SA-2 had come up and tried to shoot, but they thought that their HARMs had taken out the radar.

"So, we sent the photos over to the Tornados because they were going in there. Right after that, we were tasked to

go to Al Qaim, a super phosphate plant up in the extreme northwest corner. It was the most heavily defended target outside Baghdad. They had four SA-3 batteries and two SA-2s, plus all the AAA and low-altitude SAMs. That's where the F-15E Strike Eagle went down. We didn't feel good about going there, either. If they could bag the F-15E, they could easily get us.

"Al Qaim reminded me of the Thanh Hoa Bridge in Vietnam. Everyone tried to get it. We sent B-52s up there and they couldn't get it. The B-52s had problems because they bombed from such a high altitude. We had a jet stream from about 116 kt (133 mph; 215 km/h). The winds changed considerably down on the deck and made bomb-impact prediction difficult.

"The plant was important because it produced uranium for the Iraqis' nuclear bomb project. We had fired SLAMs at the facility, but, although we knew the SLAMs had hit it, the picture stops as soon as the missile hits, so we didn't know how badly we had damaged the building.

"It was a huge place and we tried to destroy it. Some crews had gone up there

A VF-32 F-14A waits its turn for a top-up. The 'Swordsmen' crew can relax, just briefly, before replacing the A-6 Intruder behind this USAF KC-135's boom. US Navy tactical aircraft frequently made use of USAF tanker assets during Operation Desert Storm. There simply were not enough KA-6D Intruder tankers to go around.

VF-32 Tomcats on the break, prior to recovering aboard the USS John F. Kennedy. The nearest of the three aircraft carries a TARPS pod under the belly, with an expanded chaff adaptor and an EW pod forward and with Sidewinders and Sparrows underwing. During the Gulf War, the TARPS pod still used only wet film-based sensors, although in recent years the Tomcat has flown with a Digital TARPS pod.

the preceding day but turned back because of the intense SAM activity. It was just a hornets' nest with all the sites up. As you tried to avoid one site, another would get you.

"We decided to come in at high altitude and come screaming down to 10,000 ft (3050 m) at Mach 1.2. No real flak, nothing like what they talk about over Germany in World War II.

"I had trouble believing this was this horrible target everyone talked about, like when everyone talked about going to Berlin in World War II. We started calling it 'Big Al'. 'We're going to Big Al's place.'

"The Air Force said they'd send in the Strike Eagles and take out the SAM sites. Then they got bagged! They did have some success, however.

"As we closed on Big Al, I kept saying to 'Dog', 'Faster! Faster!' although I knew the airplane was going as fast as it could.

"We had an A-7 off our wing with four HARMs, plus an EA-6B. We knew the A-7 would pre-emptively fire one HARM, but anything after that meant that more SAM sites were up. Our callsign for a HARM shoot was 'Downtown', after Colonel Broughton's book on going downtown to Hanoi.

"We heard, 'Downtown!' Then, 'Downtown, downtown!' There was no delay. That really got our hearts beating fast. There were three SAM sites up.

"We had an Expanded Chaff Adapter (ECA) on the airplane with 120 rounds of chaff. I yelled at 'Dog', 'Chaff, chaff, chaff!' We were continuously pumping chaff out.

"Before the mission, I must have talked to the Prowler crew for two hours, asking,

'Which angle do we want to go in, which sites do you think are active, is this the right angle?'

"They were confident. 'Yeah, we'll be able to protect you.'

"After the brief, I asked, rhetorically, 'You guys are going to keep us safe, right?'

"'We think we can.'

"'Wait a minute,' I said, 'You didn't say you thought you could last night!'

"'Well, we'll try our best.'

"'Don't say that!' I said. 'Say you're gonna do it. Make me feel good.'

"After we got back, one of our pilots came up to us. 'I really didn't think I would see you back.'

"Both missions were 'super-real' moments for me. I checked out my 9-mm pistol and loaded it. I wasn't going to make it easy for them to get me. This was a place we had really hit hard and the Iraqis wouldn't be happy to see me."

Commander Dave Parsons and Jon Lake

Above: During Desert Storm F-14s routinely provided strike escort for the Navy's A-6 Intruders, as well as for other aircraft. Ironically, the F-14 has now adopted many of the Intruder's attack roles since the A-6's retirement.

Left: A VF-32 F-14A banks in towards its carrier. Landing a massive F-14 on a relatively tiny carrier deck is difficult by day, and worse at night.

Above: An F-14A dispenses IR decoy flares from the launchers faired into the underside of the beaver tail. The launchers can fire chaff cartridges.

Chapter Seven

The Pilot

A VF-31 F-14D waits its turn to refuel from a USAF KC-135 tanker as the Section leader refuels. While refuelling the F-14 is stable yet responsive.

Although the F-14 force has been dramatically cut back, the adoption of new roles has given the Tomcat a new importance, and morale is high. After a period during which morale was subdued, and during which the writing seemed to be on the wall for the F-14, Tomcat pilots can once more be secure in the knowledge that theirs is a vitally important job, and the F-14 community again feels like an elite force. In this chapter a number of F-14 pilots describe flying the F-14.

"If you wanted to gain a balanced view as to the relative capability of a particular aircraft, the very last person you should ask is a pilot who flies that particular aircraft type. Every fighter pilot in the world will tell you that his is the best fighter airplane there is. Hell! He might even believe it. It's like mothers. No mother ever has an ugly baby or a stupid child, yet we all know that there are ugly babies and stupid children. Just don't ask their moms. These guys could give you the most balanced and incisive assessment of the F/A-18 or the F-16 (as long as they weren't asked to compare them to the F-14) but

they would be blind to the 'faults' in their airplane which a Hornet driver might be able to dispassionately tell you about. Right now I 'know' that the F/A-18 is the best there is, but might just be exaggerating, but I could give you a balanced unemotional view of the F-14. But ask me at the end of the course and I guess I'll be thinking that the Tomcat is the best fighter airplane in the world." The speaker was a brand-new arrival at VF-101, the Tomcat FRS, who had not even started F-14 conversion, but who had flown the F/A-18. It's an interesting health warning, and it may be worth keeping in mind, but the rest of this chapter belongs

to those who do already fly the Tomcat, and who are already 'indoctrinated'. Unfortunately, we can't name our first 'source', callsign 'Flash', interviewed while he was still serving with VF-101.

"I'd prefer not to have my name mentioned, because I was involved with some of the Libyan type stuff way back, and we're still trying to keep that a little bit quiet, at least in terms of names – there's still a lot of crazy people running around.

Cadillac of the Fleet

"The F-14 is a Cadillac to fly. I flew the Phantom for seven years and I've flown the F-14 for the last six or seven and its a quantum leap

both in technology and pilot comfort. We used to say it took a good pilot to fly an average Phantom sortie. But you can put an average pilot in an F-14 and he will fly a good Tomcat sortie. The aeroplane makes the pilot look good. The systems that are available to the RIO also are a quantum leap from what we had in the Phantom and it makes the RIOs look a lot better too. That's important, because while we all like to joke that the RIO is just the talking ballast in the back seat, he has an important job to do – he makes my coffee before the flight, holds the umbrella if it rains during the walk-around... No, seriously. As

Left: Steam rises from the catapult as a VF-84 'Jolly Rogers' Tomcat blasts off. The aircraft's tailerons are fully deflected, ready to rotate the nose as the aircraft leaves the end of the catapult.

Right: A Tomcat of VF-24 waits for the cat. The F-14A always takes off from the carrier using afterburner, while the F110-engined F-14B and F-14D can safely take off without afterburner when lightly loaded. Deck operations are extremely hazardous, and great care is taken not to expose the crew to unnecessary risks. The whole procedure is a carefully choreographed routine aimed at maximising safety and speed.

the pilot, I'm the guy who flies the airplane and at the end of the day, I'm the guy who makes the real important decisions, but he is my extra pair of eyes, and he gives me the information I need to make the decisions. A single-seat Tomcat couldn't do the same job that we do, and that's why the F/A-18 can't do everything we do.

"A lot of the processing is digitised and synthesised now and so a lot of the guess work and thinking and a lot of the art form is gone out of it. That is nice because when you're dealing with a lot of threats and when you have a lot of information to process, you need all the help from the system that you can get. Being in an F-14 squadron is unique to the Navy, we consider ourselves the pinnacle of naval aviation. The F-14 is the airplane that we consider to be the front line navy fighter, especially now with the new engines. People ask what it's like to be in a navy fighter squadron flying F-14s and I guess my stock answer is kind of like being in a motor cycle gang and yet your mother is still proud of you! We have a good time, a great time (it's fun!), yet we do a vitally important job, defending our country and defending our country's interests. Everybody is very dedicated, they are hand picked and they marry ourselves to the weapon system and it works out very well.

"And quite apart from the technology (which works real well) there is no doubt that the F-14 is a comfortable airplane to fly, and a comfortable environment to work in. And the question of comfort is vitally important on long CAPs. You want to be comfortable, you don't want to be distracted. It's a large, spacious cockpit, and it's

nicely air conditioned. Even the seat is cooled, so your fanny doesn't sweat, you know. The environmental control system in the aeroplane keeps the cockpit very comfortable.

Alert and effective

"That comfort means that we can stay alert and efficient for a relatively long period, though we don't like to keep people up more than five hours, we didn't ever like to do that. We can go longer, but after five hours, I think you're going to start losing your edge. Even on the ship, on deck alert, we don't try to keep guys focused indefinitely.

"On alert on board ship, you might be sitting in the aeroplane

waiting to go for some time. We're not sitting there with the engines turning, we're generally sitting at alert status with the aircraft powered up, the nav system aligned and ready to start engines, depending on the criticality of the event and the immediacy of the threat. Depending on the stage of alert, we can either be in the ready room waiting in flight gear, we could actually be in the airplanes, or we could even be in our racks. As long as they know where we were, it just depends on how close the threat is. At the highest state of readiness we're on the deck, in the cockpit, sitting on the cat, electrical power hooked up to the airplanes. All they have to do is fire up the engines, fire the cat – there's a

The catapult officer watches each launch from a recess in the deck. On some carriers this may be covered by a retractable cupola.

sudden bang and we're off, we already have our alignments.

"In the final stage of alert where you're actually sitting in the airplane, we don't like to leave the crews in the cockpit longer than two hours and prior to that, you can spend up to two hours in the ready room in your flight gear. That's a four hour total of alert status and that's as long as we like to go with a crew.

"In practical terms I don't know if you could say that there are any real limits to mission length. The longest mission I've flown was about six hours and that was

As the F-14 reaches the end of the catapult, the compressed nose oleo extends, kicking the nose upwards and helping the aircraft achieve the correct attitude for climbout.

the BARCAP, TARCAP and maritime air superiority roles. Only the F-14 has the legs, the range and the stand-off weapons that are required for that. The F-14 is king of the outer air battle. Closer in to the carrier you might deploy fighter-roled F/A-18s to mop up anyone lucky enough to get past the Tomcats. Both aircraft are very capable dogfighters, and in fact comparing the baseline F-14A and the F/A-18, the Hornet probably has some numbers advantages over the F-14A. But it doesn't have the range, and it doesn't have the reach, while the F-14B is more than a match for the F/A-18 even close-in, in my opinion. But bottom-line, it's not going to be easy for anyone to get past the F-14 or the F/A-18.

re-fuelling several times. That was not typical, though when we're holding a long-range CAP-type scenario, practising for an incoming threat, five or six hours is by no means an absolute limit, I mean, you're only limited by how long you have unlimited tanker assets, and at the end of the day you're only limited by the crew. That's the critical limiting factor.

"The Tomcat's primary mission is fleet air defence. What is fleet air defence? You can define it as protecting the carrier and the carrier's support ships from the airborne threat. The airborne threat consists of hostile bombers and attack aircraft, but also includes sea-

Although sometimes criticised for a lack of agility, the F-14 can turn remarkably well, albeit not as tightly as the later 'Teen-series' superfighters like the F-16 and F/A-18. This aircraft, turning hard in full afterburner, is seen with vortices forming above the wings.

skimming air to surface and cruise missiles. It's obviously best to shoot down the launch platform before it gets close enough to launch such missiles, but that can be hundreds of miles out. The F-14 was basically designed to be able to shoot down those incoming threat missiles after launch, but as it has turned out, the Tomcat is capable of doing that mission but it is also capable of hitting the launch platforms further out, before the missiles are fired, and given the choice, that's what we'd want to do.

"The keys to the capability we have lie in long range and long endurance – the ability to patrol far out from the carrier, and to hit the enemy before he presents a threat. And to do that, not only do we stand out a long way from the carrier, but we use sensors and weapons which allow us to detect, identify and then engage the

enemy while he's still as far away as possible.

"Typically a carrier deploys with a mix of F/A-18s and Tomcats. It used to be two squadrons of each, but now it tends to be one squadron of F-14s, three of F/A-18s. The F/A-18s have got a degree of fighter capability, but their mission is a little bit different. It depends on the scenario, obviously, but in the long-range type scenario, where we're trying to project power, typically you would have the F-14 operating in the escort fighter type role. But if it's a high threat environment in which you require an aircraft with a lot of self-sustained EW gear, but operating at shorter ranges you'd probably send the F/A-18s in the attack and the fighter roles. They can operate self-escort and can 'swing' from one role to the other during a strike interdiction type mission. Meanwhile, the F-14 can conduct

"For any that do, you then have the ships which protect the carrier, and these will take any 'leakers'. But it all depends on what the threat is, as to how you will go and employ those assets, how you're going to relieve them on station, what you're tanking plan is going to be, and how long you have to keep them up there. How long is the threat window going to be, two days, three days, a couple of hours? You need to know all this.

"One question I've been asked, especially with the reduction in F-14 numbers aboard the typical carrier is, 'Are there enough F-14s in the Air Wing to do the job? What with aircraft being serviced, aircraft being relieved on-station, aircraft landing, aircraft taking off, how many CAP stations can you maintain?'

It depends on the scenario, where the threat's coming from, the nature of the threat and how long we'll be exposed to that threat. But we find we can do very well if the ship is dedicated to the air defence mission. But if we've got the Air Wing carrying out surface strikes at the same time that we're providing the outer air battle then obviously the flight deck's going to be a very crowded place, there'll be a shortage of tankers, and it all gets more difficult. If you're trying to carry out both of those roles naturally you're going to face some limitations on the number of aircraft that you can operate. But if it is totally a fighter mission, then we would have no problem maintaining a grid with tankers and fighters.

Serviceability and availability tend to be very good, especially at sea, despite the more difficult conditions for the maintenance people. We have very good availability rates if we know we're going to be required to have them. Squadrons that are deployed typically see a lot better full mission-capable rates than you would see here at the airfield because they have first priority for parts, and also they are fully manned. Most squadrons are manned completely only when they go to sea, so the operating rates you'll see on those aircraft approach 90-95 per cent. Whereas here on the field, you would see numbers dramatically lower than that.

"And of course, we have to be able to fly and fight by day or night, in any weather conditions. The F-14 is a truly all-weather, day/night fighter. The sensors provide great eyes which can 'see' at any time, day or night, and in any type of weather. The weapons themselves do not rely on good weather or daylight with the exception of the gun.

Armament

The F-14 carries AIM-9 Sidewinders, AIM-7 Sparrows and the AIM-54 Phoenix. The aircraft has a very versatile weapons suit, in other words, there are various ranges the bogey has to fly through before he gets to you or to what you're trying to protect, and these range bands equate to the ranges of your weapons. The first range that he will go through, the first weapon's LAR (Launch Acceptable Region) he encounters is that of the Phoenix. That is a long-range, stand-off, radar-guided missile. It's a very versatile missile, with many modes we can launch it in. It's also very ECM resistant, in other words, its not easily fooled by electronic counter measures. Basically that missile was designed to shoot down the ASM or air-launched cruise missile. We have since found that it's not only good for that but it's also good for stand-off launches against, say, regimental strength bomber raids or against incoming fighter raids as well. The AIM-7 Sparrow missile's launch envelope comes next. Again, the AIM-7 is a radar-guided missile, but reaches out only to medium range, and requires support (constant-wave illumination) by the launch aircraft. You have to stay roughly pointing at the enemy, and you can't fire and forget, like you can with the Phoenix. It's cheaper than the AIM-54, though, and lighter, and doesn't impose the same restrictions and limitations.

Next in turn is the Sidewinder. This is the missile of choice for the dogfight. It is highly manoeuvrable and is a true fire-and-forget weapon, but is restricted to fairly short ranges. The types of Sidewinder that we are carrying now have all-aspect capability which means you can fire them at a head-on target – they don't have to be pointed directly up the bad guy's jet pipe. The Nine-Limas and the Nine-Mikes are to some degree IRCM-resistant – they have IRCM rejection modes in there to allow them to differentiate between the target and IR decoy flares. Then inside of that we have the Vulcan cannon which shoots 6,000 rounds of 20-mm a minute in its high-rate mode. That is very lethal, you get tapped with one of those and we consider it a kill. Just one round. So you've got the Phoenix for very long range, and for simultaneous use against multiple targets, you have the Sparrow for medium range, you've got the Sidewinder for close-in. dogfight range and then, of course, you've got your gun for really close-in, 'there's-the-whites-of-his-eyeballs, let's-blow-him-away' range.

Weight and drag

"Although the Phoenix is, if anything, the RIO's weapon, its carriage has a major impact on how the pilot will carry out his job. Theoretically you can carry six Phoenix missiles on the airplane, and every so often they will do it, often for a photo. Once (and I think it was only once) they even fired six off in a test. It is a theoretical capability, and if you were in danger of being swamped, several F-14s, each firing six AIM-54s could destroy an entire enemy raid – even an entire enemy air force! But it is really only a theoretical capability. Obviously we've all seen the pictures, but the question is whether it's a practical load out, and obviously it's not. The reasons it's not are to do with weight limitations and tactical flexibility. The AIM-54 missiles themselves are so heavy (so are the supporting rails), that to land back aboard you'd have to jettison any unused weapons – and they cost multi-millions of dollars each. If you didn't jettison them, you'd be too heavy to land on a carrier. You certainly couldn't come back with the maximum fuel to trap, which we try to do back at the ship. Even with four AIM-54s you'd be limited to so little fuel that you'd only have one or two looks at the deck. Anyone can bolter, so effectively you can't come back with enough fuel to happily operate off the carrier. Now at a land airfield, where you could flare for the landing, you could land with six AIM-54s. The rate of descent is much lower and a runway is of unlimited strength, and you don't have to worry about the arrester gear. And as well as being very heavy, the AIM-54s impose a drastic drag penalty, reducing your range and endurance.

Tactical inflexibility?

"And if you do carry six Phoenix, you can only carry two Sidewinders with them. Therefore, carrying six limits you to two types of weapon on board, a long-range missile and an extremely short-range missile. Where you are required to get a VID (a Visual identification), in other words where I have to see you and identify you to shoot you, obviously it pulls you inside the minimum range of the Phoenix.and perhaps outside of the range of the Sidewinder. So there you are,

F-14Ds of VF-31 break away from the camera aircraft. The basic fighting unit for the F-14 is two aircraft, though two sections (each of two aircraft) may sometimes operate together. Larger numbers of aircraft may operate in a single formation in the newly-found air-to-ground role.

Hook down, an F-14A of VF-211 joins the landing pattern, as the carrier turns into wind. The F-14 is not the most difficult aircraft in the fleet to land aboard a carrier (the massive E-2C and the heavyweight EA-6B Prowler are reckoned to present even more of a challenge). Nor is it the easiest (that honour probably falling to the F/A-18), however, and every 'trap' is a challenge, despite sophisticated aids aboard ship, direct lift control and intensive training. Landing aboard never becomes routine, and is always stressful and exciting. Small wonder, then, that Naval Aviators count up and log their carrier landings the way other pilots log flying hours. Becoming a Centurion (logging 100 carrier landings) has more significance to the F-14 pilot than logging 1,000 flying hours.

facing an enemy who maybe has a ten-mile missile aimed right at you and there's nothing you can tap him with for that portion of the intercept.

So a practical interceptor or full F-14 loadout might be two Phoenix, two Sparrow and two 'Winders. That's a good loadout, that gives you a mix you can use

An F-14D of VF-31 approaches a shore base. With everything down, the F-14 is said to resemble a giant turkey, though a still photograph cannot capture the way in which this bird's 'feathers' (spoilers, tailerons etc.) flap and 'flutter' as it flies down the approach. This is the derivation of the 'Turkey' nickname often applied to the F-14 by the crews of other aircraft types. Unusually, this F-14D is completely clean, not even carrying the under-nacelle fuel tanks which are virtually a permanent fixture on the aircraft. The US Navy remains perilously short of the definitive D-model.

throughout the whole regime. The enemy has to fly through each weapon's ideal range region before he gets to you, before he can get to what you're trying to defend. What we call a fighter load out is four and four, four Sparrows, four Sidewinders and the forward-firing gun.

"Dogfighting in the airplane is fairly neat, and while there may be airplanes out there that can out-turn us at this speed or at that altitude, our overall package is good, and because I have a RIO behind me, we do have that all-important extra pair of eyes. Cock-pit workload is nice and low, too, allowing me to retain situational awareness and to think about what I'm doing and what I need to be doing. The variable-geometry wing looks after itself, for starters,

which is a big plus. Typically when we're flying the aeroplane, wing sweep scheduling is all being done by the air data computer. The airplane does it all itself, we have it in the computer mode and its just a function of Mach and altitude and dynamic pressure, so that is gener-ally, its handsoff, no piloting action required. Now if I want to, I can sweep the wings with a button electrically or I can use a mechani-cal handle to move them too. That moves in the same sense as the wing and has a direct link to the actuator, so there are three basic wingsweep modes you can use but if you are fighting, the computer will do it all.

"We turn well at high speed, and with the wing forward, we turn pretty well at low speed too. With the Super Tomcat engines,

While it is stable and controllable on approach, the F-14 has to land on a tiny steel deck, and its hook has to snag one of four closely-spaced arrester wires, making absolute precision essential. Landing Signals Officers carefully monitor every approach.

the General Electric F110 engines even in the existing F-14 airframe (turning the F-14A into the A Plus or F-14B), we find that aeroplane is a true fourth-generation fighter in all respects. As good as it is as an interceptor, the F-14B really is equally as good as a close-in dogfighter. We find that it is virtually an equal match for an F-16, or an A-4 Fox or A-4 Super Mike type of adversary and it is definitely superior to the F-15 series. That is the hybrid F-14B, a relatively new aircraft in the fleet, yet at the same time the F-14 we should have had (and could have had) 10-15 years ago. Even the current baseline F-14A is pretty much on a par with the F-15. They're pretty closely matched airplanes and the only thing the F-14A is lacking is the engines to go along with the proven airframe. The variable-geometry wing, the manoeuvring devices, all of that makes it a very good high performance fighter airframe. All we needed to go with it was some engines that had the thrust to weight ratio and the reliability and carefree handling you take for granted today. Now we've got those, we've got a great interceptor, a great fleet air defence fighter, and a great close-in dogfighter as well.

Slow-speed fighter

"The Adversary A-4s sometimes claimed that if they could drag us slow then they could kill us, and I guess that what they said is partially true. However, the A-4 would drop his flaps, to go slow and when he did that it gave him a much more manoeuvrable airplane because obviously he increased the camber of his wing and thereby was able to increase the lift he was generating and to lower his stall speed. But that assumed that the F-14 pilot wouldn't realise what was going on, and was not going to do the same thing. When I did the same thing with the F-14, the A-4 was just as easy to beat as it was prior to lowering the flaps. With the flaps down in both aircraft the F-14 was a superior slow speed fighter to the A-4.

"And with the Alpha limits we have, we can sustain that kind of low-speed turning fight until we beat him, as long as we need do it. However, it's not the method of choice to fight somebody, not with an aeroplane with the superior thrust to weight ratio of the Tom-cat. We have other tactics that we use in fights which would preclude us from getting slow. A slow speed, close-in turning fight is not the place to be. It all gets dangerously unpredictable and you start getting problems with maintaining your situational awareness. However, many Adversary pilots took great pride in slow-speed fighting because that's seen as the A-4's forte. But after two turns it was an energy bleeder and once it made one or two turns, it was going to be slowing down rapidly, because of the design of the wing it had, and because it didn't have much thrust. The F-14 with its high aspect ratio wing does not bleed energy so much in the turn, so we can sustain energy much better. We'll go round and round until either he realises he can't stay with us or until he tries getting inside our turn. But to do that he has to get slower, he can't sustain the turn like we can. There's no reason for us to get slow, so long as we maintain our energy we can use the vertical to come back down on the enemy, and then its not a problem.

Airshow performer

"All the factors that make the F-14 a tremendous dogfighter also make it a dynamic aeroplane for an airshow. The aircraft also has tremendously large and noisy burners, and together with the variable-geometry that makes the F-14 always a crowd pleaser. Films like *Top Gun* and *The Final Countdown* have also helped to give the Tomcat the most glamorous possible image. But at the end of the day, airshow performances and

A flimsy-looking hook and a relatively thin steel cable have to bring the F-14 to a halt in a remarkably short distance, even though the pilot applies full throttle as he touches down, in case he has missed the wire, and needs to 'bolter' (go around again).

The Pilot

Landing an F-14 on a conventional runway would be an almost impossible challenge for the average flying club light aircraft pilot, yet it is child's play by comparison with the deadly business of landing aboard an aircraft-carrier. Here an F-14D of VF-31 lands at NAS Miramar. All F-14Ds used to be based at Miramar and were assigned to the Pacific Fleet, but today the whole Tomcat fleet is based at Oceana on the East Coast, and squadrons can deploy with carriers from the Atlantic or Pacific Fleets. One of the three F-14D squadrons (VF-11) has been forced to transition back to the F-14B by aircraft shortages, leaving VF-2 and VF-31 in great demand as the only F-14D units.

close-in dogfighting are not important, and they are not what the airplane is about. If someone wants to say that in a close-in fight an F/A-18 or a MiG-29 or an Su-27 or whatever is going to get me, well I'm not going to agree, but I don't need to argue. With our tactics, sensors and weapons, he's going to be dead long before we can get close enough to settle that argument. It may not be so glamorous, but I can take him out before he even knows I'm there, and in wartime, that's exactly what I'll do.

The deadly deterrent

"It's kind of neat that wherever the F-14 has stood ready to actually do its job, the presence of the aircraft has tended to have the effect of making the enemy run away. During the Libyan crisis it was immediately apparent that the Libyans had a great respect for the F-14 weapon system and for the aircraft. Their fighter participation after the initial attack on their boats was virtually nil. If Libyan fighters came out 'feet wet', it was under close GCI control, and they attempted that only when they had

full knowledge that we were nowhere in the vicinity. As soon as they picked up a Tomcat's radar signature, they were back on deck. The Libyans got stung in 1981 and since then they have been extremely wary of any direct conflict with an F-14. It is an airplane whose capabilities make it very imposing. It has a worldwide reputation as a formidable foe and that seemed to be confirmed during Desert Storm, when the Iraqis stayed away when the F-14s were in the area.

"Once you've engaged the enemy, there is the small matter of getting back aboard ship. Fortunately the F-14 is very easy to take off and very easy to land. Unfortunately it's hard to really look good landing with it because of the high lift devices and spoilers on the wing and the differential moving tail. There are a lot of moving parts on the airplane, and they all tend to move quite a bit on approach. That's why some call it the 'Turkey' – they say it looks like some fat turkey, with all it's feathers fluttering this way and that. We take a lot of pride as naval aviators in the style with which we come

aboard the ship. In fact all our landing passes are graded, your best pass is 4.0, then fair or average is 3.0 and on down the list. If you have a pass with virtually no deviations whatsoever, you get an OK or a 4.0 on that pass. An average pass with a lot of deviations about the airspeed elevation and line up would give you a 3.0 or average pass – safe but not perfect, and maybe a bit untidy. A below average pass is 2.0, what we call a no grade and that would have some pretty dramatic deviations in both line up, elevation and airspeed. Then, of course, we have a dangerous pass which we call a cut pass. If you land on a cut pass (rather than going round again) that's no points and it draws the commanding officer's attention.

Looking good

"Some airplanes are easier to look good in than others. The less they move around on the glide slope, the better they look. The Phantom was a good looking aero-plane, but it was so over-responsive to the throttle that it was very easy to kill yourself in the back of the ship at night, hitting the ramp. The F-14 floats about, and although it doesn't look as good on the glide slope, it is easier to bring aboard safely. The F-14's approach speed is slower and it responds better. The aircraft has a tendency to glide and it doesn't drop like a rock with a reduction of power, so you get a little bit more sensory feedback

before the impact actually takes place."

From Tomcat to Bombcat

Today, many young pilots are transitioning to an aircraft very different to the F-14 variously enjoyed and endured by their predecessors. Their tone can be almost obnoxiously up-beat, but it does reflect the way the Tomcat is seen today. Talk to a junior pilot on one of the current F-14 squadrons, and the chances are that he'll barely mention the outer air battle or the AIM-54. Today the F-14 is a multi-role airplane, and air-to-ground is the name of the game, as one young pilot explains.

"The Tomcat is the Navy's fighter of choice. Anywhere the USA wants to project military power, we'd send a carrier, and anywhere we send a carrier the fighter protecting it, and taking the war to the enemy is the Tomcat.

"As a Tomcat pilot, I'm the man. I am the man. I'm unbeatable air-to-air, I am shipboard recce (no-one else does it), and now (with the Bombcat) I'm King Kong in the air-to-ground game also. Bomber pukes will always claim that fighters are fun, but that bombers are important – the Tomcat today is both.

"The F-14 (F for Fighter) was purpose built for the air-to-air mission, to dominate massive volumes of airspace around the carrier and to engage and destroy enemy bombers or missileers way out,

before they could threaten the carrier. But though the outer air battle is our number one priority, the F-14 isn't just some long-range bomber-destroyer. In the F-14 I can turn and burn with anything. Period. There isn't a fighter that I won't wax in a turning fight. If it gets 'down and dirty' those wings just auto-sweep forward, out come the manoeuvre devices and I can turn as tight and slow as I need. I've got four 'Winders for close range targets, and if I need it I've got the gun. The gun is awesome – a high-speed 20-mm cannon built on the principles of the old Gatling gun, rotating the barrels to allow the maximum rate of fire without melting them. We've proved it again and again against Adversary F-5s and F-16s, air force F-15s, everyone we've come up against,

in fact. Like they say – 'Anytime Baby!'

"And the F-14 is the free world fighter with the best record against the enemy. Four-to-nothing. Khaddafi tried twice and we blew him away both times. Don't ask me about Desert Storm. The air force controlled the air battle and they made damned sure that their boys got the chances to fight the enemy. 'Nuff said.

"The Tomcat is also carrier-borne recce. Hang a TARPS pod out on station 5 and the F-14 is a photo recon bird. They're changing all that stuff right now, putting digital sensors in the pods instead of cameras, bringing the capability right up to date. One day there may be a recon Hornet, but right now, the only carrierborne reconnaissance capability we have is the

TARPS Tomcat.

"The Tomcat was designed from the start to be able to drop bombs on the enemy. There are plenty of pictures from the 1970s showing Tomcat prototypes hauling every kind of bomb, but with carrier decks full of A-6s they never cleared the airplane to fly the mission. Also, it really wasn't something a fighter pilot wanted to do. I guess we didn't know any better.

"They finally learned the lesson in Desert Storm. With no enemy airplanes to go shoot, everyone wanted to drop bombs and do some damage. The F-14 was side-lined because that wasn't really a capability we had. The Bombcat programme was already well underway, but Desert Storm added impetus. Now we're getting LAN-

The whole of the Tomcat's trailing edge is taken up by flaps, leaving roll control to differential tailplane movement, and to the differential use of spoilers. On landing the spoilers are used as lift-dumpers.

TIRN so we can find targets at night, and lase for our own laser guided bombs. When Tomcats dropped LGBs on the Serbs, they needed an F/A-18 to designate the target. Today we'd do it autonomously.

"In the air-to-ground role, I can fly a mission carrying two GBU-16s or GBU-24s, a LANTIRN pod for targeting, four AIM-9s and can still take a Phoenix on the glove and a Sparrow on the centre-line. We wear a patch that kinda says it all. 'Bombcat. No escort required.'

"Some laughed at the movie *Top Gun*, and sure, there were plenty of things to laugh at. But deep down, they told it like it is. The F-14 is where its at in carrier aviation. Every Tomcat aviator is Tom Cruise: able, confident, and aggressive. We are all Erroll Flynn in *Dawn Patrol*. We are fighter pilots. We are the elite of the fleet. By any measure. Capability, training, experience. And of course the Tomcat community takes the pick of the pilots and NFOs coming out of training. The best deserve the best. And we are the best of the best. The Cat is Back!"

The Tomcat community faces an interesting and challenging future, with new weapons, systems and sensors being integrated, and with structural changes to the F-14 fleet about to result in mixed squadrons equipped with all three frontline F-14 variants. Such changes have been greeted with easy optimism, perhaps summed up by the Tomcat's unofficial motto – 'Anytime, baby'.

Chapter Eight
The Tomcat RIO

At the time of writing, then-Lieutenant Sam Platt was a radar intercept officer (RIO) assigned as an instructor with the East Coast Fleet Replacement Squadron, VF-101 'Grim Reapers'. He was assigned to the 'Black Aces' of VF-41 onboard USS *Theodore Roosevelt* (CVN-71) during Operation Desert Storm, and is a veteran of 45 Tomcat combat missions. He returned to a front-line F-14 squadron, and is now serving in a staff appointment with COMSEVENTHFLT.

The F-14 is built around its radar, and that radar is so old that for it to be used most effectively it requires a dedicated operator. He is the Tomcat's radar intercept officer (RIO), arguably the key member of the two-man team which flies and fights the F-14. The RIO also represents an invaluable extra pair of eyes in the cockpit, helping the pilot maintain his situational awareness and lookout. An equal partner in flight, he is a naval officer qualified to wear the wings of gold as a naval flight officer, and is considered as responsible as the pilot for flying the aircraft and the mission. As he becomes more experienced, a RIO can qualify as an F-14 mission commander, leading multi-aircraft strike, fighter and reconnaissance missions. When the mission commander is a RIO, the formation leader is the lead pilot and is responsible for the safe and tactical conduct of the formation. Eventually, the successful RIO will be qualified as a strike lead, leading air wing strikes as the airborne commander.

Junior pilots are normally crewed with senior RIOs, and vice versa, to maximise expertise within each cockpit. Within a squadron, all the pilots and RIOs fly with each other, flying with their assigned aircrew members whenever scheduling allows. This standard organisation is called the squadron TacOrg.

The Tomcat is a complex aircraft, and detailed checklists are used in each phase of flight to ensure that all equipment is set up properly. Take-off checks, climb checks, air combat manoeuvring checks, descent checks and landing checks are all completed by the RIO challenging and the pilot replying to each checklist item.

The RIO's 'office'

The rear cockpit is completely filled with avionics and radar equipment; the RIO has no flight controls. There is minimum duplication of controls and systems in the front and rear cockpits. The RIO does have basic flight instruments, including airspeed indicator, barometric altimeter, standby attitude gyro and bearing, distance, heading indicator (BDH). The pilot's display of radar information is restricted to the horizontal situation display (HSD), which is a small repeat of the RIO's tactical information display

Lt Sam Platt in the rear cockpit of a VF-101 Tomcat. Following service with the 'Black Aces' during Operation Desert Storm, Sam Platt was assigned to the 'Grim Reapers' as an instructor.

(TID). Division of responsibility is necessary for all Tomcat missions, and crew co-ordination is stressed from the beginning of aircrew training.

The premium on clear, concise communication and crew co-ordination is especially high during inflight emergencies. When an emergency occurs, the RIO's first responsibility is to read aloud the immediate action procedures, known as boldface. After completing the boldface items, the crew verifies the problem, including any warning, caution and advisory lights. Problems are prioritised in the event of multiple emergencies. The RIO then reads the naval aviation training and operations procedures standardisation (NATOPS) emergency procedures to the pilot, who completes the required action.

Command ejection

These procedures are practised in simulators again and again. The RIO's situational awareness in an emergency is essential in most critical flight regimes, since the RIO is much more likely to successfully initiate ejection than the pilot. Such situations include single-engine during the catapult shot, out-of-control flight, and mid-air collision. For this reason, the normal position for the eject-command lever is aft, which automatically ejects the pilot when the RIO initiates ejection.

The Hughes AWG-9 weapons control system (WCS) is the heart of the RIO's systems. More than a radar alone, the AWG-9's analog computer integrates inputs from almost all avionics systems. The radar itself is a multi-mode system with extremely high power. It was developed simultaneously as the companion radar to the AIM-54 Phoenix missile, a long-range, multi-mode, semi-active radar guidance air-to-air missile.

The Phoenix is extremely large and weighs nearly 1,000 lb (454 kg), and is the longest-range air-to-air weapon carried by any fighter. The AIM-54 is a 'smart' weapon with impressive microelectronics for anti-jamming capability. The high pulse repetition frequency (PRF) modes give out the highest

Right: Even during inflight refuelling, operating the F-14 is very much a team game, requiring complete crew co-ordination. Here two F-14s wait their turn while another takes on fuel from a US Air Force Boeing KC-135.

power, and provide the longest-range target detections. Once the AWG-9 computer establishes a Doppler track file, the system automatically assigns a target priority, called the firing order number (FONO), to the track. This is the next target to be engaged by Phoenix, but can be altered by the RIO with the next-launch button.

Below: To refuel a US Navy aircraft, a USAF tanker must have a drogue attached to the end of its boom. Here a VF-84 'Jolly Rogers' F-14A takes on fuel from a USAF KC-135.

The Tomcat RIO

For many years the Tomcat's tanker of choice was the Grumman KA-6D Intruder, though this has now gone from the inventory, along with the A-6E bomber. This has left tanking as a secondary role for the Lockheed S-3 Viking, primarily used as an ASW platform, but also fulfilling an ever-expanding roster of other duties, from reconnaissance to ship-killing.

When a Phoenix is launched in the track-while-scan (TWS) mode, the system continues to track any other targets in the radar scan volume. Missile messages to each Phoenix in flight automatically update target information, and allow the RIO to send an active transfer command that 'cuts' the missile to the active guidance mode. When in an active mode, the Phoenix requires no support from the F-14 and the Tomcat can retire from the battle while the Phoenix continues to the target.

The AWG-9 also supports the AIM-7 Sparrow missile. The standard for a medium-range semi-active missile, the Sparrow is an impressive, flexible weapon. Comparatively light-weight and low-drag, the Sparrow is fast off the rail and has good manoeuvrability in the end game of target intercept. It is the radar missile of choice in engaged manoeuvring as a result of its high speed and short minimum range.

The AWG-9 supplies displays to the pilot and RIO, including a steering dot, for collision heading to the missile, surrounded by a variable-size circle of allowable steering error (ASE circle), which defines the area of acceptable missile launch. The RIO also has a display on his TID of maximum and minimum ranges called the launch acceptability regions (LARs). Once launched, the Sparrow tracks the reflected radar energy from the tracked target. The Sparrow is normally tracking the continuous wave illuminator (CWI) for target tracking, which allows the AWG-9 to switch

between high PRF and low PRF or pulse-tracking modes with a Sparrow in flight.

The AWG-9 also supports the AIM-9 Sidewinder. Tracking signals point the infra-red seeker head in the direction of a target when the RIO has a radar lock. This mode is called Sidewinder expanded acquisition mode (SEAM). The pilot verifies a good shot by the distinctive tone rise in his headset and by noting the placement of the seeker head position indicator in the head-up display (HUD) over the target and not over clouds, a flare or his wingman.

Fire and forget

Once launched, the Sidewinder is on its own, with no support from the AWG-9. Upon initial alignment, the AWG-9 supplies all voltages to align the inertial navigation system (INS). The INS is vital to the weapons systems for Phoenix support, for accurate employment of the M61A1 Gatling gun as well as bombing. The INS is the primary attitude platform. The RIO enters waypoints for display on the TID, to which the pilot can get destination steering on his large vertical display indicator (VDI) located on the instrument panel directly below the HUD.

The AWG-9 computers provide systems status monitoring and testing. The continuous monitor (CM) checks key systems for malfunction every few seconds. Onboard checks (OBC) is a comprehensive check of all major systems. It is run on deck and then airborne. When a system is degraded, the RIO can access computer memory locations called flycatchers to isolate the defective system. The radar and computer subsystems have built-in test (BIT) functions to isolate the specific weapons replaceable assemblies (WRAs) for replacement upon return to base.

The RIO's primary display is the tactical information display directly in front of him, just above knee

level. The large, round display shows computer-generated target tracks and own aircraft position, RIO-entered waypoints and datalink tracks. The display is selectable from ground orientation showing the aircraft in the centre with 'up' oriented to magnetic north, to attack display showing a 'pie piece' picture in which own aircraft is at the bottom flying toward the top of the display.

The TID displays all numerical information around the targets and in two large data buffers at the top of the screen. The RIO selects targets by aiming the cursor using the hand control unit (HCU). When a target is selected, it becomes bright and is said to be 'hooked'. Once hooked, the target displays a two-digit altitude number for thousands of feet on the left side of the track. Above the track is speed in Mach number. The tracks are called 'staples', from which a velocity vector projects in the direction of target heading. The vector length varies with target speed. The TID also has a TV-display position, which allows viewing of the monochromatic television camera system (TCS) in green and black.

Secondary scope

The RIO's secondary radar scope is the detail data display (DDD), located at eye level directly in front of the RIO. In high PRF modes, the DDD shows Doppler (target closure) on the vertical axis and target azimuth on the horizontal. In low PRF or pulse search mode, the vertical axis is the selected range scale and the horizontal is target azimuth. A mechanical tape display to the immediate left of the DDD shows the elevation of the radar antenna.

The DDD is the primary display for discerning individual aircraft within a tactical formation. It is also the first display that the RIO uses for recognition of electronic

jamming. After recognising the type and intensity of jamming, the RIO adjusts the radar and weapons employment to defeat the threat. The APX-76 IFF interrogator also is displayed along with radar video on the DDD. The pilot has no repeat to see what is on the DDD.

The electronic countermeasures display (ECMD) is located on the console just to the right of the RIO's knee. It displays received-threat radar warning and missile launch from the ALR-45 and ALR-50 radar warning receivers. In Tomcats equipped with the ALR-67 improved radar warning receiver, the display is located on the RIO's instrument panel on the right side. The ECMD navigation mode provides digital BDHI repeat, TACAN and destination steering, and winds determined by the AWG-9 from INS information.

Locking on

The hand control unit (HCU) is aft of the TID between the RIO's knees. The HCU is a multi-function device and controls the radar and TCS, and communicates with the AWG-9 computer. When the TID push-tile is selected the HCU controls a cursor on the TID. By positioning the circular cursor over the desired computer symbology and pulling the index finger trigger, symbols are hooked. The RIO can select targets and waypoints, or can access special functions through the TID menus. The offset button on the upper aft side of the HCU allows the RIO to reposition own aircraft symbology anywhere on the TID.

With DDD selected, the HCU controls the range gates or speed gates to take a radar lock on targets appearing on the DDD. When IR/TV is selected, the RIO can slew the television camera system. The manual rapid lock-on (MRL) button is a red button on the forward side of the HCU, and selects quick-lock-on mode for a last-chance radar lock from medium to close range. The elevation thumbwheel on the left side of the HCU provides fine control of radar elevation.

The sensor control panel (SCP) is a console to the left of the RIO's left knee. This is where the radar scan patterns are selected, as are azimuth and elevation knobs. Also located on this panel are the video tape recorder (VTR) controls, and TCS field of view and slaving controls, which slave the TCS line-of-sight to the radar lock's azimuth and elevation. Vertical scan lock-on (VSL) is a pulse rapid-lock-on mode that is selected by a switch on the left side of the SCP.

To the right of the SCP is the computer address panel (CAP) which is used to input all numerical information to the AWG-9 computer. The CAP consists of a keypad of 15 keys and 10 pushbuttons which have pre-assigned functions selected by the rotary dial at the bottom of the panel. For example, to select the built-in test functions the RIO selects the BIT category on the rotary dial and then presses the button corresponding to the specific test that he desires.

The RIO selects the appropriate radar mode on the push-tiles directly to the right of the DDD. The primary radar mode of the F-14 is track-while-scan (TWS). As its name implies, TWS provides computer tracking of up to 24 targets while scanning the entire radar scan volume for initial detection of new targets. In TWS (manual), the RIO determines the centre of the radar scan through the SCP and HCU. In TWS (auto), the AWG-9 automatically moves the centre of the radar scan volume to maintain track on any track files that have been established. A TWS track's bearing, range, altitude, speed and heading are all available to the RIO via the data buffers at the top of the TID.

Radar modes

The longest-range radar detections are achieved in pulse-Doppler search (PDS). In PDS, computer tracks are not initiated by the AWG-9. Doppler returns are displayed to the RIO on the DDD. By positioning the speed gates around the target and taking a pulse-Doppler single-target track (PDSTT), a radar lock is established, which is transferred to the AWG-9's Doppler track file. This is the most accurate altitude, speed and heading information available on the target. A lock also gives the fastest indication of a target manoeuvre.

Only one target can be locked at a time. This causes a loss of tactical awareness of any target other than the one tracked. A lock is required to guide a Sparrow missile or to guide a Phoenix in the semi-active-only mode.

Pulse search, or low PRF mode, gives extremely accurate range information and is the primary mode to break out aircraft flying in close formation. Pulse search simply transmits radar energy out and receives back the reflected pulse. No Doppler information is obtained. To determine target

speed and heading, the RIO takes a pulse single target track (PSTT). The pulse lock does not require any target closure to maintain lock. Once a lock is taken, the target information is transferred to a Doppler track file in the same way as a PDSTT.

In pulse search, the radar can be saturated by radar returns from terrain, clouds or mechanical jamming such as chaff. A PSTT lock

can guide a Sparrow in the same way as a PDSTT lock. Pulse search has the additional utility of ground mapping modes for attack and navigation, and weather avoidance capability.

The remaining radar modes are all fast acquisition modes. Pilot automatic lock-on (PAL) and manual rapid lock-on (MRL) are both 'hotbox' modes which activate a large radar scan volume, locking up

Above: An F-14D lets fly with a Sparrow from Station 4. The aircraft also carries GBU-10 2,000-lb laser-guided bombs on stations 3 and 6, with test camera pods replacing the fuel tanks on stations 2 and 7. The F-14 is not yet cleared for AMRAAM.

Below: The back-seater enjoys an excellent view, which allows the RIO to play a vital monitoring role during refuelling. Here a Tomcat refuels from a Viking, which is now the only carrierborne tanker.

The F-14's primary close-range armament is the AIM-9 Sidewinder IR-homing AAM, seen here being fired by a VF-211 F-14A (Plus).

any target Doppler detected within the volume. The pilot activates PAL through a switch forward of the throttle quadrant. Pilot lock-on mode (PLM) and vertical scan lock-on (VSL) are pulse lock-on modes, and are especially useful in gaining a radar lock in a turning dogfight after the first merge.

PLM locks up targets directly in front of the pilot's windscreen centred on the aircraft datum line (ADL), which is a reference point in the HUD. PLM is activated by the pilot. VSL is a vertically orientated rectangular scan on the axis of the aircraft's nose and its velocity vector. VSL is used when pulling toward an aircraft above the canopy, and can be activated by either the pilot or RIO.

The combination of flexible radar modes and high power make

Among the many tasks of the RIO is photographing intercepted aircraft using a hand-held camera. Here a VF-102 'Cat holds station on a Tu-16K-10-26 while the RIO takes photos for the intelligence staff.

the AWG-9 lethal in any air-to-air engagement from initial long-range detection to quick locks in close when engaged in a manoeuvring dogfight. Other avionics equipment in the rear cockpit include weapons auxiliary systems, navigation equipment and communications systems.

Chaff and flares

The ALE-39 chaff and flare dispenser is located on the RIO's right console, inboard of the IFF transponder. The ALE-39 is a programme which expends chaff in a pre-set pattern when triggered by the pilot's button on the throttles, or the RIO's thumb switches on the hand grip above the DDD. The expendables can be used singly or in a complex programme. Normally, the RIO expends chaff, and the pilot launches flares.

The AWG-15F weapons control panel is located on the panel just above the SCP. The AWG-15F controls the release and jettison of all air-to-air and air-to-ground ordnance, as well as auxiliary fuel tanks. It also is the switchboard for power to all weapons stations and weapons arming voltages. Using

the WCP, the RIO selects the type of air-to-ground weapon and the delivery method.

The RIO also selects the weapon station, type and delay of fusing, and quantity and interval of weapons dropped. If computer pilot is selected, the pilot is shown a continuously computed impact point (CCIP) for the ballistics of the selected weapon. He has a hot trigger and when the CCIP is over the target, the pilot releases the bomb. If the RIO has selected computer target, the pilot is displayed a bomb-fall line. He slews the designator diamond up or down this line over the target, and designates the target by pressing the cage SEAM button on the throttle.

Once the target is selected, the computer will determine the correct time for a release pulse and will drop the bomb when the pilot depresses his bomb button. Computer targetting allows for more aggressive aircraft movement, as well as both straight path and lofted bomb delivery.

The launch button for the RIO to shoot Sparrow and Phoenix missiles is also on the AWG-15. Although it is an aircrew prefer-

ence item, the RIO usually makes all TWS shots and the pilot shoots any missiles with a radar lock.

The TCS is an uncomplicated video system which can help identify aircraft beyond visual range (BVR). The TCS pod is a video camera with a x4 and x10 magnification lens. The camera line-of-sight can be slewed manually, but in normal tactical use it is slaved to the radar line-of-sight. When a dark target comes into the TCS field of view, the TCS automatically tracks the contrast difference between the target and background. The television picture is displayed on the VDI or the TID and can be recorded via the VTR.

Each Tomcat is equipped with either the ALR-45/50 or its replacement, the ALR-67 radar warning receiver. These systems warn the aircrew of active threat surface or airborne radar systems. The aircrew identifies the threat by sound and annunciator lights with the ALR-45/50, while the more advanced ALR-67 has a digital library of known threats that are displayed in alphanumerics on the small round display panel.

Electronic warfare

The ALQ-126B is an automatic defensive ECM suite which degrades threat radar-tracking systems with its own jamming. The APX-72 is an IFF transponder used to comply with FAA air traffic procedures. It also employs an encrypted mode which responds with a pre-set code when interrogated. This gives positive ID of friendly aircraft to any interrogating aircraft, ship, or shore facility. The APX-76 interrogator allows the F-14 to identify IFF modes 1, 2 and 3, and encrypted mode 4, on any aircraft track.

The F-14 has a full suite of navigation equipment controlled by the RIO. The ARN-84 TACAN provides bearing and range to any

A RIO of VF-84 demonstrates the extraordinary all-round view enjoyed from the Tomcat's rear cockpit.

TACAN station, be it ashore, afloat or airborne (in the case of tanker aircraft). The information is displayed on the BDHI, as well as the pilot's VDI. TACAN updates to compensate for INS are available, as is air-to-air TACAN to help in poor-weather rendezvous.

Communication is primarily the RIO's responsibility, and for voice communication two radios are available. The ARC-51 front cockpit UHF radio, or UHF No. 1, is normally used for inter-flight tactical communication. The ARC-182 UHF/VHF radio, or UHF No. 2, is used to talk to controlling agencies and is the primary radio for talking to controllers and the rest of the air wing for tactical communication. The ARC-182 is UHF and VHF capable, as well as Have Quick 2 capable for secure communication.

The ASW-27C is the Tomcat's digital datalink. It can send commands, target information and vector for the F-14 when used with the Link-4 on AAW surface ships, and E-2Cs. The datalink can be used as a fighter-to-fighter datalink (FFDL) to communicate among 4 Net aircraft. The most essential function of the datalink is the automatic carrier landing system.

Autoland

The ship's radar locks the desired aircraft and then sends azimuth and glideslope needles to

During Persian Gulf operations Tomcats (like this VF-154 F-14A) encountered Iranian P-3F Orions. As far as is known, meetings between US and Iranian Tomcats have not occurred.

the pilot on the HUD and VDI, and to the RIO's TID. The system can be coupled with the autopilot actually to fly the aircraft down the glideslope all the way to landing, although all systems must be in perfect trim to use this capability. The automated carrier landing system (ACLS) needles are the most accurate precision landing aid for the pilot and are a tremendous safety advantage when coming aboard the carrier in poor weather or at night.

A standard intercept mission illustrates the RIO's purpose and the crew co-ordination required for fighter success. The standard unit of Tomcat employment is the section of two fighters flying in formation. Assuming a combat air patrol (CAP) mission over water, the section will be in contact with an early warning radar aircraft, such as an E-2C from the carrier, or an Air Force or NATO E-3 Sentry AWACS. Receiving a vector from the controller, the lead RIO directs the section's heading and the Tomcats accelerate to a tactical speed from their low-fuel-consumption

loiter airspeed. Both pilot and RIO report 'vector checklists complete' in turn on the VTR.

'Bogey Dope'

The controller calls the bogey's (or unknown) bearing, range and altitude. (Such information is sometimes known as 'Bogey Dope'.) The RIOs are each searching the altitude blocks assigned in the pre-flight brief, normally with the lead searching the block where the expected threat will be located. Communication is a studied cadence, with the controller calling out, followed by the lead RIO, then the wing RIO. During an intercept, the callsigns used by the RIO are the pilot's callsign to avoid confusion. Once the lead has radar contact, the cadence shifts, with the lead RIO driving the comm, followed by the wing, and then the controller. The lead may stay in a high PRF mode such as TWS, while the wing goes into pulse search to break out the bogey formation.

The lead RIO asks for weapons status, which will determine

whether he can employ his long-range weapons or will have to visually identify the threat. If the response is 'red and free', or the bogey is declared to be a bandit, the lead RIO will have his pilot arm up and will employ Phoenix. The wing aircraft will normally wait for a second target break-out before launching a weapon.

If not cleared to fire, the lead RIO will manoeuvre for target aspect in order to get turning room to be in offensive position at the merge. The RIOs will try to be 'sorted' at range, i.e. locked-on to separate aircraft, prepared to launch Sparrows, and also giving their pilots a radar-lock diamond in his HUD field of view to facilitate sighting the threat aircraft. Coming into visual range, the communication burden shifts to the pilots. The RIOs have done their job if the formation is defined at the merge and they have separate locks.

Coming into the turning dogfight phase, the pilot is responsible for seeing any bogey forward of the wing line. The RIO looks for anyone behind the aircraft. Typically, the pilot will be 'pad-locked' on the bogey he is turning with, while the RIO watches his wingman and any other bogey.

An extra pair of eyes

Engaged communication between cockpits is essential to co-ordinate radar hot modes, and the RIO will give status calls to the pilot during the engagement on everything from own aircraft energy state ('You've got 220 kt') to his wingman's status ('Dog is left eight o'clock low, engaged defensive, nose low left-hand turn').

Once engaged, the fighter must look for a way out. If quick kills are not achieved, the fighters look for a neutral merge, and 'bug out'. Better to fight another day than push a poor situation.

Lieutenant Sam Platt, F-14 RIO

Chapter Nine
Tomcat Today

The success of the F/A-18 led to a general shift from single-role aircraft, and in 1987 the Naval Operational Advisory Group issued recommendations that the F-14 should be more flexibly employed, taking greater advantage of the aircraft's latent ground attack capabilities. At much the same time, industry began to look at multi-role Tomcat derivatives, perhaps realising that single-role advanced F-14s would never be funded. Grumman, however,

has been repeatedly dealt blows in its effort to keep the F-14 Tomcat on the production line. Still, the builder has offered a variety of options – some as alternatives to the NATF (Navy Advanced Tactical Fighter), others to fill the gap left by the A-12 Avenger.

In 1991, for example, Grumman had four development studies underway, all with the overriding requirement that the modifications could be retrofitted to the F-14D. Three stages of evolution have

been planned, beginning with the F-14 Quick Strike, which improves the attack capability of the F-14D by adding additional modes to the APG-71 radar, making it similar to the F-15E's APG-70. Navigation and targeting pods similar to LANTIRN would be installed, and cockpit changes would include FLIR, HUD, moving-map display and large colour displays. Software changes would allow the carriage of laser-guided bombs, stand-off SLAM missiles

Dismissals, career-haltings and a climate of suspicion followed the scandal of the notorious Tailhook Convention of 1991, eroding morale in the F-14 community – which was already declining as the force shrank. Wearing a patch like this one became impossible as the hunt for participants intensified.

and Maverick in addition to HARM and Harpoon.

A more radical update is known as Super Tomcat 21. This features redesigned aerodynamics, the main features of which are enlarged wing gloves, enlarged tailplane and reshaped slats and flaps. These would result in additional internal tankage, reduced approach speed, nil-wind carrier take-offs and vastly

VF-74 gained a brief stay of execution after its final carrier deployment, operating its camouflaged F-14Bs in the adversary role before the squadron finally disestablished.

increased range. The radar cross-section of the aircraft would be significantly reduced, while uprated F110 engines would allow 'super-cruise' (i.e. sustained supersonic cruise without afterburner), and would even incorporate thrust-vectoring. An improvement in the weapons system package would see the adoption of helmet-mounted sights and a new radar with double the power of the APG-71: FLIR pods would be installed for night-attack missions.

Attack Tomcat

A dedicated attack version of the aircraft, the Attack Super Tomcat 21, briefly received great attention as a potential successor to the cancelled A-12, adding more air-to-ground options to the basic Super Tomcat 21, possibly including the radar developed for the A-12. Due to the postponement of development of the Naval ATF, Grumman has also proposed the ASF-14, which would adopt the engines of the Lockheed F-22 within the F-14 airframe as a lower-cost alternative to NATF procurement. At the end of the day, the time was not right for these advanced Super Tomcats and they progressed no further than models and artist's impressions, although a Tomcat bomber was soon to become a reality.

The uncertain future meant that Grumman's work force of 25,500 faced immediate lay-offs of up to

4,100 people and a 'stop work' order was issued in 1991, halting future Tomcats in their tracks. Grumman merged with Northrop during 1994. It was not the end – in the Washington world of defence acquisition, nothing ever quite seems to end – but it was assuredly an undignified penultimate chapter for the US Navy's standard carrier-based fighter of the past two decades. Although production of new Tomcats was brought to a precipitous close, existing airframes had exciting new developments awaiting them.

Various experiments with new air wing compositions were undertaken during the 1980s, including an all-Grumman cruise by CVW-2, described by one F-14 RIO as "a beautiful thing, everybody had lots of gas." After the end of the Cold War, larger numbers of F/A-18s seemed to offer greater flexibility and the F-14 force began a steady contraction, while the A-6 Intruder slipped towards extinction. Air Wing 11 was the first to embark with only a single F-14 squadron

(VF-213), from June until December 1993, partnered by three F/A-18 squadrons. This proved an extremely effective mix, and attracted more support than the Hornet-less air wing trialled aboard the *John F. Kennedy*. At the peak of its deployment, the F-14 was operated by one Reserve and five regu-

Above: This is the boss-bird of the 'Fighting Renegades', seen entering the pattern. VF-24 flew the Tomcat from 1975 to 1996.

Below: Some of the US Navy's most colourful and famous fighter squadrons disappeared as the Tomcat force dwindled. Even VF-111 'Sundowners' vanished in March 1995.

lar carrier air wings assigned to the Pacific Fleet, and by one Reserve and six regular carrier air wings on the East Coast.

The dissolution of CVW-15 and the switch to a standard carrier air wing composition which included only one F-14 squadron led to the disbandment of VF-114 on 30 April 1993, VF-1 on 30 September 1993, VF-33 on 1 October 1993, VF-74 on 28 April 1994, and the West Coast RAG, VF-124, on 30 September 1994. VF-51 and VF-111 went the same way on 31 March 1995, VF-142 followed on 30 April 1995, and VF-84 disappeared on 1 October, although the latter unit's 'Jolly Rogers' name and traditions were then taken on by VF-103, formerly the 'Sluggers'. One of the last duties carried out by VF-84 was to provide aircraft for the Warner Brothers' motion picture *Executive Decision*, in which four of the squadron's aircraft intercept a hijacked Boeing 747; this followed the Tomcatís starring roles in the previous Hollywood blockbusters *The Final Countdown* and *Top Gun*. Before its disestablishment, VF-74 ('Bedevillers') spent the final months of its life as an adversary squadron, leading some to hope that the historic squadron (the Navy's first frontline F-4 unit) might have been saved.

The Reserve's VF-202 disestab-lished in October 1994, along with VF-301 and VF-302 which disappeared with the dissolution of CVWR-30 in late 1994. During 1995, only USS *Nimitz* (with CVW-9) and USS *Independence* (with CVW-5) deployed with two F-14 squadrons; *Eisenhower*, *Constellation*, *Roosevelt*, *Lincoln* and *America* all made deployments with only a single Tomcat squadron aboard. The twin-F-14 squadron air wing probably made its final appearance in 1996, when *Vinson* returned to the USA with two D-model users aboard, VF-11 and VF-31.

Air Wing Five lost VF-21 when it decommissioned in January 1996, and VF-24 disappeared from the roll of active squadrons the same year. This left only 11 front-line F-14 squadrons, with another Reserve unit and one training unit, which represented exactly half of the Tomcat's peak strength, at least in terms of the number of units. The single Tomcat squadron air wings actually deployed more than half the number of aircraft deployed by the original two-squadron wings, making it necessary to strengthen the surviving F-14 units.

Dwindling force

The dwindling force of F-14s was as active as ever, and carriers with F-14s aboard were deployed to the Persian Gulf in support of Operation Southern Watch, and to the Mediterranean in support of

It was ironic that the F-14 force was cut back just as the most capable variants of the aircraft were becoming available. Thus, relatively few aircrew got the chance to appreciate the qualities of the APG-71 radar which lay at the heart of the F-14D.

Right: The 'Bounty Hunters' were the survivors when Air Wing Two reduced to a single F-14 squadron, subsequently re-equipping with the F-14D, one of which is seen here in temporary exercise camouflage.

Below: A rainbow flash on the tail and the distinctive '00' ('Double Nuts') modex mark this aircraft out as VF-11's CAG-bird. VF-11 has recently transitioned from the F-14D (seen here) back to the F-14B.

The famous two-tailed alley cat motif has appeared in many forms on flying suit patches. This one marks its wearer as an F-14D crewman.

Provide Promise and Deny Flight. After OTEF (VX-5) tests in 1988, and front-line trials in 1990, during which F-14s of VF-24 and VF-211 dropped Mk 82, Mk 83 and Mk 84 bombs from the forward Phoenix stations, more and more F-14 squadrons adopted a secondary air-to-ground ('Bombcat') role, includ-

Right: The two F-14D squadrons of CVW-14 had similarly painted 'CAG birds'. This one served with VF-31, the 'Tomcatters', whose Felix the Cat insignia can clearly be seen superimposed on a rainbow stripe down the tailfin.

Cutbacks ensured that only F-14Ds were produced, and this allowed the formation of only three front-line squadrons, one of which has since transitioned back to the F-14B. Current plans will result in the formation of mixed squadrons of F-14Bs and F-14Ds. This aircraft is from VF-31, the 'Tomcatters'.

ing VF-2, VF-14, VF-24, VF-33, VF-51, VF-143 and VF-211. The first live ordnance drop was made by VF-24 on 8 August 1990. Unfortunately, the programme was not sufficiently far advanced to allow air-to-ground roled Tomcats to participate in Operation Desert Storm. The so-called 'Bombcat' did finally make its initial carrier deployment with VF-14 aboard the USS *John F. Kennedy* on 7 October 1992.

Going air-to-ground

The F-14 had always had a latent air-to-ground capability, although it was never used. When designing the 'rival' F-15 Eagle, engineers at McDonnell Douglas were directed that the aircraft should be kept light, optimised for the fighter role, and 'not a pound for air-to-ground' became something of a project slogan. By contrast, Grumman always accepted the need for air-to-ground capability, and devoted some time and resources to ensure that the F-14

could, if required, operate in the fighter-bomber role. Bombs were fitted to some of the early prototypes, largely for publicity purposes, and the AWG-15 (air-to-ground attack system) weapons control panel was fitted from the start, although it was viewed by fleet Tomcat crews as nothing more than a jettison and AAM launch panel. As early as 1973, a Tomcat flew with 18 Mk 82 bombs, Sparrows, Sidewinders and Phoenix.

The Navy had the A-6, and as one RIO remembered, "They were professionals at dropping bombs. We would have seriously invaded their turf. And there is no doubt that working air-to-ground detracts from your air-to-air proficiency. Look at the F/A-18 – jack of all trades, master of none. They are overworked because they have too few pilots and too many toys to learn. That's what's driving so many of them out of the Navy!"

The adoption of an air-to-ground role happened remarkably

quickly, as changing air wing compositions saw the retirement of the A-6 Intruder and the expansion of F/A-18 numbers aboard each carrier. The F/A-18 is a superb air-to-ground aircraft, but lacks payload/range capability. The use of the F-14 as a long-range bomber to augment the F/A-18 was felt to be essential if the air wing was to retain its full capability after the withdrawal of the A-6, which was originally to have been replaced by the cancelled General Dynamics A-12.

Clearing weapons

For a time, there were shortages of bomb racks and sometimes only one F-14 squadron aboard each carrier had a secondary 'Bombcat' role, while the other had a TARPS commitment. Elsewhere, whole air wings were 'Bombcat'-qualified, while other F-14 air wings were not. Even before air wings reduced to a single F-14 unit, all remaining squadrons took on both roles.

The basic 'Bombcat' carried only unguided, free-fall air-to-surface weapons, exploiting a latent air-to-ground capability which the F-14 had incorporated from the first flight. Weapons cleared for use by the F-14 included the 500-lb Mk 82 in its original low-drag configuration, and in Snakeye or BSU-86 high-drag guise. The aircraft could also carry various types of 1,000-lb Mk 83 bomb (including versions with the BSU-85 Air Inflatable Retard) and the 2,000-lb Mk 84. Interestingly, since the infamous *Forrestal* accident in 1976, these weapons have worn an ablative coating in Navy service which is designed to burn in a fire, preventing bombs from simply heating up until they explode. This practice was gradually adopted after a number of ship-board fires during and after the Vietnam War. Mk 77 fire bombs may have been cleared for use with the F-14, but do not appear to have reached fleet units, which do not use any FAE weapons.

Lethal ordnance

Weapons that are in use include various versions of the Mk 7 dispenser. They include the anti-armour Mk 20, Mk 99 and Mk 100 Rockeye, and the CBU-78 Gator (filled with 15 BLU-92/B anti-personnel and 45 BLU-91/B anti-tank mines), but not the anti-personnel CBU-59 (containing BLU-77 mines). Although it is an impressive enough multi-role fighter-bomber, the 'Bombcat' F-14's pure air-to-ground capability could not compare with that of the

An NAWC F-14A delivers four BSU-86 finned Mk 82 500-lb bombs in a steep dive. The F-14 tends to carry bombs in the 'tunnel' on racks which replace the Phoenix pallets.

These two flying suit patches celebrate the Tomcat's transformation into a multi-role fighter-bomber, capable of performing the air-to-ground role unescorted. The right-hand patch deliberately mimics a well known F/A-18 design, reflecting the intense rivalry between the communities.

Intruder it was supposed to be replacing. The 'Bombcat' was not compatible with any of the stand-off or guided weapons routinely carried by the A-6E, from the AGM-84 Harpoon and SLAM, the AGM-65 Maverick and the AGM-Walleye to the AGM-88 HARM, or laser-guided bombs like the GBU-10, GBU-12 and GBU-16. Perhaps most significantly, the 'Bombcat' had no equivalent to the Intruder's undernose TRAM turret, which was a fully-articulated sensor incorporating a laser range-finder and marked target seeker, a laser designator and a FLIR. This gave the A-6E a formidable night-attack capability, and also provided the aircraft with the ability to des-

ignate targets for its own LGBs. The 'Bombcat' was not originally even cleared to carry LGBs, and when this capability was added (with GBU-10, -12, -16 and -24) the aircraft initially relied on other aircraft to designate its targets.

Although any Tomcat has the AWG-15 weapons control system, and can thus carry bombs, some aircraft have undergone a specific Multi-Mission Capability (MCAP) upgrade. This consists of a coupling of the existing radar and cockpit displays with a MIL STD 1760 digital databus, together with the new Programmable Tactical Information Display System (PTIDS). The computer can be loaded from the cockpit or from a point in the nose gear bay.

The addition of the laser-guided bomb to the Tomcat brought with it an entirely new precision attack capability. The first such weapon

approved for use with the F-14 was the 1,000-lb GBU-16, in early 1994. At the same time, it was decided that the Tomcat should be able to designate its own targets, and that it should have a night air-to-ground capability. Thus LGB integration was accompanied by an urgent programme to find a basic FLIR and laser designator for the aircraft, not least to allow it to take over from the Grumman A-6E Intruder, then beginning to be withdrawn from the fleet.

LGB testing

Before such equipment could be developed and integrated, the Tomcat began using LGBs, albeit by day, and albeit with other aircraft types acting as designators. The 'Sluggers' of VF-103 had the honour of being the first precision 'Bombcats' on 2 May 1994, when two aircraft dropped a total of three GBU-16s on the Capo Frasca range off the coast of Sardinia; F/A-18s and A-6s from CVW-17 were 'spiking'.

Appropriately, it was VF-41 (the first to take the F-14 into action in the air-to-air role) which became the first Tomcat squadron to drop live ordnance in anger. The 'First to Fight' thereby also became the

'First to Strike'. During a Mediterranean cruise, the squadron participated in NATO/IFOR air strikes against Serbian targets. On 5 September 1995, two VF-41 F-14s dropped GBU-16s on an ordnance depot from 50° dive attacks, with accompanying F/A-18s 'lasing' the target with their AN/AAS-38A Nite Hawk designators. The 'Black Aces' delivered 24,000 lb (10885 kg) of bombs during their deployment, including 10 1,000-lb GBU-16s. The 'Bombcat' had finally been blooded.

The US Navy's A-6E Intruder made its final carrier deployments aboard the USS *Carl Vinson* and the USS *Enterprise* at the end of 1996. When VA-75 'Sunday Punchers' aboard the *Enterprise* made the Intruder's last operational sorties, they operated alongside 'Bombcat'-configured F-14As from VF-103 'Jolly Rogers'. They were the most capable air-to-ground Tomcats in the fleet, and were the first F-14s to receive a basic day-night air-to-ground and autonomous PGM capability. Funding for the advanced Super Tomcats

This NAWC F-14D, with test camera pods under the intakes, is seen dropping a GBU-10 from station 6, with another still on station 3.

Above: The introduction of LANTIRN has given the F-14 a real night-attack capability, although bad weather presents problems to IR-based sensors, meaning that the LANTIRN Tomcat cannot fully replace the capabilities of the A-6E TRAM Intruder.

Right: This sequence of photographs shows the first GBU-16 launch (made by Commander Hnarakis and Lieutenant Commander Slade) by a VF-41 F-14 against the Vieques Island range.

described earlier remained impossible to find, but the basic in-service F-14D was able to achieve a degree of night-attack capability, and on a shoestring budget. Plans to give the in-service F-14 a night-attack

A VF-143 'Pukin Dogs' F-14A drops a 1,000-lb Mk 83 AIR retarded bomb during early 'Bombcat' trials. LANTIRN has now transformed the F-14's once-limited attack capability.

capability (to allow the aircraft to replace the A-6) had been abandoned in 1994, when funding was withdrawn, although funding for integration of the Joint Direct Attack Munition (JDAM) remained safe. This was a bitter blow, since it was felt that the F-14 urgently needed some kind of FLIR and laser designator with which the aircraft could operate at

night and use LGBs autonomously. The US Navy thus decided to see whether a FLIR could be integrated into the F-14 cheaply enough to fit within the funding allocated for JDAM integration. This inferred the use of an existing system, and the Loral Nite Hawk (used by the F/A-18C/D) and the Martin-Marietta LANTIRN (used by the F-15E and F-16C) were

carefully examined by the US Navy.

Despite the commonality advantages promised by the Nite Hawk, the LANTIRN was selected because of its wider field of regard (a 150° cone from the pod's boresight) and its superior magnification and optional fields of view. For target acquisition, the LANTIRN pod has a wide (5.87°) FoV with

This NAWC Tomcat is seen dropping a salvo of Mk 20 Rockeye cluster bombs from the 'tunnel' during clearance trials.

Left: *This NAWC (AD) F-14A is seen test dropping two 1,000-lb GBU-16 LGBs during February 1994, after the Tomcat had been cleared to drop Mk 80 series GP bombs.*

x4.1 magnification (compared to a narrower FoV with only x4 magnification for Nite Hawk). For target identification and tracking, the narrow FoV (1.68°) gives x10 magnification, while an electronically enhanced expand mode (which is useful for precise positioning of the laser) allows a x20 magnification. The laser operates at 1.56 microns for training, and 1.06 microns in combat.

LANTIRN integration

Fairchild Defense came up with a series of design drawings for a hand-control interface using off-the-shelf hardware and innovative new software to integrate a single Low Altitude Navigation and Targeting Infra-Red for Night (LANTIRN) pod with the F-14. The

aircraft software did not need any modification. In the face of some scepticism, Lockheed Martin was asked by Vice Admiral Richard Allen, COMNAVAIRLANT, to demonstrate the system on a fleet aircraft. The aircraft was an F-14B MCAP (Multimission Capability)-configured aircraft drawn from VF-103 (AA/213), and was modified by a joint team from Martin and the US Navy, headed by Captain Dale Snodgrass, Commander Fighter Wing Atlantic. A prototype hand control interface was mated to a LANTIRN pod (loaned by the USAF) at Fairchild's Germantown, Maryland plant in February 1995, and this was then shipped to Oceana for fitting to the aircraft, which had already been modified to carry a GPS antenna. This antenna was linked to a Litton GPS/IMU (Inertial Measurement Unit) which was itself incorporated into the LANTIRN pod as an Integrated Targeting System (ITS), to avoid the need for the pod to be boresighted to the aircraft, or linked to the aircraft's own analog INS. The LANTIRN pod was carried on the starboard wing glove pylon, with the stub pylon still able to carry an AIM-9 Sidewinder. The use of its own internal GPS

A VF-14 aircraft fires a salvo of 5-in Zuni rockets off the Virginia coast in August 1996. (The 5-in Zuni is being withdrawn in favour of 2.75-in rockets.) The Tomcat community is receiving a Zuni capability as a result of its emerging forward air controller (airborne) (FAC(A)) mission.

A new dimension in F-14 'Bombcat' operations has come with the addition of 2,000-lb GBU-24B/B hard-target penetrator LGB capability.

allowed the pod to find targets without a radar or aircraft-based INS hand-off. The IMU serves a navigation function, but also measures the smallest movements in yaw, velocity and pitch and uses them to stabilise the FLIR's line of sight and picture. In the F-15E and other LANTIRN platforms, the IMU is airframe- rather than pod-mounted, making it less easy to stabilise the LANTIRN's line of sight.

Satellite navigation

During LANTIRN operations, the Tomcat can be navigated to the target area using its own onboard INS, or the pod's GPS. If the target's position is known, the pod's own GPS will automatically point the FLIR at the target, and can provide the pilot with steering commands. They can be displayed overlaid on the VDI (Vertical Display Indicator), superimposed on the FLIR picture. The RIO designates the target using the pod's laser after the pilot releases the weapon, and the pod performs its own BDA by videoing the impact. LANTIRN can be used against targets of opportunity, when the RIO selects the cue-to-HUD mode. This locks the LANTIRN's line of sight to a fixed position in the HUD, and the pilot then manoeuvres that 'dot' onto the target, which the RIO then acquires and identifies. Alternatively, in 'snowplough' mode the LANTIRN's FLIR is depressed by 15°, with the RIO monitoring the picture to search for targets.

The F-14B testbed first flew with LANTIRN on 21 March 1995, in the hands of Commander Alex Hnarakis (VF-103's XO) and his RIO, Lieutenant Commander Larry Slade. The pod worked well, and the F-14B MCAP's big-screen PTIDS actually gave a better picture than was possible in the F-16 or F-15E. After a series of shakedown flights, the aircraft dropped four laser-guided training rounds (LGTRs) on the nearby Dare County range, scoring three bullseyes and a miss. The miss had been dropped outside the LGTR's wind limitations. Four inert GBU-16s dropped at the same range all scored bullseyes. Four live GBU-16s were then dropped at the Vieques range, Puerto Rico, and three of these scored bulls, the fourth missing due to an unrelated guidance failure. VF-103 was

awarded the first Vice Admiral Allen Precision Strike Trophy (named after the retiring admiral who had driven the programme to reality) for its part in clearing the LANTIRN for service use in fewer than 10 months.

A contract for the supply and integration of LANTIRN was negotiated in late 1995, and the first pod was ceremonially accepted by John Dalton (Secretary of the Navy) at Oceana on 14 June 1996. The LANTIRN pod contains its own computer, with all necessary ballistics data, but must interface with the aircraft's AWG-15 via a MIL STD 1553B digital databus, which has to be added to non-MCAP F-14As and F-14Bs if they are to carry the pod. Very few aircraft have been fitted with PTIDS, but this does not prevent the use of LANTIRN, although image quality is severely degraded on the F-14's standard displays. PTID can, of course, display AWG-9 radar

displays and can record them for later analysis. The new displays are being fitted fleet-wide.

VF-103, which traded its 'Sluggers' identity for the 'Jolly Rogers' identity of the disestablished VF-84, began intensive LANTIRN training. During a mini-cruise between 26 April and 17 May 1996, the squadron exercised with the Royal Navy, and even spiked targets for RN Sea Harriers. VF-103 deployed to the Adriatic aboard the USS *Enterprise* on 28 June, with nine of its 14 aircraft being LANTIRN-equipped. Six of these aircraft were further modified to use MXV-810 'Cat's Eye' NVGs, which allow a crew to 'look into the turn' while the FLIR continues to look forward. The addition of NVGs also allowed the squadron's FAC (A) aircrew to practise their art, even during night operations. VF-103's LANTIRN 'Bombcats' were deployed to the Adriatic in support

of Operations Deny Flight and Deliberate Force, following earlier deployments by VF-41 and VF-102.

During VF-103's cruise, the squadron flew over Bosnia and Iraq. LANTIRN was found to have applications beyond the designation of targets for LGBs. The pod proved extremely useful for reconnaissance, recording GPS coordinates for targets. LANTIRN even proved useful in the air-to-air role, with a wider field of regard than the TCS, and may have a longer range. In all roles the MXV-810 NVGs proved highly successful, but the F-14 fleet is already receiving the alternative ANVIS-9 NVG system, with a wider FoV, a tripled light amplification, and a lower unit cost.

LANTIRN confers a degree of night capability, but has no all-weather application, since low cloud and rain severely degrade FLIR imagery. However, the D

'Bombcat' weapons can be carried in the 'tunnel', on modified Phoenix pallets. However, TARPS-capable F-14s cannot carry LANTIRN.

Above and left: The most significant change to the rear cockpit of the 'Bombcat' is the addition of the 8 x 8-in (20 x 20-cm) programmable tactical information display (PTID) which can display radar and LANTIRN information for the RIO. The PTID's side-stick hand controllers (left) were originally manufactured for the A-12 programme and withdrawn from storage for the 'Bombcats'.

model Tomcat's radar is soon to gain the same modes and capabilities as that of the F-15E, which will transform the aircraft into a true all-weather precision attack platform. The APG-71 already has more memory than the APG-70, and it has been estimated that $800 million would give an air-to-ground mapping capability of extraordinary resolution. Moreover, the JDAM and JSOW (Joint Stand-Off Weapon) are both reliant on GPS for guidance, and pre-launch target updates require a GPS-equipped launch aircraft. The LANTIRN Tomcat is today the only aircraft in the US Navy inventory with a suitable GPS. A

current F-14 RIO asserted that, "We are now definitely multi-mission, helping keep us on the cutting edge, and now with LANTIRN pods we're the King Kong of the air-to-ground role, and that's counting all tactical aircraft, bar none! We are getting a multitude of new toys in the next few years to help us maintain our new position as King Kongs of the strike game. It truly has been a renaissance for the F-14 and we are again seeing ourselves on the ATO as major players, and not just as space-fillers!"

It was soon possible to concentrate the much-contracted F-14 force at a single base, and the

Pacific Fleet squadrons at Miramar began to disband or prepare for a move across the continent to NAS Oceana. The Pacific Fleet training unit, VF-124, was disbanded on 30 September 1994 (the last day of FY 1994), when VF-101 at Oceana took over responsibility for training all F-14A aircrew. The Atlantic Fleet FRS parented a new detachment at Miramar for the purpose of training new aircrew for the F-14D, which was used only by the Pacific Fleet squadrons. The first unit to move was VF-2, which changed home port to Oceana on 1 April 1996. This also marked the arrival at Oceana of the F-14D, and marked the end of the need for a separate training unit at Miramar. Accordingly, VF-101's Miramar Detachment returned to Oceana in October 1996, alongside the five surviving front-line Pacific Fleet squadrons. The move, which was completed by June 1997, involved the relocation of VF-211 in August 1996, VF-11 and VF-31 in November 1996 and VF-213 in May 1997. This left Oceana as the Navy's sole Tomcat base, though VF-154 with CVW-5 is based at NAS Atsugi in Japan when not deployed aboard the Seventh Fleet carrier *Independence*.

Even as morale within the Tomcat community reached an all-time high, fate conspired to demonstrate that the aircraft still had its problems. Within a four-week period, three Tomcats were lost in acci-

dents, prompting a 72-hour safety stand-down from which only VF-102 was exempted, to allow them to fly off USS *America* after their Mediterranean cruise. These accidents brought F-14 losses to a massive 144, of 632 delivered. All aircrew had to undergo training in out-of-control flight procedures, flight discipline/SOPs, spin procedures, checklist compliance, crew co-ordination, the ejection decision process, and mission risk analysis before they flew again. The first accident (on 29 January 1996) proved to be a result of pilot error, the aircraft crashing into a civilian home when the pilot (an NFO-to-pilot retread) failed to recover from a steep dive following vertigo, while the last (on 22 February) was the result of a technical failure, although the crew ejected safely. More serious was the accident on 19 February, which killed Commander Scott 'Scooter' Lamoreaux (a former Tomcat squadron commander serving as air operations officer for CruDesGru 3). The aircraft exploded during a supersonic flyby, while in Zone 4/5 afterburner.

Operating restrictions

The accident prompted major operating restrictions for the F-14B and F-14D, including a restriction in the use of afterburner below 10,000 ft (3050 m) for the F-14B, and a speed limit of 550 kt (630 mph; 1015 km/h) below 10,000 ft for the F-14D, or below 17,000 ft (5180 m) when Phoenix pallets were fitted. The problem was traced to blockage of fan duct airflow by a rotated turbine frame turnbuckle. This turnbuckle was redesigned from a round to an elliptical shape. As the new turnbuckle was retrofitted the afterburner restrictions were gradually

This F-14A of the NAWC is seen launching from the US Navy's newest carrier, the John C. Stennis.

*Sea trials of the F-14 **DFCS (Digital Flight Control System)** testbed proved highly successful, and the system is likely to be retrofitted fleet-wide.*

lifted, and today the F-14B and F-14D and their engines have a clean bill of health. The TF30 of the baseline F-14A remains a troubled engine, however, and during one recent carrier deployment one 14-aircraft squadron experienced seven compressor stalls in one month.

The F-14 community is also handicapped by a shortage of the best and most capable versions, especially the F-14D. Only 55 F-14Ds were built, and five were lost in service. Others are used for training by VF-101. The shortage of D model Tomcats is so acute that VF-11 transitioned back to the F-14B in late 1996, leaving only two D-equipped squadrons. From FY 1998 it is intended that five squadrons (VF-2, VF-102, VF-143, VF-103 and VF-31, in that order) will transition to a mix of F-14Ds and F-14Bs. VF-2 will be the first 'mixed' squadron to deploy, in August/September 1999.

Improvements to the F-14 will certainly continue, even if new versions do not emerge. In the air superiority and fleet air defence roles the F-14 will remain in service until it is replaced by a new

interceptor, but in other roles replacement will happen sooner. The introduction of the F/A-18E/F will probably render the aircraft surplus to requirements in the attack role, despite the Tomcat's slightly better payload/range characteristics, and despite the money now being spent on LANTIRN and other systems and mods.

New recce systems

In the reconnaissance role, the TARPS-equipped F-14 will be replaced by 50 ATARS (Advanced Tactical Air Reconnaissance System) systems acquired for the F/A-18E/F. ATARS will be nose-mounted and will include a low-altitude sensor covering a 140° arc below the aircraft (used below 3,000 ft/915 m). The medium-altitude sensor (for use at altitudes up to 25,000 ft/7620 m, and up to 5 miles/8 km from the target) provides limited stand-off capability.

The IRLS is primarily intended for night reconnaissance. The reconnaissance management system, designed by the UK Division of Computing Devices International, is based on that of the RAF's Tornado GR.Mk 1A and can automatically activate the sensors, scan and stabilise images and process them to a common format for recording and transmission by datalink. A separate podded LOROP sensor may be acquired to augment ATARS, while the aircraft will also have the Phase 2 APG-73 radar, which has an impressive high-resolution SAR capability. Since the A/F-X was cancelled in 1993, the F-14 will have to serve until at least 2008 in the fighter role, and will not begin to be replaced by the F/A-18E/F in its other roles until 2001 at the earliest. The F/A-18E/F's importance as a Tomcat replacement can be gauged by the fact that the first

E model prototype wore the insignia of a former Tomcat squadron (VF-142 'Ghostriders') on its port tailfin, with an F/A-18 unit insignia (VFA-131 'Wildcats') to starboard.

The F-14 looks set to remain in widespread service into the next century, when the aircraft will be celebrating 35 years at the sharp end. Fortunately, even the baseline F-14A (which remains in fairly widespread use alongside F-14Bs and F-14Ds after the recent emasculation of the Tomcat fleet) is a highly capable fighter-interceptor, and remains able to defend its carrier battle group against any credible threat – a continuing tribute to the men who created the immortal Tomcat.

Jon Lake, Julian Lake and Robert F. Dorr

*This **NAWC F-14D** was one of the aircraft used in trials aboard the Stennis **during 1996, before the carrier deployed operationally.***

Chapter Ten

'Bombcats' over Bosnia ...and beyond

The war in Bosnia marked the operational debut of the F-14 in its new multi-role incarnation – as the 'Bombcat'. Lt Todd Parker, a RIO with VF-41, provides the personal view which forms the backbone of this examination of the F-14's most recent operational exploits.

Following the end of the Gulf War, the US Navy returned to its routine of peacetime training and operational commitments, though it soon became clear that with the end of the Cold War confrontation between the USA and the Soviet Union, the world had become a more unstable and more dangerous place. Feuding and revolution erupted within a number of former Soviet client states and allies, which might once have been kept inert by pressure from the USSR, in case they had escalated into more dangerous conflicts. With the benefit of hindsight, it soon also became clear that the war to liberate Kuwait had not been brought to a properly resolved conclusion. With Saddam Hussein still in power, the UN had to supervise and monitor the destruction of prohibited weapons of mass destruction, while in the north and south of Iraq, the Iraqi regime car-

ried out military operations against its own people, Kurd and Marsh Arab alike. This was not something to which the international community could acquiesce, and multi-national operations were quickly established to protect 'No-Fly Zones' over the areas, to try to prevent further military operations and to allow humanitarian relief operations to be undertaken without interference from the Iraqi military.

The US Navy had a crucial part to play in these operations, using aircraft from its aircraft-carriers operating in the Mediterranean and the Red Sea. With the failure of US-sponsored covert attempts to topple Saddam Hussein, even more emphasis was placed on monitoring and enforcing UN resolutions relating to Iraq, and on maintaining a strict regime of sanctions. While tensions remained high in the Middle East and eastern Mediterranean, further hotspots followed

Below: Author of this chapter Lt Todd Parker poses with friend and pilot Lt Jesse Fox during the 1995 cruise. Parker flew with another pilot on the mission described.

Above: The 'Black Aces' went to war during Operation Deliberate Force, with an initial two-aircraft strike on 5 September 1995, using GBU-16 laser-guided bombs.

within months of the completion of Desert Storm.

Perhaps the most significant of these was in the Balkans, where Yugoslavia rapidly began to fragment, torn into separate states by its ethnically, religiously and politically diverse population.

UN intervention

First of the regions of the former Federal Republic of Yugoslavia to secede was Slovenia in 1991, after a short but violent civil war, followed by Croatia. Slovenia rapidly returned to a peaceful normality, but bitter conflict continued in Croatia, largely due to the presence of two major Serb enclaves within the territory of the new republic, Slavonia and Krajina. The first UN intervention in the former Yugoslavia came in the form of peacekeeping/ceasefire-monitoring forces in Croatia.

Once Croatia and Slovenia had demanded their independence, it was only a matter of time before Bosnia-Herzegovina followed suit. Here, if anything, the situation was even more complex than in the other areas, since half of the population were Muslims, and the rest were broadly equally divided between Croat and Serb. The bloody civil war which began in April 1992 was more often than not a two-sided struggle between Serb and Muslim, with the Croats usually supporting the Muslims.

Carriers in the Adriatic

While remaining neutral, the UN did recognise the new Muslim government in Sarajevo, and began a humanitarian airlift into the new state, while simultaneously trying to uphold an arms embargo against

the Serbs, and particularly attempting to prevent the flow of arms into Bosnia. Forces involved in these operations were primarily based at Italian airfields, though US Navy aircraft-carriers also played their part, operating in the Adriatic. Operation Sky Monitor began in November 1992, and monitored the ban on military flights in Bosnian airspace. This gave way to Operation Deny Flight in March 1993, when the UN authorised its air commanders to forcibly prevent Serbian and Bosnian Serb attacks. From 22 June 1993, allied aircraft were authorised to fly close air support missions in support of UN peacekeepers, and armed CAS aircraft began flying 'cab-rank' type patrols, ready to respond to the call

for action. Carrierborne F-14s were heavily involved in the policing of the UN-imposed 'No-Fly Zones', and in providing air cover for transport aircraft conducting humanitarian relief operations. The Tomcats flew regular combat air patrols, looking for violations of the UN resolutions, and for unauthorised air activity by the combatants. NATO generally kept pairs of fighters airborne at two CAP stations for 24 hours per day, day-in, day-out. This had the desired effect, keeping the Bosnian Serb air force on the ground at Banja Luka, and preventing violations of Bosnian airspace by the Krajina Serb's air arm, based at Udbina. Serb helicopters were frequently found violating Bosnian airspace, but

Above: One of VF-41's F-14s refuels from an air force KC-10, as a USAF F-16 waits its turn to top off its tanks, 'somewhere off the coast of Bosnia'. Before the Deliberate Force strikes, VF-41 flew TARPS, XCAS and even FAC(A) missions.

inevitably landed when challenged, resuming their activities once NATO fighters had left the area. USAF F-16s shot down four Serb Galebs in February 1994, but, generally, the rules of engagement were too tightly drawn to allow the F-14s to engage the enemy.

Below: A pair of VF-103 F-14s cruises over the Adriatic during a training mission (note the blue-coloured Sidewinder drill rounds). During Bosnia operations F-14s routinely refuel from USAF KC-135s.

'Bombcats' over Bosnia

The work, though useful, was thus somewhat tedious and generally uneventful until August 1994, when attacks on Serb ground targets began in earnest. There was some useful training value even during the unproductive CAP missions however, with the Tomcat crews getting the opportunity to fly beside a wide variety of allied aircraft, and to take on gas from a very wide range of tanker types. Once offensive operations began, the F-14's role was increased dramatically in scope, with aircraft flying pre- and post-strike recce missions using the TARPS pod, and with the 'Bombcat' capability finally being exploited.

The message from Commanding Officer, VF-41 to Commander, Fighter Wing, US Atlantic Fleet was deceptively powerful in its simplicity: Maybe not a Zuni through the sunroof, but how about four GBU-16s on an ammunition storage depot, TOT (time on target) 16.15 local. This historic flight would mark the culmination of a remarkable rebirth of the F-14.

Lieutenant Todd Parker was a RIO with VF-41 during that squadron's 1995-1996 Adriatic cruise, as he describes.

A lethal team

Anyone familiar with naval aviation, and the continually evolving persona it undertakes, knows that change is not only constant but necessary. As theatres follow a sinewave pattern of action and intensity, and corresponding threats upgrade and shift, the carrier battle group is the pre-eminent force to meet the challenges head on. Responding unlike any other force in the world in its combination of speed and intensity, the carrier air wing is the sword of the warrior that is the battle group. Accelerating the upcoming retirement of one of the distinguished members of this lethal team – the A-6 Intruder – identified a shortfall in the air wing's capability. The carrier air wing projects power, and power projection equals bombs on target. All other missions support attack. The demise of the A-6, combined with the A-12 cancellation, meant that the number of aircraft capable of using air-to-ground ordnance had to be increased with existing aircraft. Thus began the five-year metamorphosis of the Tomcat from fleet air defender and strike escort to a multi-mission, self-escorted strike-fighter unparalleled in naval aviation in its combination of performance, precision, and payload, day or night.

As recently as six or seven years ago, anyone who said Tomcats would be patrolling the skies of the former Republic of Yugoslavia loaded with laser-guided bombs awaiting strike, close air support (CAS), or forward air controller (airborne) – FAC(A) – missions would have been called insane. Yet here I was, just 20 miles (32 km) southeast of downtown Sarajevo, en route to a target with two 1,000-lb laser-guided bombs known as GBU-16s.

Normally, at five months and one week into a cruise, one has seen and done just about everything there is. Not this time. The night before what was to be our last port visit, we felt that familiar rumble of the propeller shafts, and noticed that the ship's heading was due west, not the north-northwest heading that would have taken us to Rhodes. Several days earlier, Bosnian Serb artillery had shelled a market in Sarajevo, in clear violation of United Nations' restrictions. Once again, our presence in-theatre was requested.

'Black Aces' go to war

First though, a little background on how we got to this point.

I had been a radar intercept officer (RIO) in VF-41 for three years when we deployed in March 1995 as a member of Carrier Air Wing Eight on board USS *Theodore Roosevelt* (CVN-71). This team had proved its lethality in the Gulf War, and those of us who had missed that opportunity were eagerly anticipating our shot. Things had been quiet in Bosnia for many months, primarily because of the winter weather, but we knew that the spring thaw usually meant increased hostilities. From the Tomcat standpoint, we were especially excited about the chance to employ a truly multi-mission capable aircraft. In addition to our standard combat air patrol and fleet air defence roles, we would be flying exercise close air support (XCAS), tactical reconnaissance, and the newly emerging Navy mission of FAC(A).

After an uneventful six-week stint in the Red Sea and the Persian Gulf, we transitted back through the Suez Canal to the Adriatic, with tensions in the area rising as expected. Once on station, we immediately began planning contingency operations, for clashes between the Bosnian Serbs and Bosnian Muslims were already occurring daily. Unfortunately, the first four missions that launched off the carrier – all CAS and FAC(A) missions – were as anticlimactic as the three months that followed. In what became a routine drill for aircrew and planners alike, we would plan all night for a bombing mission we were certain would launch at first light, only to be shut down, sometimes literally, just before launch. This is not to say there were not exciting moments, such as the shootdown of USAF F-16 pilot Captain Scott O'Grady by a surface-to-air missile, the one-night bombing of ammunition storage depots in Pale by the Marines and Air Force, the Bosnian Serb takeover of Zepa and Srebenica, and the two-day offensive by the Croatians to reclaim the area in Eastern Croatia that the Krajina Serbs had claimed as theirs for two years. Each event brought an intense 24- to 36-hour planning period, followed by the wait for the word to launch, which never came. As might be expected, after doing this many times over three months, morale can suffer, and it became increasingly difficult to muster motivation to plan a mission that we doubted would ever launch. But, plan we did.

On to the eastern Med

The time between these larger-scale events was by no means boring. The air wing flew daily missions as tasked by the Combined Air Operations Center in Vicenza, Italy. EA-6B Prowlers patrolled the sky providing electronic protection. E-2 Hawkeyes were the 'eye in the sky', acting as the command, control and communications link between Navy aircraft and the joint command and control system. S-3Bs and ES-3As provided electronic support. F/A-18 Hornets provided CAP, XCAS and HARM support. Tomcats flew XCAS, TARPS and FAC(A) missions 'feet dry', but along with all other UN aircraft they were restricted to 'feet wet' for CAP missions. Whenever possible, the carrier would pull in for a quick port visit in Corfu or Trieste, but there was always the tether of a short recall to worry about.

En route to what was supposed to be our second-to-last port visit in Marseilles, Saddam Hussein's two sons-in-law decided to defect, which proved to be the beginning of a dramatically altered last two months of cruise. Instead of pulling into port, we transited from the

GBU-16 bombs (laser-guided 1,000-lb Mk 83s) nestle under a Tomcat during Bosnia operations. Navy bombs differ from those of the USAF by having a grey ablative coating for fireproofing.

Adriatic to the eastern Med and stationed ourselves off the coast of Israel. By 28 August the situation had defused, and we finally got the OK to start our trek west. The next stop would be our last port visit in Rhodes, followed by a turnover with USS *America* (CV-66) in the western Med, and finally the trip home. But, as mentioned earlier, late that evening the propellers started churning the water faster than usual, and *Roosevelt* sped back to the Adriatic.

Returning to the warzone

We assumed that – like in every other instance of increased hostilities – we would plan all night only to see another opportunity lost. What made this instance different, and therefore even more difficult, was that we were supposed to be pulling into port and then on our way home. Instead, we were returning to an uncertain area with even more uncertain intentions. However, it was not our job to

question those intentions, so once again we began the now-familiar planning exercise.

Even though the first events manned up, and even launched, we still did not believe that anything would actually happen. So when the first aircraft returned shortly after 02.00 on 30 August with its racks and rails empty, we could hardly contain our surprise and excitement. Finally, after so much hard work and so little return, we were getting the chance to prove ourselves.

The main question on our minds was, "How can we get the Tomcats to play?"

At that point, our role of suppression of enemy air defences (SEAD) was critical, and our TARPS flights were crucial for the intelligence picture, but the opportunity to be the first F-14 to drop live ordnance in combat was the gold at the end of the rainbow. Once the Combined Air Operations Center was aware that Tom-

cats could indeed drop air-to-ground ordnance, the question became how and when it would be best to do so. At the time, we were not carrying the LANTIRN pod, which now provides Tomcats with a day or night, self-escort, self-lased precision-guided munitions (PGM) capability. We were still a lethal day iron-bomb dropper, and we could employ any of the laser-guided bombs as long as someone lased the target for us.

An initial target was finally identified – an ammunition depot in eastern Bosnia. Because of potential collateral damage issues, this was a PGM target only, which meant that the Tomcats would drop their LGBs off a buddy-lase from a Hornet. We were not surprised that the 'food chain' theory applied here, with this historic flight being top heavy rank-wise.

Two F-14s launched with the Hornet flight, yet there was still the question of whether drop authority would really come for this unusual

delivery tactic. Imagine the feeling of excitement when, two hours later, those same two Tomcats came back with their belly stations empty, except for the dangling arming wire that remains after the release of an electrically fused weapon. The review of the FLIR tapes (the same tapes commonly seen on television on CNN) proved that the planning and diligence had paid off: two bombs, two direct hits, and a history-making day for VF-41 and the Tomcat community at large.

Dumb-bomb targets

The success of this mission set the stage for future ones. The next live-ordnance flight for the Tomcats was a dumb-bomb target, selected carefully for its relative isolation and lesser potential for

'Bombcat' Boss in Bosnia

Commander Bob Brauer, USN, Officer Commanding, VF-41 'Black Aces', was interviewed shortly after his return from the Adriatic:

"I've been flying the F-14 since 1982, and have accumulated over 2,200 flying hours in the aircraft. My total time is about 3,800 flying hours. During the summer and fall of 1995 we flew a lot of missions operating off the coast of Bosnia as part of Operation Deliberate Force. We – VF-41 – were the only Tomcat squadron aboard the USS *Roosevelt*, along with three squadrons of F/A-18 Hornets. (They were VMFA-312, VFA-15 and VFA-87.)

"In September 1995 we had the opportunity to make the F-14's first-ever delivery of air-to-ground ordnance in combat. We delivered laser-guided munitions and free-fall Mk 82 bombs. I got to participate in the first strike, which involved one section of F/A-18s and one section of F-14s, flying as mixed sections. The F-14s each carried two 1,000-lb laser-guided bombs, and the Hornets carried the same load. That was the first time we had a chance to do the laser delivery in a mixed section, though we had previously done a lot of practice on this at NAS Fallon and while working Deny Flight in the Arabian Gulf. The first time we actually got to do this with live bombs was in Bosnia. There was no air-to-air threat at the time. The surface-to-air threat was significant in some areas, but had been pretty well beat down.

"On the day of the first strike the weather was a big factor, and it continued to be a factor into the winter months. As we launched off the ship and headed in over the coast, it didn't look like the strike was going to go because of an undercast. But about 10 miles (16 km) out from the target the weather cleared, and we could see the target well out.

"We rolled in at a very steep angle, from high altitude, against some ammunition facilities. The F-14s dropped while the F/A-18s lased. We egressed the target area having achieved absolutely superb results from direct hits, and there were impressive secondary explosions.

"It was an incredible feeling as the 1,000-lb bombs kicked off the aircraft. Even in a 50° dive and at nearly 500 kt (575 mph; 925 km/h) you could feel the release. I pulled the nose up, rolled and looked back over my shoulder to see the bombs impact on the target.

"I can recall another mission over Bosnia in which some of our junior pilots were able to go in on the target and drop Mk 80 series bombs, with excellent results. They picked up some very valuable experience.

"The F-14s are now getting LANTIRN pods. VF-41 will get a LANTIRN capability in the next few months and will deploy with it when we do our major cruise in April 1997. Then we will be able to lase our own bombs and lase for someone else as well.

"One major benefit of all of this is the fact that the F-14 can launch with a heavy load of laser munitions and can also bring it all back aboard if something like bad weather prevents us from reaching the target area. This is a distinct edge we have over the F/A-18 Hornet, which has similar carriage capabilities. But due to fuel and weight considerations the Hornet has to get its bombs off, and if for some reason they can't drop their ordnance they must jettison it before landing back on the carrier. Another plus for the F-14 is that it can carry a very significant air-to-air load: a Phoenix, a Sparrow and some Sidewinders, plus a couple of 1,000-lb LGBs. It can fight its way to the target, drop the bombs and fight its way back out. It's a self-escort mission for us!"

Warren Thompson

'Fast Eagle 101' was the aircraft assigned to VF-41's skipper, Cdr Bob Brauer, interviewed above. It is seen here about to launch from the deck of the USS Theodore Roosevelt for the Tomcat's first live bombing mission against Serb targets during Operation Deliberate Force. The 'Black Aces' of VF-41 have now set two important operational milestones in the Tomcat's long and glorious career. It was VF-41 which shot down two Libyan Su-22 'Fitters' over the Gulf of Sidra in August 1981 – marking the F-14's first air combat victories. Some 14 years later, the same squadron became the first to drop bombs on enemy targets from the same aircraft type. VF-41 could justifiably claim to be the 'first to fight' in either Tomcat or 'Bombcat'.

collateral damage. This particular target happened to be a radio-relay station on top of a mountain. Three Tomcats ingressed on a self-escort mission, and, after making two passes each over the sight, all tasked targets were destroyed with four Mk 83 1,000-lb unguided bombs each. Tomcat bombing missions continued throughout the week, until they became almost routine. Weather was a significant factor, and it became luck of the draw whether an individual Tomcat pilot or RIO got his chance to be part of history.

In the meantime, Tomcats continued to fly other missions in support of the effort. Most notable were the TARPS missions, generally flown in co-ordination with strike missions to provide immediate feedback on the success of the operations. The nature of these missions often caused them to be the most dangerous flown in-

Below: VF-84 deployed to the Adriatic aboard the USS Roosevelt between March and September 1993, alongside three F/A-18 units.

country. Tasking typically included targets just attacked, or significant threat locations, which meant that these aircraft were often asked to fly into an aroused hornets' nest. Combine this with the lower altitudes for TARPS flights, and you have a recipe for excitement.

One particular ridgeline south of Sarajevo over which we were routinely tasked to fly was especially notable for the high surface-to-air threat activity coming from it. On one flight over this ridgeline, the crews noticed AAA fired at them, a relatively common experience. What they did not see this time was the shoulder-fired SAM, which was launched from behind them but did not reach them. It was not until they returned to the carrier that they saw their passage southeast of Sarajevo recorded live on CNN, complete with a missile smoke-trail rising up toward their aircraft before trailing off behind them. Despite these dangers, TARPS missions continued daily, and proved to be crucial for intelligence gathering.

In the meantime, the *America* battle group had arrived on station eager to turn over and participate in the action. The majority of the *Roosevelt* battle group had already begun its journey home, with only the carrier and its Aegis escort remaining. The *America* battle group immediately assumed the duties of protecting both carriers, while *Roosevelt* and *America* began their turnover.

Carrier turnover

Normally, a turnover lasts only one or two days, but these were not normal circumstances. The CAOC wanted uninterrupted carrier air missions, yet was concerned about *America* picking up the full load of duties on its first day on station in an unfamiliar region. The turnover therefore lasted several days, with *Roosevelt* initially flying all of the missions and *America* picking up an increasingly larger share.

On the evening of 11 September, the rumours began circulating that the next day *Roosevelt* would

be released to transit back home. Even though we were already two weeks late for the scheduled start of our return, everyone had mixed feelings about leaving. We were anxious to return home, but no one really wanted to leave the theatre. Several of us in the Tomcat squadron were especially disappointed, since we had not yet dropped live ordnance in combat, and it appeared we would not get the chance. So I went to sleep that night with conflicting emotions.

I had only slept for two hours when the phone rang, and I was told to come up to the ready room immediately. We had just received word that the CAOC had ordered one more strike from the *Roosevelt*, to be launched first thing in the morning. We had spent the last several nights attempting to beat down the threats – in the western

and northern parts of Bosnia with HARMs and Tomahawk cruise missiles – and now there was a priority target that was deemed reasonably safe to bomb. The request for a mixed F/A-18/F-14 strike package was approved, and we began flight planning well after midnight. By 04.00 we were tired but satisfied with the plan, and we retired to our staterooms for a few hours of rest before the mission launched.

I awoke feeling excited and alert, despite the few hours of sleep I had managed to log. We briefed for the flight, and as we manned up the aircraft we were relieved that there were no changes to the mission. The plan was relatively simple: eight targets at an ammunition

Below: VF-102 'Diamondbacks' was the F-14A squadron aboard the USS America, which replaced the Roosevelt on station in the Adriatic in September 1995. Apart from Kennedy (which deployed in 1992) all carriers had only one F-14 unit.

'Bombcats' over Bosnia

Below: Tomcats wait on the deck of the **Roosevelt** between sorties, while one of the carrier's **SH-60Fs** hovers alongside. The **SH-60F** has replaced the **SH-3** in the inner-zone **ASW** and plane-guard roles.

Below: From May 1992, there was always a US Navy carrier on duty in the Adriatic. The ships involved were successively the **Saratoga**, the **Kennedy**, the **Roosevelt**, the **America**, the **Saratoga**, the **Washington**, the **Roosevelt**, the **America**, and, from September 1995, the **Roosevelt** again. The F-14's formidable night/all-weather capabilities made the aircraft a particularly useful addition to Operation Deny Flight.

Above: VF-102 had an eventful Adriatic cruise, but did not have an opportunity to engage the enemy. The America's air wing included three F/A-18 units, one of them (VMFA-251) from the USMC.

Left: F-14As of VF-102 'Diamondbacks' are seen ranged on the deck of the USS America in the Adriatic. America was replaced on station by the Roosevelt, carrying the F-14As of VF-41, 'Black Aces'.

storage depot, one for each aircraft. The Hornets would each lase their own target and would then reattack to buddy lase for their Tomcat wingmen. I was the fourth aircraft in the lead division, which would be followed shortly after by the second division.

Approaching the target, the excitement grew as we realised our pre-flight chart study had paid off and we had found the target. The first three attacks went off without a hitch, scoring direct hits with secondaries observed. We set up for our attack, ensuring that we were meeting our pre-planned parameters exactly.

Pickle button

When we reached our release point, with confirmation of a good lase from the Hornet, my pilot pressed the pickle button. After what seemed like a millennium, but was actually only milliseconds, the clunk-clunk of two 1,000-lb laser-guided bombs coming off resonated beautifully through the aircraft. We jinked off target and looked down to check for threats and spot our hits. Fortunately, we were nearly directly abeam our target when the bombs hit, and two enormous explosions verified what we already sensed – this mission was a success. We headed back to the carrier, hearing over our tactical frequency that the second division had achieved similar success. When we got back on board and reviewed the tapes, the success of the mission was overwhelming. Of the eight targets, seven were completely destroyed, with no restrike required.

After the excitement of the flight began to diminish, and we settled back into our routine, the ship's intercom whistled with the familiar sounds preceding a message from the captain. Instead of the usual, "Good evening, this is the captain," we heard music accompanying the words "Westbound and down, loaded up and trucking ... we got a long way to go, and a short time to get there."

Minutes earlier, the captain had received the OK to pack up and ship out. The ship, due home in eight days, would require almost record-breaking speed to get there on time. Miraculously, the approval came for 'all ahead, warp speed', and without the rest of the battle group to slow the ship down, *Roosevelt* wasted no time. It wasn't until it was all over that everyone really had a chance to reflect on what we had been a part of, and to realise that we in VF-41 had become a part of Tomcat history. The 'Black Aces', with the first F-14 air-to-air kills in 1981, had been the 'First to Fight', and now 14 years later we had been the 'First to Strike'.

Lieutenant Todd Parker
Lieutenant Parker is a RIO currently assigned to Strike Weapons and Tactics School, Atlantic (SWATSLANT)

Grumman F-14
Tomcat Operators

United States Navy

Today the US Navy no longer has two separate F-14 Tomcat forces, one supporting COMNAVAIRLANT and one supporting COMNAVAIRPAC. Instead, the US Navy has a single F-14 fighter wing based at NAS Oceana; it provides aircraft for deployments on both Atlantic and Pacific fleet carriers, coming under the control of COMNAVAIRLANT or COMNAVAIRPAC when deployed. COMNAVAIRLANT is responsible for providing combat-ready forces to fleet commanders operating from the North Pole to the Antarctic and between the USA's eastern seaboard and the Indian Ocean. The numbered fleets in COMNAVAIRLANT's area of responsibility are the Second in the Atlantic and the Sixth in the Mediterranean. COMNAVAIRPAC is responsible for providing combat-ready forces to fleet commanders operating from

the North Pole to the Antarctic and between the Indian Ocean and the Pacific Coast of the USA. The numbered fleets in COMNAVAIRPAC's area of responsibility are the Third and the Seventh. All fleet Tomcat squadrons are controlled by Fighter Wing Atlantic (Fighter Wing One) at NAS Oceana when shore-based, but deploy with numbered air wings (CVWs) when deployed aboard the carriers of the Atlantic Fleet. The sole FRS (Fleet Replenishment Squadron) is now VF-101, which does not deploy and thus is not listed in the order of battle below. Since September 1994, VF-101 has become the single Tomcat training unit, following the disestablishment of VF-124. Similarly not included in the order of battle below are the various test and trials units. The US Navy has reduced its front-line strength from 11 to 10 air wings and from

This section (pair) of F-14As is from VF-102 'Diamondbacks', an Oceana-based squadron which has become the sole Tomcat unit within Air Wing One. The squadron's aircraft have worn a variety of toned-down markings, including dark and light grey unit insignia, and (on some aircraft) dull red. The USA inscription at the base of the rudder is noteworthy, and reflects the unit's then-assignment to the USS America, now retired. Air Wing One now serves aboard the USS George Washington.

two to one Reserve air wings. The reductions have affected the F-14 community disproportionately, since most air wings have reduced from two to one F-14 squadrons, gaining an extra F/A-18 unit to give additional fighter-attack capability. CVW-6 and CVW-15 have now disappeared, as has the second Reserve wing, CVW-30. Some F-14 operators have already disbanded, including VF-1 'Wolfpack', VF-21 'Freelancers', VF-24 'Fighting Renegades', VF-33 'Starfighters', VF-51 'Screaming Eagles', VF-74 'Bedevilers', VF-111

'Sundowners', VF-114 'Aardvarks', VF-124 'Gunfighters', VF-142 'Ghostriders', VF-191 'Satan's Kittens', VF-194 'Red Lightnings', VF-202 'Superheats', VF-301 'Devil's Disciples', and VF-302 'Stallions'. Only Air Wings Eight and Fourteen have second F-14 squadrons, and each may lose a squadron, bringing the front-line strength to only 10 units.

The next development in the F-14 community will be the formation of mixed squadrons, operating both F-14Bs and F-14Ds alongside each other.

One of VF-103's F-14As launches from the USS Ranger. Ranger has since decommissioned, and the 'Sluggers' have transitioned to the re-engined F-14B with Air Wing 17 aboard the Eisenhower, and have taken over the identity and distinctive skull-and-crossbones markings of the decommissioned VF-84 'Jolly Rogers'. In this guise, VF-103 has pioneered the latest and perhaps most important development in the F-14 community for many years – the introduction of LANTIRN, which transforms the aircraft into a potent night attack aircraft, with a genuine autonomous precision strike capability.

The Fleet F-14 community today

Air Wing One (USS George Washington – CVN-73)
VF-102 'Diamondbacks' F-14B (AB-100)
Air Wing Two (USS Constellation – CV-64)
VF-2 'Bounty Hunters' F-14D (NE-100)
Air Wing Three (USS Theodore Roosevelt – CVN-71)
VF-32 'Swordsmen' F-14A (AC-100)
Air Wing Five (USS Independence – CV-62)
VF-154 'Black Knights' F-14A (NH-100)
Air Wing Seven (USS John C. Stennis – CVN-74)
VF-143 'Pukin' Dogs' F-14B (AG-100)
Air Wing Eight (USS John F. Kennedy – CV-67)
VF-41'Black Aces' F-14A (AJ-100)
VF-14 'Tophatters' F-14A (AJ-200)
Air Wing Nine (USS Nimitz – CVN-68)
VF-211 'Fighting Checkmates' F-14B (NG-100)
Air Wing Eleven (USS Kitty Hawk – CV-63)
VF-213 'Black Lions' F-14A (NH-100)
Air Wing Fourteen (USS Carl Vinson – CVN-70)
VF-11 'Red Rippers' F-14B (NK-100)
VF-31 'Tomcatters' F-14D (NK-200)
Air Wing Seventeen (USS Dwight D. Eisenhower – CVN-69)
VF-103 'Jolly Rogers' F-14B (AA-200)
Air Wing Twenty (Atlantic Fleet Reserve air wing, NAS Fort Worth, Joint Reserve Base)
VF-201 'Hunters' F-14A (AF-100)

VF-1 'Wolfpack'

The first of the front-line Pacific Fleet F-14 squadrons to form, VF-1 was formally commissioned on 14 October 1972, receiving its first F-14As on 1 July 1973. The squadron's first deployment with Air Wing 14 was aboard the USS *Enterprise* and took place between 12 September 1974 and 19 May 1975, the first F-14 embarking for pre-cruise training on 18 March 1974. Together with the F-14As of sister squadron VF-2, VF-1's 12 Tomcats flew 20 operational combat air patrol missions in support of Operation Frequent Wind, the evacuation of Saigon. The aircraft were fired upon by 37-mm AAA, but were not hit. Nor did they have the opportunity to use their weapons in anger. During the WestPac tour, VF-1 flew a total of 850 sorties, and clocked up 1,400 flying hours. Unfortunately, the squadron also lost two F-14As after engine failures, but in both accidents the crews were able to eject successfully. These accidents signalled the fan-blade containment problems which plagued early versions of the TF30 turbofan. Second and third WestPac cruises (between 30 July 1976 and 28 March 1977, and 4 April and 3 October 1978) were made aboard the USS *Enterprise*.

VF-1 transferred to CVW-2 and USS *Ranger* (CV-60) in September 1980, embarking for WestPac/Indian Ocean cruises between 10 September 1980 and 5 May 1981 (for the Iranian and Afghan crises) and 7 April and 18 October 1982. During 1982, VF-1 won the CNO safety award for five years and 17,000 flying hours without an accident, as well as the prestigious Admiral Joseph Clifton award for the Navy's top fighter squadron (this returned to VF-1 in 1990, along with a Battle E). The squadron remained with Air Wing Two during a subsequent 13 January to 1 August 1984 cruise aboard USS *Kitty Hawk* (CV-63), and then moved back to *Ranger* (albeit still with Air Wing Two) later that year, undertaking NorPac cruises (18 August to 20 October 1986, and 2 March to 29 April 1987), and WestPac/Indian Ocean cruises (14 July to 29 December 1987 and 24 February to 24 August 1989) with CVW-2. VF-1 was able to add to its reputation between cruises, most notably in 1988 when exercises against USAF F-15s went exceptionally well, three squadron crews graduated from 'Topgun', and four AIM-54s and 10 AIM-7s were fired.

During the Gulf War, VF-1 embarked aboard *Ranger* with CVW-2 for an Indian Ocean/Persian Gulf cruise between 8 December 1990 and 8 June 1991, and was the only F-14 unit to gain an aerial victory.

One of the squadron's aircraft (162603/NE-103), flown by Lt. Stuart Broce and with RIO (and squadron CO) Lt Cdr Ron McElraft, scored the Tomcat's only air-to-air victory in Desert Storm by downing an Iraqi Mil Mi-8 'Hip' helicopter on 6 February 1991. The apparent lack of success of the Tomcat during Operation Desert Storm was mainly due to coalition policy of assigning target aircraft to F-15s; the F-14 was strictly constrained to an escort role. The F-14's lack of fully USAF-compatible IFF was a major factor in determining where the F-14s could patrol.

A further CVW-2/*Ranger* cruise was undertaken in the Indian Ocean and Persian Gulf between 1 August 1992 and 31 January 1993, participating in Operations Southern Watch and Provide Relief, after relieving *Independence* in the Gulf on 15 September. This was, however, to be the squadron's final deployment. With the rundown in the Tomcat fleet, and with USS *Ranger* slated to be among the first of the US Navy's carriers to embark only a single F-14 squadron, VF-1's proposed conversion

to the F-14D and planned transfer to the USS *Constellation* were cancelled. VF-1 finally disestablished on 1 October 1993, having dropped out halfway through the conversion training cycle and transferring some personnel to sister unit VF-2, leaving

CVW-2 with a single F-14 squadron. Other sources suggest that VF-1 disestablished one day earlier, on 30 September 1993 (the last day of the fiscal year). Either way, the 'Wolfpack' and its famous 'Wichita' callsign were no more.

Above: A VF-1 F-14A escorts a prowling 'Bear-F Mod 2'. The Tomcat's ability to intercept its targets far out from the carrier is highly prized.

Above: In 1978, VF-1's F-14As were almost as colourful as they had been when the squadron received its Tomcats, with red and white insignia over a glossy light gull grey finish. Only the white undersides and control surfaces were missing. By 1980 only a tiny wolf's head, with no tail stripes, was carried.

Left: For a squadron normally known as the 'Wolfpack' it was appropriate that the animal should have featured so prominently on the unit's flying suit patch and aircraft tail markings. Many find it hard to believe that Fighter Squadron One no longer exists.

Above: In May 1977, VF-1's CAG-bird received a disruptive splinter camouflage – colloquially known as the 'Heater-Ferris' scheme – invented by artist Keith Ferris, and amended by a US Navy F-14 pilot named Heatley. The pattern incorporates a black 'false canopy' under the nose.

Right: Another experimental camouflage scheme worn by VF-1 Tomcats was this three-tone grey camouflage. Unit insignia was applied in a paler grey.

VF-2 'Bounty Hunters'

First formed on 1 July 1922, VF-2 was the first naval fighter squadron to be deployed aboard an aircraft-carrier (the USS *Langley*, CV-1). The squadron's use of a red, white and blue diagonal stripe (the carrier's marking) dates from this period, although the stripe is now often applied now in three shades of grey. The unit flew Vought VE-7SF, Boeing FB-1 and Curtiss F6C-1 fighters. From 1 January 1927 (when the squadron disbanded and recommissioned on the same day) until the beginning of World War II, the unit was known as the 'Fighting Chiefs' or the 'Chiefs' Squadron' because – in an unusual and farsighted experiment – its pilots were all enlisted men. The enlisted pilots were transferred to instructor's duties or commissioned after Pearl Harbor. The squadron disestablished on 1 July 1942, after its carrier, the *Lexington*, was lost at Coral Sea. A third VF-2 commissioned on 2 June 1943 with F6F Hellcats, serving with great distinction

Seen in August 1977, this 'Bullets' F-14A wears a variation of the original squadron colour scheme with the traditional squadron badge displacing the tailcodes onto the inner faces of the tailfins.

aboard *Enterprise* and *Hornet*, destroying 261 enemy aircraft in air-to-air combat before disestablishing on 9 November 1945.

The fourth VF-2 was established as an F-14 unit on 14 October 1972, receiving its first aircraft in July 1973. Unusually, the squadron had no history with the F-4 Phantom or F-8 Crusader, having been dormant since the end of World War II. The squadron's history closely followed that of its sister squadron VF-1, the 'Bounty Hunters' partnering the 'Wolfpack' with CVW-14 and CVW-2 for cruises aboard the *Enterprise, Ranger* and *Kitty Hawk* between 1974 and 1993. VF-2's aircraft suffered the

same engine failures as those of VF-1, caused by the fan blade containment problem, but fortunately VF-2 escaped the aircraft losses which bedevilled VF-1's first cruise. During the first cruise, between September 1974 and May 1975, like VF-1, the 'Bounty Hunters' flew combat air patrols during Operation Frequent Wind, the final humiliating evacuation of the last US personnel from Vietnam. They did not engage the enemy, but made history as the last Navy fighters involved in the long and costly Vietnam war. VF-2 provided about half of the aircrew involved in the 1976-77 ACEVAL/AIMVAL evaluations at Nellis AFB.

though they transferred to VX-4 ('Evaluators') for the duration of the evaluation. The other aircrew came from VF-1. The squadron also provided some of the aircraft (Block 90 F-14As) involved in the evaluation, these being painted in the splinter-pattern 'Ferris' camouflage scheme. Between them, VF-1 and VF-2 provided three constituted sections, each with two crews.

During the squadron's second cruise, however, things did not go so smoothly, and VF-2 lost an aircraft in a landing accident off the Philippines.

By May 1981, VF-2 had returned to form, and won the COMNAVAIRPAC Battle E awarded to the best West Coast fighter unit, and the Mutha trophy awarded to the best Miramar-based F-14 squadron, also winning the 1981 ComFitAEWWingPAC fighter derby and clocking up its 10,000th accident-free flying hour. TARPS-configured Tomcats were taken on charge during 1981, with VF-2 aircrew returning to 'school' with VF-2 to learn to use the new system and the techniques involved in flying tactical reconnaissance missions. The seven-month 1982 cruise aboard the *Ranger* (beginning in March) allowed the squadron (the second West Coast TARPS unit to deploy) to develop many of the procedures later adopted fleet-wide as SOPs by the F-14 TARPS squadrons.

Adoption of the tactical recce role did not

Left: By 1986, the red, white and blue 'Langley stripe' had been reduced in size and moved to the fin, as a background to the skull-and-crossbones badge. The stars were in toned-down grey, and moved from the rudders.

Below: Old and new: CAG and squadron commander's aircraft have tended to retain high-visibility markings, with the full-colour nose stripe.

At first sight the present VF-2 squadron commander's aircraft (actually an F-14D) could be mistaken for one of the unit's original F-14As.

This skull insignia has been an occasional feature of VF-2's markings throughout the F-14 era.

The flying suit patch of VF-2 has hardly changed since the unit's pre-war days as the 'Fighting Chiefs'.

bring with it any let-up in the primary fighter role and, as if to demonstrate this, on 2 June 1984 VF-2 became the first unit to make a carrier launch while towing an air-to-air gunnery target banner.

During a 1986 WestPac cruise aboard the *Ranger* the squadron intercepted Soviet IA-PVO and VVS Sukhoi Su-15 'Flagons' and MiG-23 'Floggers' as well as Tupolev Tu-16 'Badger' and Tupolev Tu-95/-142 'Bear' bombers. One year later, a VF-2 F-14A clocked up *Ranger*'s 260,000th carrier landing.

Between 8 December 1990 and 8 June 1991, VF-2 accompanied VF-1, its sister squadron, on a WestPac/Indian Ocean/Persian Gulf cruise aboard USS *Ranger* (CV-61) as part of Air Wing Two, flying BarCAP, MiGSweep and MiGCAP sorties in support of Operation Desert Storm. The squadron failed to score any air-to-air victories, but its work was roundly praised and greatly appreciated, especially by the bomber crews who received 'escort services' from the 'Bullets'. 1991 also saw the award of the Mutha trophy, and one of the unit's pilots clocked up a record number of F-14 traps (126 in a year), and a record

West Coast, active-duty career total of 744 traps. 1991 also saw victory in the High Noon gunnery competition, and a full work-up in the 'Bombcat' role, culminating in a historic 28 August mission in which an aircraft fired an AIM-7, strafed a ground target with its gun and dropped a pair of Mk 83 bombs.

On its return to Miramar after the August 1991 to January 1993 CVW-2 Persian Gulf cruise, VF-2 bade farewell to the *Ranger*, which decommissioned, and began conversion to the F-14D.

With its unrivalled history (including its status as the Navy's first carrier fighter squadron) and TARPS mission, VF-2 was bound to be the survivor when Air Wing Two was reduced to a single F-14 squadron.

The 'Bullets' (VF-2's tactical callsign) spent 1994 preparing for deployment aboard *Constellation* as part of CVW-2, and undertaking a Pacific cruise between 6 May and 30 June 1994. The squadron made another similar cruise which ended in May 1995. The squadron then moved from Miramar to Oceana in April 1996, where the unit became one of the first to operate a mixture of F-14Bs and F-14Ds.

Above: Even in the most toned-down colour scheme VF-2 Tomcats retained a small red, white and blue 'Langley stripe' with two stars.

Below: Looking for all the world like one of the squadron's original F-14As, this F-14D (seen over Iraq) was the unit's 1996 CAG-bird.

VF-11 'Red Rippers'

Although not known as VF-11, the 'Red Rippers' commissioned at Hampton Roads on 1 February 1927, flying the Curtiss F6C-3, but quickly transitioned to the Boeing F4B-1. Since then the squadron has operated 25 different fighter aircraft types, served on 21 carriers, and fought in both theatres during World War II, and then in both Korea and Vietnam. The 'Red Rippers' began a long association with Grumman aircraft in 1933 with the FF-1. The squadron flew Grumman fighters continuously for the next 17 years, with only a brief break with the Vought F4U Corsair. Wartime service saw the 'Red Rippers' flying the F4F Wildcat and the F6F Hellcat, first aboard *Ranger* and *Wasp* in support of the invasion of North Africa and off Norway, then in the Pacific, winning three Presidential Unit Citations in the process. Post-war, the 'Rippers' flew Corsairs and Bearcats, transitioning to F2H-1 Banshees in May 1950. The squadron deployed to Korea aboard the USS *Kearsarge* and subsequently flew air cover during the Suez and Lebanon crises. VF-11 became the 'Red Rippers' (callsign 'Ripper') in February 1959, commissioning at Cecil Field with the F8U-1 Crusader, and taking over the 'Rippers' distinctive hogshead badge and proud traditions. During the Crusader era, the squadron flew missions during the Dominican crisis

July 1966 saw a move to Oceana and the F-4B Phantom, and eventually VF-11 transitioned to the F-4J. The squadron transitioned to the F-14 during 1980, making its final F-4 cruise in May of that year and opening a new era for the Navy's longest continuously serving fighter squadron (VF-14 is older, but has spent some time as a bomber unit). By the time the squadron transitioned to the F-14, the aircraft were being delivered in an overall grey colour scheme, and not the original gull grey and white. Pairing with sister squadron VF-31 (longtime sister squadron with F-4 Phantoms), VF-11 joined CVW-3 aboard USS *John F. Kennedy* (CV-67), making its

first cruise with the new aircraft type between 4 January and 14 July 1982. A mini-cruise in the Atlantic followed during May and June of 1983, with the unit participating in NATO's Operation Ocean Safari. A full-scale Mediterranean cruise began on 27 September 1983, beginning with a rare visit to Latin America for joint exercises with the Força Aérea Brasileira, still as part of CVW-3 aboard the *Kennedy*. VF-11 flew combat air patrols during the 4 December 1983 US Navy airstrikes on Syrian positions in the Lebanon, during which two aircraft from the 28-strong package were shot down.

The squadron next made a short Caribbean cruise in July 1984. That same year, the unit was honoured with the award of both a Safety S and a Battle E. VF-11 'Red Rippers' and its sister squadron VF-31 moved to CVW-6 aboard the *Forrestal* (longtime home to the squadron during the F-4J era, with CVW-17) on 1 April 1985. The squadron made cruises in the Mediterranean, North Atlantic and Gulf (2 June to 10 November 1986, 28 August to 9 October 1987, and 8 April to 20 April 1988), receiving the 1986 Clifton Award for safety. During the 1986 cruise, the squadron exercised with the Egyptian and Turkish air

forces, giving plenty of opportunity for high quality dissimilar air combat training. *Forrestal* took VF-11 into the Mediterranean and Indian Ocean from 25 April until 7 October 1988, the squadron receiving a Meritorious Unit Commendation and an Armed Forces Expeditionary Medal in 1988, after conducting 108 straight days of sustained operations in the Indian Ocean and Persian Gulf in support of Operation

One of VF-11's new F-14Ds wears unit markings in a grey almost as light as the camouflage itself, for minimum conspicuity.

Earnest Will.

On 4 November 1989, VF-11 and VF-31 together deployed with CVW-6 aboard the *Forrestal* for a winter cruise to the Mediterranean, returning home on 12 April

Below: VF-11 received its F-14s in the overall gull grey colour scheme, as seen on these two aircraft patrolling near San Diego.

Right: Sharkmouths are a routine addition to fighters, and VF-11 even uses one officially. The significance of these warthog jaws is unknown.

1990. During the winter of 1990, the squadron sent a detachment to Luke AFB, for air combat training with the F-15s and F-16s of the USAF's 58th TFW.

The 'Red Rippers' deployed to the Caribbean aboard the *Forrestal* between 29 November and 23 December 1990, before visiting the Mediterranean again from 30 May 1991, still with Air Wing Six aboard the *Forrestal*. The squadron had been prepared to deploy at a moment's notice, but missed Operation Desert Storm. However, the 1991 cruise brought with it operational flying in support of Provide Comfort over northern Iraq, and the squadron dispatched a single aircraft to Le Bourget for static display during the Paris air show. Also during this cruise, 'Red Rippers' Tomcats exercised with IDF/AF aircraft, involving much low-level overland flying. When the *Forrestal* completed this, its 21st and final, cruise on 21 December 1991, it became the Navy's training carrier. Its air wing was disestablished, and its two Tomcat squadrons moved to the West Coast, where they re-equipped with F-14Ds. After completing a three-month transition syllabus at NAS Miramar, with VF-124, the 'Red Rippers' stood up in early July 1992 as the first fleet F-14D 'Super Tomcat' squadron.

Lt Dave Burnham and Lt Cdr Paul Pompier made the first fleet F-14D flight on 6 July. F-14Ds were deployed to Alaska to participate in Exercise Cope Thunder later in 1992. The squadron subsequently joined CVW-14 for service aboard USS *Carl Vinson* (CVN-70). 'Gold Eagle' (*Vinson*'s callsign) began a WestPac cruise on 18 February 1994, sailing from San Diego to Pearl Harbor, and then on to Yokosuka. Rough seas and a pitching deck provided a challenging background against which the squadron prepared for its first F-14D night traps, while flying MiG sweeps, TarCAP and TARPS missions, and attack missions during which the APG-71, JTIDS and IRST were used to 'shoot down' orange force F-15 Eagles. *Vinson* went on to the Persian Gulf in support of Operation Southern Watch, and returned home on 15 August 1994. This cruise marked the first deployment by the F-14D to the Persian Gulf.

In addition to their normal fighter duties, the 'Red Rippers' performed all the

necessary R&D work to make the F-14D fully compatible with the use of NVGs, for the night attack, night AFAC and night SAR roles. The squadron spent February 1996 at sea aboard the *Vinson* for Composite Unit Exercise B, during which the squadron successfully dropped a Mk 82, at night, using NVGs. Celebrations were cut short however, when the squadron lost an F-14, with its pilot and Cdr Scott Lamoreaux (a RIO from the staff of Cruiser-Destroyer Group 3). This accident led to a two-day fleet-wide grounding of the F-14.

During 1996, FITRON 11 completed a number of successful missile exercises, most notably with the AIM-7 Sparrow. The effectiveness of this ageing weapon was demonstrated in early May, when a squadron F-14 downed a Tactical Air Launched Decoy (TALD) launched by another squadron aircraft.

VF-11's last cruise aboard the *Vinson* began on 14 May 1996, and again began as a standard Westpac cruise, but which involved virtually a whole summer of support for Operation Southern Watch. The squadron escorted USAF Boeing B-52 Stratofortresses when they launched cruise missiles against Iraqi targets during Operation Desert Strike in September 1996. The squadron also flew numerous patrols in support of the 'No-Fly Zone', which had been extended. The cruise gave an opportunity for live AIM-9 Sidewinder firings, which were entirely successful.

Returning to the USA, VF-11 launched all nine of its F-14Ds from the *Vinson* off the coast of southern California on 11 November. They then flew, with USAF

Above: The traditional 'hogshead and thunderbolt' insignia of the 'Red Rippers' is proudly worn by the squadron's aircrew.

The 'Red Rippers' badge has scarcely changed since the squadron's formation in 1927. It is seen here on the tailfin of an F-14. The red fin-cap has been a welcome splash of colour on VF-11's Tomcats for most of the type's service career, in defiance of the general toning down.

tanker support, non-stop across the USA to NAS Oceana, the squadron's new home.

In 1997, VF-11 transitioned to the F-14B, as a result of a shortage of F-14Ds, but will probably soon become a mixed squadron operating both versions. This left VF-11 operating a different Tomcat variant to its sister squadron VF-31, leaving the way clear for transfer to a different air wing. Reports suggest that VF-11 will transfer to CVW-7 aboard the USS *John C.Stennis*.

Below: This F-14D wears the distinctive markings of VF-11, and is seen at the unit's old base of Miramar.

Below: Due to a shortage of F-14Ds, VF-11 transitioned to the F-14B during early 1997, leaving the Navy with only two F-14D squadrons. Current plans will almost certainly see the return of the D-model to VF-11, since many squadrons are due to re-equip with a mix of Tomcat variants. It is unlikely that TF30- and F110-engined aircraft will ever serve together in a front-line unit, however.

Grumman F-14 Operators

VF-14 'Tophatters'

VF-14 is the oldest continuously active squadron in the Navy, with a history dating back to September 1919 (albeit with periods as bomber, patrol and training units). It transitioned to the F-14A under the auspices of VF-124, together with sister squadron VF-32. The squadron (callsign 'Camelots') moved to Miramar during Christmas 1973 for conversion and finally returned to Oceana on 1 September 1974. The first Tomcats had started to arrive at Oceana in July 1974. Conversion to the F-14A was especially appropriate, since the squadron's original insignia was a grinning tomcat, in white tie and top hat.

VF-14 made the F-14's first Mediterranean cruise from 28 June 1975 to 27 January 1976, marking the first time that the E-2C and F-14 had been deployed together. The two aircraft proved to be a winning combination, and one which has provided US Navy carrier battle groups with unequalled air defence capability ever since. For this first cruise the squadron deployed aboard USS *John F. Kennedy* (CV-67) as part of CVW-1. Engine-related problems reduced

serviceability and availability, but the only F-14A actually lost ran off the deck when an arrester wire failed.

VF-14 made North Atlantic, Mediterranean, Caribbean, Atlantic, Mediterranean and Mediterranean/Indian Ocean cruises aboard the *Kennedy* (respectively from 2 September to 9 November 1976, 15 January to 1 August 1977, 7 November to 13 December 1977, 20 January to 22 March 1978, 29 June 1978 to 8 February 1979 and 4 August 1980 to 28 March 1981) before being reassigned to CVW-6, with whom the squadron deployed aboard USS *Independence* for a Mediterranean cruise (7 June to 22 December 1982), Caribbean cruises (6 June to 21 July 1983 and 15 August to 16 September 1983) before a full-scale Caribbean/Mediterranean/North Atlantic cruise which lasted from 18 October 1983 to 11 April 1984, and which involved the squadron in combat operations in two separate areas. Beginning in the Eastern Caribbean, VF-14 flew 82 combat CAP and escort missions in support of Operation Urgent Fury (the US invasion of Grenada) between 23 October and 5 November.

The *Independence* then proceeded to the

Eastern Mediterranean, where more trouble was brewing. Although VF-14 was not actively involved in the 4 December airstrikes against Syrian positions in the Lebanon, it did fly BarCAP missions in support of the operation, and flew escort for VF-32's TARPS birds. An Atlantic/Caribbean cruise followed between 20 August and 9 September 1984, with a final pre-SLEP (service life extension programme) Mediterranean/Indian Ocean cruise aboard USS *Independence* between 16 October 1984 and 19 February 1985.

Reassigned to CVW-3 on 1 April 1985, VF-14 undertook a Mediterranean cruise aboard the *Kennedy* between 18 August 1986 and 3 March 1987, before returning for a second full-scale cruise between 2 August 1988 and 1 February 1989. Between these two cruises, the squadron visited the Caribbean (aboard the *Kennedy* again) between 4 and 17 December 1987. During this deployment, VF-14 participated in Sea Wind '88 (a bilateral exercise with Egypt) and Display Determination '88, a NATO exercise in Italian airspace. These exercises were followed by African Eagle '88, flying against the F-5Es of the Moroccan air force, which reportedly proved to be somewhat

tougher opposition than had at first been anticipated.

Between 4 January and 1 February, VF-14 visited the Caribbean again, and then on 15 August 1990 VF-14 joined the other squadrons of CVW-3 for a short-notice deployment aboard the *Kennedy* in support of Desert Shield, sailing into the Red Sea. The carrier returned home on 28 March 1991. The squadron deployed as part of CVW-3 on the brief post-SLEP shakedown cruise of the *Kitty Hawk* between 26 August and 17 September 1991.

The 'Tophatters' had transitioned to the 'Bombcat' role by the spring of 1992, and practised air-to-ground operations during its next carrier deployment to the Mediterranean (again as part of Air Wing Three aboard the *Kennedy*) which began on 7 October 1993 and ended on 7 April 1993. It became the first East Coast squadron to launch from a carrier while carrying Mk 80-series bombs. During the cruise the squadron also flew CAPs in support of the Provide Promise emergency relief aid drops in Bosnia-Herzegovina, and received BDU-45s for its 'Bombcat' role. *Eisenhower* hosted VF-14 and the squadrons of CVW-3 for a brief Caribbean cruise between 17

Above: After losing its original high-visibility markings – which were applied to aircraft in the original grey and white scheme and which consisted of a red chevron on the fins – VF-14 was left with a simple top hat badge in a small disc.

Left: The fin chevron was reintroduced in outline form during the late 1980s. This aircraft has a small top hat emblem on its underfuselage fuel tanks, a common location for Tomcat unit insignia to be repeated.

Right: A pair of VF-14 F-14As is seen during the Independence era. During the time aboard the 'Indy', VF-14 were involved in the US operations over Grenada (Operation Urgent Fury), flying various CAP and escort missions during the US airstrikes. This famous cruise continued with action in the eastern Mediterranean, the first time two conflicts had been covered in a single cruise. VF-14 Tomcats did not take any great part in operations over Lebanon, being restricted primarily to BarCAP defence of the battle group and in reconnaissance escort sorties for TARPS aircraft.

VF-14's top hat badge is one of the best-known unit insignias in the world. When it had first appeared it was worn by a grinning cat.

May and 1 July 1994.

Some rumours suggested that VF-14 would transfer to CVW-17 to replace VF-103, although this did not happen, and the squadron is now with CVW-8.

The squadron detached from CVW-3 on 1 April 1994, joining Fighter Wing Atlantic while waiting reassignment. It continued the full run of training, including regular carrier qualification detachments. During 1995, the squadron tested the Tomcat in the air-to-ground rocket programme, principally using the 5-in Zuni. 1995 was a good year for the unit, which celebrated 76 years of service and won the 'Fighter Fling Banner Blaster' award for their air-to-air gunnery skills. During 1996, VF-14 formally joined CVW-8 and rejoined the USS *John F. Kennedy* (CV-67). No sooner had it done so than the squadron was temporarily attached to another carrier, the brand-new *John C. Stennis,* making a shakedown cruise in March. May saw the squadron victorious in the Fighter Wing Bomb Derby, and in June the unit began a 40-day cruise aboard the *John F. Kennedy* to Ireland and England.

The 'Tophatters' have won two Presidential Unit Stations, the Navy Unit Commendation, two Meritorious Unit Commendations, five Battle Stars, four CNO Safety Awards and six COMNAVAIRLANT Battle Es, during their long and proud history.

Above and above right: The 'Tophatters' wore this colourful scheme when they first transitioned to the F-14, though the red tail chevron vanished by 1977, leaving a small black hat; all colour disappeared in 1977-78, leaving the hat in toned-down grey. The chevron eventually reappeared in outline form.

Right: This 'Tophatters' F-14 (hook already down for landing) wears the colour scheme introduced in the late 1980s.

Below: This VF-14 F-14A is seen landing on the John C. Stennis during the new carrier's March 1996 shakedown cruise. From time to time, the unit's F-14s are seen with a colourful marking on the inner faces of the fins.

Grumman F-14 Operators

VF-21 'Freelancers'

VF-21 'Freelancers' converted to the F-14A under the auspices of VF-124, the West Coast RAG. It received its first Tomcat in November 1983 and was formally established as an F-14 unit on 15 March 1984. Paired throughout the Tomcat era with VF-154, its partner from F-4 Phantom days, the unit made an early hit in 1984 when it won that year's Boola Boola trophy (awarded for the best AAM readiness of a Pacific Fleet fighter squadron), having chalked up a 100 per cent success rate with its AIM-7s and 83 per cent with AIM-9s.

The squadron joined CVW-14 aboard USS *Constellation,* sailing with it from 18 August to 15 November 1984 and from 6 to 16 December 1984 in the eastern Pacific. A full WestPac/Indian Ocean cruise followed, between 21 February and 24 August 1985, with a short NorPac (northern Pacific) cruise with Air Wing 14 aboard the 'Connie' between 4 September and 20 October 1986. The ship next sailed for a WestPac and Indian Ocean deployment between 11 April and 13 October 1987. A similar cruise was again undertaken by VF-21 between 1 December 1988 and 1 June 1989. CVW-14 next made a NorPac cruise between 16 September and 19 October.

In 1990, VF-21 transferred with Air Wing 14 to USS *Independence* and sailed on a WestPac, Indian Ocean and Persian Gulf deployment from 23 June to 20 December, supporting the opening phase of Operation Desert Shield. The carrier was the first on the scene in the Persian Gulf (passing through the Straits of Hormuz on 2 August 1990) for participation in any necessary operations, but left the area before hostilities broke out. During this time, the CAG aircraft from each CVW-14 squadron wore a black tail with multi-coloured bands.

VF-21 was awarded a Safety S by CNO for its excellent safety record up to 1989 (and later won another in 1992). In 1991 VF-21 was transferred, along with CVW-14 and the *Independence,* to Japan to replace *Midway* as the sole carrier home-ported outside the USA. The 'Indy' sailed from CONUS on 5 July 1991 for Pearl Harbor, subsequently departing Hawaii for Japan on 22 July. Six days later the ship arrived in Japan, where it remained on cruise until 11 September 1991. It undertook three brief WestPac cruises by 15 April 1992, when the ship began a full WestPac/Indian Ocean/Persian Gulf cruise.

VF-21 had transferred to Air Wing Five (still aboard the *Independence*) at Pearl Harbor on the way out to Japan. During this cruise, the *Independence* visited Australia to participate in the celebrations commemorating the 50th anniversary of the Battle of the Coral Sea, before going on to help police the newly established 'No-Fly Zone' over southern Iraq (Operation

Southern Watch) and finally returning home on 31 December 1992. Four more mini WestPac cruises followed before 'Indy' again carried VF-21 and Air Wing 5 on a full-scale WestPac and Indian Ocean cruise between 17 November 1993 and 17 March 1994, including participation in Operation Southern Watch and the Somalia crisis.

VF-21 disestablished in January 1996.

Rumours suggested that the squadron would then convert to the F/A-18 Hornet as VFA-21, retaining the 'Freelancers' name and traditions, but this has not occurred, and now looks unlikely. The disappearance of VF-21 took CVW-5 down to a single Tomcat squadron, and left the 'Black Knights' of VF-154 as the sole Japan-based F-14 Tomcat unit.

Above: VF-21's original Tomcat colour scheme included a black anti-dazzle panel which extended back over the canopy rails, and swept forward over the radome, tucking back below the nose. This radome decoration was removed from about 1985.

Right: With tailcodes moved to the rudders, a VF-21 Tomcat launches from the **Constellation,** *on which it served as part of CVW-14. The yellow tail chevron acts as a background for the unit's sword and lion rampant badge. The overall light grey colour scheme was soon replaced.*

Below: This VF-21 F-14A wears a rare badge on its tailfin inner faces, with a cartoon dog superimposed on the stars and stripes, and the caption 'Oop Ack baby'. Reports suggest that VF-21 is to become an F/A-18 unit, as VFA-21.

VF-24 'Fighting Renegades'

Converting to the F-14A in November 1975 and discarding single-seat F-8J Crusaders, VF-24 (callsign 'Nickel') joined Air Wing Nine as partner to VF-211, on 1 March 1976. Once known as the 'Red Checkertails', the unit soon switched to the 'Fighting Renegades' nickname to avoid confusion with its sister squadron. The first F-14 unit to win the coveted Mutha award (for the best Pacific Fleet fighter squadron) in March 1977, VF-24 began its first carrier deployment with a WestPac cruise between 12 March and 21 November 1977, aboard USS *Constellation*. The squadron received the Clifton Award for flight safety in July 1978, having received a second successive Mutha in March.

Between 26 September 1978 and 17 May 1979, VF-24 again embarked with Air Wing Nine aboard the *Constellation*. The unit flew extensive 'blue water' (no diversion) operations on the WestPac/Indian Ocean cruise, during a period of tension caused by the Yemen crisis. The squadron entered the 1980s making a WestPac and Indian Ocean deployment with CVW-9 and the 'Connie' from 26 February until 15 October 1980.

During this cruise, CVW-9 provided support for Operation Eagle Claw, the abortive US attempt to rescue the hostages held in the US embassy in Teheran. *Constellation*'s aircraft were roughly painted with black and red recognition stripes on the wings as a protection against friendly fire. *Constellation* was replaced on 'Gonzo Station' by USS *Midway* on 27 June, but made a hasty return when *Midway* was damaged in a collision and had to head for port to effect repairs. The next year VF-24 left on another WestPac deployment, starting on 20 October 1981 and returning on 23 May 1982. The 'Renegades' next joined USS *Ranger*, with the rest of Air Wing Nine, and undertook an Indian Ocean cruise between 15 June 1983 and 29 February 1984.

On 20 May 1985, one of VF-24's Tomcats (159593/201) became the first F-14 to clock up 3,000 flight hours, a notable achievement. Later that year, on 24 July, the squadron sailed on another WestPac/Indian Ocean cruise on the *Kitty Hawk*, returning on 21 December.

Still as part of CVW-9 aboard USS *Kitty Hawk*, VF-24 made a round-the-world cruise from 31 January 1987 to 29 July 1987, this marking the last cruise of the *Kitty Hawk* before its SLEP. The unit then transferred, still as part of Air Wing Nine, to USS *Nimitz* and made a WestPac and Indian Ocean deployment between 2 September 1988 and 2 March 1989, operating in support of Operation Earnest Will, protecting tankers in the Persian Gulf. A NorPac cruise was next, lasting from 15 June 1989 until 9 July. The 'Renegades' transitioned to the F-14A+ during spring/summer 1989, becoming the first West Coast squadron to do so, before undergoing refresher training aboard the *Nimitz* in June. BuNo. 162911 was the squadron's first F-14A+. That same year, the squadron won the Boola Boola award. In the summer of 1990, the squadron began to develop tactics and techniques for the air-to-ground mission, becoming the first front-line fleet squadron to drop bombs (four Mk 84s) from the Tomcat on 8 August 1990.

The squadron took its F-14A+s on a WestPac/Indian Ocean cruise aboard USS *Nimitz*, as part of CVW-9, between 25 February and 24 August 1991, just too late to participate in Operation Desert Storm. This cruise included exercises with Thailand and Malaysia, and also provided plenty of trade in the shape of Soviet 'Bears' and

'Fitters' for the wing's two Tomcat units to intercept.

Once back in the United States, on 30 September 1991 the unit's F-14A+s demonstrated their new-found 'Bombcat' role at NAS Fallon, where VF-24 developed the FRS training syllabus and trained its own crews in the air-to-ground role. VF-24 next became the first West Coast fighter squadron to complete the Advanced Attack Readiness Program (AARP), although by this time – June 1992 – the unit had transitioned back to the F-14A, the F-14Bs being consolidated into the Atlantic Fleet.

The WestPac/Persian Gulf cruise by *Nimitz* which began on 4 February 1993 saw VF-24 deploy again as part of Air Wing Nine, subsequently flying missions in support of Operation Southern Watch over southern Iraq. Equipped with TARPS pods, VF-24 undertook reconnaissance missions over the contended territory. A year later, the unit was at Nellis flying Red Force missions during Red Flag. A final WestPac cruise began on 1 December 1995, and included operations in the South China Sea during Taiwan's first elections, deterring aggression from mainland China. VF-24 disestablished on 31 August 1996, following a host of other historic units into oblivion.

Right: Carrying a pair of AIM-54 Phoenix missiles, an F-14A of VF-24 launches from NAS Miramar. The curving chevron on the fin was originally red, outlined in black, but had been toned down by 1978 (except on CAG- and boss-birds). Full-colour, large-size stars and bars were retained into the 1980s, when the tactical blue-grey colour scheme began to appear, and when VF-24's aircraft received a smaller, more angular tail chevron.

Left: VF-24's CAG aircraft taxis at NAS Fallon during June 1981, with black tailfins and a red tail chevron. The red nine, surrounded by stars, indicates assignment to CVW-9. A black S, with red shadow, indicates the award of a Safety S to the squadron. CAG aircraft traditionally wear the 00 ('Double Nuts') Modex.

Below: This VF-24 F-14A+ wears water-based temporary camouflage for participation in a shore-based bombing exercise. The aircraft is named Camel Smoker and carries a bomb tally in red. Such temporary colour schemes are by no means rare on the F-14, although they tend to be carried only for very short periods.

VF-31 'Tomcatters'

VF-31 is the US Navy's second oldest fighter squadron, and had the unique distinction of scoring air combat victories in World War II, Korea and Vietnam. It began F-14 conversion with VF-101 on 8 September 1980. This ended a record-breaking 24-year association with the USS *Saratoga*. The squadron received its first F-14s on 22 January and its first TARPS-equipped aircraft soon afterwards. The squadron (callsign 'Bandwagon' or 'Felix') officially stood up with Tomcats on 4 June 1981, joining VF-11 as part of Air Wing Three.

Kennedy took CVW-3 to the Indian Ocean and Mediterranean from 4 January to 14 July 1982, and on exercises in the Atlantic and Mediterranean from 27 September 1983 to 2 May 1984. It found itself in an unexpectedly hostile situation when it was called to readiness at 'Bagel Station' off the coast of Lebanon, to support the US presence in Beirut. On 3 December two of the squadron's TARPS aircraft came under fire, this triggering a retaliatory Alpha Strike against the offending Syrian positions during which an A-6 and an A-7 were lost. The cruise also resulted in two F-14 losses for VF-31, with one crew killed. Transferring with VF-11 to CVW-6, the squadron deployed to the Mediterranean again between 2 June and 10 October 1986, sailing with USS *Forrestal*. Forced to sail within sight of the coast to boost morale, the ship remained in a super-heightened state of readiness by often-predicted suicide attacks by boat and even air.

From 28 July until 9 October 1987, the unit undertook a NorLant deployment, followed by a further NorLant/Mediterranean/Indian Ocean cruise between 25 April and 7 October 1988. CVW-6 next made a Mediterranean cruise from 4 November 1989 until 12 April 1990, returning there for another deployment from 30 May to 21 December 1991, after a brief Caribbean cruise between 29 November and 23 December 1990.

The 'Tomcatters' remained with CVW-6 and undertook the same cruises as their sister squadron, VF-11, flying much the same sort of missions but with the added tactical recce commitment made possible by the unit's handful of TARPS-capable F-14As. The May-December 1991 Mediterranean cruise aboard the *Forrestal* provided particularly useful training opportunities, and saw the squadron undertake low-level exercises with the Israeli air force.

The squadron moved to the West Coast upon the retirement of the *Forrestal* and the consequent disestablishment of Air Wing Six, and began to transition to the F-14D in early 1992. VF-31 officially joined CVW-14 aboard USS *Carl Vinson* (CVN-70) in July, and began training using the first five of its F-14Ds from 8 July. Introduction of the

Above: Felix the Cat adorns the tailfins and fuel tank noses of this VF-31 'Tomcatters' F-14A. During 1981 the tail insignia was replaced by a simple tailcode.

Right: By 1991, most VF-31 Tomcats had low-visibility markings, with tailstripes in dark grey, although radomes remained black.

F-14D brought about a slight change in colour scheme for the squadron, since only the CAG-bird retained the unit's traditional black radome, most other aircraft being delivered with radomes in light grey. F-14Ds went on cruise aboard the *Vinson* between 18 February 1994 and 15 August 1994, making a WestPac/Indian Ocean/Persian Gulf cruise and participating in Operation Southern Watch.

The 'Tomcatters' returned from their second WestPac cruise (aboard *Vinson*) in late 1996, having flown in support of Operations Southern Watch and Desert Strike (the B-52 ALCM raids against Iraqi targets). On returning to the USA, the squadron moved back across the continent to Oceana, where the F-14 force is now concentrated.

VF-31 retained its F-14Ds when sister-unit VF-11 converted to the less capable F-14B, but is likely to become a mixed unit, operating both types, if current plans go ahead. It has been reported that VF-31 may transfer from CVW-14 to another carrier air wing, leaving VF-11 with the *Vinson*. In fact, both squadrons remained with CVW-14 in mid-1997, and VF-31 expected to cruise aboard the *Abraham Lincoln* in mid-1998. Reports that one of the two squadrons would disestablish during FY 1997 seem to have been erroneous.

Right: Although wearing toned-down markings, this VF-31 F-14D features a larger-than-normal Felix insignia.

VF-31's famous Felix the Cat insignia dates back to the squadron's 1935 origins as VF-1B.

Below: This VF-31 F-14A has its tail stripes and Felix applied in grey, instead of the original red and black. The aircraft even lacks the squadron's traditional black radome, which was a feature of even most toned-down schemes.

Above: The original full-colour squadron markings of VF-31 are now seen only on aircraft assigned to the CAG and to the squadron CO and XO.

VF-32 'Swordsmen'

VF-32 traces its roots back to the redesignation of VF-4A in August 1948, after which it flew F8F Bearcats, F4U-4 Corsairs, F9F Panthers, F-8 Crusaders, and the F-4 Phantom. VF-32 converted to the F-14 at Miramar during early 1974, but as an Atlantic Fleet squadron it moved back to Oceana after conversion. In those early days, the squadron marked its aircraft with broad yellow tailbands and a sword extending up the rudder. The squadron's first deployment was with USS *John F. Kennedy* on a Mediterranean cruise which began on 29 June 1978, as part of CVW-1. The squadron then undertook the same pattern of cruises and deployments as its sister unit, VF-14. The squadron made Tomcat history by participating in Exercise Red Flag during 1979. Air Wing One sailed again with 'Big John' between July 1980 and 28 March 1981. VF-32 (callsign 'Gypsy') then joined CVW-6 and deployed aboard its new home, USS *Independence,* from 7 June 1982 to 22 December. This was 'Indy's' first extended deployment with F-14s. In mid-1982, VF-32 made early and effective use of its TARPS capability, recording Harpoon missile strikes on a target ship in a trials operation known as Harpoonex '82.

Operation Urgent Fury, the US invasion of Grenada in October 1983, was supported by the *Independence* and CVW-6. F-14s from VF-32 undertook their normal roles of fleet air defence and air superiority. After Grenada, the *Independence* continued on to the Mediterranean for a cruise lasting from 18 October 1983 until 11 April 1984, during which VF-32 TARPS aircraft flew the first live BDA sorties since the Vietnam War, photographing the damage caused by the December 1983 strike against Syrian positions in the Lebanon. This historic cruise marked the first time that the F-14 participated in two conflicts during one cruise. The *Independence* next took its air wing to the Mediterranean and Indian Ocean from 16 October 1984 until 19 February 1985. On 1 January 1989 two of VF-32's crews added to the F-14A's laurels by downing a pair of Libyan MiG-23s in an incident which marked the F-14's third and fourth kills, but which remains controversial to this day. Some aver that the Libyan aircraft were 'Flogger-Es' incapable of carrying a BVR missile, and were thus not presenting a threat when engaged.

The squadron played a major role during Operations Desert Shield and Desert Storm, especially in the vital TARPS tasking. Between 7 October 1992 and 7 April 1993, the squadron embarked with CVW-3 aboard the *Kennedy* for another Mediterranean cruise. The squadron remained partnered with VF-14 with CVW-3, assigned to the *Eisenhower,* but has now moved with CVW-3 to the USS *Theodore Roosevelt,* while VF-14 has moved to CVW-8 and the USS *John F. Kennedy.* The squadron retains F-14As, which still use the callsign 'Gypsy', and has recently been operating with the new Digital TARPS pod, proving the new equipment, ironing out the problems and effectively laying the ground work for the Tomcat's new reconnaissance capabilities. Digital TARPS will finally free the F-14 from its dependence on wet film processing support, improving the speed with which imagery can be delivered to the user.

Above: For years, VF-32 used as its badge a version of Grumman's 'Tomcat' insignia, in pirate's costume and leaning on a sword.

Above right: By 1989, VF-32 had reverted to a simple sword insignia on the fins of its F-14s. Such a sword was originally carried on the aircraft's rudders and then, from 1979, across the fin.

Right: VF-32 Tomcats in their original colour scheme had broad yellow fin bands and swords on the rudders.

Above: The original VF-32 colour scheme incorporated yellow tail stripes and a black canopy surround and spine, though it was destined to have only a short life, before 'toning down'.

Below: VF-32's CAG-bird at the time of the Gulf War had black tailfins with yellow stripes and a yellow sword, and even reintroduced the black spine and canopy surround.

Right: VF-32's traditional badge incorporates a sword (held by a lion) and a yellow band, together with Navy wings and the motto 'God and Country'. It is worn with pride.

Above: During its period aboard the Independence, VF-32 adopted a colour scheme which combined the Grumman 'Tomcat' insignia (in piratical garb, with a cutlass) with the traditional yellow bands, though these were very narrow.

Grumman F-14 Operators

VF-33 'Starfighters'

VF-33 accepted its first F-14s in December 1981 (when it was known as the 'Tarsiers'), having transitioned to the aircraft with VF-101. It was declared operational in January 1982, six months after the conclusion of its last F-4J cruise. The squadron mirrored VF-102, making a series of cruises as part of CVW-1 aboard USS *America*. Between 24 March and 18 April 1986, during a Mediterranean cruise with Air Wing One aboard the *America*, VF-33 flew operations off the coast of Libya, crossing Colonel Khadaffi's 'line of death' by entering the international waters of the Gulf of Sirte, which were claimed as territorial waters by Libya. These operations culminated in Operations Prairie Fire and El Dorado Canyon (air strikes against Libyan targets).

Between 6 January and 19 February 1987, the squadron embarked on the *Theodore Roosevelt* for a brief shakedown cruise in the Caribbean, then continued to partner VF-102 aboard USS *America*. During late 1988 the squadron, officially redubbed the 'Starfighters' (although the 'Tarsiers' nickname lingered on unofficially), teamed up with the F/A-18C-equipped VFA-82 'Marauders' to act as threat aircraft against USAF F-15s, F-16s, F-111s and A-10s. The two squadrons later practised mixed-section tactics against VF-45 prior to another carrier deployment aboard USS *America*. As part of CVW-1, VF-33 made a NorLant and Caribbean cruise from 11 May to 10 November 1989. USS *America* next sailed with a composite CVW-9, transiting the Horn from west to east between 12 February and 7 April 1990. On this cruise VF-33 was the only F-14 squadron embarked.

Between 28 December 1990 and 18 April 1991, VF-33 again deployed with CVW-1 aboard USS *America* for a Mediterranean/Red Sea/Persian Gulf cruise, and flew operations in support of Operations Desert Shield and Desert Storm. The squadron initially flew strike escorts and MiGCAPs while the *America* was in the Red Sea, switching to the fleet air defence role when the carrier took up position in the Persian Gulf. Another cruise aboard USS *America* with CVW-1 began on 21 August 1991. This was a brief deployment into the Atlantic for Exercise North Star, and the carrier returned to port on 11 October.

A further cruise between 2 December 1991 and 6 June 1992 took the *America* and Air Wing One into the Mediterranean, where the two F-14 squadrons had the opportunity to practise dissimilar air combat against Tunisian F-5Es and Spanish navy AV-8Bs. For VF-33, however, the writing was on the wall, and the squadron disbanded on 1 October 1993, leaving VF-102 as CVW-1's sole Tomcat unit.

*Top: VF-33's **CAG**-bird is seen in 1988. Ordinary squadron aircraft were similarly marked from April 1984, before which the lightning bolt and star were in black outline form only. For a brief initial period, these markings were applied in yellow on a black fin panel, with a grey tip and leading edge.*

Above: The VF-33 CAG-bird, 1992-style, wore markings similar to the original 1981-type squadron markings.

Left: The 'Starfighters' final colour scheme had a toned-down lightning bolt on the black fins and on the forward fuselage. The forward fuselage lightning bolt had not been seen since 1981, when it was yellow, outlined in black.

VF-41 'Black Aces'

VF-41's distinguished history began on 1 June 1945, when it was commissioned at NAS Chincoteague, Virginia, flying the F4U Corsair. In July 1948 the squadron became VF-3B, and VF-41 that September. VF-41 received jets (in the shape of the F2H Banshee) in May 1953, converting to the radar-equipped, missile-armed F3H-2 Demon in 1959. The squadron transitioned to the Phantom in February 1962, participated in operations during the Cuban Missile Crisis and made a seven-month combat cruise off Vietnam, flying fighter, escort, day and night interdiction, reconnaissance and SEAD missions. During the mid-1970s, the squadron participated in peacekeeping operations following the end of the Yom Kippur War. Throughout the late 1970s and 1980s, VF-41 'Black Aces' (callsign 'Fast Eagle') sailed as part of CVW-8 aboard USS Nimitz.

The squadron began conversion to the F-14A in April 1976, and was declared operational with the new type in December. A successful ORE cleared the way for an eight-month maiden cruise which began in December 1977 and ended on 20 July 1978. Further cruises aboard Nimitz followed, with a 10 September 1979 to 26 May 1980 Mediterranean/Indian Ocean cruise supporting Operation Evening Light in Iran, and diverting to the Indian Ocean in response to the Afghan crisis. This cruise included a record 144 continuous days at sea. There followed a work-up NorLant deployment beginning on 14 May 1981. Tragedy struck when a Marine EA-6B crashed onto the deck of the Nimitz, killing three crew from VF-41 and destroying three of the squadron's F-14s.

This was followed by a Mediterranean cruise beginning in August. The squadron soon found itself in action against the Libyan air force on 19 August 1981. Cdr Henry M. ('Hank') Kleeman and Lt David Venlet (in F-14 Modex 102), along with Lt Larry 'Music' Musczynski and Lt(jg) Jim 'Amos' Anderson (in Modex 107), claimed a pair of Libyan Su-22s with their AIM-9 Sidewinders. After days of the F-14s hassling with Libyan fighters attempting to close on the battle group, the two Su-22s went too far, firing a missile at the pair of Tomcats. The missile did not guide, and in retrospect some analysts believed the lead F-14 crew may have mistaken a tank being jettisoned for a missile launch. Whatever the truth, the action sealed the fate of the Libyan pilots. These represented the first kills by the F-14, and the first US Navy kills since the Vietnam War. They came at just the right time for the Tomcat squadrons, seemingly confirming the start of a new era for the aircraft, which at last seemed to be leaving many of its early troubles behind it. The engagement with the Libyan fighters marked the first air-to-air battle between variable-geometry fighters and provided a much-needed boost to morale and to recruiting.

1982 saw the squadron gain three major awards – a Battle E, a Safety S and the Clifton Trophy – while conducting another Mediterranean cruise between November 1982 and May 1983, and a one-month Caribbean shakedown for the new USS Carl Vinson during May/June. The Joseph P. Clifton Trophy is probably the most prestigious and important prize that can be awarded to a Tomcat unit, being given annually to the US Navy's best fighter squadron. VF-41 stayed with Air Wing Eight aboard the Nimitz and undertook a Mediterranean cruise in 1985, from 8 March to 3 September, during which the squadron tested minor improvements made to the M61A1 cannon. Nimitz returned to the north Atlantic with VF-41 between 15 July and 16 October 1986.

For a round-the-world cruise, VF-41 transferred to USS Roosevelt along with the rest of CVW-8, departing on 30 December 1986 and returning on 26 July 1987. CVW-8 formally transferred to the Theodore Roosevelt in October 1987, and the squadron made a brief Caribbean deployment from 8 March to 8 April, before going on a full NorLant deployment aboard Roosevelt between 25 August and 11 October 1988. A second cruise, this time to the Mediterranean, began on 30 December 1988 and lasted until 30 June 1989. On both this and the previous NorLant cruise, Roosevelt carried an 'experimental' air wing comprising 20 F-14s, 20 F/A-18s and 20 A-6s, as opposed to the then-standard 24 F-14s, 24 A-7s and 10 A-6s. This maximised both the carrier's strike and air combat potential through the F/A-18's impressive 'swing' capability. Such an air wing (which soon became known as the 'Roosevelt Wing') became the US Navy's preferred composition until recently, when the realities of the post-Cold War world dictated an even more flexible structure with one enhanced F-14 squadron and three multi-role F/A-18 units.

At the end of 1988, CVW-8 sailed for the Mediterranean (on 30 December) and returned the following year on 28 June. 1989 was a good year for the 'Black Aces', the squadron gaining a Safety S from the CNO and a COMNAVAIRLANT Battle E. Between 19 January and 23 February 1990, CVW-8 conducted a Caribbean shakedown cruise for the new Abraham Lincoln (CVN-72).

Between 28 December 1990 and 28 June 1991, the squadron deployed aboard USS Theodore Roosevelt as part of CVW-8 for a Mediterranean/Red Sea/Persian Gulf

Above: The first F-14As delivered to the US Navy were in glossy light grey, with white undersides and control surfaces. On these aircraft, squadron markings were extremely colourful, as exemplified by this red-striped VF-41 aircraft, which wore its tailcodes inside a massive black ace of spades.

Right: The late 1970s saw the introduction of an overall gloss light grey finish, on which squadron markings were reduced in size. This was replaced by a matt version of the same colour. The VF-84 aircraft in the background shows the next phase in Tomcat markings, wearing the overall matt blue-grey tactical camouflage on which all markings were toned down, applied in slightly different shades of grey with little contrast and no colour.

Below: This pair of VF-41 F-14As illustrates the standard and CAG/squadron commander colour schemes as applied during 1992. The far aircraft is painted in the original light grey paint, and has small patches of colour on its fintips, and on unit markings, warning stripes, etc., together with enlarged full-colour star and bar. Both aircraft have an attractive, tapering anti-dazzle panel with stripes, which extends back aft of the canopy.

Grumman F-14 Operators

cruise. *Roosevelt* sailed on 28 December 1990, and was joined by nine F-14s of VF-41 the following day. The carrier arrived in the Gulf on 19 January, and the two Tomcat squadrons flew MiGSweep, TarCAP, MiGCAP and HVACAP missions, eventually roaming widely over southern Iraq but still without finding any enemy aircraft to down. By the war's end, the squadron had amassed 1,500 combat flying hours, with an unprecedented 100 per cent sortie completion rate. The 'Black Aces' remained in the Arabian Gulf and Red Sea until April to enforce the Desert Storm ceasefire. It then repositioned to the Mediterranean to give air cover to the forces providing assistance to Kurdish refugees in northern Iraq as part of Operation Provide Comfort.

VF-41 left the *Roosevelt* to join CVW-15 aboard USS *Kitty Hawk*, departing for a RimPac cruise on 22 June 1992. During this deployment, the squadron participated in exercise Tandem Thrust '92. This Pacific sailing was followed by another WestPac cruise from 3 November 1992 until 3 May 1993.

The squadron has since rejoined CVW-8, which is now reassigned to the *Roosevelt*. The squadron was not embarked for a March 1993 cruise, supplanted by USMC Hornets, but remained on 72-hour standby. In the spring of 1994 the squadron's establishment grew to 14 aircraft and it made an Atlantic cruise between 19 May and 29 June 1994.

On 22 March 1995 the squadron again deployed aboard the *Roosevelt*. During this cruise, VF-41 flew combat operations in Deliberate Force over Bosnia, then over Iraq as part of Southern Watch. Deliberate Force saw VF-41 become the first 'Bombcat' unit to drop ordnance 'in anger'. VF-41 took over the TARPS commitment upon the disbandment of VF-84.

Above: One of the more traditional flying suit patches worn by the aircrew of VF-41 incorporates the ace of spades and a red stripe, as worn on the aircraft above right.

Right: A 'Black Aces' F-14A 'Bombcat' refuels from a USAF tanker high over Bosnia. The squadron became the first F-14 unit to drop bombs in combat, with laser designation provided by F/A-18 Hornets.

Below: The 'Black Aces' current markings have a tapering red flash behind the traditional 'death card', as seen on this VF-41 aircraft.

VF-51 'Screaming Eagles'

Although not a particularly old unit, the 'Screaming Eagles' do have the distinction of having had the longest continuous service of any fighter squadron in the Pacific Fleet. VF-51 'Screaming Eagles' was commissioned in August 1948 as VF-3S 'Striking Eagles' with the renumbering of VF-5A. The Screaming Eagle insignia dated back further, however, having first appeared on the Curtiss F6C-4 in 1927. The original 'Screaming Eagles' flew the Boeing FB-5, F3B-1, F4B-4, and the Grumman F2F-1 and F3F-3. The squadron flew Wildcats at Guadalcanal before introducing the F6F into fleet service. The squadron subsequently transitioned to the F4U Corsair, and was aboard the USS *Franklin* when it was damaged by *kamikazes*. The squadron followed the usual pattern of equipment and re-equipment, operating F8F Bearcats, FJ-1 Furies, F9Fs, FJ-3 Furies, F11F Tigers, F4D Skyrays, various F-8 Crusader variants and the mighty F-4 Phantom.

But VF-51's existence was far from routine. With the FJ-1, the squadron was the first fleet unit to operate jets from a carrier. During the Korean War, VF-51 made

the first Navy kills of the conflict, two of the squadron's Panthers downing a pair of Yak-3s. The unit's Crusaders participated in the Vietnam War, flying secret air-to-ground missions into Laos from June 1964. In 1968, VF-51 F-8Hs shot down a pair of MiG-21s (winning the unit the prestigious Clifton Trophy, as the Navy's best fighter squadron), and in 1971, the squadron's new F-4 Phantoms accounted for four MiG-17s. The Phantoms were subsequently used during the USS *Mayaguez* rescue mission.

The squadron, callsign 'Eagles', took delivery of its first F-14A on 16 June 1978, at Calverton, converting from the F-4N under the guidance of VF-124. The squadron made its first cruise aboard the *Kitty Hawk* with CVW-15, departing for a WestPac deployment on 30 May 1979. The cruise was eventful, the carrier coming to action stations and holding off the Korean coast following the assassination of President Park, and then taking station off Iran in response to the kidnapping of 60 Americans by revolutionary Iran. A subsequent eight-month WestPac cruise lasting from 1 April until 23 November 1981 saw *Kitty Hawk*'s

air wing notch up some notable achievements. CVW-15's aircraft logged 1,600 traps over the course of 3,400 flying hours. Every crew on board became centurions (logging 100 traps) and at peak sortie rate 785 hours were flown over just 22 days – much of it during monsoon conditions.

VF-51 gained a Boola Boola award in 1983, and that same year the squadron temporarily transferred, along with Air Wing 15, to the East Coast for embarkation aboard the new USS *Carl Vinson*, which was due to transfer to the Pacific Fleet. The newly commissioned carrier's first deployment took it, and VF-51, on a round-the-world cruise from 1 March 1983 until 29 October 1983. This cruise involved the squadron in many exercises, including air-to-air combat missions against Moroccan F-5Es. The following year VF-51's F-14s made two short USS EastPac cruises aboard *Vinson* before embarking for a full WestPac cruise on 18 October 1984, to visit Australia and participate in Fleet Ex '85 in the new year. During that cruise, VF-51's Tomcats became the first US Navy aircraft to intercept a Soviet air force Tu-22 'Blinder' (on 2 December 1984), and subsequently its aircraft encountered curious Su-15s and

MiG-23s, intercepting these with the aid of their powerful new Northrop TCS sets. This cruise also saw VF-51 make the first F-14 day and night automatic carrier landings.

During 1985, VF-51 was heavily involved in the filming of the Hollywood motion picture 'Top Gun'. This took place at NAS Miramar, from where the 'Eagles' also flew as aggressors in Red Flag 85-5.

Vinson took Air Wing 15 on another WestPac cruise from 12 August 1986 until 5

Below: VF-51's first F-14As were delivered in the overall glossy grey scheme, and were decorated with red-striped black tailfins, with grey leading edges. CAG aircraft differed only in having multi-coloured stripes replacing the red ones.

Bottom: The adoption of toned-down markings has been accompanied by a variety of styles of unit insignia, including plain horizontal stripes in dull red or dark grey, and stripes with the unit's star and eagle superimposed, as seen here.

Grumman F-14 Operators

February 1987, returning for a second such deployment between 15 June and 14 December 1988, which continued into the Indian Ocean. VF-51 made an unusual combined NorLant and WestPac cruise (albeit an extremely short one) between 5 September and 8 November 1989. This was followed by a WestPac/Indian Ocean deployment from 1 February to 31 July 1990.

In 1990 the 'Eagles' picked up the Mutha Trophy and a Battle E, as well as winning the West Coast Fighter Derby and the ECCM trophy.

The planned transition of VF-51 and its long-term partner unit VF-111 to the F-14D (as the first F-14D squadron) was cancelled when defence cuts halted the F-14D conversion programme. This meant that only the more senior squadrons (VF-2 and the two units transferred from East to West Coast on the disestablishment of CVW-6, VF-11 and VF-31) received the new variant.

Instead, the 'Eagles' moved, along with CVW-15, to USS *Kitty Hawk* (CV-63). Together they sailed east-to-west around Cape Horn from 18 October 1991 until 11 December, during which time the Tomcats were able to fly DACT missions against Venezuelan, Chilean and Argentine fighters.

Although the squadron did not participate in Operation Desert Storm, a far-reaching cruise from 3 November 1992 until 3 May 1993 took VF-51 to the Indian Ocean and

The 'Screaming Eagles' have worn a variety of toned-down colour schemes, with thin red and thin blue tailbands, or sometimes grey.

Persian Gulf, where Air Wing Fifteen flew in support of Operation Provide Relief and Southern Watch. Another cruise began on 24 June 1994.

CVW-15 disbanded on 31 March 1995, along with both of its Tomcat squadrons. There had been speculation that only VF-111 would disband, but, in the end, there were to be no survivors of the air wing's disappearance. Although it had a short life, VF-51's career has been most distinguished and full of great achievements, yet it too has become a casualty of restructuring following the end of the Cold War, accompanying some of the US Navy's most famous units into retirement.

Below: VF-51's F-14s were wearing this colourful scheme in the late 1970s, and survived longer without being toned-down than most other units. It was not until 1985 that most of the unit's aircraft lost their distinctive black tailfins.

VF-74 'Bedevilers'

VF-74 was formed on 15 February 1950, by the redesignation of VF-92 at Quonset Point. The squadron operated Grumman F8F Bearcats, but soon transitioned to F4Us, F9Fs, F4D Skyrays and then became the first Atlantic Fleet F-4 Phantom squadron. VF-74 'Bedevilers' (callsign 'Devil') began conversion to the Tomcat (from the F-4S) in February 1983, receiving its first aircraft in June and becoming fully operational in October 1983. The squadron embarked aboard *Saratoga* for a brief shakedown in the Caribbean between 26 January and 21 February 1984, then remained with CVW-17 (its parent unit during the Phantom era) and *Saratoga* for its maiden F-14 cruise, a 1984 Mediterranean deployment lasting until 20 October 1984.

Right and above: Had VF-74 not been disestablished, it would have fallen foul of current regulations which prohibit the use of satanic insignia or names by US military units. This devil's head badge was worn by VF-74 aircraft and aircrew.

VF-74 was again aboard the *Saratoga* for its August 1985 Mediterranean cruise. The ship participated in Exercise Ocean Safari '85 on its way out, chopping to Sixth Fleet control on 7 September and then taking part in Exercise Display Determination '85. The squadron also played a minor part in Operation Prairie Fire in March 1986 and in Operation El Dorado Canyon on 15 April 1986. The squadron also participated in the amazing air-to-air capture of the *Achille Lauro* hijackers.

Saratoga switched to Seventh Fleet control in November, after making the first night transit of the Suez Canal by a US carrier. The ship returned to the Mediterranean for operations off the Libyan coast during January, February and March, dropping out from the Sixth Fleet on 5 April and returning home. As part of its Mediterranean cruise in 1985/1986, this time with CVW-17 on the *Saratoga*, VF-74 flew strike CAPs during HARM shoots against Libyan missile sites. Over this period VF-74 was at sea between 25 August 1985 and 16 April 1986, returning for another Mediterranean cruise from 5 June 1987 until 17 November 1987. A 12-day detachment to NAS Roosevelt Roads for missile practice ended on 16 November 1988.

Right: A VF-74 F-14A wears temporary desert camouflage, seen during June 1987. The last of the Atlantic Fleet F-14 units, VF-74 received toned-down F-14As.

VF-74 sailed with the rest of Air Wing Seventeen aboard the USS *Saratoga* when it departed Mayport to join the *Independence* (with CVW-14) and the *Kennedy* (CVW-3) for participation in Operation Desert Storm, still operating alongside its long-time sister unit VF-103 'Sluggers'. While still in the closing stages of conversion to the F-14A+, the squadron departed for this war cruise on 7 August 1990 and returned home on 28 March 1991.

VF-74 made a subsequent cruise (with its aircraft now formally redesignated F-14Bs) aboard the *Saratoga* between 6 May and 6 November 1992. The squadron next deployed (with the rest of CVW-17) aboard USS *Constellation* for a post-SLEP shakedown cruise.

With the transition of CVW-17 to a single F-14 squadron, VF-74 was left without a role, but the unit was not immediately decommissioned and continued to fly from NAS Oceana. This led many to hope that the squadron might be saved, and might find a new air wing assignment.

Instead, between its last cruise and its disestablishment, VF-74 operated mainly in the adversary role, its aircraft adopting an unusual disruptive pattern, blue-grey camouflage scheme. The squadron finally disestablished on 28 April 1994, joining the roster of once-proud fighter squadrons which disappeared in the early 1990s.

Above: The Olympic rings on the nose of VF-74's CO's Tomcat, pictured in 1992, are of unknown significance. The squadron markings are usually applied in shades of grey, with only the lightning bolt itself in red. Unit commanders are traditionally assigned the 01 Modex.

Right: For the last months of its career as an F-14 unit, VF-74 served in the adversary role, and its aircraft were painted in two-tone disruptive camouflage, with red Modexes, in an approximation of the most common MiG-29 and Su-27 colour schemes.

Grumman F-14 Operators

VF-84 'Jolly Rogers'

VF-84 'Jolly Rogers' (callsign 'Victory') began conversion to the F-14 during October 1975, under the supervision of VF-101 at Oceana. The unit finally stood up with the Tomcat in mid-April 1977, when it was officially reassigned to Air Wing Eight, along with sister squadron VF-41, whose pattern of carrier deployments it mirrored. Decorated with a massive skull-and-crossbones on their fins, the squadron's F-14As were early achievers, chalking up an impressive 752.9 flying hours over only 23 days on an early (1978) cruise with CVW-8 aboard USS *Forrestal*. By 1980 VF-84 was aboard USS *Nimitz* making a NorLant, Mediterranean, Indian Ocean deployment with transits via the Cape of Good Hope and

Persian Gulf, returning home from 'Gonzo Station' on 26 May. Had Operation Eagle Claw not been abandoned as a result of the disaster at Desert One, when *Nimitz*-based RH-53Ds collided with a C-130 and had to be left in the desert, VF-84 would have undoubtedly had a role to play in the US hostage rescue.

The squadron assumed a TARPS reconnaissance commitment during 1981, flying TARPS missions over the Persian Gulf, and became the first Tomcat TARPS unit in either fleet to deploy the new pod operationally. Further cruises included an August 1981 to February 1982 Mediterranean deployment, a November 1982 to May 1983 deployment, and a 1985

Mediterranean cruise which saw the unit participating in Exercise Bright Star, and standing by in case required for action generated by the hijacking of a TWA Boeing 727 at Athens. Unfortunately, the 'Jolly Rogers' were unable to achieve the success of their sister unit, VF-41, during the 1981 cruise, none of their hassles with Libyan fighters giving an opportunity to open fire under the prevailing Rules of Engagement.

In 1982, the *Nimitz* spent some time on 'Bagel Station' off the Lebanese coast supporting the Marine garrison in Beirut. This involved constantly steaming within sight of the Lebanese coast, to provide maximum moral support for the US Marines in Beirut, and maintaining a 24-hour alert against suicide attacks and other terrorist threats.

Later (but still as part of CVW-8) VF-84 made a NorLant cruise aboard USS *Nimitz* between 15 August and 16 November 1986, which included extensive air combat exercises with a number of opponents including the Royal Norwegian air force. The squadron next undertook a round-the-world cruise from 30 December 1986 to 26 July 1987, incorporating a stop for missile practice at NAS Roosevelt Roads. During 1988 the squadron and the rest of Air Wing Eight transferred to the *Roosevelt*. A NorLant cruise was next, between 25 August and 11 October 1988, followed by a Mediterranean deployment from 30 December 1988 to 30 June 1989. During 1989 a VF-84 Tomcat and crew made history by becoming the first fleet aircraft to make an arrested landing on the new carrier *Abraham Lincoln* (CVN-72). On board the USS *Theodore Roosevelt*, the 'Jolly Rogers' sailed to the Red Sea, Persian Gulf and Mediterranean from 28 December 1991 until 28 June 1992, missing out on participation in Operations Desert Storm and Desert Shield but flying CAPS and sweeps over Iraq in support of UN operations in the area.

Between 11 March and 8 September 1993, VF-84 was the sole F-14 unit deployed during *Roosevelt*'s Mediterranean cruise in support of the Special Marine Air-to-Ground Task Force. By 1993, some reports were suggesting that VF-84 would disband in mid-1995, but other sources suggested that the unit would replace VF-143 with CVW-7. In fact, the squadron did decommission during October 1995, but the 'Jolly Rogers' traditions and insignia then passed to VF-103, along with the famous bones of a former 'Jolly Rogers' ensign.

Left: The 'Jolly Rogers' can trace their traditions back to the wartime VF-17, via a takeover of VF-61 in the 1950s. The original 'Jolly Rogers' were among the most successful users of the F4U Corsair, one of which is seen here in VF-17 colours, escorting a modern 'Jolly Rogers' F-14A.

Right: VF-84's F-14As lost their black fins and black/yellow nose markings around 1982, when low-visibility markings and tactical camouflage were introduced. The markings crept back gradually during the mid-1980s, with restoration of the nose stripe (albeit in toned-down form). During the late 1980s, coloured fintips appeared on CAG-assigned aircraft, initially in yellow and later in red. Only on CAG and CO aircraft have full-colour markings reappeared.

Left: The last VF-84 colour scheme is completely toned down, with all squadron insignia applied in dark grey over the tactical blue-grey camouflage. The squadron was the TARPS-equipped unit within Carrier Air Wing Eight, and continued to serve alongside the 'Black Aces' of VF-41. VF-84 disbanded as part of the current drawdown of the F-14 force, which will end when all CVWs have been reduced to a single F-14 squadron.

Top right: *For many years, VF-84 was partnered by VF-41 (the 'Black Aces') as the fighter component of Air Wing Eight, principally aboard the USS Nimitz. Here, Tomcats from the two squadrons formate for the camera.*

Below right: *This VF-84 F-14A has empty Phoenix pallets under the fuselage, but carries a Sparrow and a Sidewinder under each wing, with auxiliary fuel tanks under the intake ducts.*

Far right: *The stylised skull and crossbones badge of VF-84 as applied to 'toned-down' squadron Tomcats. This aircraft also carries a Battle E and black fin-caps. Air wing codes were carried on the inner faces of the tailfins.*

Above: *Inevitably, VF-84's flying suit patch has the Grumman 'two-tailed cat' caricature in piratical regalia, leaning on a skull.*

Above: *The 'skull-and-crossed bones' flag (the Jolly Roger) was the insignia of pirates for many years, and is worn proudly by 'Jolly Rogers' aircrew (today VF-103).*

Right: *Two VF-84 F-14As show off the original 'high-vis' colour scheme used by the 'Jolly Rogers'.*

Below: *The switch to single F-14 squadron air wings saw the end of 200-series Modexes. This VF-84 F-14A wears old-style high-visibility colours because of its assignment to the CAG.*

Grumman F-14 Operators

VF-101 'Grim Reapers'

Until late 1994, VF-101 (callsign 'Gunfighter') was the East Coast fleet replenishment squadron for the Tomcat, responsible for training pilots and NFOs before they join Atlantic Fleet fighter squadrons. Permanently assigned to the training role from 1958, VF-101 successively acted as a training unit for the F4D Skyray, the F3D Skyknight and F3H Demon, and the F4H Phantom, operating from Key West and Oceana. A purely Phantom training operation for most of the 1960s and 1970s, VF-101 stood up as an F-14 component at NAS Oceana in 1975. The unit organised a replenishment training programme for future F-14 pilots, backseaters and maintenance personnel, although VF-124 had already started training Tomcat crews (including those from the first Atlantic Fleet units) from 1973. By March 1977, such training was the sole responsibility of VF-101, which had finally discarded the last of its Phantoms by redesignating the F-4 element as VF-171 on 5 August 1977, formally becoming the East Coast F-14 RTS during that summer.

VF-101's first intake of aircrew was for VF-41 and VF-84, these two units entering the conversion process in mid-1976 and standing up in February 1977. VF-101 did not train all the Atlantic Fleet squadrons, VF-14, VF-32, VF-142 and VF-143 converting under the auspices of VF-124 'Gunfighters' at Miramar. It did, however, oversee the conversion of VF-11, VF-31, VF-33, VF-74, VF-102, VF-103, VF-201 and VF-202, and today provides suitably trained replacement air and ground personnel for all fleet F-14 squadrons. This involves the unit in converting aircrew to the new aircraft type (including carrier landing training), and giving rudimentary tactical and weapons training. As such, VF-101 makes numerous short deployments to sea, although its aircraft seldom stay on a carrier overnight. Known as the 'Gunfighters' for many years, VF-101 finally gave up that nickname in the winter of 1982 to avoid the clash with rival VF-124, instead using the 'Grim Reapers' identity. As the only Atlantic Fleet F-14 squadron not assigned to a carrier air wing, VF-101's aircraft have always worn the same 'AD' tailcode, although markings have changed frequently over the years.

F-14A+s (since redesignated F-14Bs) were taken on charge in 1988, these being used to train aircrew for F-14B squadrons from both Atlantic and Pacific Fleet units, until all F-14Bs were consolidated on the East Coast. VF-124 similarly took responsibility for all F-14D training.

On 12 September 1990, VF-101's CO dropped a pair of live Mk 84 bombs, demonstrating the squadron's new-found 'Bombcat' capability, and inaugurating the start of strike warfare training by the unit. VF-101 was tasked as model managers for the Tomcat Strike Fighter programme, undertaking to develop the air-to-surface training syllabus while also training fleet squadrons and replacement aircrew. This has since become a vital part of the Tomcat's role. VF-101 is the destination for RAF Tornado ADV aircrew flying the F-14 on exchange tours with the US Navy.

The dramatic post-Cold War drawdown of the Tomcat force has resulted in a much-diminished need for F-14 aircrew, and it was decided that to continue to maintain separate conversion training units for each fleet would be an unaffordable luxury. Accordingly, it was decided to disband one

Above right: VF-101's initial marking consisted of a broad red tail band, bordered in blue, with 'AD' tailcodes edged in gold. The tailband had disappeared by 1978, leaving aircraft with an extremely plain finish.

Right: This F-14A carries the personal 'Moon-equipped' insignia of Commander Moon Vance, with a crescent moon on the tailfins and bloodshot eyes on the nose. The markings were painted on both sides of the aircraft.

Below: Before the present 'Grim Reapers' markings were adopted, VF-101's Tomcats seldom wore badges. This aircraft, with its winged anchor motif, was an exception.

Far right: One of VF-101's Tomcats is pulled into a steep climb, 'burners blazing.

Right: The 'Grim Reapers' insignia goes back to 3 June 1942, when Fighter Squadron 10 commissioned with F4F Wildcats, which it took to war.

of the two units, VF-124 drawing the short straw, probably provoking the later decision to combine the F-14 force at NAS Oceana. VF-101 is the surviving Tomcat training unit and initially maintained a detachment at Miramar with F-14Ds, as VF-101 Det West, after the West Coast FRS, VF-124, disbanded in September 1994. The West Coast detachment returned to Miramar during 1996, with the F-14D front-line units.

Below: VF-101's CAG-bird wears the squadron's 'Grim Reaper' insignia in red and black. VF-101 has never had very colourful markings.

Today, VF-101's syllabus is divided into five phases, and follows a building block approach. The initial stage is the FAM (familiarisation) phase. Next the trainees move to the WCS (Weapons Control Systems) phase, before moving on to the Strike phase, usually completed through detachments to El Centro or Fallon. The TACTICS phase follows, and is the heart of the replacement training syllabus. It is completed at Key West, which enjoys superior weather and range availability. The final make-or-break part of the course is the CQ (Carrier Qualification) phase. Obviously a Tomcat pilot or RIO who cannot safely fly the aircraft aboard a carrier cannot complete

Below: One of VF-101's F-14Ds flies over the Florida Keys. The tactical phase of the conversion phase finishes with sorties flown from NAS Key West.

Right: This VF-101 Tomcat was the first aircraft to land aboard the carrier Stennis, in January 1996, piloted by Lt Dave Dobbs.

his training, and cannot become a productive member of the F-14 community. The contents of each phase differ slightly according to which course is being conducted (Fleet A, Fleet B, Fleet D or A/B to D transition). The Det West course was an abbreviated version of the Fleet D course. VF-101 is proud of its status as the sole producer of F-14 aircrew, and as the heart of the Tomcat community. During 1996-97, several of VF-101's F-14s wore the markings of disbanded F-14 squadrons, keeping their traditions and insignia alive, albeit briefly and in a low-profile manner.

Grumman F-14 Operators

VF-102 'Diamondbacks'

The 'Diamondbacks' (callsign 'Diamondback') began transitioning to the F-14 during July 1981. Its first traps were made aboard the *America* during May 1982, by which time the squadron was virtually fully operational, having completed conversion smoothly despite the need for specialised training with the TARPS pod.

The squadron deployed with CVW-1 aboard the *America* in the Atlantic/Caribbean (30 May 1982 to 8 July 1982) and North Atlantic/Mediterranean (23 August to 4 November 1982), before its first full Mediterranean/Indian Ocean cruise which included operations in support of the US peacekeepers between December 1982

and June 1983. Despite the squadron's relative inexperience, its performance on the cruise was enough to win it a handsome trophy from Grumman, in recognition that it was that year's top Atlantic Fleet TARPS squadron. Embarked on USS *America* as part of CVW-1 from November to December 1983, VF-102 provided a presence in the Caribbean following Operation Just Cause in October of that year. February 1984 saw a 20-day Caribbean exercise, again aboard *America*, before a full Central America/Mediterranean/Indian Ocean cruise was undertaken between April and November 1984.

CV-66 and CVW-1 went to sea for Ocean

Safari in the North Atlantic for a period which included the whole of September 1985. Between 10 March 1986 and 14 September 1986, VF-102 again saw action, this time in support of operations against Libya, during which VF-102 aircraft were fired upon by Libyan SA-5s and anti-aircraft artillery during Operation Prairie Fire. The squadron then flew top cover for the 15 April 1986 El Dorado Canyon airstrikes against Libyan targets. During February 1987, VF-102 participated in *Roosevelt*'s shakedown cruise in the Caribbean, then flew in Exercise Solid Shield '87, which gave the unit opportunities for practising DACT with USAF F-15 Eagles. 1988 saw a brief Atlantic deployment (from 21 March to 6 May 1988). Still as part of Air Wing 1, VF-102 sailed with the *America* on a Caribbean

and NorLant cruise between 8 February 1989 and 3 April 1989, a Mediterranean and Indian Ocean cruise from 11 May 1989 until 10 November 1989, and a Red Sea to Persian Gulf deployment from 28 December 1990 to 18 May 1991 – the latter for combat in Operation Desert Storm.

In 1990 the 'Diamondbacks' earned the Grand Slam award. The following year they sailed on a NorLant cruise from 21 August until 11 October, participating in Exercise North Star. Later that year Air Wing One and the *America* sailed for a NorLant/Mediterranean/Red Sea and Persian Gulf deployment between 2 December 1991 and 6 June 1992.

Between 11 August 1993 and 5 February 1994, VF-102 was the sole F-14 unit deployed with CVW-1 aboard USS *America*

Above: VF-102's F-14As wear a band of red diamonds around the forward fuselage, and have traditionally used a diamond on the fin in which to display the appropriate CVW tailcode. Here a Phoenix- and Sidewinder-armed aircraft prepares to launch from USS America during September 1984. VF-102 is tasked with tactical recce duties, as well as fleet air defence. The aircraft depicted typifies VF-102's standard colour scheme, although aircraft did briefly have the squadron markings applied in shades of grey.

Left: Illustrating the CAG/squadron commander scheme used in 1984 is this F-14A, which has white diamonds on its red rudders, as well as the usual nose band and wing glove diamonds. A small number of aircraft in each squadron (usually those allocated to the CAG, CO and XO) retained colourful markings after the 1980s toning-down.

Right: The 1990s have seen a slight increase in the use of colourful squadron markings, still of limited extent and still tending to use dull shades. The overall light grey colour scheme has been reintroduced widely. This VF-102 F-14A has the full complement of diamonds, with the unit's rattlesnake marking applied in the fin diamond, and a small solid diamond replacing the hyphen in the VF-102 squadron designation on the ventral fin.

for a Mediterranean cruise, sister squadron VF-33 having disbanded on 1 October 1993. During this deployment, the squadron participated in operations supporting Operations Provide Promise and Deny Flight, and then Operation Restore Hope, off the coast of Mogadishu, Somalia, before going on to support Operation Southern Watch in southern Iraq. The squadron transitioned to the F-14B in June 1994. The 'Diamondbacks' 1995-96 Mediterranean cruise aboard the *America* included sorties in support of Operation Deliberate Force and won the squadron its first Battle E.

Right: Even with toned-down national insignia, VF-102 has often retained its traditional red diamonds.

Below: Some F-14 toned-down colour schemes have seen unit insignia applied in a lighter tone than the base camouflage colour.

Above: The VF-102 badge seen in toned-down form on the fin of a squadron Tomcat, complete with the 'AB' tailcode of Air Wing One, and the 'USA' of USS America.

Left: One of VF-102's new F-14Bs. The squadron has been among the first to be equipped with LANTIRN, which allows autonomous use of LGBs and more precise night attack navigation and weapons delivery. The F-14B has increased thrust.

Above: This rattlesnake badge is worn with pride by the squadron's aircrew. The diamondback is a species of rattlesnake.

Below: VF-102 transitioned to the F-14B in 1994, and has now gained LANTIRN capability, transferring (with CVW-1) to the CVN-73 USS George Washington. The squadron was the first to train with LANTIRN F-14Bs at NAS Fallon.

VF-103 'Sluggers', now 'Jolly Rogers'

VF-103 commissioned in 1952 as the 'Sluggers', flying the F4U Corsair. The squadron subsequently transitioned to the F9F Cougar, the F8U Crusader, and the F-4J and F-4S Phantom. Highlights of the squadron's history included the only night MiG kill of the Vietnam War. VF-103 (callsign 'Clubleaf') transitioned to the F-14 during 1983, under the auspices of VF-101. The squadron spent the winter of 1983/1984 preparing to go to sea aboard the USS Saratoga, which had just emerged from a long SLEP, as part of Air Wing Three. Also during 1983, the squadron received a CNO Safety S. The ensuing April-October 1984 shakedown cruise was spent with the Sixth Fleet, not least because of the continuing tension in the Lebanon. VF-103, again partnered by VF-74, undertook a Mediterranean and Indian Ocean cruise aboard the Saratoga between 25 August 1985 and 16 April 1986. On 10 October 1985, VF-103 aircrews intercepted the Egyptair airliner carrying the hijackers of the Achille Lauro, forcing it to land at NAS Sigonella, where the terrorists were arrested. This action earned the squadron a Navy Unit Commendation.

The Saratoga carried VF-103 to the Mediterranean again from 24 March 1986 to 15 April, operating in support of the US strikes against Libya. The squadron won the COMNAVAIRLANT Tactical Reconnaissance Trophy in 1986. A 1987 cruise brought the opportunity for ACM flying with French Super Etendards, while

Right: This VF-103 'Sluggers' F-14B has its 'AA' tailcode applied in highly stylised form. The old 'arrow' tail badge was replaced by the more intricate 'club and cloverleaf' insignia shortly before the Gulf War.

Below: This F-14A of VF-103 wears the simple stylised arrow marking applied to the unit's F-14s (in one form or another) for most of its existence as the 'Sluggers'.

the TARPS aircraft were able to photograph the Soviet helicopter cruiser Kiev from close quarters.

On 15 August 1988 the squadron began a temporary deployment aboard USS Independence, rounding the Horn and arriving at San Diego eight weeks after departure. The squadron then rejoined the Saratoga for a further Mediterranean/Red Sea cruise, which was undertaken between 7 August 1990 and 28 March 1991, before which VF-103 had traded in its A model Tomcats for F-14A+s, taking these to war in Operation Desert Storm. One of the squadron's aircraft, flown by pilot Lt Devon Jones and RIO Lt Lawrence Randolph 'Rat' Slade, was shot down by an SA-2, the pilot being rescued by a force of USAF A-10s and MH-53s and the RIO being taken prisoner by the Iraqis. The squadron won the COMNAVAIRLANT Battle E for 1991, this following the award of the 1990 CNO Safety Award.

Before its participation in Desert Storm, VF-103 adopted new-look markings, with a club and arrow insignia on the fins replacing

Above: This VF-103 F-14B wears the revised 'Jolly Rogers' scheme applied to the squadron's aircraft (in various forms) from 1 October 1995. Full colour schemes are not restricted to CAG, CO and XO aircraft, but neither are they universal.

the original arrowhead device. The unit began intensive training in the air-to-surface role following its return from the Gulf. Still equipped with the F-14B (as the F-14A+ was redesignated in the autumn of 1991), VF-103 flew in support of Operation Provide Promise along with the other squadrons of CVW-17 from USS Saratoga from 6 May 1992 until 6 November that same year. 1992 was an exceptional year for the 'Sluggers', the squadron winning a CNO

Right: The 'club and cloverleaf' insignia of VF-103 (complete with baseball bat and stylised F-14) is now no more than a memory, VF-103 having taken over the insignia and traditions of the 'Jolly Rogers' in October 1995, on the disbandment of VF-84.

Above: With the assumption of the 'Jolly Rogers' identity once associated with VF-84, the aircrew of VF-103 now wear this flying suit badge, almost identical to the old VF-84 patch. The 'Sluggers' identity has gone.

Safety S, and a second consecutive COMNAVAIRLANT Battle E. The squadron was the first F-14B unit to employ air-to-ground weapons while flying from an aircraft carrier. The squadron demonstrated the Tomcat's reach in the air-to-ground role during its cruise, hitting targets on Egypt's Wadi Natrun range after a 1,700 nm transit. Sister squadron VF-74 disestablished on 28 April 1994, leaving VF-103 as CVW-17's only Tomcat unit. VF-103 had deployed alone for the final cruise of the 'Super Sara', which began on 12 January 1994 with a scheduled decommissioning date of 20 August.

Some expected VF-103 to leave the fleet for about two years, perhaps to convert to the advanced F-14D or, according to some reports, while its aircraft were further upgraded to some unspecified interim configuration. In fact, during 1994, VF-103 pioneered the introduction of the LANTIRN laser targeting pod on the Tomcat, giving the aircraft an autonomous PGM capability for the first time. During its 1994 deployment VF-103 became the first Tomcat unit to deliver LGBs, dropping two on the Capo Frasca range on the Sardinian coast on 2 May 1994, with CVW-17 Hornets and Intruders providing target designation. On its return to the USA, VF-103 provided

the trials aircraft for the initial Tomcat/LTS demonstrations, and Commander Hnarakis and Lt Cdr Slade made the first live drop (on the Vieques Island range during March 1995).

VF-103's traditional sister unit (VF-74) was not the only casualty of the downsizing of the F-14 force and the scaling-down of air wings from two 10-aircraft squadrons to one 14-aircraft squadron. Among the squadrons which disappeared were some of the Navy's most famous and historic fighter units. With one exception these units went into oblivion. On the disbandment of VF-84 in October 1995, however, VF-103 took over the insignia and traditions of the 'Jolly Rogers', and its aircraft were quickly repainted with the disbanded squadron's traditional skull-and-crossbones badge, and it was the 'Sluggers' tradition and insignia which disappeared.

Following the successful LANTIRN demonstrations, VF-103 became the first squadron to deploy with the new equipment, initially for a two-week joint fleet exercise with the Royal Navy (between 26 April and 17 May 1996), and then for a full six-month deployment (again aboard *Enterprise*). Nine of the squadron's 14 aircraft were modified to carry LANTIRN, six

also being compatible with MXV-810 Cat's Eyes NVGs. The squadron flew missions in support of Operation Decisive Endeavor over Bosnia, and then moved on to participate in operations in support of Operation Southern Watch. VF-103 is likely to be among the first units to re-equip with a mixture of F-14Bs and F-14Ds.

Above: VF-103's traditional marking is a yellow arrow, but on the F-14 this has usually been presented in outline form only, except on CAG and CO aircraft. This F-14A also has full-colour, full-size national markings.

Above: A pair of VF-103 F-14Bs patrols shortly before Operation Desert Storm. The 1991 Gulf War marked the first US Navy combat loss of an F-14, one of VF-103's aircraft falling victim to an SA-2. Fortunately, both crew ejected safely, one being rescued and the other being taken prisoner.

Right: When it transitioned to the F-14A+ (now known as the F-14B), VF-103 adopted a new squadron marking, with a curving arrow bisecting a clover leaf, superimposed on a baseball bat. The aircraft wears a small 'S' on the lower part of the fin, signifying the award of a Safety S. VF-103 is the sole surviving Tomcat squadron within CVW-17, partner squadron VF-74 having disbanded.

VF-111 'Sundowners'

VF-111 (callsign 'Sundowner') was established as VA-156 on 4 June 1956. It was redesignated VF-111 on 20 January 1959, and flew F11F-1s, F8U-2Ns, F-8Cs, F-8Hs, F-4Bs and F-4Ns, winning a fearsome reputation, most notably over Vietnam, where the squadron flew several cruises with F-8 Crusaders and F-4 Phantoms. A small detachment from VF-111, known as 'Omar's Orphans', deployed aboard the USS *Intrepid* during 1967-68, and one of the detachment pilots (Lt Tony Nargi) downed a MiG-21. The squadron had adopted the insignia of the old VF-111 (disestablished on 19 January 1959) but, while the new VF-111 can carry on the traditions of the old VF-111, which dates to World War II, it cannot claim that squadron's lineage. The original VF-111 had originated as VF-11 in October 1942, and the original squadron picked up their nickname for their performance in downing aircraft decorated with Japan's rising sun insignia. The squadron transitioned to the F8F after the war (retaining a flight of Hellcats for recce duties) and then transitioned to the F9F-2 Panther. The squadron's CO, Lt Cdr W. T. Amen, downed a MiG-15 on 9 November 1950, marking the first USN kill of the Korean War. The squadron also flew the last navy strike of the Korean War, on 27 July 1953.

The squadron began F-14A operations in 1978, replacing its F-4J Phantoms, and deployed aboard USS *Kitty Hawk* on 30 May 1979. This cruise with CVW-15 was extended until 15 February 1980 to enable *Kitty Hawk* to remain in the Arabian Sea off Iran during the hostage crisis, and also to observe any Soviet activity in Afghanistan. Following a second WestPac and Indian

Ocean cruise with the same carrier (between 1 April and 23 November 1981), the 'Sundowners' and the rest of CVW-15, including sister squadron VF-51, shifted to USS *Carl Vinson*, carrying out a world cruise (its first with TARPS F-14s) between 1 March and 29 October 1983. This took them from Norfolk to Alameda through the Caribbean, around the Cape of Good Hope via the Indian Ocean to Australia. En route the carrier spent time on 'Gonzo Station' off the coast of Iran and with the US Sixth Fleet off Lebanon.

During a brief EastPac cruise from 14 May to 28 June 1984, VF-111 participated in Exercise RimPac '84, and later that year a second such cruise (between 31 July and 22 August) took the squadron to Readex 4-84. At the end of 1984, VF-111 sailed for a WestPac and Indian Ocean deployment, departing on 18 October and returning on 24 May 1985.

Just prior to its 1986/87 WestPac and Indian Ocean deployment (from 12 August to 5 February), still with CVW-15 aboard the *Vinson*, one of the 'Sundowners' pilots had an embarrassing experience: on 5 May 1986 he landed on the wrong aircraft-carrier (USS *Constellation*) when meaning to land aboard the *Vinson* (then some 12 miles away) during daylight carquals.

VF-111's next deployment was another EastPac, WestPac and Indian Ocean cruise between 15 June and 14 December 1988, which included Operation Earnest Will. During this sailing, VF-111 flew more than 1,000 sorties and more than 2,000 flying hours, amassing 1,025 traps. The cruise also saw the first trials of the new KS-135A high-altitude camera and the 610-mm lens.

CVW-15 and VF-111 next travelled on a

Left: Sharkmouths have been a common sight on 'Sundowner' Tomcats, particularly during the late 1970s and early 1980s.

Below: Throughout their lives (always spent with CVW-15), VF-111's aircraft have been assigned the Modex code 200.

Above: During the mid-1980s, the 'Sundowners' went the way of all US Navy Fleet squadrons and were reduced to flying grey Tomcats with a 'colour scheme' that only hinted at their former glory.

Left: In 1989, VF-111's specially-painted CAG-bird sported a far more graphic 'sunburst' tail and 'Miss Molly' nose art. VF-111 was then part of CVW-15 aboard USS Carl Vinson.

combined NorPac and WestPac sailing from 5 September 1989 until 8 November (participating in Exercise PacEx '89), followed by a WestPac and Indian Ocean deployment between 1 February 1990 and 31 July (participating in Exercise Team Spirit '90). In December 1991, the US Navy cancelled plans for VF-111 and VF-51 to be the first fleet squadrons to operate the F-14D Super Tomcat.

Returning to USS *Kitty Hawk* with CVW-15, VF-111 made an east-to-west sailing around the Cape of Good Hope between 18 October and 11 December 1991. From 3 November 1992 to 3 May 1993, VF-111 made an Indian Ocean and Persian Gulf cruise in support of Operations Restore Hope and Southern Watch. On 24 June 1994 VF-111 departed with the *Kitty Hawk* and CVW-15 on a WestPac, Indian Ocean and Persian Gulf deployment again involving Operation Southern Watch. This was VF-111's last cruise, as the squadron disestablished at Miramar on 31 March 1995. This saw the end of arguably the most colourful F-14 squadron, whose aircraft had always been decorated with gaudy sharkmouths and which had often featured sunburst ventral fins tailfins.

Below: VF-111's traditional, official badge shows Japanese fighters going down in flames in front of a rising sun, reflecting the squadron's World War II success.

VF-111's trademark sunburst insignia.

The VF-111 CAG-bird has often worn a full-colour red and white sunburst over the whole vertical tailfin. This has sometimes been centred at the base of the leading edge, and sometimes at the centre of the fin root, as seen here.

VF-114 'Aardvarks'

The history of VF-114 (callsign 'Aardvark') can be traced to the July 1934 commissioning of VB-5B, through subsequent identities as VB-2 and VB-11, and post-war redesignations as VA-11A and VA-114. The squadron subsequently became VF-114 on 15 February 1950. The squadron's ant-eating mascot, named 'Zot', is a replica of the 'BC' comic strip aardvark. A 2-ft (0.6-m) replica carved out of wood

The VF-114 official insignia.

Gruman F-14 Operators

was encased and prominently displayed in the squadron ready room. The squadron flew F4Us from the *Philippine Sea* in Korea, subsequently transitioning to the F9F-2 Panther, the F2H Demon and the F3H Demon before the squadron became the first Pacific Fleet F-4B squadron.

After five cruises in Vietnam (during which the squadron destroyed five enemy aircraft) the squadron began transitioning to the F-14A Tomcat on 15 December 1975 from the F-4J Phantom. Transition to the Tomcat was completed 1 January 1977, and the 'Aardvarks' made their first cruise with CVW-11 aboard USS *Kitty Hawk* (CV-63) in the western Pacific, departing on 25 October 1977 and returning home on 14 May 1978. Mediterranean cruises aboard

USS *America* as part of CVW-11 followed in 1979 (13 March to 22 September) and 1981 (14 April to 12 November) – an unusual series of events for a West Coast squadron. The latter trip, which took CVW-11 to the Indian Ocean, saw USS *America* become the largest USN vessel to transit the Suez Canal. Before returning on 12 November 1981, VF-114 logged 3,100 flying hours and 1,500 traps. With the same air wing, the squadron subsequently joined USS *Enterprise*, fresh from its three-year overhaul, in 1982. Together they sailed on a NorPac, WestPac and Indian Ocean cruise from 1 September 1982 until 28 May 1983. That year the squadron was awarded the Mutha trophy.

VF-111 stayed with Air Wing Eleven

aboard the *Enterprise*, deploying in 1986 for a WestPac, Indian Ocean and Mediterranean cruise between 15 January and 12 August. From this cruise, VF-114 adopted Modex codes in the 100 series, replacing its previous 200-series codes.

1987 saw VF-114 depart for a short NorPac sailing (25 October to 24 November), followed by a WestPac and Indian Ocean sailing in 1988 (5 January to 3 July, for Operation Praying Mantis). In 1989 VF-111 embarked on a round-the-world cruise (including Operation Classic Resolve) from 17 September 1989 to 16 March 1990. The squadron retired its traditional orange flying suits in September 1990, but orange-coloured beer continued to be served at squadron functions, and the orange flying

suits were reintroduced in early 1992.

The 'Aardvarks' next deployed with CVW-11 aboard USS *Abraham Lincoln* for its round-the-Horn cruise from Norfolk to its new home port of Alameda. Departing on 25 September 1991 and arriving on 20 November, *Lincoln* carried a composite air wing. The squadron next left for a full-scale WestPac, Indian Ocean and Persian Gulf cruise with CVW-11 aboard 'Honest Abe' on 28 May 1991, returning home on 25 November 1991. On this deployment, VF-114 flew in support of Operation Fiery Vigil, on what was to be VF-114's last Tomcat cruise

In 1991 VF-111 gained a Safety S, and the Mutha Trophy in 1993. The 'Aardvarks' were disestablished on 30 April 1993.

Above: 'Bear' intercepts were once a common part of an F-14 squadron's life, as the Soviet aircraft kept an eye on US Navy activities or transitted en route to bases in Cuba, Africa and Vietnam. Here an 'Aardvarks' Tomcat escorts an AV-MF Tu-95RT 'Bear-D' near the Philippines in March 1983.

Right: By the mid-1980s, VF-114 had toned down (slightly) by deleting its orange fintips and ventral fins, while still flying orange-striped gloss grey Tomcats.

VF-124 'Gunfighters'

VF-124 (callsign 'Gunslinger') was established as VF-53 on 16 August 1948 and became VF-124 on 11 April 1958, when elements of VF-53 and VF-194 were merged. The introduction of the new generation of swept-wing fast jets necessitated a major expansion of the US Navy's training machine, and the formation of VF-124 reflected this. In June 1961 the squadron moved from Moffett Field to NAS Miramar. As a fast-jet training unit, VF-124 operated virtually every version of the Vought F-8 and took delivery of the last example built in 1964. For many years the squadron was referred to as 'Crusader College', providing combat training for all F-8 fleet replacement pilots as well as basic, refresher and maintenance training. In addition, VF-124 had the supplementary task of providing fighter support for the USAF's Air Defense Command, a task which it carried into its F-14 days.

The 'Gunfighters' were the West Coast fleet replenishment squadron with the task of training Tomcat pilots and RIOs for the Pacific Fleet. In 1970, the former Crusader training squadron stood up to become the first Tomcat FRS, although the first F-14A did not arrive until 8 October 1972 as the unit was busy establishing the infrastructure for future F-14 operations. In 1973 it was a VF-124 F-14 that appeared at the Paris Air Salon, where it gave a series of very impressive flight demonstrations and was hailed as the star of the show. Crews from VF-1 and VF-2 had the honour of participating in the first Tomcat conversion course, commencing that same year. The first carquals were undertaken aboard USS *Kitty Hawk* in 1974. The next customers were VF-14 and VF-32. These units were Atlantic-based squadrons, and California-based VF-124 had the unusual distinction of training two more Atlantic fighter squadrons (VF-142 and VF-143) before VF-101 assumed the responsibility for training pilots and RIOs for the remaining Atlantic Fleet front-line squadrons. From then on VF-124 handled the conversion of eight regular Pacific Fleet squadrons. These were (in order) VF-24 and -211 (CVW-9), VF-114 and -213 (CVW-11), VF-51 and -111 (CVW-15), and VF-21 and -154 (CVW-14). In 1976, the squadron trained crews (mostly instructor pilots) from the Imperial Iranian Air Force. TARPS training began in 1980. Between 1984 and 1985, two Reserve squadrons (VF-301 and -302) gave up their F-4S Phantoms, under VF-124's expert supervision. VF-124 trained the first USAF exchange aircrews in 1985.

In the years that followed VF-124 masterminded replacement crew training for the Pacific Fleet, while maintaining an enviable safety record. On 18 January 1983, VF-124 passed 25,000 accident-free flying hours, a remarkable achievement for a unit so closely involved with the Tomcat's troublesome early years, and in training many relatively inexperienced pilots and RIOs. Soon afterwards, in March, the 'Gunfighters' completed three years of flight operations without major mishap, despite

Left: During the 1970s, typical VF-124 markings comprised the unit's twin 'swoosh' on the fins, echoed by the stripes on the top surface of the wings and elevators. Both the Modex number and tailcode had white drop shadows.

Below: For the 1986 Reconnaissance Air Meet at Bergstrom AFB, several of VF-124's F-14s gained temporary camouflage applied with a broom.

Below: This Tomcat was a show aircraft during 1987. With VF-124's Distinguished Unit Citation below the canopy rail, a yellow Safety S was also carried on the port side. On the tail could be found the ubiquitous 'Tomcat' character and the legend 'Fightertown USA' – an allusion to NAS Miramar.

Below right: Smaller fin stripes were adopted during the 1980s, as worn by this black-tailed F-14 in 1989.

Grumman F-14 Operators

the number of inexperienced 'nugget' aircrew that passed through its hands. In that time, crews logged 18,150 sorties and over 2,700 traps. By 1987, the squadron had reached a total of 68,000 mishap-free flying hours, when the CO, Cdr Jay 'Spook' Yakeley, logged his 3,000th F-14 flying hour.

The squadron accepted its first F-14D Super Tomcat on 16 November 1990 at Miramar, and was for many years the sole F-14D FRS, reflecting the concentration of the D-model within the Pacific Fleet. The squadron sent four of the new F-14D Super Tomcats aboard the *Nimitz* on 2 October 1991 for the D model's first fleet carrier qualifications. Although two Pacific Fleet squadrons briefly flew the F-14A+, the decision was soon taken to concentrate the A+ in Atlantic Fleet squadrons, and VF-124's involvement with the variant was very limited.

In 1991, VF-124 acquired a small number of Beech T-34C Turbo Mentors for use as spotter aircraft on target ranges, and for AFAC training. The squadron began 'Bombcat' air-to-ground training in 1991-1992.

With the change from two 10-aircraft F-14 squadrons per air wing to one 14-aircraft squadron, many Tomcat units were disestablished. The training requirement was significantly reduced, and the decision was taken to centralise all F-14 training within a single FRS. Almost simultaneously, the US Navy decided to concentrate all remaining front-line F-14 squadrons at NAS Oceana. This spelled the end for the Miramar-based Tomcat wing, and removed the need for a separate West Coast FRS.

Accordingly, VF-124 was disestablished on 30 September 1994 (the last day of the fiscal year), passing over the entire Tomcat training commitment to VF-101 on the East Coast, although the latter unit then maintained a West Coast Detachment with F-14Ds until the West Coast Tomcat community had almost completed its move from Miramar ('Fightertown USA') to Oceana. The squadron made its last cruise aboard USS *Ranger* on 11 March 1993.

Above: This patch was worn by many Tomcat crews (from various squadrons) before and immediately after the move from Miramar.

Right: This VF-124 F-14A wears one of the earliest Tomcat colour schemes. The aircraft is painted gull grey and white overall, while the squadron markings consist of sweeping red flashes on the tailfins and with triple red stripes on the tailplanes and wingtips.

Left: VF-124's 'Gunfighters' nickname dated from its heritage as an F-8 Crusader FRS. Although the F-14 has an internal cannon, it is best known as a missileer.

Right: This pair of VF-124 F-14As was specially decorated for air show and display appearances, and has the unofficial squadron insignia superimposed on the aircraft's yellow tail flashes. The fins are black, while the ventral fins, canopy frames and anti-dazzle panels were black, edged in yellow.

Below: The early VF-124 tail stripes were gracefully curved, but were soon replaced by straighter, tapering angular stripes. These were applied in red on some aircraft, but were toned down in black or grey on others.

VF-142 'Ghostriders'

VF-142 (callsign 'Dakota') was established as VF-193 on 24 August 1948, and was redesignated VF-142 on 15 October 1963. The 'Ghostriders' transitioned to the F-14A Tomcat at Miramar, CA, in 1974. Prior to this, the unit had flown the F-3B Demon, and it had then undertaken six combat cruises in Southeast Asia, chalking up several North Vietnamese MiG kills with its F-4Bs and then F-4Js.

While becoming an F-14 user, the squadron shifted from the Pacific to Atlantic Fleet with Oceana, VA, as its new home base. Formerly, the squadron had flown the F-4J Phantom. As part of CVW-6, the 'Ghostriders' made their first carrier deployment aboard USS *America*, from 15 April until 25 October 1976. Air Wing Six and elements of the US Sixth Fleet were involved in Operation Fluid Drive, the emergency evacuation of US civilian personnel from Beirut's worsening civil war that year. VF-142 provided top cover for the operation.

Next came a south Atlantic cruise (10 June to 19 July 1977) and a Mediterranean cruise (29 September 1977 to 25 April 1978). The 'Ghostriders' then shifted in 1979 from CVW-6 aboard USS *America* to CVW-7 aboard USS *Dwight D. Eisenhower*, making their first sailing between 16 January and 13 July. This was *Eisenhower*'s first deployment with the Mediterranean Sixth Fleet. The *Eisenhower*'s Indian Ocean and Arabian Sea cruise of the following year (15 April to 22 December 1980) was also a notable one. At a time of tension in Iran and Afghanistan, VF-142 embarked for 317 days including a continuous underway time of 251 days. Only a single port stop was made (five days in Singapore) and the ship spent two unbroken periods at sea, of 93 and 153 days, establishing a new record. During this time, VF-142 logged 3,673 flight hours and 1,813 arrested landings.

In 1981 VF-142 and CVW-7 participated in NATO's Exercise Ocean Venture on a cruise which lasted from 17 August to 7 October. This was followed by a Mediterranean deployment between 5 January and 13 July 1982, which coincided with Israel's invasion of Lebanon. VF-142 returned to the Mediterranean from 27 April until 30 November 1983, supporting the US Marine peacekeeping contingent in Beirut, and its F-14s participated in Exercise Bright Star in Egypt that year also.

VF-111 made a Mediterranean cruise with CVW-7 and *Eisenhower* between 11 October 1984 and 8 May 1985, and the unit was awarded a Battle E in 1984. Later in 1985, the 'Ghostriders' sailed from the Caribbean to the North Atlantic for Exercise Ocean Safari '85, departing on 8 July and returning to port on 8 September. During 1985 DACT exercises, the squadron scored a 61:1 kill:loss ratio. In 1987 the squadron made a brief Caribbean and South Atlantic deployment between 16 June and 28 July.

VF-142 made a Mediterranean cruise between 29 February and 29 August 1988, and later that year the 'Ghostriders' made detachments to NAS Key West and Roosevelt Roads for gunnery and EW training, and for missile firing, respectively.

The squadron took its new F-14A+s aboard the *Eisenhower* with CVW-7 for a Mediterranean and Red Sea cruise which lasted from 8 March to 12 September 1990. This was the first carrier deployment of the F-14A+, which was redesignated F-14B on 1 May 1991. Paired with VF-143, the squadron remained with 'Ike' and CVW-7 during Desert Shield on a cruise which included a 7 August 1991 transit of the Suez Canal. The carrier, air wing and squadron withdrew from the Persian Gulf region before the start of the war with Iraq. Afterwards, between 26 September 1991 and 2 April 1992, VF-142 made a Mediterranean, Red Sea, Persian Gulf and North Atlantic cruise, during which it took part in NATO's maritime Exercise Teamwork '92.

The squadron took its F-14Bs aboard the brand-new USS *George Washington* (commissioned on 4 July 1992) for its shakedown cruise from 3 September to 23 October 1992. VF-142 then withdrew from the fleet for two years to upgrade its aircraft. The 'Ghostriders' returned to active duty for the *Washington*'s first operational cruise (along with CVW-7), departing on 20 May 1994 to participate in the D-Day commemorations and, subsequently, in Operation Deny Flight.

Above: During its 'colourful' years in the 1970s, VF-142's aircraft were bedecked with yellow and black stripes and yellow 'piano keys' on the rudders. On the reverse of the fins the F-14s carried a yellow lightning bolt and an array of coloured stars denoting the squadron colours within USS America's air group. Note the Safety S (in squadron colours) on the nose.

Right: The grey and white scheme gave way to overall grey in the late 1970s, and at the same time VF-142 adopted a whole new look. Gone were the garish markings, in favour of the graphic 'Grim Reaper' as depicted on the unit badge. The 'AG' tailcode reflects the new posting aboard USS Eisenhower.

This was, however, to be the 'Ghostriders' final cruise. Owing to cutbacks in the US Navy's fighter squadrons, CVW-7 lost one of its two Tomcat units. VF-142 was the obvious choice, with its supernatural/satanic nickname, which offended the peculiar brand of Christian political correctness which swept through the US forces in the 1990s. Accordingly, VF-142 disestablished at Oceana in April 1995.

Below: At the height of the toning-down of US Navy markings, even the CAG-birds were relatively dowdy. Here, VF-142's CAG-assigned F-14A is seen landing aboard the Eisenhower, with only its fin-caps in yellow.

Left: VF-142's aircraft wore a badge consisting of a death's head and a skeletal arm holding a cutlass.

Above: A fully toned-down F-14B of VF-142 is seen aboard the Eisenhower, shortly after Desert Storm.

VF-143 'World Famous [Pukin'] Dogs'

VF-143 (callsign 'Taproom') traces its history to VF-871, a Reserve squadron called to active duty for the Korean War on 20 July 1950, with its F4U Corsairs. The squadron flew F9F-2s, F9F-8s, and F3H-2s, using the designations VF-123 and VF-53. Its real history began as late as June 1962, with the redesignation of VF-53 ('Griffins') and its conversion to the F4H-1 Phantom. The squadron's unusual nickname dates from those days, when an officer's wife (perhaps the CO's) exclaimed that the unit's griffin badge "looked more like a puking dog!" VF-143 first went to sea aboard USS *Constellation* in February 1963, for a WestPac cruise. The following year,

Below: Two of VF-143's earliest F-14As wear the original 'high-visibility' colour scheme applied to the squadron's initial aircraft. The blue fin flash did not survive for long, and had vanished by the end of the 1970s.

operating as part of CVW-14, the squadron became involved in the Gulf of Tonkin incident and flew in the Peace Arrow attacks on North Vietnamese naval facilities on 5 August that year. Having moved on to F-4Js in the years that followed, the 'Pukin' Dogs' finally gave up their Phantoms for the F-14A Tomcat at Miramar, CA, in 1974, while converting from the Pacific to Atlantic Fleet, having amassed seven deployments to Vietnam.

As part of CVW-6, VF-143 made its first F-14 carrier deployment aboard USS *America* (to the Mediterranean) from 15 April until 25 October 1976. During this time VF-143 provided top cover and CAPs for the evacuation of US nationals from Lebanon. After a subsequent south Atlantic cruise (10 June to 19 July 1977) and Mediterranean cruise (29 September 1977 to 25 April 1978), VF-143 shifted in 1978 to CVW-7 aboard USS *Dwight D. Eisenhower*. Together with CVW-7, it made its first deployment (a Caribbean sailing) between 18 September and 26 October 1978. At that

time, *Eisenhower* was the US Navy's latest aircraft-carrier. VF-143 next travelled to the Persian Gulf for GulfEx '79, the last time any US unit could do so; the entire cruise lasted from 14 November to 4 December 1978.

Eisenhower, CVW-7 and VF-143 next made a Mediterranean deployment between 16 January and 13 July 1979. The 'Pukin' Dogs' then sailed from the Indian Ocean to 'Gonzo Station' during a 15 April to 22 December 1980 cruise when it replaced USS *Nimitz* after the ill-starred Operation Eagle Claw. Tension was running high in the area and VF-143 spent 152 days continuously at sea. The following year, VF-143 made a brief NorLant cruise, between 17 August and 7 October, to participate in NATO's Exercise Ocean Venture. This was followed by a Mediterranean cruise commencing on January 1982 – during which time Operation Peace for Galilee, Israel's invasion of Lebanon, was under way. The squadron exercised its new-found TARPS capability with three aircraft so equipped, and finally returned to port on 13 July.

VF-143 returned to the Mediterranean in 1983, from April to December, joining the US Sixth Fleet off Lebanon and participating in Exercise Bright Star '83. VF-143's Tomcats provided air defence, 'intercepting' US F-4s, F-16s and B-52s at very long range from the carrier. At the same time, Tomcats flew simulated attack missions against Egyptian airfields while providing reconnaissance coverage courtesy of their TARPS pods. The 'Pukin' Dogs' next made two brief Caribbean and NorLant deployments – 7 May to 20 June and 9 July to 9 September (for ReadEx 2-84) – before returning to sea aboard the *Eisenhower* for a Mediterranean cruise commencing on 11 October 1984. During this time, VF-143 again found itself observing the worsening situation in Lebanon, although the US Marine ground presence there had finally been withdrawn in February, following

The 'World Famous Pukin' Dogs' official badge actually shows a griffin, and not a dog at all.

Right: This F-14B wears the toned-down insignia of the 'World Famous Pukin' Dogs', with CVW-7 tailcodes and the 'Ike' legend of the USS Dwight D. Eisenhower. VF-143 uses similar markings today.

Above: The insignia of the 'World Famous Pukin' Dogs'. The 'AG' code indicates CVW-7.

terrorist bombings and retaliatory airstrikes. VF-143 returned home on 8 May 1985.

To take part in Ocean Safari '85, VF-143 embarked on a Caribbean and NorLant cruise between 8 July and 8 September 1985. After a lengthy break from sea-going operations, VF-143 returned to CVW-7 and 'Ike' for a 1988 Mediterranean cruise between 29 February and 29 August. While at sea, the squadron used its TARPS capability to photograph the Soviet warship *Baku*, a 'Kiev'-class carrier. On 26 May 1989, VF-143 began transitioning to the F-14A+ TARPS-equipped Tomcat with the delivery of its first aircraft (BuNo. 161441), and soon thereafter became fully equipped with A+ models. Paired with VF-142, the squadron remained with the same carrier and air wing during Desert Shield, on a Mediterranean and Red Sea cruise which lasted from 8 March until 12 September 1990. All were withdrawn before the start of the war with Iraq in January 1991. 1990 was a good year for VF-143, which won the Arleigh Burke Award, the DoD Phoenix Award for

maintenance excellence, the Tac Recce Trophy, and a Battle E.

In May 1991 the squadron became the first Fleet Tomcat squadron to drop live bombs from a (newly designated) F-14B. VF-143 then resumed Atlantic Fleet duties with a Mediterranean, Persian Gulf and NorLant cruise from 26 September 1991 to 2 April 1992, incorporated Exercise Teamwork '92.

Later that year VF-143, along with CVW-7, transferred to USS *George Washington* for its shakedown cruise in the Caribbean from

3 September to 23 October. The *Washington* returned to the Caribbean, briefly, with the 'Pukin' Dogs' from 19 January to 18 February 1994 before embarking on its maiden operational cruise on 20 May 1994. VF-143 was another of Air Wing 7's squadrons that participated in the D-Day commemorations of June 1994 before sailing for the Mediterranean and Operation Deny Flight. VF-143 survived the reduction of CVW-7 to a single F-14 squadron, but was directed by higher authority to drop the 'Pukin' from the

squadron's title. Thus, officially at least, VF-143 is now the 'World Famous Dogs', though the unit's original name is still widely used and universally recognised.

A cruise beginning in December 1995 saw the squadron flying over Bosnia in support of Operation Decisive Endeavor, and over Iraq in support of Operation Southern Watch. The squadron sailed on the maiden deployment of the *John C. Stennis*, cruising with LANTIRN, NVGs and the new Digital TARPS pod.

Above: Wearing Air Wing Seven's 'AG' tailcode, this F-14A from 'Pukin' Dogs' displays the blue fin flash and stripes long associated with the unit. While the stripes were generally carried on both sides of the fin, the winged 'Pukin' Dog' appeared on the outer surfaces only. Throughout the 1970s these were standard markings for VF-143, but this aircraft was specially painted in 1989 when the 'low-vis' rules were relaxed slightly.

Left: As early as 1981, half of VF-143's Tomcat fleet had adopted this scheme. Squadron markings were applied in light grey over the blue-grey finish, but national insignia is almost invisible.

Grumman F-14 Operators

VF-154 'Black Knights'

VF-154 (callsign 'Blacknight') was established on 1 February 1951 when Reserve squadron VF-837 was called to active duty for the Korean War. The squadron was designated VF-154 on 4 February 1953. The unit flew F9Fs, FJ-3 Furies, F-8 Crusaders and finally F-4 Phantoms, moving to NAS Miramar in 1959. The emblem of the 'Black Knights', showing an armoured knight at parade rest holding shield and sword, was designed by Lieutenant Junior Grade John Miottel in 1957 and drawn by cartoonist Milton Caniff of 'Steve Canyon' fame. The squadron recorded five deployments to Vietnam, with F-8s and F-4s.

The 'Black Knights' transitioned to the Tomcat and, as the last US Navy squadron to adopt the F-14, made the fastest transition of any Phantom squadron. By 1984 VF-154 was operational with its full complement of 12 F-14s, including three TARPS-equipped aircraft.

VF-154 made its first cruise, an EastPac deployment, as part of CVW-14 aboard USS Constellation, between 18 October and 15 November 1984 for FleetEx 1-85. This was followed by an even shorter sailing lasting from 6 to 16 December 1984, for Exercise Kernel Usher '85.

The 'Black Knights' went to sea 'for real' with the Constellation from 21 February to 24 August 1985 on a WestPac and Indian Ocean cruise. In 1986 VF-154 participated in Exercise Marcot '86 during a NorPac deployment of 4 September to 20 October. A 1987 'Connie'/CVW-14 WestPac and Indian Ocean deployment from 11 April to 13 October took VF-154 to 'Gonzo Station' near the Gulf of Oman and included intercepts of Iranian P-3F Orions and flights in support of Operation Earnest Will.

VF-154 made another WestPac and Indian Ocean deployment from 1 December 1988 to 1 June 1989. On 16 September 1989 VF-154 sailed, still with CVW-14, on a NorPac deployment and returned on 19 October. Paired with VF-21, the squadron operated aboard USS Independence (with CVW-14), the first carrier to arrive for Desert Shield in August 1990. This deployment lasted from 23 June to 20 December so the squadron missed Desert Storm.

In August 1991, VF-21 joined VF-154 aboard the Independence, which relieved the Midway as the sole aircraft-carrier home-ported at Yokosuka, Japan. 'Indy' departed for Japan on 5 August, arriving in Pearl Harbor on 22 August. Six days later it set sail again, reaching its final destination on 11 September. VF-154 was then operating as part of CVW-5. It embarked on a WestPac sailing between 15 October and 24 November 1991, followed by a similar cruise between 9 and 21 December. The following year, the Independence became the last US Navy carrier to visit Subic Bay in the Philippines, carrying VF-154 on a WestPac cruise from 2 to 31 March.

VF-154 sailed, via Australia, for an Indian Ocean and Persian Gulf deployment and participated in Operation Southern Watch from 15 April to 13 October 1992. Several brief WestPac cruises followed in 1993 – 25 to 30 January, 15 February to 25 March (Exercise Team Spirit '93), 11 May to 1 July, and 21 September to 14 October.

Between 17 November 1993 and 17 March 1994, VF-154 was deployed aboard the Independence for a WestPac and Indian Ocean cruise supporting US operations in Somalia and Operation Southern Watch. On 28 May 1994, VF-154 departed for RimPac '94, with CVW-5 and the Independence, returning on 4 July. The squadron is presently forward deployed at NAF Atsugi, with the USS Independence. Despite being a latecomer to the F-14, VF-154 has survived the mass decommissionings and disbandments of the last few years, unlike VF-21 'Freelancers', its traditional sister unit.

Above: Grumman's caricature twin-tailed cat appears in full armour in this 'Black Knights' flying suit patch.

VF-154 carried over its markings from the Phantom to the Tomcat, adopting black and red fin stripes. The shield is a more recent addition, compensating for the lack of colour on current aircraft. Extending the anti-glare panel from the nose to behind the cockpit has long been a VF-154 trademark, although this is now done in a 'toned-down' fashion.

Left: VF-154 has never decorated its aircraft with very colourful markings, restricting them to black and red fin chevrons.

Below: The more formal and more traditional version of the VF-154 badge is also worn as a flying suit patch.

VF-191 'Satan's Kittens'

VF-191 (callsign 'Hellcats') was founded in July 1942 as VF-19. The squadron's only wartime deployment was with USS *Lexington* (CV-16) in July 1944 with the Grumman F6F Hellcat as its equipment. After a four-month cruise as part of Air Group Nineteen, the squadron's tally reached 155 air-to-air kills and 25 ships sunk, an impressive record. Even more impressive was the fact that not one of the dive- and torpedo-bombers escorted by the squadron was ever lost to enemy action. The unit saw action again in Korea (with F8Fs) in 1950, when they were remarkably joined by aircraft from the 'Blue Angels' – the only time the US Navy's aerobatic display team has gone to war. Following this fighting, VF-191 graduated from the FJ-3 Fury to the F11F Tiger and then to the F-8 Crusader, with which it flew the bulk of its missions on 'Yankee Station' over Vietnam. VF-191 made only a single cruise with the F-4 before being disestablished on 1 March 1978. During its brief career, the squadron had established a reputation for efficiency and many expected it to reappear eventually.

'Satan's Kittens' were finally re-established on 4 December 1986 and trained with VF-124 to become one of two new F-14 squadrons (along with VF-194) intended to operate with the newly established CVW-10 aboard USS *Independence*, which moved from the East Coast to replace USS *Kitty Hawk*. The squadron actually undertook carquals in the eastern Pacific aboard USS *Enterprise* with F-14As from 24 July until 5 August 1987, but this was the only time that VF-191 went to sea.

'USS *Independence*' titles appeared on some of the squadron's assigned Tomcats in 1987/88 but no cruise was ever made. Instead, VF-191 and its sister squadron VF-194 became the victim of US Navy cuts which saw the elimination of one carrier air wing (inevitably the brand-new CVW-10). As a result, after a brief flirtation with the F-14, VF-191 itself was disestablished on 30 April 1988. Plans for VF-191 to stand up to become the third F-14D squadron (along with VF-51 and VF-111) were cancelled, and the unit had only one existence with the Tomcat and only ever flew the baseline F-14A.

Aircrew assigned to VF-191 remember it as a happy and well-led unit, although some of the aircraft assigned for training were old and somewhat troublesome.

Right: VF-191's colourful badge of a 'satanic' black cat riding a pitchfork and wielding lightning bolts was never applied to the squadron's F-14s, which wore a simple red (or grey) diamond on each rudder. VF-191 lasted only 17 months as an F-14 squadron, and never made a full operational carrier deployment. Had the squadron survived, its name would doubtless have had to have been changed in recent years, since any satanic references are now strictly banned in unit names or insignia. Air Wing 10 promised to be a great unit, and its Tomcat squadrons were well led and had excellent morale. Unfortunately, that was not enough.

Right: Some of VF-191's F-14As were painted in low-visibility colours, with unit insignia applied in grey. This VF-191 F-14A was photographed shortly before the unit disappeared, on approach to NAS Miramar.

Right: The squadron CO's F-14A seen here has a refined fin stripe, which dipped down at its leading edge. Aircrew flying helmets were similarly decorated.

Below: The red fin markings carried by VF-191 'Satan's Kittens' Tomcats during 1987 and 1988 had a rather temporary appearance. Even more short-lived were the 'USS Independence' titles and 'NM' tailcode of Carrier Air Wing Ten, as seen on this aircraft at NAS Miramar in January 1988. This aircraft has simple chordwise bands which run straight across the fin tips, each with three white diamonds superimposed.

VF-194 'Hellfires', later 'Red Lightnings'

Like its sister squadron VF-191, VF-195 (callsign 'RedFlash') has its origins in World War II as a Grumman F6F Hellcat squadron. Established in 1942 as VF-20, it was redesignated VF-9A after the war in 1947, by which time the squadron was operating the Grumman F8F Bearcat. In 1949 the unit was subjected to yet another change in identity, this time becoming VF-91. Embarked on USS *Philippine Sea* (CV-47) during the Korean War, VF-91 flew 1,938 combat missions with Grumman F9F-2 Panthers.

Over the years that followed, VF-91 flew the F9F-6 Cougar, the FJ-3 Fury and finally the F-8 Crusader. VF-91 was the first West Coast squadron to stand up with the Crusader, and also the first US Navy squadron to deploy aboard a carrier with the new aircraft type. On 1 August 1963 the squadron was renamed again, becoming VF-194 'Hellfires'.

The 'Hellfires' went to war in Vietnam with USS *Bon Homme Richard* as part of Air Wing Nineteen, and later served aboard USS *Ticonderoga* (again) and USS *Oriskany*. Having seen action over Southeast Asia,

VF-194 became the last US Navy squadron to give up its F-8s, in favour of the F-4J Phantom.

The squadron's only Phantom cruise was made with Air Wing Fifteen aboard USS *Coral Sea*, commencing in February 1977. On returning from that deployment, VF-194 was finally disestablished on 1 March 1978.

The unit's brief association with the Tomcat began at NAS Miramar on 1 December 1986, when VF-194 was recommissioned as one of the new fighter squadrons for the new Air Wing Ten, formed in response to a Navy requirement for a 13th front-line air wing. CVW-10's intended operational home was to be USS *Independence,* which began a major SLEP (service life extension programme) in 1985, emerging in 1988. VF-194's aircrew trained with VF-124 at Miramar, and then began working up at NAS Fallon. The squadron briefly went to sea in the summer of 1987 (24 July-5 August), flying from USS *Enterprise* with CVW-10, but this was destined to be the unit's only deployment.

Independence's name appeared on some of VF-194's Tomcats, as it did on some

VF-191 aircraft, reflecting plans to send CVW-10 on a full deployment. The squadron performed well during its brief existence but, along with VF-191 and the rest of Air Wing Ten, the 'Red Lightnings' were disestablished on 30 April 1988 due to US Navy budget cuts. For a brief period it seemed as though production of the F-14D might lead to an increase in size of the overall Tomcat fleet. Plans to re-establish the squadron as the fourth F-14D squadron, following VF-51, VF-111 and VF-191 were, however, cancelled when the F-14D programme itself was cut short.

The squadron was born and died while Tomcat squadron markings were at their most restrained. The unit's official badge was a lightning bolt passing through an Ace of Spades playing card, with the motto 'Dictum Factum' (translated by the unit as 'No sooner said than done!') but this did not appear on the squadron's F-14s. Instead, these had a simple red lightning bolt piercing the 'NM' tailcode of CVW-10. The markings were revised with a larger lightning bolt and with the tailcode moved to the base of the rudder before the

Above: Like most F-14 squadrons, VF-194 had a variety of squadron flying suit patches, including one based on Grumman's classic cartoon ('Anytime Baby') cat.

squadron disestablished, but many of the aircraft with these more prominent markings had them applied in toned-down shades of grey, and not in red at all.

Left: VF-194's CAG-bird is seen in flight. Few of the squadron's aircraft were ever as colourful as this, although less restrained markings would doubtless have evolved had the squadron enjoyed a longer life.

Below: VF-194 was lucky to get to sea, but between 24 July and 5 August 1987 the short-lived squadron operated its Tomcats from the deck of USS Enterprise in the eastern Pacific. The unit's simple red lightning bolt markings are seen here on the VF-194 CAG-bird, as it takes the wire aboard 'Big E'. Other aircraft originally had a more involved decoration, with the lightning bolt intersecting the tailcode. The squadron badge showed an ace of spades pierced by a lightning bolt. The unit's motto was Dictum Factum – which roughly translates as 'No sooner said than done'.

VF-201 'Hunters'

VF-201 (callsign 'Hunter'), established 25 July 1970, was one of two Naval Air Reserve squadrons formed at NAS Dallas to operate the F-8 Crusader as part of Carrier Air Wing Twenty, itself formed as part of the reorganisation of the Naval Reserve. The aim was to produce a complete Reserve-manned air wing ready to deploy to a carrier in the event of a national emergency. VF-201 flew the Crusader until February 1976, when the squadron transitioned to the F-4 Phantom. VF-201 then flew the F-4N until 1984, and the F-4S until 1987. VF-201 flew its last F-4S (BuNo. 155732) to the 'boneyard' in December 1987, transitioning to the F-14A. Many doubted that the Reserve would be able to operate the maintenance-intensive and complex F-14 (using many of the same arguments which had once been raised against USMC procurement of the aircraft), but the doubts and fears proved ill-founded.

F-14 aircrew and ground crew training actually began in October 1986, under the auspices of VF-101 at NAS Oceana. The squadron accepted its first aircraft (BuNo.

158634) in early 1987. As the squadron worked up to full strength it carqualled aboard the USS *Forrestal*.

VF-201 and VF-202 were formed as part of Reserve Air Wing Twenty (CVWR-20), the Atlantic Fleet Reserve CVW. The wing made the first of its two sea-going active-duty training deployments aboard USS *Forrestal* between 14 and 26 June 1987, with the F-14A. This was followed by a similar Atlantic sailing between 24 July and 3 August 1989, aboard USS *Dwight D. Eisenhower*.

One aircraft received by the 'Hunters' was the last F-14A built (BuNo. 162711) before production shifted to the F-14A+ (now F-14B) model. The US Navy Reserve fighter force has been in the forefront of recent cutbacks, which included the disestablishment of one of the two Reserve CVWs in 1994, and the consequent disbandment of both West Coast Reserve Tomcat units. VF-202 disappeared in December 1994, falling victim to the reduction of CVWs from two to one Tomcat squadron. Thus VF-201 is currently the only

surviving F-14 Reserve unit – clinging on with Reserve Air Wing Twenty. The squadron expanded in size by about 25 per cent and had its pick of the finest officers and enlisted personnel from the original four Reserve F-14 squadrons. No front-line Reserve fighter squadrons are left on the West Coast, as the dissolution of CVWR-30 in late 1994 means that only VFC-13 (with the F/A-18) remains in that part of the world.

As well as being the only Reserve F-14 squadron, VF-201 has also gained new responsibilities and capabilities, making it arguably the single most valuable unit in the entire Reserve. In 1993, the squadron completed Adversary Level II training, allowing the unit to provide quality adversary support for the fleet, compensating, in part, for the massive drawdown in the adversary force. During that same year, the squadron won a prestigious Battle E, and added a Safety S the following year.

In early 1994, the 'Hunters' further expanded their capabilities into the air-to-surface arena. VF-201 is now fully-qualified in the 'Bombcat' role, and was actually the first F-14 unit to participate in and pass a

Part of the unofficial 'Texas air force', VF-201's tail markings leave no doubt as to where the squadron's heart lies. On 'low-vis' aircraft the tail flashes and map are black, with a white code. The recent dramatic reductions in the US Navy Reserve call into question how much longer these markings will be seen.

mine readiness inspection in October 1994. VF-201 took over the TARPS role from the disbanding VF-202.

Now based at NAS Fort Worth JRB (Joint Reserve Base), the squadron has as its insignia a sword against a Texas flag and a formation of four aircraft, though aircraft wear a simple outline map of Texas. The squadron's location in Texas allows it relatively easy access to both Atlantic and Pacific Fleets.

VF-201 will soon gain LANTIRN and Digital TARPS capabilities and in the longer term may even receive upgraded aircraft – perhaps F-14Bs and F-14Ds, although it currently has only the F-14A.

Below: The official insignia of VF-201 incorporates the 'Lone Star' flag of Texas, the 'Lone Star State'.

Right: The VF-201 CAG-bird shows off the full-colour version of the squadron's markings.

Below right: This VF-201 F-14A wears the toned-down version of the unit's markings.

The squadron tail marking consists of an outline map of Texas with the CVWR-20 tailcode of 'AF'.

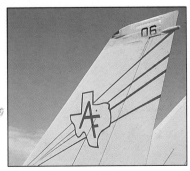

VF-202 'Superheats'

VF-202 was established on 1 July 1970 to fly F-8H Crusaders as part of a new Reserve Carrier Air Wing (CVWR-20). It was one of two Reserve squadrons formed at Dallas (the other being VF-201) and transitioned to the F-4N Phantom in April 1976. The squadron acquired the F-4S Phantom in 1984, subsequently becoming the last USN unit to operate a Phantom from a carrier (making the last F-4 trap aboard the USS *America* on 21 October 1986). The squadron replaced its F-4S Phantoms with the F-14A Tomcat, converting to the new type between March 1987 and January 1989, flying its last F-4S (the Navy's last tactical F-4) to the 'boneyard' on 14 May 1987. Phantoms soldiered on in the recce and test roles, but this was the end for the Phantom fighter in US Navy service.

The squadron insignia is a horse's head (a knight chess piece) in black against a white star and yellow field, with the legend 'Fighting 202', but this is worn very small on the fin-caps of the unit's aircraft, which are instead dominated by the distinctive state flag on their rudders.

The squadron accepted its first F-14A on 10 April 1987. Most of the unit's jets were drawn from temporary storage, or came from modernisation or upgrade at the Naval Air Rework Facility, but the squadron's initial complement also included two brand-new jets, fresh off Grumman's Calverton production line. In May 1988, the 'Superheats' concluded their transition to the Tomcat with carrier qualifications aboard USS *America* off the Virginia coast.

The 'Superheats' were the TARPS squadron for Reserve Air Wing Twenty (CVWR-20). The squadron participated in the USAF-sponsored 1988 Reconnaissance Air Meet (RAM '88) at Bergstrom AFB, TX, performing well against highly experienced opposition, despite their newness to the reconnaissance game.

The following year, VF-202 made its only active-duty training cruise. Embarked aboard USS *Dwight D. Eisenhower*, VF-202 deployed to the North Atlantic between 24 July and 3 August 1989, alongside its sister squadron VF-201 and the rest of CVWR-20. VF-202 was TARPS-equipped (with three F-14As) and became the first 'Bombcat'-trained Reserve squadron in 1993. Unfortunately, cuts in the US Navy Reserve forces saw the unit disestablished officially

on 31 December 1994. The squadron had actually ceased operations some time before this 'official' date, however, passing many of its personnel and some of its aircraft on to the surviving Reserve Tomcat unit, VF-201. The TARPS role passed to VF-201, which had also transitioned to the air-to-ground role.

The Reserve F-14 squadrons confounded expectations by coping well with the sophisticated and complex F-14, although they operated away from the front-line F-14 bases, with a high proportion of reservist personnel. Their competence matched their sky-high morale.

Top: Wearing almost imperceptible 'low-vis' fin markings, this 1988-vintage VF-202 Tomcat still manages to display its 'Lone Star State' roots, with a heavily toned down version of the state flag on the outer faces of its rudders. Tomcat colour schemes have gone through a number of incarnations, with light and dark greys predominating at different times and with markings toned down (darker) or toned up (lighter).

Above: Seen here in 1991, this more colourful gloss-grey aircraft (its '201' Modex singling it out as the squadron commander's) carries a Distinguished Unit Citation, Battle E and Safety S, along with the Texas state flag on its fin. VF-202 was the TARPS-capable squadron of Reserve Air Wing 20, with a trio of TARPS-compatible aircraft and a proportion of recce-trained crews. The TARPS F-14 replaced the Reserve's dedicated RF-8G.

Below: Like all fleet squadrons, VF-202 maintains the tradition of painting its CAG and CO's aircraft in full colour markings. This aircraft even has the larger, full-colour star-and-bar national insignia. Traditionally, CAG aircraft wear the distinctive 00 ('Double Nuts') Modex, with the CO's aircraft carrying 01, and the XO's taking 02. These aircraft are often the only ones to wear full-colour squadron insignia, and then only in peacetime.

Right: The fact that VF-202's F-14As always wore the latest camouflage colour scheme sometimes disguised the fact that their aircraft included some of the oldest F-14As still active in the fleet. Even when equipped with the oldest F-14As, wearing the drabbest colour schemes, VF-202's intense unit pride demanded that the Texan flag be applied to the tails. The USAF's Texas-based ANG units have a similar penchant for displaying the state insignia.

VF-202's official badge is a knight chess-piece on the Texan 'Lone Star' insignia.

One of the unofficial flying suit patches used by the 'Checkmates'.

Above: One of VF-211's F-14Bs is seen at Miramar. The squadron used the F-14B only very briefly before reverting to F-14As.

Above: VF-211's unusual official badge is often worn by squadron aircrew as a flying suit patch, as shown here.

VF-211 'Fighting Checkmates'

VF-211 (callsign 'Checkmate') traces its history to VB-74 'Bomb-a-Toms', established on 1 May 1945, and acquired its current designation on 9 March 1959. The 'Checkmates' stood up as an F-14A squadron at Miramar on 1 December 1975, following months of preparation and after operating the F-8J Crusader.

The squadron's maiden flight in a Tomcat was made on 23 December 1975. VF-211's first F-14A carrier landing was made aboard USS *Constellation* in June 1976. As part of Carrier Air Wing Nine, and paired with VF-24, the squadron made its first cruise aboard *Constellation* between 12 April and 21 November 1977. A second WestPac and Indian Ocean cruise followed from 26 September 1978 to 17 May 1979. During this cruise, the Shah fled Iran in the face of the Islamic Revolution. In March the battle group took up station off Aden, in response to the fighting between North and South Yemen.

During its Indian Ocean cruise of 26 February to 15 October 1980, VF-211 spent 110 days on 'Gonzo Station' in response to the Teheran hostage crisis, and later participated in Exercise RimPac '80. On 15 October 1980, the squadron was selected for the TARPS mission, becoming the first West Coast squadron so-equipped. VF-211 returned from a subsequent WestPac and Indian Ocean cruise (20 October 1981 to 23 May 1982) with 100,000 ft (30480 m) of TARPS film. For its combat readiness record over three cruises and shore deployments, VF-211 was awarded a COMNAVAIRPAC Battle E. In July 1983, still with the same air wing (CVW-9), the squadron began a cruise aboard USS *Ranger*. For this WestPac and Indian Ocean deployment, VF-211 was at sea from 15 July 1983 to 29 February 1984. Unusually, this cruise began with the *Ranger* involved in surveillance missions off Central America, before staging via Hawaii three weeks later. A subsequent WestPac and Indian Ocean cruise was made with CVW-9 aboard the *Kitty Hawk*, from 24 July to 21 December 1985.

Embarked with the *Kitty Hawk*, VF-211 undertook a round-the-world cruise from 3 January until 29 June 1987 – *Kitty Hawk*'s last before its SLEP. The unit then moved to USS *Nimitz* (along with CVW-9) for a WestPac and Indian Ocean deployment, in support of Operation Earnest Will, from 2 September 1988 until 2 March 1989. VF-211 began transition to the F-14A+ (now designated F-14B) Tomcat in April 1989, but later reverted back to the F-14A due to a lack of F-14Bs, which prompted the US Navy to concentrate all F-14Ds with the Pacific Fleet and all F-14Bs with the Atlantic Fleet. VF-211 remains TARPS-capable.

A NorPac cruise for NorPacEx '89 (15 June to 9 July 1989) and a WestPac, Indian Ocean and Persian Gulf deployment (25 February to 24 August 1991) came next, including operations in support of Desert Storm. In June 1992, VF-211 became the first West Coast Tomcat squadron to complete the Advanced Attack Readiness Program (AARP), and transitioned back to the A-Model Tomcat that same year. During the WestPac, Persian Gulf cruise which began on 2 February 1993, the squadron flew recce missions in support of Operation Southern Watch and supported the presence in Somalia. VF-211 returned home on 1 August 1993. In February 1994, it operated from Nellis during Red Flag 94-2. VF-211 moved to NAS Oceana in August 1996, where it gained NVG and LANTIRN capability.

Above right: Today VF-211 has reverted to the F-14A, having briefly operated F-14Bs between 1989 and 1992. Some of the squadron's aircraft wear full-colour markings, usually with toned-down national insignia.

Right: A 'Checkmates' F-14A taxis 'off the wire' aboard USS Constellation during its 1980 cruise, when VF-211 was later on station off Iran.

Above: In 1986 several VF-211 aircraft wore temporary brown and green camouflage over their normal colour scheme for exercises at NAS Fallon. VF-211 was among the first with 'Bombcats'.

Right: From 1989 until 1992, VF-211 flew the F-14B (F-14A+), when the F-14B was concentrated within the Atlantic Fleet. Toned-down or full-colour, VF-211's Tomcats have always been among the smartest.

VF-213 'Black Lions'

VF-213 (callsign 'Blacklion'), established 22 June 1955, stood up with the F-14A Tomcat at Miramar in September 1976, replacing the F-4B Phantom. On 25 October 1977, the squadron embarked on its first cruise with Tomcats as part of CVW-11 aboard USS *Kitty Hawk*, followed by a WestPac sailing until 15 May 1978. During this period, VF-213 contributed significantly to the 16,000 hours flown by Air Wing Eleven while embarked.

VF-213 was next temporarily detached to the Atlantic Fleet for Mediterranean cruises aboard USS *America* (again with CVW-11).

The first of these departed Norfolk on 13 March 1979 and returned on 22 September 1979, followed by a 1981 cruise between 14 April and 12 November, taking in the Indian Ocean. In 1982, the squadron acquired the tactical reconnaissance role and took delivery of its first TARPS-equipped aircraft. With the same air wing, the squadron subsequently went on a NorPac, WestPac and Indian Ocean cruise with USS *Enterprise* (its first after three years overhaul) in 1982-83 (departing on 1 September and returning on 28 May). During this deployment, the 'Black Lions' used their new-found TARPS capability to photograph numerous Soviet Pacific Fleet surface ships and submarines. In March 1983 the 'Black Lions' chalked up a remarkable 17,000 accident-free flying hours.

VF-213 was then back on the West Coast and its 1984 cruise with the *Enterprise* was another WestPac and Indian Ocean sailing. Changing its Modex codes from 100 series to 200 series, VF-213 next departed for a WestPac and Indian Ocean cruise from 12 January to 13 August 1986, followed by a brief NorPac deployment between 25 October and 24 November 1987, all with CVW-11. The squadron then made a WestPac and Indian Ocean cruise between 5 January and 3 July 1988 (including

Operation Praying Mantis), during which time Commander Greg 'Mullet' Gerard became the first Tomcat pilot to log 2,000 flying hours on type.

VF-213 embarked on a round-the-world cruise from 17 September 1989 until 16 March 1990, its last deployment with USS *Enterprise*. While at sea VF-213 flew operations for Operation Classic Resolve.

VF-213 and the other squadrons of CVW-11 then transferred to USS *Abraham Lincoln's* round-the-Horn cruise between 24 September and 20 November 1990. This gave opportunities for DACT with Argentine and Chilean fighters, although the *Lincoln* had only a reduced 'split' air wing onboard for this transit to the West Coast.

CVW-11 was embarked in full strength for the maiden WestPac and Persian Gulf cruise of the *Abraham Lincoln*, which began on 28 May 1991 and lasted until 25 November. During this cruise VF-213 acted as adversaries for Omani Jaguar and Hawker Hunter squadrons, flew TARPS missions over Iraq and also provided support for Operation Fiery Vigil.

1992 saw the award of the Mutha Trophy, and the beginning of 'Bombcat' training in May. CVW-11 was the first single Tomcat squadron air wing, and a slightly expanded VF-213 partnered three F/A-18 units. A WestPac, Indian Ocean and Persian Gulf cruise aboard the *Lincoln* began on 15 June 1993, and ended on 15 December. During this deployment VF-213 flew missions for Operation Southern Watch and also in support of the US contingent in Somalia. From October 1995 the squadron cruised with CVW-11 aboard the USS *Lincoln* (CVN-72) and cruised aboard the USS *Kitty Hawk* (CV-63) from August 1996 until February 1997.

Left: This VF-213 F-14A, seen here circa 1978, is a classic example of a period US Navy colour scheme. The black lion of the squadron badge gained two tails in recognition of the Tomcat's twin fins.

Below: Between 1986 and 1987 several of VF-213's Tomcats received temporary disruptive grey or brown-green camouflage.

VF-301 'Devil's Disciples'

VF-301 (callsign 'Devil'), which is also called the 'Fighting Infernos', was established 1 October 1970 as a Reserve squadron at Miramar and part of Reserve Air Wing Thirty. The squadron patch shows a red smiling satanic figure holding a pitchfork.

The unit was first commissioned on 3 January 1944 with the F4U-1 Corsair. VF-301's World War II history is brief – the squadron made a short deployment aboard USS *Steamer Bay* and a shore-basing at Luganville Airfield, Esperitu. VF-301 was disestablished on 1 August 1944. In October 1970 the squadron was resurrected as one of two Reserve units at NAS Miramar, CA, and equipped with the F-8 Crusader. Then, as later, they were part of CVWR-30. In 1974 transition to the F-4B began, followed by the F-4N in February 1975. CVWR-30 finally exchanged its clapped-out F-4Ns for CVW-14's surplus F-4Ss in November 1980.

The squadron began the transition to the F-14A in 1985, although its first aircraft had arrived in October the previous year. The change-over from Phantom to Tomcat was a lengthy one and the F-4 remained in service with the 'Devil's Disciples' well into 1985. VF-301 received early production F-14s drawn from aircraft delivered to the Navy as far back as 1973 and 1974. In total, the unit was allocated 12 Tomcats.

The squadron began conversion to the Tomcat even before the commissioning of the short-lived squadrons of CVW-10, VF-191 and VF-194, marking the importance of the F-14 to the Reserve. Many doubted the wisdom of equipping Reserve fighter squadrons with an aircraft as 'difficult' and challenging as the F-14, but critics were to be silenced by VF-301's early success with the aircraft. Although not sea-going squadrons, the Reserve F-14 units nonetheless had to maintain the same degree of operational proficiency as front-line units – including carrier operations – and carquals were regularly practised.

On 21 April 1985, VF-301 made the first Reserve deployment of the Tomcat, taking five aircraft to Yuma, AZ, for air-to-air training. The first deployment at full squadron strength was made for training at NAS Fallon, NV, beginning 4 August 1985.

US Navy Reserve fighter squadrons traditionally made two-week active-duty training (AcDuTra) cruises to keep up their carrier skills. VF-301 made its first such deployment between 15 and 26 January 1986, in the eastern Pacific aboard USS *Ranger*, as part of CVWR-30. Subsequent

Above: This VF-301 three-ship displays the current blue-grey paint scheme and 'low-vis' squadron markings. When the unit was making the transition to 'low-vis' markings, the arrow head on the fin was originally all-black, but has now been reduced to a simple outline.

Left: VF-301's original tail markings comprised a black arrow outlined in red, as seen on this high-gloss Tomcat (in 1986) partnered by a VFA-195 Hornet.

cruises were held at two-year intervals and all in the same area. Between 10 and 22 August 1988, the 'Devil's Disciples' went to sea with USS *Enterprise*.

Its next sea-going deployment was aboard USS *Nimitz* from 6 August to 16 August 1990, and the *Nimitz* was again VF-301's host for its last AcDuTra cruise between 15 and 24 August 1992. Such training cruises were invaluable, and inevitably resulted in all air- and deck-crew returning fully carrier-qualified, ready to take their place at the front-line if ever called upon to do so.

CVWR-30 was done away with by budget

cuts in 1994 (leaving almost no West Coast Reserve fighter units).

VF-301 was disestablished in December 1994, although its TARPS-equipped sister unit, VF-302, lingered on for some months more.

Had the squadron not been disestablished, it would have inevitably faced a name change – for a squadron to call itself the 'Devil's Disciples' in the United States today is judged to be too offensive to the fundamentalist Christian right. VF-301's name and traditions, of course, were in no way indicative of satanism, but merely reflected a once-popular means of gaining a

fearsome image, but times have changed, and it seems unlikely that squadrons will ever again use names like 'Satan's Kittens', 'Ghostriders', or 'Devil's Disciples'. In this atmosphere, even VF-101's 'Grim Reapers' appellation must be in some doubt.

VF-302's red devil badge has never been applied to the squadron's F-14s, which instead wore a black-edged red arrow on the tailfins, or a gray outline arrow in the case of 'toned-down' aircraft. This was carried rather higher on the fin than the similar device once used by VF-103, and was less symmetrical.

Below: When toned-down, VF-301's markings sometimes appeared as a solid grey arrow, but more usually as a grey outline.

Below: A VF-301 F-14A manoeuvres on the deck of the USS Nimitz during one of the regular periods of AcDuTra (Active Duty Training) conducted by all Reserve squadrons. The F-14 Reserve squadrons won an enviable reputation, but only one remains active today.

*Above: In 1986 VF-302's **CAG-bird** appeared in these colourful markings. The aircraft wore an overall gloss-grey scheme, and the squadron's 'stallion' insignia appeared on the rudders.*

Above: VF-302's standard F-14s were among the most non-descript in the fleet. In 1994 the squadron fell victim to the severe cuts in the US Navy Reserve, and was disestablished in December.

VF-302 'Stallions'

VF-302 (callsign 'Stallion'), established 21 May 1971, was a Reserve squadron at Miramar. The squadron badge comprised a red and black shield on a yellow background bearing a black stallion's head and a red sword, with the legend 'Fighting 302'. Like its sister squadron VF-301, the 'Stallions' were commissioned at Miramar as a result of the major reorganisation of the US Navy Reserve in the early 1970s. The squadron was first equipped with the Vought F-8K, until November 1973. VF-302 then became the first US Navy Reserve squadron to

operate the Phantom. By February 1974 it was active with 12 F-4Bs and undertook its first AcDuTra cruise with the type at the end of the month. The early F-4Bs were replaced from late 1975 by reworked F-4Ns, which remained in use until the advent of the F-4S in 1981. By 1984 VF-302 had been selected as the second US Navy Reserve squadron for the F-14.

The squadron began the transition to the F-14A Tomcat in 1985, with the first aircraft arriving in April. Like those allocated to VF-301, VF-302's Tomcats were rather

vintage machines. By 1986 the full complement of 12 F-14As had been delivered. The 'Stallions' are paired with VF-301 as part of CVWR-30 but, unlike its sister squadron, Fighting Three Zero Two was assigned the TARPS reconnaissance mission. In line with similarly equipped fleet squadrons, VF-302 operates three TARPS F-14s. The F-14 is designed to operate in tandem with the E-2 Hawkeye, and VF-301 and -302 were unable to exploit their full potential until the the latest model E-2Cs were released to the US Navy's Reserve early-warning squadrons (in Miramar's case, this was VAW-78, the 'Fighting Escargots'). The squadron participated in the USAF-

sponsored 1988 Reconnaissance Air Meet (RAM '88) at Bergstom AFB, TX. Its active-duty training cruises mirrored those of VF-301; 15 to 26 January 1986 (USS *Ranger*), 10 to 22 August 1988 (USS *Enterprise*), 6 to 16 August (USS *Nimitz*) and 15 to 24 August 1992 (USS *Nimitz*).

Like VF-301, the 'Stallions' have fallen victim to the drawdown in US Navy strength and the squadron was disestablished at Miramar in December 1994.

The official, formal flying suit patch of VF-302 'Stallions'.

Right: Whereas the Atlantic Fleet Reserve F-14 squadrons were based in Texas, far from the other COMNAVAIRLANT Tomcat units, CVWR-30's F-14s shared the Miramar flight lines with the active-duty Pacific Fleet Tomcat units. NAS Miramar no longer has any based F-14s, and Oceana is the main home of the 'Turkey'.

*Below: This VF-302 is in what cynics refer to as the F-14's optimum dogfighting configuration, carrying nothing but an AIM-9 acquistion round and a **TACTS** pod. When lightly loaded, the F-14 is a formidable opponent, but is no match for the later 'teen-series' air-superiority fighters.*

Grumman F-14 Operators

Naval Strike and Air Warfare Center (previously Navy Fighter Weapons School)

The Navy Fighter Weapons School ('Topgun') at NAS Miramar provided air combat training for fleet fighter pilots, and acted as the centre of the US Navy's dedicated adversary force. It provided training and standardisation for the adversary units and ran the 'Topgun' course. This took hand-picked crews from the fleet and put them through an intensive air combat course, balanced between practice (fighting the school's instructors) and theory, learning about enemy tactics and equipment. 'Topgun' graduates then returned to their squadrons, where they passed on their knowledge and skills.

Established in the wake of the influential Ault Report, which analysed US Navy losses and the poor kill ratio being achieved by fleet fighter squadrons in actual air-to-air combat over Vietnam, 'Topgun' was a 'hands-on' training course as close to actual combat as was possible, with highly experienced instructor pilots flying representative adversary aircraft using enemy tactics in realistic training scenarios.

The introduction of the F-14 to the Navy Fighter Weapons School was made possible by the surplus of aircraft created by squadron disbandments, and provided an aircraft capable of simulating the BVR threat posed by the MiG-29, MiG-31 and Su-27, as well as by potentially hostile Western types.

Adversary units have traditionally opted not to use aircraft types already in fleet use, since the value of fighting a dissimilar aircraft type is greatly appreciated. However, an F-14 can be an accurate representation of a potential threat, and that makes it useful.

The NFWS began to incorporate strike fighter instruction into its curriculum in June 1995, but this served only to emphasise the need for an overall tactical air warfare centre, providing multi-role training for the fighter, attack and associated communities. The Carrier Airborne Early Warning School ('Topdome') moved to Fallon to join the Naval Strike Warfare Center at the end of 1995, and the NFWS moved from Miramar in June 1996. The three units merged to form the Naval Strike and Air Warfare Center, which officially established on 11 July 1996.

The new unit was intended to provide more 'seamless' training for strike-fighter aircrews. According to the unit's commander, RADM Bernard Smith, the Navy needed "to establish a strike fighter mindset with attack and fighter attitudes. Our goal is unity of purpose, with excellence in training and tactics development."

The unit's aircraft wear a new insignia, consisting of the old NFWS 'gunsight and MiG-21' badge superimposed on the lightning bolt used by the Strike Warfare Center. These aircraft include F-14s, F/A-18s and even HH-60s.

The 'Topgun' course has been transformed into a Strike Fighter Tactics Instructor course, rather than a dedicated Fighter Tactics course, reflecting more accurately the needs of the newly multi-role tasked fleet Tomcat squadrons.

Above: FWS aircraft use a variety of colour schemes loosely based on those worn by potential real-world adversaries. This FWS F-14As wears a pseudo-'Flanker' scheme. Closely matching the Su-27 in size and shape, the F-14 can also replicate the BVR multi-sensor capability.

Below: This FWS F-14A wears the unit's badge, showing a MiG-21 centred in a gunsight pipper. An F-14 crewed by FWS instructors, versed in Soviet tactics and simulating a MiG-31, is a very different matter to going 'head-to-head' with squadron mates.

Above: Wearing convincingly realistic Iranian camouflage and national markings, this unique FWS F-14A was not the single genuine Iranian-standard F-14A embargoed before delivery, which served (albeit in standard US Navy colours) with VX-4.

VX-9 'Vampires' (previously VX-4)

VX-4 (callsign 'Vandy') was established on 15 September 1952 to undertake testing of air-launched guided missiles, and became the Navy's main air-to-air fighter operational test and evaluation unit. Throughout its life VX-4 was based at Point Mugu, CA. VX-4 was the first US Navy Tomcat operator and, over the years, between seven and 12 aircraft were on strength for systems evaluation and tactics development. VX-4 was allocated Tomcats after the type received a preliminary evaluation at the hands of the NATC, Patuxent River.

In the Tomcat's primary role of fleet defence, its missile armament is of the utmost importance. VX-4 was instrumental in proving the F-14's AWG-9/AIM-54 Phoenix system, particularly the latest AIM-54C. VX-4 was closely involved with AIM-9L

Sidewinder all-aspect, short-range AAM programme. Other missile work undertaken in the Tomcat's earlier days was the ACEVAL/AIMEVAL (Air Combat Evaluation/Air Intercept Missile Evaluation) programme. Six F-14s were detached to Nellis AFB in the late 1970s. Flying under VX-4 auspices, in conjunction with USAF types, they were instrumental in formulating the AMRAAM (Advanced Medium-Range Air-to-Air Missile) requirement finally fulfilled

Like several other US Navy Tomcat units, VX-4 experimented with a variety of camouflage schemes during the 1980s. This unmarked F-14A (BuNo. 158978) was seen at NAS Fallon in June 1985.

Concealing its identity well, BuNo. 159831 was another of VX-4's 1985 camouflage experiments, again using water-soluble distemper. The only markings visible over its roughly applied reddish-brown and olive green stripes is the Modex '45', which appears in black on the nose.

by the Hughes AIM-120. VX-4 was the first unit to operate the Tomcat's undernose TCS (Television Camera System), a passive electro-optical system which extends the 'eyeball' range of the F-14 pilot up to 100 miles (161 km).

VX-4 was an important part of the F-14D 'Bombcat' trials, and by the early 1990s the squadron had two F-14Ds in service alongside seven F-14A/Bs and a mix of F/A-18s. In a departure from its previous guided-weapons work, the F-14D programme took the 'Evaluators' into the realm of 'dumb' bombing as the squadron undertook Mk 80 series free-fall bomb separation tests. More recently, VX-4 passed the AN/ALR-67 radar warning receiver fit for use in time to see combat during Operation Desert Storm.

The squadron was relatively large, with 39 officers including three Marines and a USAF exchange officer, 281 enlisted men and five civilians. VX-4 is perhaps best known for its use of the 'Playboy Bunny' as

an aircraft marking. The 'Bunny' has appeared on its F-14s, and in pre-F-14 days VX-4 operated two Phantoms (an F-4J and an F-4S) permanently in an all-over gloss black scheme with white 'playboy markings' – the infamous 'Black Bunnies'. The first Tomcat (BuNo. 158358) to appear in a similar (matt) black scheme was painted for a VX-4 change of command ceremony. With the bunny logo on the tail, the aircraft wore VX-4's 'XF' tailcode on a red fintip band, flanked by white stars. No actual serial was carried. By all accounts the scheme was

popular with everyone but an unimpressed admiral, and the (water-soluble) paint was removed after two days. Since then it has reappeared sporadically on various F-14s to mark a number of special occasions.

VX-4 was to have been formally disestablished, on 29 April 1994, but this was delayed until 30 September. As part of the major changes sweeping through the US Navy, VX-4 was combined with sister unit VX-5 'Vampires' to form the aptly numbered VX-9 (formally established on 29 April), headquartered at NAWS (Naval Air

Warfare Station) China Lake, where VX-5 was chiefly involved in fixed- and rotary-wing air-to-ground ordnance testing and tactics. VX-4's role has now been taken over by VX-9 Det Point Mugu. The unit maintains detachments at both Point Mugu and China Lake but uses the bat insignia of VX-5 ('Vampires') on its aircraft. Although the Tomcat has been in service for many years, ongoing improvements and developments necessitate a constant OT&E effort, most recently with the 'Bombcat', LANTIRN and Digital TARPS projects.

Right: An important part of VX-4's trials work was done at sea. The squadron made several deployments aboard USS Enterprise, most recently as part of its F-14D evaluations. Here a very understated VX-4 F-14D 'Super Tomcat' launches from 'Big E'.

Below: One of the least public US Navy units, VX-4 was responsible for some of the Navy's best known aircraft – the 'Black Bunnies'. BuNo. 161444 was one of VX-4's longest serving F-14As and is seen here in high-gloss 'Black Bunny' guise (complete with AIM-54C Phoenix), at Point Mugu in October 1987. Political correctness has seen an end to use of the Playboy logo.

Naval Air Warfare Center (Aircraft Division) – formerly NATC and NADC

The Naval Air Warfare Center is a part of the US Naval Air Systems Command (Navair). Since 1 January 1992 the operations of the former Naval Weapons Center (NWC) at China Lake and the Pacific Missile Test Center, at Point Mugu, have come under the aegis of the Naval Air Warfare Center, as the Naval Air Warfare Center (Weapons Division), while those of the former Naval Air Test Center at Patuxent River, the Naval Air Development Center at Warminster and the Naval Engineering Center at Lakehurst have become elements of the Naval Air Warfare Center (Aircraft Division). These five main components of the NAWC now undertake the wide range of aircraft, weapons, engineering and systems testing

and development previously allocated to 32 different organisations.

The Naval Air Warfare Center at Patuxent River was established in January 1992 by redesignation of the Naval Air Test Center. Its primary task is to test all new aircraft entering naval service, or any new variants of aircraft, or any new equipment entering service on naval aircraft, to determine their suitability for operational use. The unit also develops systems, servicing procedures and even computers. This necessitates close liaison between NAWC and the relevant manufacturers. Divided into Strike Aircraft, Fixed-Wing Aircraft and Rotary-Wing Aircraft Test Directorates, the NAWC maintains a number of F-14s on charge, including some

NF-14s that have been permanently converted for test duties. Operational testing carried out at NAWC has included (in 1982) take-off trials using a 6° ski-ramp. The NAWC also parents the USN Test Pilot's School.

VX-4 'Evaluators' at Point Mugu were parented by the NATC, and served as a fast-jet operational test and evaluation squadron, taking on the evaluation process as new aircraft or systems neared service entry. One officer described VX-4's role in the following words: "We test it, rock it, roll it, slam it, jam it, beat it, drop it and then ram it aboard the boat." VX-4 evaluated the F-14's Northrop TCS, and the aircraft itself when it began to be used in the 'Bombcat' role.

The former Naval Air Development Center at Warminster, Pennsylvania, is tasked with enhancing technology, improving existing equipment by refining software and hardware. It develops avionics and instrumentation for US Navy aircraft, and has frequently had examples of the F-14 on strength. Its current fleet includes a single F-14A.

Wearing an interesting two-tone grey colour scheme, with high-conspicuity orange tailfins, this F-14 serves with the NAWC (Aircraft Division) at Patuxent River.

Naval Air Warfare Center (Weapons Division)

Of particular relevance to the Tomcat community are the Naval Air Warfare Center (Weapons Division), China Lake (formally the NWC) and the Naval Air Warfare Center (Weapons Division), Point Mugu (formally PMTC).

China Lake (six miles east of Inyokem, California) is a major research development and test centre for naval weapons. It includes fully instrumented range facilities, with a variety of targets and even nuclear range facilities (no longer in use). It has

seen a wide range of guided, powered and free-fall ordnance tested for the US Navy. VX-5 'Vampires' was an operational test and evaluation squadron responsible for the development of weapons and tactics, and was parented by the Naval Weapons Test

Center at China Lake. It is not believed that VX-5 ever operated the F-14. VX-5 disestablished on 29 April 1994 and its aircraft and personnel became a detachment of the newly formed VX-9. VX-4 disestablished on 30 September, becoming another VX-9 detachment. Now that VX-5 and VX-4 have been amalgamated, the unit's Tomcats are based at China Lake with VX-9.

The Pacific Missile Test Center at Point Mugu, now an element of the Naval Air Warfare Center (Weapons Division), has been a Tomcat operator since the early 1970s. A missile test facility has been at the California base since 1946, with firing ranges stretching out to sea and telemetry instrumentation located on nearby Laguna Peak. Before the PMTC came the Naval Missile Center (NMC), which was a Tomcat operator from the type's earliest days. In 1972 the first AIM-54 firings were undertaken by an NMC F-14 (BuNo. 157983). NMC aircraft wore a variety of colour schemes, including a tail badge with a swan clutching a missile. Later, the NMC crest appeared on the fin, superimposed on a dark blue and red chevron with the legend 'NMC'.

In the mid-1970s the PMTC was established. Its aircraft wore a blue tail band with the unit's triangular dark blue and gold eagle and anchor badge. On the whole,

This line-up of prototype and early production F-14As was photographed at Patuxent River. One of the aircraft wears the insignia of the Naval Missile Center, soon after redesignated as the PMTC. A large test fleet allowed rapid progress.

PMTC Tomcats wore the same light grey colour scheme with white undersides as fleet F-14s of the period did. At least one F-14 appeared in an experimental grey 'splinter camouflage' with toned-down markings. Tomcats from VX-4 flew alongside the PMTC's own aircraft. The targets for both units were usually QF-86 and QF-4 drones launched from San Nicolas Island, near the coast.

Right: This NAWC F-14A illustrates the drab markings currently applied to F-14s of the former PMTC, with a toned-down NAWC tail stripe. The unit has a mix of Tomcat sub-variants on charge.

Below: This PMTC F-14A carries Phoenix missiles under wings and fuselage, in the Point Mugu circuit. PMTC markings are here carried on a mid-blue tail band, but were later toned down.

NASA (National Aeronautics and Space Administration)

Two different F-14As have been used by NASA in support of two quite separate research programmes at the Administration's Dryden Flight Research Facility at Edwards AFB. The first of these was an F-14A (BuNo. 157991, actually the last of the 13 pre-production aircraft) which wore its 'last three' in lieu of an officially allocated NASA serial, after arriving on 8 August 1979. The aircraft participated in a joint US Navy/Grumman/NASA investigation into low-altitude, high-Alpha flight with asymmetric thrust settings, which was of obvious application to the then-troubled F-14 community that was suffering more than its share of spinning accidents, many caused by single engine failures and the consequent thrust asymmetry. The ARI (aileron-rudder interconnect) was enhanced to help prevent wing rock, and to help prevent departure or spinning. Different shaped wing gloves were trialled on the aircraft, and flip-up canards were added on the nose, with an anti-spin parachute in a package attached to the beaver tail fairing and an undernose air data sensor projecting from the empty IRST housing. The aircraft completed its highly successful flight test programme on 1 June 1984, after 23 flights and 254 high AoA manoeuvres, including 54 engine-out stalls. It was often flown as a single-seater. The aircraft returned to the US Navy at Patuxent River on 6 September 1984, by which time it had gained Dayglo

NASA's 'first' Tomcat, serialled NASA 991, passes over the famous dry lake bed on approach to the Administration's Dryden flight facility, at Edwards AFB. The aircraft was returned to the Navy at Patuxent River on 6 September 1984, but had already been replaced by a second F-14A, which remained on NASA's boks until 11 September 1987. Today, NASA is not a Tomcat operator.

orange tailfins, tailplanes and outer wing panels.

A second early F-14A had arrived at NASA from Patuxent River on 8 April 1984. The aircraft (BuNo.158613) lost its '7T' tailcode, but retained its -201 Modex and was also allocated the NASA serial 834. Operating in support of a joint research and development programme with NASA's Langley Flight Research Center, the aircraft was used for a variable-sweep flight transition experiment, of little direct benefit to the F-14 Tomcat. The aircraft had its

tailfin cores, inboard spoilers and wingtips painted in high-conspicuity Dayglo orange, and flew with one wing painted white to allow dye-flow visualisation. The aircraft lacked any undernose sensor package, and had the production-standard wing glove fairings, unlike the earlier F-14A used by NASA. The aircraft finally returned to Patuxent River on 11 September 1987, after an extension to its two-year loan period.

Some scientists apparently favoured using an F-14 as the basis of the MAW (mission adaptive wing) later tested on an

F-111. It is likely that future experiments will see the return of the Tomcat to NASA's fleet, especially as squadron disbandments mean large numbers of early F-14As becoming surplus to Navy requirements. As two-seaters able to carry a wide range of stores, and with a wide performance envelope and reasonable payload/range characteristics, the F-14 variants would make useful general hacks and chase aircraft, though they are more expensive to operate and less useful than F-16s or F/A-18s, which are similarly widely available. At the moment no F-14s are flying in NASA colours.

Grumman F-14 Operators

Iran

The Imperial Iranian Air Force took delivery of 79 F-14As (BuNos 160299-160377, IIAF serials 3-863 to 3-892 and 3-6001 to 3-6050) before the revolution which toppled the Shah and halted delivery of the last aircraft. This example (BuNo. 163078, IIAF serial 3-6050) was stored at AMARC for some years, and was then issued to VX-4. Cut off from spares support, serviceability of Iran's F-14As was poor, although this steadily improved. Fortunately, the Iranians received only 284 of the 714 AIM-54As they had ordered. A number of aircraft (with their Phoenix missiles) were almost certainly delivered to the Soviet Union in exchange for Soviet-built aircraft and weapons, and Soviet help in maintaining the F-14s themselves. After a period during which the lack of spares and a shortage of skilled manpower progressively reduced aircraft availability, and during which the handful of F-14As were used primarily as mini-AWACS platforms, the number of F-14As active with the Islamic Republic of Iran Air Force have apparently risen dramatically. The type saw active service during the Iran/Iraq war (when at least one was lost, to a Mirage F1). By 11 February 1985, the IRIAF was able to mount a 25-aircraft flypast over Teheran's Azadi Square. Spares and support may have been obtained as a result of Colonel North's Irangate dealings, from organised crime and from Israel. The type may now be operational in the long-range intercept role, and may even equip or partially equip more than the original two squadrons based at Isfahan and Shiraz before the revolution. The early aircraft have been reserialled in the 3-60** range, including 3-6063 and 3-6064.

Below: Imperial Iranian Air Force F-14As refuel from one of the nation's Boeing 707-3J9C tankers.

Right: Iranian F-14As had no covers over their inflight-refuelling probes, a distinctive recognition feature. Here an IIAF Tomcat refuels from a drogue trailed by one of the air arm's Boeing 707 tankers.

Below: Iranian Tomcats were delivered in this attractive three-tone desert camouflage, but many have since been repainted in an air superiority blue-grey colour scheme. IIAF titles on the forward fuselage have been replaced by IRIAF titles.

Above: Staff aircrew of VF-101 pose in front of some of the squadron's Tomcats. VF-101 is now responsible for the training of all F-14 aircrew, since the integration of the Atlantic and Pacific Fleet Tomcat communities.

Three of VF-101's F-14s return to base in close formation. Close formation flying is great for the camera, and for practising precise manoeuvring, but no longer has any tactical significance.

F-14 Tomcat Training

The sole Tomcat conversion and training unit today is VF-101 'Grim Reapers', based at NAS Oceana and responsible for the training of all F-14 aircrew, 'nuggets' fresh from training and more experienced pilots and RIOs returning to the type, or transitioning from other aircraft types. Trainees are known as 'replacements' because they are trained to replace pilots and RIOs already serving with a squadron. There is no dual-control model of the F-14, so a pilot's first flight in the aircraft is made with an instructor able only to offer advice from the rear cockpit, and not able to take control or demonstrate manoeuvres. VF-101 offers a number of different courses, which vary according to which Tomcat variant the student is destined to fly when he (or she) reaches a fleet fighter squadron. When some squadrons gain a mix of F-14Bs and F-14Ds it may be assumed that a new course will be offered, tailored to prepare crews for both variants.

VF-101 regards itself as having two 'customers', the first being the replacement aircrew, who they train in the best possible learning environment, and the second customer being the fleet squadrons. Every member of VF-101 treats each Replacement as if they are to be their next wingman 'because one day they might be', and enormous pride is taken in conducting the syllabus of lectures, briefings, debriefings, simulator rides and training flights.

The VF-101 syllabus is divided into five phases, following a building block approach and taught by staff pilot and RIO instructors. The initial familiarisation (FAM) phase covers systems, basic handling, switchology and emergency procedures. The latter must be known 'Cold' without reference to 'flip-cards'. Each 'replacement' is continuously assessed and evaluated during the phase.

'Replacements' then move to the Weapons Control Systems (WCS) phase, which introduces basic intercept tactics, the use of ECM, and basic air-to-air gunnery skills, and prepares the student for the subsequent phases. The aircrew are taught how to employ the radar effectively, and how to recognise appropriate Launch Acceptability Ranges, as well as intercept geometries and tactical communication.

'Replacements' then move on to the Strike phase, which is usually completed through detachments to El Centro or Fallon to take advantage of better weather, and greater opportunities for live weapons employment, with plentiful range slots. The Strike phase includes low-level tactical flying and navigation as well as high-, medium- and low-level delivery techniques, and SAM and small-arms defence.

The Tactics phase represents the heart of the F-14 'replacement' training syllabus. It is completed at Key West, which enjoys superior weather and range availability. The aim of the phase is to teach expert employment of the F-14 in its primary fighter mission, preparing the aircrew to participate in power projection scenarios in a number of roles. The phase builds on the tactics learned in the WCS phase, and the delivery techniques taught in the strike phase, complicating the 'replacements' lives by adding in manoeuvring threat aircraft and simulated SAMs. Tactical employment of the radar is taught, together with BFM (Basic Fighter Manoeuvring) in realistic mission scenarios. 'Replacements' even begin briefing

The Strike and Tactics phases of the VF-101 replacement training syllabus involve participation by dissimilar threat aircraft, as did the syllabus offered by VF-124, one of whose aircraft is seen here with an adversary TA-4.

some of the missions flown.

The final make-or-break part of the course is the CQ (Carrier Qualification) phase. Obviously a Tomcat pilot or RIO who cannot safely fly the aircraft aboard a carrier is of no possible use to a front-line F-14 squadron and cannot complete his training. The CQ phase qualifies replacement pilots in day and night carrier operations, and provides both pilots and RIOs with a full working knowledge of carrier operational procedures, including all aspects of flying an F-14 around and landing on a carrier.

The contents of each phase differ slightly according to which course is being conducted (Fleet A, Fleet B, Fleet D or A/B to D transition). The Det West course was an abbreviated version of the Fleet D course.

Carrier qualification represents the final hurdle for the 'replacement' Tomcat aircrew. If they cannot get their aircraft back aboard a carrier safely, by both day and night, they are of limited usefulness to a front-line F-14 squadron. Here, a VF-114 F-14 begins a dusk mission.

Gruman F-14 Tomcat Variants

Design 303 variants

The F-14 was born because of the failure of the Naval TFX, the F-111B, for which Grumman had been the principal sub-contractor. The F-111B was too complex, too heavy, too slow, never right for the carrier mission and unlikely to be rendered so despite herculean efforts. Not even a costly Colossal Weight Improvement Program (CWIP) could transform this aircraft into a shipboard interceptor. The Pentagon scrapped the TFX, the notion of commonality and the F-111B programme, although the US Air Force version of the 'one eleven' has since matured into a potent low-level, long-range bomber.

In October 1967, at the height of the war in Vietnam, Grumman proposed that a new airframe be developed to accommodate the avionics, missile, engines and weapon system of the discredited F-111B. Between the F-111B and the new proposal, the AN/AWG-9 had picked up new fighter-attack modes, gained in flexibility and lost a staggering 600 lb (272 kg) in weight, and took to the air in a modified TA-3B Skywarrior during April 1970. The new airframe promised to be vastly superior to the F-111B in all regimes. The Grumman proposal came just as the Navy was restating its requirement for a fleet interceptor, and the VFX-1 requirement was

Vought's unsuccessful VFX proposal is seen in mock-up form, complete with rather unconvincing dummy AIM-54 missiles.

formulated around the new design, with the contemporary VFX-2 requirement describing the same aircraft with advanced technology engines. VFX-2 eventually resulted in the F401-engined F-14B. Design 303 was primarily designed around an armament of four AIM-7 missiles, although the AIM-54 Phoenix grew in importance, especially after the development of low-drag pallet carriage of the big missiles, which minimised the impact on the basic fighter role.

Grumman's long record of development with the XF10F-1 Jaguar, F11F-1 Tiger and F-111B gave the Bethpage, New York, manufacturer – long the US Navy's key supplier of carrier-based warplanes – a significant advantage over any other manufacturer which might have wanted to produce a new-generation fighter/interceptor, especially one using a VG wing. Competition had to be encouraged, however, and other companies were eager for a production order. When a Request for Proposals (RFP) went out to the aerospace industry in July 1968, calling for a two-seat, twin-engined, Phoenix-armed carrier interceptor, North American, LTV, McDonnell and General Dynamics all submitted designs.

Grumman's design was refined from the single-finned 303-60 through the 303A, 303B, 303C (submerged engines and high-set wing), 303D (submerged engines and low-set wing), 303E (single fin), 303F (submerged engine), and 303G (without Phoenix) before arriving at the final configuration with twin fins, widely

separated podded engines and high-set wing. Single-seat configurations were even examined, although the design numbers of these are unknown. On 14 January 1969, with the award of a development contract covering six prototypes and 463 production aircraft, Grumman's design 303E became the VFX winner and was designated F-14.

In this artist's impression of the 303E in US Navy markings, some differences between this aircraft and the F-14 can be detected.

Below: The unsuccessful North American VFX proposal.

YF-14A

There were at least two full-scale mock-ups before the first actual YF-14 prototype was built. The original mock-up had a single tail, and a later version introduced the now-familiar twin fins shortly before the design was frozen, in March 1969. Development was expedited through the use of a detailed mock-up, known as EMMA (Engineering Mock-up Manufacturing Aid), that was built like a real aircraft, albeit without external skinning but, since it would never fly, using cheaper manufacturing methods. Thus,

Below: The 12th YF-14A had the numeral 1 painted on its fin and was known as aircraft 1X, taking over the flight test responsibilities of the ill-fated first prototype.

Right: Streaming hydraulic fluid, the first YF-14A returns to Calverton during its doomed second sortie on 30 December 1970, which ended in complete hydraulic failure on final approach. The aircraft was totally destroyed, but both crew members ejected safely.

Below right: The second YF-14A refuels from one of Grumman's fleet of converted A-6 Intruder tankers, which were used to extract the maximum benefit from each test sortie. The candy-striped nose boom carries test instrumentation air data sensors.

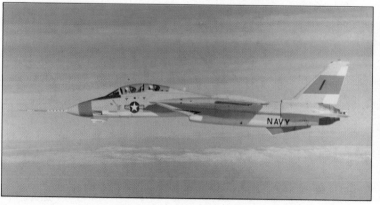

bulkheads were sand cast instead of milled, but they were aluminium and they were real bulkheads. This allowed Grumman engineers to locate hydraulic lines, electrical wires and systems, and to use EMMA to produce patterns and even to fit-check the TF30 engines. The first prototype itself was rolled out at the Grumman plant in December 1972.

Twelve prototypes were procured (individual flight test responsibilities are detailed in the main text) with Bureau Numbers from 157980-157991. These wore large sequential numerical codes from 1-11 on their tailfins, with the last being painted as 1 and known as 1X. The first prototype began taxi trials at Calverton on 14 December 1970, with high-speed taxi trials six days later. On 21 December, company chief test pilot Robert Smythe and (in the backseat) project test pilot William ('Bob') Miller made the first flight, two wide circuits of the airfield with the wings in the forward position, and laden with four dummy Sparrow missiles. A more definitive 'first' flight was begun by Miller and Smythe on 30 December 1970 but was to prove disastrous, the Tomcat experiencing a primary hydraulic system failure. Miller manoeuvred back towards a landing, using the nitrogen bottle to blow down the landing gear when the secondary hydraulic system failed, too. The two men ejected a mere 25 ft (8 m) above the trees, suffering only minor injuries – but the first Grumman Tomcat was destroyed.

A 'fix' to the Tomcat's hydraulic systems proved relatively easy to accomplish, the cause having been a fatigue failure of a hydraulic pipe caused by resonance and a loose connector. The loss of the first aircraft caused a delay in envelope-expansion tests and high-speed developmental flying, but the programme moved forward with almost its original momentum. On 24 May 1971, Smythe took the second Tomcat aloft.

The first five and the last (No.12, 157991, which took over the responsibilities of the first aircraft after its crash) were funded in FY69, and 157985-157990 in FY70. The individual aircraft had different model or 'Block' numbers, being F-14A-01-GR (Block 1), F-14A-05-GR (Block 5), F-14A-10-GR (Block 10), F-14A-15-GR (Block 15), F-14A-20-GR (Block 20), F-14A-25-GR (Block 25), F-14A-30-GR (Block 30), F-14A-35-GR (Block 35), F-14A-40-GR (Block 40), F-14A-45-GR (Block 45), F-14A-50-GR (Block 50), and F-14A-55-GR (Block 55). The seventh aircraft, 157986 (F-14A-30-GR), was later converted to serve as the F401-engined F-14B prototype. Aircraft from the first

production lot of F-14As were also assigned to the flight test programme, in order to hasten the transition to service.

The12 prototypes had different flight test responsibilities. The No. 1 aircraft was assigned the low-speed regime and the critical stall/spin trials. For the latter, the aircraft was fitted with retractable canard foreplanes on the upper sides of the nose, ahead of the windscreen, and initially the wings were locked at 20°, the intakes were locked open, and an anti-spin parachute was fitted to the boat tail fairing. Wind tunnel tests (actually carried out in NASA Langley's spin tunnel), trials of models dropped from helicopters and computer analysis had shown a tendency towards flat spins, with very high rates of rotation, so Grumman was not prepared to take chances. No. 2 later tested the F-14's gun. No. 3 flew envelope-expanding trials with steadily increasing loads and speeds, and acted as the structural test vehicle. Nos 4, 5 and 6 went to NAS Point Mugu, the fourth for integration of the AWG-9/AIM-54 system, the fifth for systems, instrumentation and compatibility tests, and the sixth for weapons system and missile separation work. Of these, No. 5 was lost during a Sparrow separation on 20 June 1973. No. 7 became the test ship for the F-14B with F401 engines, while No. 8 was used to test the production configuration and to provide contractual guarantee data.

Nos 9 and 11 went to Point Mugu for radar evaluation and auxiliary system trials (including ACLS), respectively. No. 11 also flew air-to-ground gunnery trials.

No. 10 was delivered to the Naval Air Test Center at Patuxent River, and from there it was flown on structural trials and then carrier-compatibility work. During preparation for an air display, the aircraft crashed into the sea, killing the pilot, Bob Miller, who was flying the aircraft solo.

No. 17 replaced this aircraft on carrier-compatibility tests just, as No. 12 (redesignated No. 1X) had replaced the first prototype on high-speed flight trials. This aircraft was the most comprehensively instrumented of the test Tomcats, able to transmit up to 647 measurements back to the ground, and fitted with hydraulic 'Shakers' for flutter testing. 1X had exceeded Mach 2.25 by December 1972. 1X was actually the third F-14 to fly.

The 11th YF-14A sits on the deck of the USS Independence *during initial carrier suitability trials.*

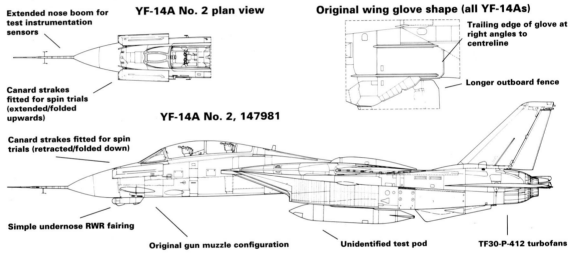

Extended nose boom for test instrumentation sensors

YF-14A No. 2 plan view

Original wing glove shape (all YF-14As)

Trailing edge of glove at right angles to centreline

Canard strakes fitted for spin trials (extended/folded upwards)

Longer outboard fence

YF-14A No. 2, 147981

Canard strakes fitted for spin trials (retracted/folded down)

Simple undernose RWR fairing

Original gun muzzle configuration

Unidentified test pod

TF30-P-412 turbofans

F-14A

Production of the baseline F-14A for the US Navy was spread over 18 Production Blocks and 15 Fiscal Years (FY71-FY85) and totalled 545 aircraft.

Minor changes were incorporated throughout the production run and, although such changes were introduced 'on-the-line', they were often retrofitted to earlier aircraft. Such changes included beaver tail and airbrake configuration, undernose sensor fit, and even gun bay purging vents. Early Tomcats were also equipped with a gimbal-mounted AN-ALR-23 infra-red detection set which could be slaved to the radar or used independently to scrutinise areas not being scanned by radar. The IRST was particularly useful for detecting rocket-engined stand-off missiles, and afterburning targets at higher altitude, or for situations when use of radar was tactically unsound or impeded by heavy ECM. Angular tracking was more accurate than with radar, providing better target elevation and azimuth data than radar. It was sufficiently accurate to allow it to be used for missile launch.

This sensor was replaced by the Northrop AAX-1 Television Camera Set, or TCS, which can be likened to a high-resolution closed-circuit TV with telephoto lens, following a 1977 evaluation of F-14s equipped with the broadly similar TISEO, then in use on USAF F-4E Phantoms. The success of this led to trials by VF-14, VF-32, VF-24 and VF-211 aboard *Kennedy* and *Constellation* with Northrop's TVSU, which was in turn developed to become the TCS.

TCS is a passive electro-optical sensor

An early F-14 in Canadian markings reflects CAF interest in the aircraft as an F-101 Voodoo replacement in the long-range air defence role.

which gives the pilot an ultra-long-range telescope able to spot an enemy visually and identify him early. TCS is operated via a stabilised, gimbal-mounted closed-circuit television system. Two separate cameras are used for the two modes: wide angle for target acquisition, and close-up for target identification. The TCS is normally slaved to

the radar, and automatically locks on to the first target acquired. The NFO can also manually control the unit in the target identification mode, steering the lens with a joystick. The picture can be projected onto the radar display. Under a $12.5-million contract, Northrop began deliveries of the first 36 TCS systems in late 1983, the first

examples being operated by VX-4 at NAS Point Mugu, California. Subsequent orders rose to 133.

Some credit the TCS with enough definition to allow the F-14 crew to identify the weapons being carried by an enemy aircraft, which would be of great tactical value. On a hazy day, however, natural

Grumman F-14 Tomcat Variants

Top and above: The pilot's and NFO's cockpits of the F-14A look rather dated by modern standards, with their analog instruments and old-fashioned displays.

conditions apply. From Block 65, the TF30-PW-412A engine was fitted. The production-standard wing glove fairing with shortened outboard wing fence was introduced with 158978 (first Block 70 aircraft), while the beaver tail and airbrake were modified from

159421 (first Block 75). Earlier aircraft had their beaver tails cut down (with dielectric fairings removed) to a similar shape. The last Block 85 aircraft (159588) introduced the new AN/ARC-159 UHF radio in place of the AN/ARC-51A, while from 159825 (the first Block 90) a small angle of attack probe was added to the tip of the nose radome, while high AoA performance was also improved by the provision of automated manoeuvre flaps. These aircraft introduced changes to the vertical display indicator group, and the provision of improved fire extinguishers and fire suppressors. During Block 95, the TF30-PW-414 engine was installed, actually

starting with 160396 instead of the first aircraft of the batch, as was initially planned. This engine was retrofitted to early aircraft and improved maintainability and reliability, with redesigned fan blades and a 'containment shell' around the whole turbine section. From Block 100, a slip clutch and coupler installation was added in the flap/slat system, as well as fuel system changes, AWG-9 reliability improvement measures, and a raft of anti-corrosion improvements, including seals, baffles and drain holes. The AN/ALQ-126 antennas were added to the beaver tail and below the wing gloves from the last aircraft of Block 110

The F-14A's primary task is to intercept bombers and missile carriers far away from the carrier battle group. Here an M-4 'Bison' becomes trade for a 'Diamondback' F-14A.

(161168). The first production installation of TCS was incorporated in 161597 (the first Block 125 aircraft).

Twenty early Block 60/65 F-14As were refurbished and modified to Block 130 standard for service with VF-201 and VF-202 at NAS Dallas. These were 158613 - 618,

Inside the F-14A

Radar antenna
The AN/AWG-9 uses a simple slotted planar array antenna, on which can be seen four horizontal IFF antenna dipoles.

Intakes
The F-14A's TF30-414 turbofan engines draw air through fully-variable intakes. These sharp-lipped, highly-swept intakes are set well out from the fuselage (to minimise the chance of ingesting sluggish boundary layer airflow) and incorporate three automatically-actuated ramps that vary the volume (and thus the speed) of air entering the intake duct. Massive spills are located in the roof of each intake.

Powerplant
The F-14A was originally powered by the Pratt & Whitney TF30-P-412 turbofan. This has since been replaced by the TF30-P-414 with steel containment cases around the fan stages, and by the further improved TF30-P-414A which was less prone to compressor stalls but which has proved more smoky than early engines.

Radome
The radar antenna is protected by a radar-transparent radome, tipped by a small pitot probe.

Missile
The primary air-to-air armament of the F-14A is the Hughes AIM-54 Phoenix missile. This incorporates its own radar for active terminal homing.

Cannon
The Tomcat's internal gun is a six-barrelled General Electric M61A1 Vulcan cannon, installed in the port side of the lower forward fuselage, with feed from a 675-round drum below the rear cockpit.

158620, 158624, 158626 - 637.

In 1988, the US Navy embarked on an ambitious programme to equip all F-14, F/A-18C/D and T-45 aircraft with the Martin-Baker SJU-17A/V NACES (Naval Aircrew Common Ejection Seat), partly to achieve a greater degree of commonality and partly because the newer seat (also with 'zero-zero' capability) offers higher velocity escape, at speeds of 700 kt (803 mph; 500 km/h) in level flight and 600 kt (688 mph;

428 km/h) in any attitude. The new seat dispenses with the optional face blind handle employed on its predecessor. Because production of the Tomcat was abruptly halted in February 1991, the Navy halted installation of the new ejecton seat in the F-14, except in the new-build and converted F-14Ds.

A single early F-14A was converted to JF-14A configuration for test duties. Four F-14As were converted to serve as F-14D

prototypes, 18 F-14As have been converted to F-14D(R) standards by Grumman and NADEP Norfolk, and 32 others were converted to F-14A+/F-14B configuration. Five to seven more F-14B conversions have been funded in FY92 ($143 million), with Grumman and NADEP Norfolk competing for the contract to install Grumman-built conversion kits. A further $175 million allocated in FY93 should fund 12 more conversions. Originally, plans called for the

conversion of 400 F-14As to F-14D standard. Installation of Tape 115B or 116 software to all surviving in-service F-14As from May 1991 gave full conventional ground attack capability and led to the 'Bombcat' nickname.

The F-14MMCAP (previously F-14A++) upgrade is a $392-million 1992 proposal for a Multi-Mission Capability Avionics Programme to be applied to surviving

The nozzle of the TF30 engine is covered by 'turkey feathers' that are rather more complex than those which make up the nozzle of the F110-PW-400.

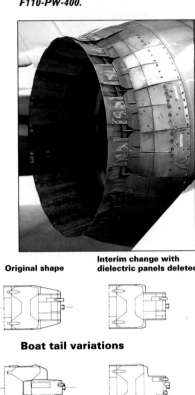

F-14A approach configuration

Production standard wing glove fairing, with extended outboard fence, from Block 70

AN/ARC-159

Early aircraft (pre-Block 90) initially lacked nose pitot

TF30-P-412A from Block 65

Arrester hook deployed

Undercarriage extended, no load

Early undernose fairing with ALQ-100 and IRST

Original shape

Interim change with dielectric panels deleted

F-14A underside plan

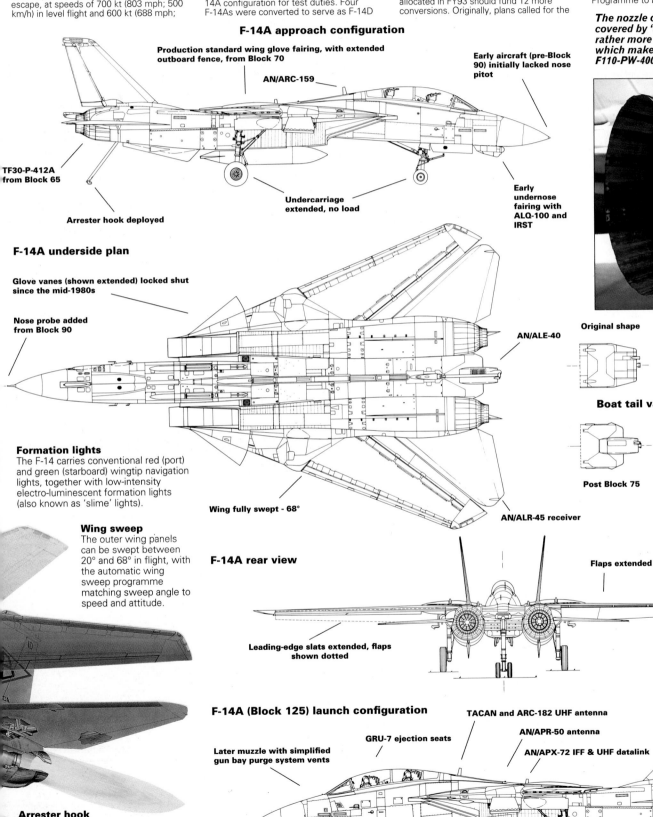

Glove vanes (shown extended) locked shut since the mid-1980s

Nose probe added from Block 90

AN/ALE-40

Boat tail variations

Post Block 75

Definitive production standard

Wing fully swept - 68°

AN/ALR-45 receiver

Formation lights
The F-14 carries conventional red (port) and green (starboard) wingtip navigation lights, together with low-intensity electro-luminescent formation lights (also known as 'slime' lights).

Wing sweep
The outer wing panels can be swept between 20° and 68° in flight, with the automatic wing sweep programme matching sweep angle to speed and attitude.

F-14A rear view

Flaps extended

Leading-edge slats extended, flaps shown dotted

F-14A (Block 125) launch configuration

TACAN and ARC-182 UHF antenna

GRU-7 ejection seats

AN/APR-50 antenna

Later muzzle with simplified gun bay purge system vents

AN/APX-72 IFF & UHF datalink

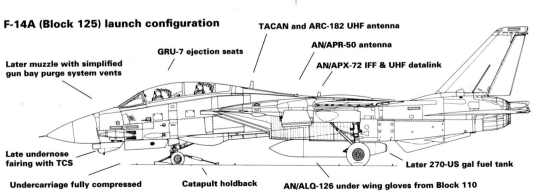

Arrester hook
The F-14 is provided with a highly-stressed, steel arrester hook to allow it to operate from carrier decks. The hook pivots left and right, as well as hinging up and down, which is helpful in crosswinds or off-centre arrivals.

Late undernose fairing with TCS

Undercarriage fully compressed

Catapult holdback

AN/ALQ-126 under wing gloves from Block 110

Later 270-US gal fuel tank

An F-14A on the catapult. The aircraft lacks a probe at the radome tip and has the early production gun bay purging vents.

This F-14A of VF-301 'Devil's Disciples' from NAS Miramar has been retrofitted with a radome-tip probe, but still retains the early gun bay vents. It has only a simple RHAWS antenna below the nose.

F-14As. This will add an AN/ALR-67 RWR system, provision for a Bol chaff dispenser, addition of a programmable tactical information display in the rear cockpit, and modification of the existing analog 5400 mission computer with digital capabilities from the F-14D AN/AYK-14. Twin Mil Std 1553B databuses will also be added. The validation aircraft is due to be redelivered in June 1994, with the first 'production' upgrade emerging from NADEP Norfolk in January 1995. The programme will last until 2002, when the Navy plans a so-called 'Block One' upgrade, which would add an attack FLIR (that will also add laser designation capability), the F-14D's HUD, an NVG cockpit, the AN/ALE-50 towed decoy, and an integrated GPS.

Further conversions/upgrades to F-14D, F-14B or to one of the advanced strike configurations remain at least theoretically possible.

Block Number	BuNos	Fiscal Year	Total
60 (F-14A-60-GR)	158612 - 158619	FY71	8
65 (F-14A-65-GR)	158620 - 158637	FY71	18
70 (F-14A-70-GR)	158978 - 159006	FY72	29
75 (F-14A-75-GR)	159007 - 159025	FY72	19
	159421 - 159429	FY73	9
80 (F-14A-80-GR)	159430 - 159468	FY73	39
85 (F-14A-85-GR)	159588 - 159637	FY74	50
90 (F-14A-90-GR)	159825 - 159874	FY75	50
(F-14A-05-GR)	160299 - 160328	For Iran	30
(F-14A-10-GR)	160329 - 160360	For Iran	32
(F-14A-15-GR)	160361 - 160378	For Iran	18
95 (F-14A-95-GR)	160379 - 160414	FY76	36
100 (F-14A-100-GR)	160652 - 160696	FY77	45
105 (F-14A-105-GR)	160887 - 160930	FY78	44
110 (F-14A-110-GR)	161133 - 161168	FY79	36
115 (F-14A-115-GR)	161270 - 161299	FY80	30
120 (F-14A-120-GR)	161416 - 161445	FY81	30
125 (F-14A-125-GR)	161597 - 161626	FY82	30
130 (F-14A-130-GR)	161850 - 161873	FY83	30
135 (F-14A-135-GR)	162588 - 162611	FY84	24
140 (F-14A-140-GR)	162688 - 162711	FY85	24

One of the stars of the film 'Top Gun', wearing fictitious and already rather eroded squadron markings, has the later single-strip upper and lower gun bay vents.

Some later aircraft, like this TCS-equipped, crudely-camouflaged F-14A from VF-213 'Black Lions', have later F-14D-style NACA-type gun bay venting system inlets.

Above: A Naval Fighter Weapons scheme features 'Flanker' camouflage for adversary training.

Below: Wearing smart two-tone grey, this CBU-toting F-14A serves with the Strike Test Directorate.

F-14A (TARPS)

Forty-five aircraft were built with the Tactical Air Reconnaissance Pod System Capability Retrofit Installation (AFC712PT), which enabled them to carry the TARPS reconnaissance pod. The Navy had previously relied upon aircraft designed specifically for the reconnaissance role, primarily the RF-8G Crusader. TARPS, however, could be fitted to the rear left Phoenix station of any Tomcat 'wired' for it, the current total being about 50 aircraft, with one of the two F-14A squadrons on each carrier usually having three reconnaissance-configured ships. All F-14Ds can carry TARPS.

Designed for a low-to-medium altitude reconnaissance role, the pod contains a KS-87 frame camera (vertical or forward oblique), a KA-99 panoramic camera giving horizon-to-horizon coverage, and an AAD-5 infra-red line scanner. The TARPS pod also includes an AN/ASQ-172 data display system for putting event marks on the sensor's film output to aid later interpretation. TARPS Tomcats accommodate pod controls in the rear cockpit and the aircraft provides power and air conditioning to the pod. TARPS became operational in 1981. Original trials TARPS pods were converted from external fuel tanks, which are a commonly carried Tomcat store.

The TARPS aircraft were 160696, 160910, 160911, 160914, 160915, 160920, 160925, 160926, 160930, 161134, 161135, 161137, 161140, 161141, 161146, 161147,

A TARPS pod undergoes maintenance, slung under the belly of a Patuxent River F-14A.

161150, 161152, 161155, 161156, 161158, 161159, 161161, 161162, 161164, 161168, 161270, 161271, 161272, 161273, 161275, 161276, 161277, 161280, 161281, 161282, 161285, 161604, 161605, 161611, 161620, 161621, 161622, 161624 and 161626. Seven more (158614, 158620, 158637, 159591, 159606, 159612 and 160696) were modified retrospectively. Three TARPS aircraft are usually assigned to each recce-capable F-14 squadron. Several more F-14As have sometimes been described as being TARPS capable, including 158978, 160916, 160921, 161138, 161143, 161144, 161149, 161153, 161165, 161167, 161278, 161283, 161286, 161430, 161601, 161625, 161864, 161866 and 161868.

A VF-102 'Diamondbacks' F-14A banks away to show the belly-mounted TARPS pod.

F-14A-GR (Iran)

From the beginning, Grumman had searched for other customers for the Tomcat and first proposed a long-range interceptor version to the US Air Force. In the 1970s, when the Shah of Iran (himself a pilot and infatuated with high-tech hardware) was striving to become the dominant force in the Persian Gulf, Teheran exhibited considerable interest in the Tomcat and other Western fighters. Iran also looked seriously at the F-15 Eagle and, soon afterwards, placed firm orders for the F-16 Fighting Falcon and the Northrop F-18L, land-based version of the F/A-18 Hornet. A few voices were warning that the Shah's fascination for top-of-the-line weaponry was growing excessive and that rumbles of discontent from the country's population threatened turmoil ahead. Iran, however, was a long-term ally that directly bordered on what was later dubbed 'the evil Empire', and was a major supplier of oil to the USA; in any event, arms sales were decided in personal conversations between the Shah and President Nixon, and Imperial Iran's ambitious armament programme forged ahead.

In the competition for the Shah's favour, the Tomcat gained an edge when a strong showing was made at the 1973 Paris air show, and by a personal demonstration for the Shah at Andrews AFB, in late 1973. Iran's case was not hindered when, in August 1974, the Iranian Melli bank stepped in with a loan when Congress voted to cut off the loan which was then keeping Grumman afloat. Motivated in part by incursions by Soviet MiG-25 'Foxbats' flying from bases on its northern border, the Imperial Iranian Air Force (IIAF) became the first and only foreign purchaser of the Tomcat, ordering 40 aircraft in June 1974 and 40 more in January 1975. The Iranian Tomcats were virtually identical to US Navy F-14As (with different harness locks and a diluter demand oxygen system), as were their Phoenix missiles, except for deletion of the ECCM (electronic counter-countermeasures) suite.

At the time, the General Accounting Office and other watchdog agencies were accusing Grumman of cost overruns in the Tomcat programme – a charge which seems to arrive with every major aircraft

An Iranian F-14A in flight. Iran is thought to remain the only foreign operator of the Tomcat, although rumours suggest that two F-14s were evaluated by Israel and may have been retained.

procurement – and the Iranian order helped to level the Tomcat's price and silence the critics. The first Iranian Tomcats were delivered to Mehrabad air base on 27 January 1976, and eventually equipped a peak of four squadrons at Khatami and Shiraz. After 79 of the 80 Tomcats had been delivered, aircraft No. 80 being retained for trials, the Persian state was swept by revolution, culminating in the fall of the Shah. This killed off all prospects for the repeat order for 70 more F-14s which had been discussed, and led to dramatic changes for the Imperial Iranian Air Force, which became the Islamic Republic of Iran Air Force (IRIAF). Many pilots and groundcrew were purged, and the force was suddenly cut off from its prime source of equipment, spares, support and training. It managed to keep most of its F-4D and F-4E Phantoms operational even during the 1980-88 war with Iraq, but this was largely due to clandestine assistance from Israel, which also operated Phantoms.

The Tomcat force never proved very effective, since only a small number could be kept airworthy, many aircraft being grounded through shortages of brakes and tyres. They did see some action, however,

The star-and-bar and H35 on the fin, applied for the long ferry flight, did little to disguise the intended destination of this desert-camouflaged F-14A at Calverton during 1977. One of the Iranian Tomcats was retained for trials.

often in a mini-AWACS role. Several were lost. Two are known to have been downed by Iraqi Mirage F1s, and another fell to a MiG-21. One was claimed on 4 October 1983, another on 21 November, and more single examples on 24 February and 1 July 1984, while on 11 August 1984 Iraq claimed to have shot down three F-14As. Iranian

F-14s are known to have claimed at least three Iraqi fighters in return, including a MiG-21 and two Mirage F1s. A rumour persists, despite the revolution's anti-Communist bent, that one F-14 was secretly whisked from Iran to the Soviet Union for study. Other stories suggest that this aircraft was flown to the USSR by a

Grumman F-14 Tomcat Variants

disaffected pilot. Perhaps more damagingly, Iran received 284 of 714 AIM-54 Phoenix missiles it had ordered, some of which were passed on to the USSR, where they proved of inestimable value to development of the AA-9 'Amos' missile.

Iranian Tomcats were officially F-14A-GRs, and were produced between Block 90 and Block 95 (F-14A-90-GR and F-14A-95-GR). They did not differ greatly from their Block 95 US Navy counterparts, and were delivered with virtually full carrier equipment, although some more sensitive systems, including the radar, ECM and AIM-54 missiles, were downgraded. The tactical software tape was unique to foreign sales aircraft. The AN/ARA-63 ILS was removed, as were the KIT-1A, KIR-1A and KY-28 cryptographic systems and the catapult abort mechanism. Crew equipment was also revised, with USAF-style harness attachments, including a centrally opening lap belt and new survival kit, and a chest-mounted oxygen regulator (normally panel-mounted) The covers over the inflight-refuelling probe were removed, giving the

A pair of Iranian F-14As refuels from one of that country's Boeing 707-3J9 tankers, the latter equipped with wingtip-mounted Beech 1800C wing pods.

only major external difference between Iranian and contemporary US Navy F-14s, although the arrester hook on Iranian aircraft was also given a sharper point, with much-reduced edge radius. The last Iranian F-14 was not delivered and was taken over by the US Navy as 160378. Allocated US Navy Bureau Numbers (160299 - 160378), the aircraft were assigned Iranian serial numbers 3-863 to 3-892 and 3-6001 to 3-6050.

It is easy to underestimate the number of F-14s remaining active with the IRIAF. Even as early as 1985, 25 were available for a mass flypast over Teheran, and serviceability and spares supply has probably improved since then, with the aircraft being accorded a high priority due to their capability and operational utility.

Left: Most Iranian F-14s have uncovered inflight-refuelling probes, as shown in this impressive line-up of Iranian F-14Bs.

Right: The US Naval Fighter Weapons School operates at least one standard USN F-14 in Iranian markings. This is not the aircraft built for Iran, whose delivery was halted by an embargo and which eventually reached the Pacific Missile Test Center.

F-14A IMI

The F-14 was proposed in 1971 as a contender for the USAF's Improved Manned Interceptor requirement for an F-106 replacement. A mock-up was constructed using the Model 303E mock-up as a basis, but with the addition of enormous conformal fuel tanks. USAF interest in the Tomcat was spurred by its very long range, which exceeded that of the F-15, and the capabilities of its AN/AWG-9 fire control system and the performance of the associated AIM-54 Phoenix missile. The F-14A IMI was eventually defeated by its very high price.

This F-14A IMI mock-up features four external fuel tanks, a single semi-conformal belly tank, and a combination of two underwing AIM-7 Sparrows and four belly-mounted AIM-54 Phoenix AAMs. Such a configuration gave range and combat persistence.

JF-14A

A single early F-14A, 158613, was assigned to test duties under the designation JF-14A.

F-14B

From the very start it was realised that the TF30-powered Tomcat would be somewhat underpowered, and would thus be best suited to being an interim aircraft, on which the Navy could gain experience while a more powerful variant was developed. Accordingly, a VFX-2 requirement (which became the F-14B) was written, describing an up-engined version of the TF-30-powered VFX-1 (which became the F-14A). It was estimated that development of an up-engined version would give 40 per cent better turn radius, 21 per cent better sustained *g* capability and 80 per cent greater radius of action. The engine chosen was the Pratt & Whitney F401-PW-P400, a derivative of the JTF-22 Advanced Technology Engine that also spawned the F100 used by the F-15 and F-16. The naval F401 used the same core, with a larger fan and afterburner, and a single-stage aft of the three-stage fan designed to supercharge the

The seventh YF-14 served as the prototype for the proposed F-14B. The F-14A was initially conceived to be an interim type, and the 67 aircraft originally ordered were to have been brought up to F-14B standard, with F401 engines. The latter engine was also to have powered the more advanced multi-role F-14C, some of which were to have gone to four US Marine Corps fighter squadrons.

core. As well as providing a degree of commonality with the USAF's standard fighter engine, the F401 offered lower weight and better specific fuel consumption than the TF30, and delivered 16,400 lb st (72.95 kN) dry thrust, and a staggering 28,090 lb st (125 kN) in reheat. This marked an increase of 16,000 lb st (71.17 kN) reheat thrust over the basic F-14, and raised the thrust to weight ratio from a modest 0.75:1 to more than unity.

It had originally been intended that only the first 67 Tomcats (including prototypes) would be TF30 powered F-14As, and that all subsequent aircraft would be built to VFX-2 standards, powered by the new advanced technology engine and designated F-14B. Existing F-14As would then be re-engined with the new powerplant. The eventual projected total was for over 700 aircraft, including aircraft for four Marine fighter squadrons, but many of these, it was felt, would be of the advanced multi-mission F-14C variant. The 469 aircraft initially contracted for were to have been procured in eight lots, of six, six, 30, 96, 96, 96, 96 and 43 aircraft. On this basis, unit cost (in 1970) was set at $12.4 million.

The seventh YF-14 was converted to serve as the F-14B prototype, flying on 12 September 1973. Some reports suggest that the aircraft first flew with an F401 in one nacelle only, but Grumman has recently stated that the aircraft flew only with two F401s installed from the very beginning. The engine proved too ambitious, however, and ran into many problems (failing its initial flight rating tests in 1975).

The Tomcat was already running into criticisms based mainly on its cost escalation, so costly and public engine development problems were the last thing the US Navy needed. Accordingly, they decided to stick with the TF30 and cancel the F-14B, while the USAF pressed ahead and set about slowly solving the similar problems which beset their version of the engine. Given the benefit of a crystal ball, or 20-20 hindsight, many might have preferred to stick with the F401 (whose Air Force equivalent suffered similar problems but eventually came good) rather than stay with an engine which remains both troublesome and lacking in thrust, and which forced a later (and thus more costly) switch to another new engine, the F110-GE-400. The F-14B prototype was put into storage, later emerging as the F-14B Super Tomcat to test the F101-DFE and its production derivative, the F110-GE-400.

The F-14B prototype waits at Calverton, virtually complete, for the installation of its F401 engines. The aircraft was the seventh of the YF-14s, and was probably the most valuable of the prototype batch, laying the groundwork for the later F-14A+ and F-14D versions, which transformed the Tomcat into the aircraft it always promised to be.

F-14B Super Tomcat

Ongoing problems with the TF30 engine (and, coincidentally, with the F100 used in US Air Force F-15s and F-16s) had led to the examination of a number of possible replacements, including the General Electric F101-X, the Pratt & Whitney F401-PW-26C, and both afterburning and non-augmented versions of the Corsair's Allison TF41, the TF41-912-B32 and -B31, respectively. No money was available for a formal competition, however, and it was not until 1979 that a development contract was awarded for a common USAF/USN future fighter engine.

In an effort to build up General Electric (which was felt to be lagging behind Pratt & Whitney in advanced fighter turbofan development), the company was given a development contract to produce a common USAF/US Navy fighter engine that might replace the TF30 in the F-14, and the F100 in the F-16. The resulting F101-DFE (Derivative Fighter Engine) was based on the core of the basic F101 being developed for the B-1 bomber, with a fan scaled up from that fitted to the F/A-18's highly successful F404. The same Tomcat that had been the original F-14B prototype, the seventh of the YF-14s, BuNo. 157986, was picked to evaluate the F101-DFE. As the so-called 'Super Tomcat' the aircraft made its first flight in its new configuration at Calverton on 14 July 1981, with the new engines installed in both nacelles and painted up with 'Super Tomcat' tail logos. At the same time, an F-16 (the so-called F-16/101) was already flying with the new engine, the first FSD F-16A, 75-0745, having initially flown with the new powerplant on 19 December 1980. This paved the way for the eventual F110 engine installation in the F-16C. Tests with the F101-DFE in the Super Tomcat were finally completed in the autumn of 1981.

The test programme showed impressive performance gains, including a highly significant 62 per cent increase in intercept radius, and useful gains in take-off performance that promised to allow unreheated carrier launches. A second aircraft allocated to the development programme, F-14A 158630, was deemed to be unnecessary. It was probably never fully converted, and was returned to standard F-14A configuration for further US Navy service. The engine's promise was such that a derived design, the F110-GE-100, was put into production for the F-16C, and a related version, the F110-GE-400, was selected to power the F-14D and the planned F-14A+. The Super Tomcat was

Originally YF-14A No. 7, 157986 successively served as the F-14B prototype with F401-P-400s, as the F-14B Super Tomcat with F101-DFEs, and as the de facto A+/D prototype with F110-GE-400s. External configuration, sensor pods etc. changed to reflect this, although the colour scheme remained constant.

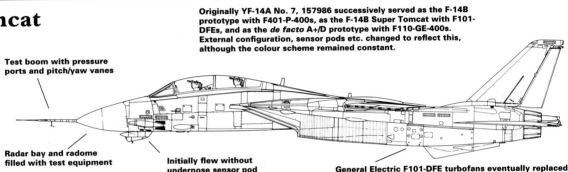

Test boom with pressure ports and pitch/yaw vanes

Radar bay and radome filled with test equipment

Initially flew without undernose sensor pod

General Electric F101-DFE turbofans eventually replaced by lengthened, productionised F110-GE-400s

F-14B Super Tomcat

re-engined again, flying with the F110-GE-400 as the F-14D engine prototype, gaining a representative undernose sensor package. With the F110-GE-400 the aircraft made another 'maiden' flight on 29 September 1986. In this guise the hardworking aircraft was flown to 762 mph (1226 km/h) and 35,000 ft (10836 m) by test pilot Joe Burke.

Right: The F-14B (originally YF-14 No. 7) is seen here flying with F101-DFE engines in both nacelles as the Super Tomcat prototype.

Laden with 1,000-lb Mk 83 bombs, fuel tanks and AIM-7 Sparrow and AIM-9 Sidewinder missiles, the Super Tomcat is seen here during the F-14D development programme.

F-14B (formerly F-14A+)

Designed as an interim improved Tomcat under the designation F-14A+, pending availability of the full-standard F-14D, it was originally envisaged that all F-14A+s would eventually become F-14Ds. Modifications to some secondary structure permit the installation of the General Electric F110-GE-400 turbofan in the new variant. This engine was developed from the USAF's DFE F110 tested in the Super Tomcat, described above.

The F110 is almost completely installationally interchangeable with the TF30, needing just an extra 50-in (127-cm) section downstream of the turbine (because the newer engine is much shorter, basically 182 in/462 cm compared with 236 in/600 cm). Almost the only other change was rearrangement of the engine accessories and their drive gearbox, plus minor modification to the surrounding F-14 secondary structure. The costs involved were modest. Diameter of the GE engine is actually less, at 46.5 in (118 cm), yet airflow at take-off is increased from about 242 to 270 lb (109 to 122 kg) per second. This increases power in a similar ratio, nominally to 29,000 lb (129 kN), although the Navy -400 engine is matched to F-14 requirements at 27,000 lb (120 kN). This not only dramatically improves all-round combat performance, but it enables catapult take-offs to be made in MIL power (without afterburner).

This backs up the great increase in power by a significant reduction in fuel consumption, because fuel burn in afterburner is multiplied by about four. Thus, at a round figure, the mission radius is increased by the new engine by no less

Below: Wearing markings indicating a recent or forthcoming deployment aboard the USS Nimitz, an F-14B of VF-211 'Fighting Checkmates', laden with a full load of six AIM-54C Phoenix missiles, gets airborne. The Pacific Fleet F-14B squadrons transitioned back to F-14As when it was decided to rationalise the Tomcat fleet with As and Ds on the West Coast, and As and Bs on the East Coast.

than 62 per cent. Time to high altitude is reduced by about 61 per cent. Not least, the F110 allows the pilot to forget about the engines during air combat and slam the throttle shut or wide open no matter what the angle of attack or airspeed.

While the TF30 was an advanced engine for the 1960s, the F110 shows the progress made in the intervening 20 years. The TF30 has a total of 16 stages of compression, the three-stage fan rotating on the same shaft as the six-stage low-pressure compressor. The F110, in contrast, has only 12 stages in total, comprising a three-stage fan and a nine-stage high-pressure compressor, yet, with hundreds of blades fewer, the overall pressure ratio of 31 is much higher than that of the older engine, which equates with better fuel economy. A further index of

progress is overall length. The comparative figures given previously show how modern engines can burn fuel in a shorter distance, and this is particularly true of the afterburner. The distance from the augmentation fuel nozzle rings to the end of the exhaust nozzle of the F110 is not much over half that of the TF30, but it was cheaper to add an unnecessary extra section to the F110 than to shorten the F-14.

Other changes include removal of the wing glove vanes, cockpit changes, the installation of the new AN/ALR-67 RWR with antennas below the wing gloves, installation of a new Direct Lift Control/Approach Power Control system, and redesign of the gun bay, incorporating a gas purging system, with NACA-type inlets

replacing the original grilles. A fatigue/ engine-monitoring system and AN/ARC-182 V/UHF radios are installed. The modernised and modified radar fire control system is redesigned AN/AWG-15F. Six aircraft were involved in F-14A+ development, including the hard-working test-ship, former F-14B Super Tomcat 157986, which made another landmark first flight on 29 September 1986 with the F110GE-400 engine. Piloted by Joe Burke at Grumman's Calverton facility, 157986 reached 762 mph

AIM-54s wait to be loaded onto a VF-211 F-14B. The NACA-type inlets for the gun bay gas purging system can clearly be seen aft of the muzzle.

This F-14B belongs to VF-103 'Sluggers', one of two F-14B units that participated in Operation Desert Storm, losing one aircraft.

Right: Apart from its F110-GE-400 engines (with different nozzles) and the lack of glove vanes, the F-14B is outwardly similar to the F-14A.

(1226 km/h) and 35,000 ft (10836 m) during this 54-minute trial run. Success with tests of the F110 powerplant led to a $235-million contract on 15 February 1987, the first of several for production of the GE powerplant. The Navy took delivery of its first production GE F110GE-400 engine for the F-14A+ on 30 June 1987.

The first FSD F-14A+ to fly was 162910,

on September 1986. The same aircraft later flew in full F-14A+ production configuration on 14 November 1987. The F-14A+ was redesignated F-14B on 1 May 1991, the original F-14B then serving as an F-14A+ development aircraft, leaving its designation 'free'. Thirty-eight F-14A+s were newly built, as detailed below. None of these aircraft were TARPS-capable.

Block Number	Bu Nos	Fiscal Year	Total
145 (F-14B-145-GR)	162910 - 162927	FY86	18
150 (F-14B-150-GR)	163217 - 163229	FY87	15
155 (F-14B-155-GR)	163407 - 163411	FY88	5

With a temporary desert camouflage applied in water-soluble paint, and with nose art proclaiming it to be the 'Thief of Baghdad', this Tomcat belonged to VF-24, one of two West Coast F-14B units.

Above: An F-14B of VF-101 'Grim Reapers' turns belly-on to the camera to show off its load of iron bombs.

Right: Before its disbandment, VF-74 pressed its F-14Bs into service in the adversary role, with a hastily applied camouflage scheme.

In addition to the newly-built F-14A+s, 32 aircraft were produced by conversion from F-14A airframes. The conversions were allocated the sequential KB- series identifications KB-1 to KB-32 (respectively F-14As 161424, 161426, 161429, 161418, 161287, 161428, 161433, 161417, 161419, 161440, 161444, 161427, 161416, 161442, 161437, 161441, 161421, 161422, 161425, 16159, 161601, 161430, 161608, 161432, 161434, 161435, 161438, 161851, 161871, 161610, 161870 and 161873). KB-1, -3, -6, -8, -13, -16, -18, -20, -22, -23 and -30 were equipped to carry TARPS. KB1-7 were funded in FY1986, KB8-25 in FY1987 and KB26-32 in FY1987 (purchase of kits) and FY1988 (installation of kits). About 17 more conversions have since been funded. Grumman has been funded to produce 11 conversion kits, with an option on eight more. Grumman and NADEP Norfolk are competing for the contract covering the installation of these kits.

Most F-14Bs may be upgraded under the same depot-level MMCAP update programme as some surviving F-14As, and are also potential targets for the Navy's proposed Block 1 upgrade.

F-14B (formerly F-14A+)

**F-14B
rear view**

Wings in oversweep (72°) position

F110-GE-400 nozzle fully closed

F110-GE-400 nozzle fully open

Standard F-14A avionics and radar

GRU-7 ejection seats

Wing glove vanes deleted

Same antennas as late F-14A

Standard late undernose sensor pod with TCS and ALQ-126

NACA-type inlets for gun bay purging system, also on very late F-14As

General Electric F110-GE-400 turbofans (nozzle closed)

Undernose sensors
The F-14 has carried a variety of sensors in pods below the forward fuselage. These have included a simple ALQ-100 RWR antenna, an IRST, the IRST with RWR underslung, or the Northrop TCS with underslung RWR.

Radar
The F-14B is fitted with the AN/AWG-9 fire control system, which consists of a powerful pulse-Doppler radar capable of simultaneously tracking up to 24 targets and engaging up to six, with a two-way datalink, computers, cockpit displays and (originally) an IR detection system. The radar was based on the AN/ASG-18 developed for the F-108 and uses a slotted planar array antenna.

Grumman F-14B

This F-14B wears the markings of VF-74 'Bedevilers', an Atlantic Fleet Tomcat unit which was disestablished on 1 July 1994, having spent the last few days of its existence flying in the adversary role. The 101 'Modex' identifies this as the skipper's aircraft, the CAG being assigned Modex 100 and the XO getting 102. Like many Tomcat squadron commander's aircraft, this F-14B has more colourful unit insignia (applied in black, red and yellow) and has full-colour national insignia.

Wing
A massive one-piece carry-through structure of electron beam-welded titanium alloy spans the upper centre-section of the F-14. The use of an all-welded structure reduced weight and limited the chance of cracking around the (absent) bolts and bolt-holes. At each end are the spherical pivot bearings and actuators for the variable-geometry outer wing panels.

Datalink
The ASW-27B provides for the automatic display of targets detected by ships, an E-2C Hawkeye or other F-14s, while simultaneously transmitting data on its own contacts. This can give the F-14 crew the reassurance of a 360° view of the area around them, which is also useful in enhancing tactical awareness. ASW-27B is also compatible with the Boeing E-3 Sentry and the Basic Air Defense Ground Environment.

Flight controls
The wing has full-span leading-edge slats and trailing-edge flaps in three sections, the inboard sections usable only with the wing swept forward. Four-section spoilers are fitted immediately ahead of the two outer flap sections.

Tail surfaces
The F-14 has conventional rudders on the trailing edge of each fin, with all-moving tailplanes moving symmetrically for pitch and differentially for roll control.

Powerplant
The F-14B is powered by a pair of 23,100-lb st (102.75-kN) General Electric F110-GE-400 turbofans. As well as giving commonality with the engines used by later variants of the F-16, the new engine is less prone to compressor stalls than the TF-30, and is considerably more economic.

Computer network
The radar and the other elements of the fire control system are linked via the Computer Signal Data Converter. This controls the Central Air Data Computer (which programmes wing sweep), the HUD, the datalink, the INS and the computerised cockpit displays. Most of the computers are digital, but analog computers are used for the AFCS and for fuel management.

F-14C

The F-14C was a proposed advanced version of the F-14B, with the same engines but with more advanced avionics and weapons systems.

Underwing pylons
The pylons under the wing gloves can carry either a single Phoenix or AIM-7 Sparrow, in each case with the option of a single AIM-9 Sidewinder on the stub 'shoulder' pylon.

Above: This new-build F-14D of VF-31 'Tomcatters' is in landing configuration, but with the arrester hook raised for an airfield landing. The squadron uses Felix the cat (carrying a bomb) as its insignia, a traditional badge going back to before World War II.

F-14D

The F-14D designation was originally applied to an unbuilt, austere version of the Tomcat, proposed at a time when the spiralling cost of the baseline F-14A was causing great concern. The F-14D we know today was first announced in 1984, and was conceived as an advanced Tomcat derivative with improved digital avionics. The F-14A+ was simultaneously conceived as an interim lower-cost supplement, which would be produced primarily by conversion of existing airframes.

The success of the F-14B Super Tomcat/F101-DFE combination led to an early decision (in February 1984) that the new variant would be powered by the 27,600-lb st (122.8-kN) F110-PW-400, the productionised version of the DFE engine, to take advantage of the promised improvement in performance, and to free the new variant from reliance on the TF30 turbofan that had proved so troublesome. This gave a 30 per cent lower fuel consumption in reheat, a 50 per cent increase in intercept radius and a 33 per cent greater CAP endurance. The increased thrust allowed carrier take-offs in dry power, a useful safety feature and particularly significant at night, when the bright flames generated by a typical 'burner take-off defeats any measures taken to darken the ship. The F-14B Super Tomcat prototype was re-engined with this powerplant, which introduced a 50-in (127-cm) plug in the afterburner section to move the heavy fan and compressor sections of the lighter, shorter engine further forward to maintain

The F110-PW-400, the powerplant used by the F-14D, has distinctive 'turkey feathers'. The nozzle is seen here in the fully open position, making an interesting comparison with the picture at the top of the page.

Above: With basic F-14A-style TF30 turbofans still fitted, the first prototype F-14D takes off on its first flight in US Navy hands, on 8 December 1987.

Below: The boat-tail of an F-14D features the high-band AN/ALQ-165 RHAWS antenna and the fuel dump pipe. Bays for tandem chaff/flare dispensers can just be seen.

A VF-124 'Gunfighters' F-14D rests on the Miramar flight line, its cockpit shown here. The heavily framed and separate windscreen and quarterlights seem especially anachronistic in an era when most modern fighters (even including the latest variants of the Mikoyan MiG-31 'Foxhound') feature a frameless, wraparound windscreen. The cockpit of the F-14D has, however, been extensively redesigned internally, with a new head-up display and with two multi-function display screens replacing some of the analog instrumentation in the F-14A's cockpit.

centre of gravity tolerances, and to allow installation in existing F-14s without major structural changes. The heavy sections of the engine actually moved forward only 39 in (99 cm), since the afterburner nozzles were mounted 11 in (28 cm) further back than on the F-14A. The re-engined F-14B made its first flight with the new engines in 1986, and later received other elements of the F-14D upgrade including the General Electric/Martin-Marietta dual undernose TCS/IRST sensor pod.

The avionics changes of the F-14D are actually the most important elements of the upgrade, and dramatically improve the combat capability of the F-14 in its primary intercept role, where all-out performance is of secondary importance. The F-14D is equipped with AN/APG-71 radar, which is essentially based on the hardware of the original AN/AWG-9, but with digital processing and NVG-compatible displays. The aircraft also has a multibus systems architecture with dual AYK-14 computers, AN/ALR-67 radar warning receivers, and provision for JTIDS. An AN/ASN-139 digital INS, and a digital stores management system are provided. All F-14Ds have expanded ground attack capability, and all are fitted with Martin-Baker Mk 14 NACES ejection seats.

Four prototypes were converted from F-14As, while the re-engined F-14B Super Tomcat was also involved in engine development work, first flying with F110-GE-400 engines on 29 September 1986. The first (PA-1 161865) made its maiden flight on 23 November 1987 and had F-14D APG-71 radar, digitised avionics and cockpit, but retained TF30-PW-414 engines. It was used for COM/NAV display system integration, radar systems testing, and datalink integration. The second (PA-2

Below: Externally, the F-14D can be distinguished from other variants by the General Electric/Martin-Marietta twin side-by-side sensor pods undernose, which house the Northrop AN/AXX-1 TCS to starboard and the General Electric Aerospace Electronic Systems AN/AAS infra-red search and track sensor to port (seen here with a solid cover, perhaps indicating that the equipment is not fitted). These were ordered in 1993 for installation before 1996.

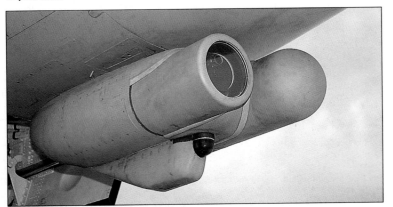

Right: The F-14D backseater has a single multi-function display screen in addition to his radar scope. Dual controls and emergency flight instruments are also fitted.

Making a rare visit to a carrier deck is one of VF-124's F-14Ds. The squadron is the West Coast Tomcat training unit, and is equipped with both F-14As and F-14Ds. No F-14D training is undertaken on the East Coast, and the Atlantic Fleet has no F-14D squadrons.

161867) was the only one of the four FSD aircraft actually fitted with F110-GE-400 engines, and had the same radar and avionics. It flew on 29 April 1988 and was used for radar and avionics integration, environmental systems integration, TARPS integration and radar fault isolation and verification trials. The TF30-PW-414-engined third and fourth prototypes (PA-3/ 162595 and PA-4/161623) made their maiden flights on 31 May and 21 September 1988, respectively, and were used for radar and stores management integration, ECM and RWR testing, and IRST and TCS integration, plus live weapons firing (PA-3) and JTIDS development and systems verification (PA-4). A TA-3B also took part in the flight test programme. The first prototype was delivered to VX-4 in May 1990.

Thirty-seven of the planned 127 F-14Ds were completed (as detailed below) before the programme was cancelled as an economy measure in 1989. The first of these was rolled out on 23 March 1990, and the last was delivered on 20 July 1992. Another 18 F-14Ds were produced by conversion of F-14As, and this total of only 55 aircraft was sufficient to equip three front-line squadrons and part of the Pacific Fleet training unit, VF-124. After a false start, in which VF-51 and VF-111 received Ds, VF-2 'Bounty Hunters' and the two units of Air Wing Six (VF-11 'Red Rippers' and VF-31 'Tomcatters') became the three F-14D units, each with a mix of new-build and remanufactured aircraft. A handful of prototype and early test F-14Ds have been redesignated as NF-14Ds and serve with a number of dedicated test units.

With the F-14Bs, the in-service F-14Ds are scheduled to receive some elements of

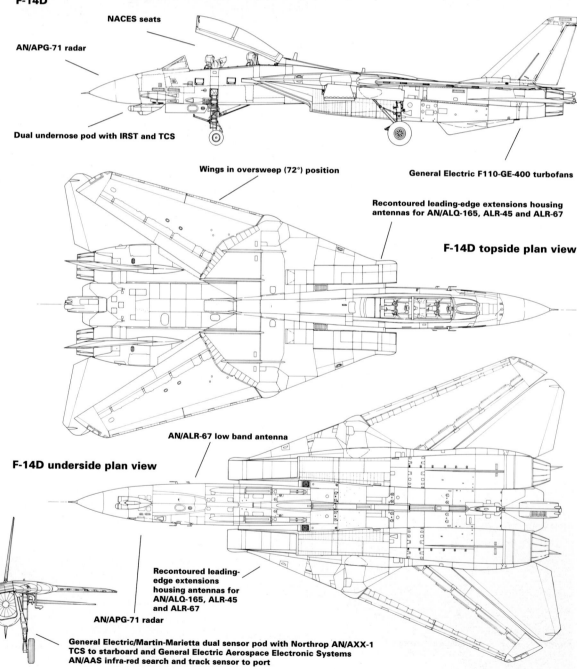

F-14D

NACES seats

AN/APG-71 radar

Dual undernose pod with IRST and TCS

Wings in oversweep (72°) position

General Electric F110-GE-400 turbofans

Recontoured leading-edge extensions housing antennas for AN/ALQ-165, ALR-45 and ALR-67

F-14D topside plan view

AN/ALR-67 low band antenna

F-14D underside plan view

F-14D front view

Recontoured leading-edge extensions housing antennas for AN/ALQ-165, ALR-45 and ALR-67

AN/APG-71 radar

General Electric/Martin-Marietta dual sensor pod with Northrop AN/AXX-1 TCS to starboard and General Electric Aerospace Electronic Systems AN/AAS infra-red search and track sensor to port

the planned Block 1 upgrade (other elements are already present in the F-14D), including GPS from FY95, a digital flight control system, AN/ARC-210 radios from FY98, and probably an attack FLIR, plus the AN/ALE-50 towed decoy.

Above: *From directly head-on, the only way of distinguishing between the F-14D and earlier variants is by looking at the side-by-side dual undernose sensor pods. This VF-124 aircraft is seen taxiing at NAS Miramar, the West Coast home of the Pacific Fleet F-14 community.*

Block Number	Bu Nos	Fiscal Year	Total
160 (F-14D-160-GR)	163412 - 163418	FY88	7
165 (F-14D-165-GR)	163893 - 163904	FY89	12
170 (F-14D-170-GR)	164340 - 164357	FY90	18

Right: *The distinctive heraldic shield of VF-11 'Red Rippers' is scarcely visible on the fin of this extremely toned-down aircraft. Most squadrons have a couple of aircraft with more colourful markings, sometimes even with full-colour national insignia. Unusually, this F-14D is parked with its inflight-refuelling probe extended.*

Above: *When it transitioned to the F-14D, VF-2 adopted new markings, consisting of a skull with stars in its eye sockets, superimposed on twin stripes.*

F-14D inboard profile

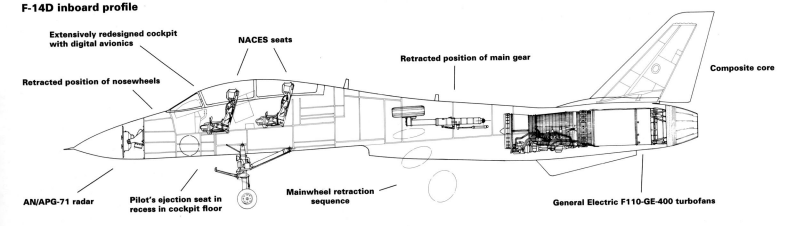

Extensively redesigned cockpit with digital avionics

NACES seats

Retracted position of main gear

Composite core

Retracted position of nosewheels

AN/APG-71 radar

Pilot's ejection seat in recess in cockpit floor

Mainwheel retraction sequence

General Electric F110-GE-400 turbofans

Grumman F-14 Tomcat Variants

F-14D(R)

The first of a planned 400+ F-14As for rebuild to F-14D standards under the designation F-14D(R) was delivered to Grumman in June 1990, the second following in September. The rebuild cycle was scheduled to take some 15 months, and eventually would have given the US Navy a Tomcat fleet consisting almost entirely of F-14Ds and F-14Bs. These ambitious plans were abandoned due to budgetary constraints. The six aircraft contracted for in FY90 were safe, but the 98 F-14D(R)s funded between FY91-FY95 (12, 18, 20, 24 and 24 aircraft) were cancelled, although the FY91 aircraft were later reprieved, to give a total of 18 conversions, all of which have now been redelivered from both Grumman and NADEP Norfolk.

The conversions were allocated the sequential DR- series identifications DR-1 to DR-18 (respectively 161159, 159610, 161158, 159613, 159600, 161166, 159629, 159628, 159619, 159592, 161133, 159595, 161154, 159603, 159635, 159633, 159618 and 159630). 159608 and 159631 were assigned as alternate aircraft for F-14D conversion. Like the F-14D, the F-14D(R) is scheduled to receive the relevant portions of the Block 1 upgrade.

The 18 F-14Ds produced by conversion of existing F-14As have been split between all three current front-line F-14D squadrons, comprising VF-2 'Bounty Hunters', VF-11 'Red Rippers' and VF-31 'Tomcatters'. All Pacific Fleet units home-based at NAS

Miramar, VF-51 and VF-111 each received a handful of F-14Ds but reverted to F-14As when the two squadrons of Air Wing Six (VF-11 and VF-31) swapped from East Coast to West Coast to become the first two operational F-14D units.

Above: A pair of remanufactured F-14D(R)s of VF-2 sits aboard the Constellation. The only way of telling remanufactured from new-build F-14Ds is by looking at the BuNo., and most squadrons have a mix of both types. Only by looking at minor differences in antenna configuration is it possible to differentiate these aircraft from the F-14B.

Conversion Nos	Conversion by	Fiscal Year	Total
DR-1 to DR-4	Grumman	FY90 (Lot I)	4
DR-5 to DR-6	NADEP Norfolk	FY90 (Lot I)	2
DR-7, 9, 10, 11, 13, 16, 18	Grumman	FY91 (Lot II)	8
DR-8, 12, 14, 17	NADEP Norfolk	FY91 (Lot II)	4

Below: An F-14D(R) of VF-11, the 'Red Rippers', manoeuvres on the deck of the USS Abraham Lincoln. Only three front-line squadrons use the F-14D, which is a considerably more advanced version of the Tomcat featuring advanced avionics as well as more powerful engines.

F/A-14D

The latest Tomcat upgrade proposal is designated F/A-14D and is designed to produce an upgraded strike derivative of the F-14D, by conversion of existing airframes, to replace A-6 Intruders, with no effect on planned F/A-18E/F procurement. If funding is made available in FY94, the programme could be launched in 1995, with deliveries for operational evaluation within two years of the programme start. Approximately $1.5 billion would be required for the upgrade of 54 F-14Ds to the new configuration, or $9.2 billion for 250 aircraft converted from F-14D, F-14B and even F-14A airframes.

Grumman proposes the F/A-14D upgrade as an alternative to the Block 1 upgrade to existing F-14As and F-14Bs, and envisages a four-stage programme, with the last three stages being incorporated as field modifications. Grumman's plan would bring all the aircraft involved up to a virtual F-14D standard, with F110 engines, AYK-14 computer, digital avionics and a new wiring harness. This would eliminate the high-maintenance analog systems that would be retained under the Navy's proposed Block 1 upgrade.

Grumman's seven-month first stage would also add an attack FLIR, Mil Std 1760 wiring for compatibility with advanced weapons like JSOW, a programmable tactical information display, a 'night vision' one-piece windscreen, stealth measures to reduce frontal RCS, and a dry bay foam system for fuel tank protection. Finally, the AYK-14 computer will be upgraded with a new XN8 memory module.

The second stage of the programme will add the AN/ALE-50 towed decoy, a navigation FLIR, and a full night vision cockpit, with many elements from the F/A-18D and night attack AV-8B, including a colour digital moving map. The HUD would be converted to use a Raster scan, allowing it to present FLIR data, and an inert gas generator would fill fuel tanks with nitrogen as fuel is consumed.

The third stage would add software modes from the F-15E's AN/APG-71, including Doppler beam sharpening, synthetic aperture, sea surface search, moving target indication, and a terrain-following mode.

The fourth stage would add the advanced weapons like JDAM and JSOW.

NF-14D

The former second and fourth prototype F-14Ds (161867 and 161623) and early

F-14Ds 163415/16 have been permanently assigned to test duties under the designation NF-14D. They were respectively operated by the Naval Air Warfare Center/Weapons Division (formerly PMTC), the

Naval Air Warfare Center/Aircraft Division (formerly NATC) and by VX-4 (163415 and 163416). The N prefix infers a level of modification which makes it impossible to return the aircraft to operational status.

161867 was never a true F-14D, in that it retained TF-30 engines, while 161623 never received the dual undernose sensor pod. The two later NF-14Ds are much closer to the definitive production F-14D.

One of the four NF-14Ds, 161623, was originally F-14D PA-4. It is now in service with the Strike Aircraft Test Directorate, having initially been allocated to the NATC (which became the NAWC/AD) after conversion to NF-14D standards.

The former F-14D PA-2, now an NF-14D, is seen during early service with the Pacific Missile Test Center. The aircraft has the full-standard F-14D powerplant but lacks the distinctive dual undernose sensor pod fitted to production F-14Ds.

F-14T

The F-14T was a very austere, very basic F-14 derivative designed as an alternative to the increasingly costly F-14A and F-14B. The type competed for an order with a navalised version of the less expensive USAF F-15 known as the F-15N, and also competed with the option of procurement

of upgraded F-4s. The aircraft would have offered only Sparrow and Sidewinder armament, and would have offered little advantage over the ageing F-4 Phantom. The lack of capability offered by the F-14T led to less radically downgraded F-14 variants.

F-14X

The F-14X designation covered a group of slightly less radically degraded Tomcats, some of which had no AIM-54 capability, and some of which had the simultaneous target-tracking capability halved from 24 to 12. DLC, glove vanes and APC (Approach Power Compensator) were removed. The

Westinghouse WX-200, WX-250 or Hughes APG-64 were the fire control system options.

High Israeli attrition rates in the 1973 war led to the type's cancellation, the US Navy preferring to equip its carriers with the best-available aircraft.

F-14 Optimod

The Optimod F-14 was a proposed austere F-14 using one of three different computers with the AWG-9, giving a reduced level of capability. It was intended to reduce the

unit price of the aircraft, which at one time threatened procurement for the US Navy. It may also have been proposed to some export customers.

RF-14

The RF-14 designation originally covered a proposed reconnaissance derivative of the F-14A, presumably equipped with internal sensors. It was

eventually abandoned in favour of equipping lightly modified (i.e., rewired) standard F-14s with external TARPS pods.

Quickstrike

Drawdowns in Naval Aviation funding and the cancellation of the A-12 as an A-6 replacement have led to a number of plans to offer the F-14 as a long-range strike fighter. Such plans have resulted in the 'Bombcat' modification to F-14As, and the incorporation of a high level of ground attack capability in the F-14D.

They have also resulted in Grumman offering a succession of proposed new strike fighter variants as competitors to the F/A-18E/F, which has been selected as the successor to the A-6. The first of these variants was the Quickstrike, which was a minimum-change FLIR-equipped aircraft with more radar modes for its APG-71 radar,

including synthetic aperture and Doppler Beam Sharpening for mapping, bringing it closer to the APG-70 used by the F-15E. Four fuselage hardpoints each had five sub-stations, while the two wing pylons had two. Navigation and targeting pods similar to LANTIRN would be installed, and cockpit changes would include FLIR, HUD, moving-

map display and large colour displays. Software changes would allow the carriage of laser-guided bombs, stand-off SLAM missiles and Maverick, in addition to HARM and Harpoon. The cockpit was NVG-compatible, and had colour displays, including a digital moving map.

Super Tomcat 21

The Super Tomcat 21 was proposed as a more radical update, a multi-role fighter alternative to the Naval ATF, offering 90 per cent of the capability at 60 per cent of the cost. It was to have incorporated all Quickstrike improvements, with further cockpit and sensor improvements, and a significantly reduced radar cross-section, plus it was to have been powered by improved F110-GE-129 engines which would allow 'supercruise' (i.e., sustained supersonic cruise without afterburner), and which would even incorporate thrust-vectoring. An APU was also planned. The type was to also to have been fitted with enlarged tailplanes (with extended trailing edges giving greater area), new extended wing gloves housing additional internal fuel, and increased-lift slotted flaps and extended-chord slats to allow nil-wind carrier take-offs or take-offs at higher weights. A single point

maintenance panel and other improvements were to have reduced MMH/FH figures by 40 per cent. An improvement in the weapons system package would have seen the adoption of helmet-mounted sights and a new radar with double the power of the APG-71. FLIR pods would have been installed for attack missions.

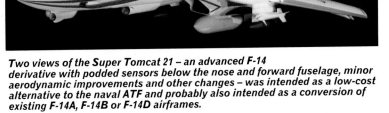

Two views of the Super Tomcat 21 – an advanced F-14 derivative with podded sensors below the nose and forward fuselage, minor aerodynamic improvements and other changes – was intended as a low-cost alternative to the naval ATF and probably also intended as a conversion of existing F-14A, F-14B or F-14D airframes.

Attack Super Tomcat 21

A proposed dedicated Mach 2-capable strike aircraft, the Attack Super Tomcat 21 was based on the Super Tomcat 21, but with thicker outer wing panels housing extra fuel, provision for larger external fuel tanks, and further refinements to the high

lift system to give a 15-kt (18-mph; 27-km/h) reduction in approach speeds. These included redesigned, composite, single-slotted Fowler flaps and a blunter, composite, extended-chord slat. The aircraft was to have had the Norden radar

developed specifically for the GD/McDD A-12. The Attack Super Tomcat 21 has received great attention as a potential successor to the cancelled A-12, a highly advanced but much-troubled flying wing intended as a stealthy naval attack aircraft.

ASF-14

Due to the postponement of development of the Naval ATF, the ASF-14 was proposed as an evolutionary development of the F-14 but with ATF systems, armament and powerplants, and intended as a lower-cost, lower-risk alternative to the Naval ATF.

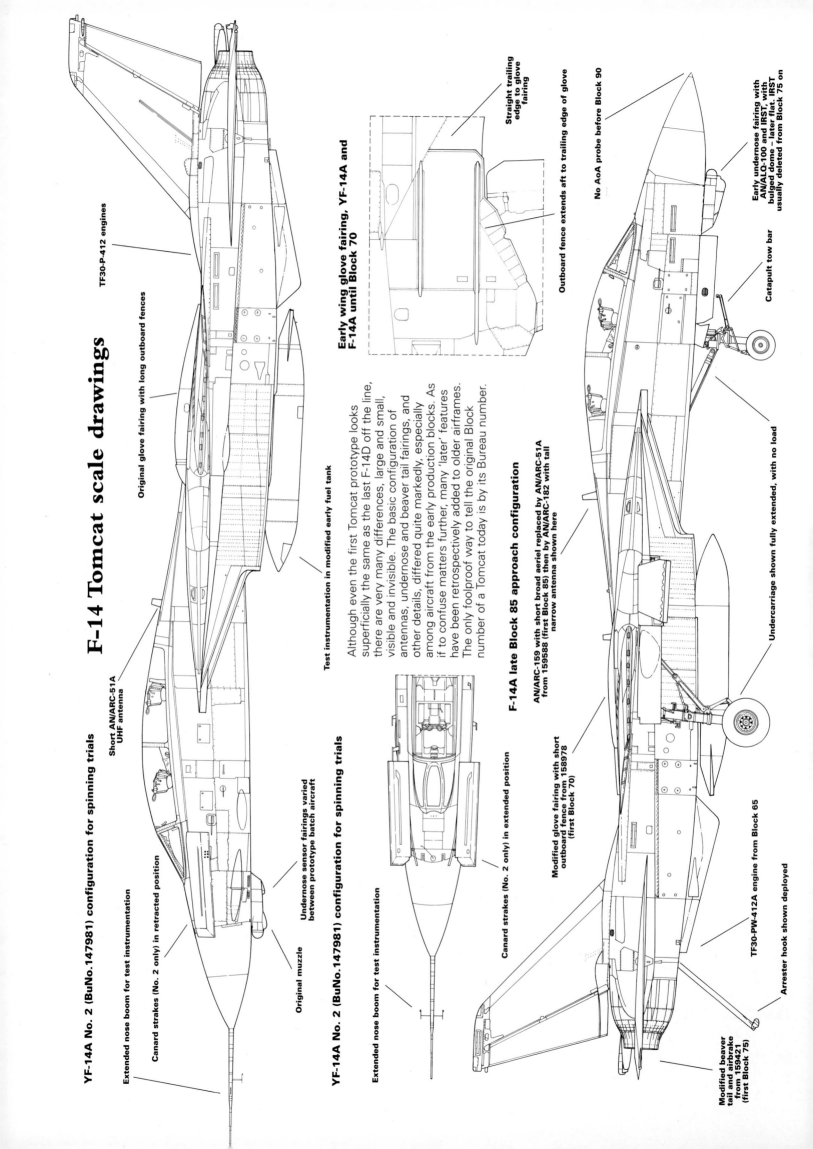

F-14 Tomcat scale drawings

YF-14A No. 2 (BuNo.147981) configuration for spinning trials

TF30-P-412 engines

Original glove fairing with long outboard fences

Short AN/ARC-51A UHF antenna

Extended nose boom for test instrumentation

Canard strakes (No. 2 only) in retracted position

Original muzzle

Undernose sensor fairings varied between prototype batch aircraft

Test instrumentation in modified early fuel tank

YF-14A No. 2 (BuNo.147981) configuration for spinning trials

Extended nose boom for test instrumentation

Canard strakes (No. 2 only) in extended position

Early wing glove fairing, YF-14A and F-14A until Block 70

Straight trailing edge to glove fairing

Outboard fence extends aft to trailing edge of glove

Although even the first Tomcat prototype looks superficially the same as the last F-14D off the line, there are very many differences, large and small, visible and invisible. The basic configuration of antennas, undernose and beaver tail fairings, and other details, differed quite markedly, especially among aircraft from the early production blocks. As if to confuse matters further, many 'later' features have been retrospectively added to older airframes. The only foolproof way to tell the original Block number of a Tomcat today is by its Bureau number.

F-14A late Block 85 approach configuration

AN/ARC-159 with short broad aerial replaced by AN/ARC-51A from 159588 (first Block 85) then by AN/ARC-182 with tall narrow antenna shown here

Modified glove fairing with short outboard fence from 158978 (first Block 70)

No AoA probe before Block 90

Early undernose fairing with AN/ALQ-100 and IRST, with bulged dome – later flat. IRST usually deleted from Block 75 on

Catapult tow bar

Undercarriage shown fully extended, with no load

Modified beaver tail and airbrake from 159421 (first Block 75)

TF30-PW-412A engine from Block 65

Arrester hook shown deployed

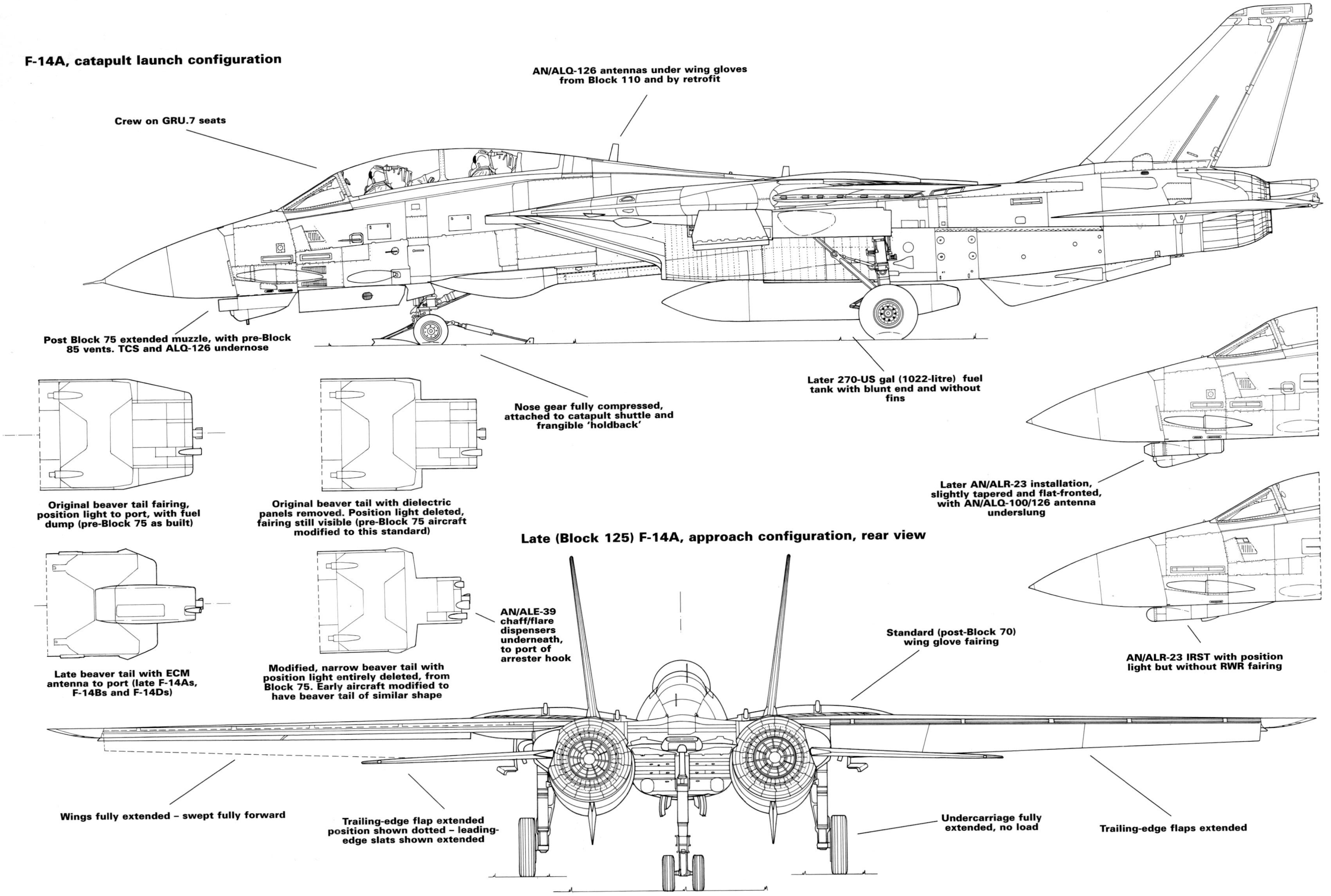

F-14A, catapult launch configuration

Crew on GRU.7 seats

AN/ALQ-126 antennas under wing gloves from Block 110 and by retrofit

Post Block 75 extended muzzle, with pre-Block 85 vents. TCS and ALQ-126 undernose

Original beaver tail fairing, position light to port, with fuel dump (pre-Block 75 as built)

Late beaver tail with ECM antenna to port (late F-14As, F-14Bs and F-14Ds)

Nose gear fully compressed, attached to catapult shuttle and frangible 'holdback'

Original beaver tail with dielectric panels deleted. Position light fairing still visible (pre-Block 75 aircraft modified to this standard)

Modified, narrow beaver tail with position light entirely deleted, from Block 75. Early aircraft modified to have beaver tail of similar shape

Later 270-US gal (1022-litre) fuel tank with blunt end and without fins

Later AN/ALR-23 installation, slightly tapered and flat-fronted, with AN/ALQ-100/126 antenna underslung

AN/ALR-23 IRST with position light but without RWR fairing

Trailing-edge flaps extended

Standard (post-Block 70) wing glove fairing

Undercarriage fully extended, no load

Late (Block 125) F-14A, approach configuration, rear view

AN/ALE-39 chaff/flare dispensers underneath, to port of arrester hook

Trailing-edge flap extended position shown dotted – leading-edge slats shown extended

Wings fully extended – swept fully forward

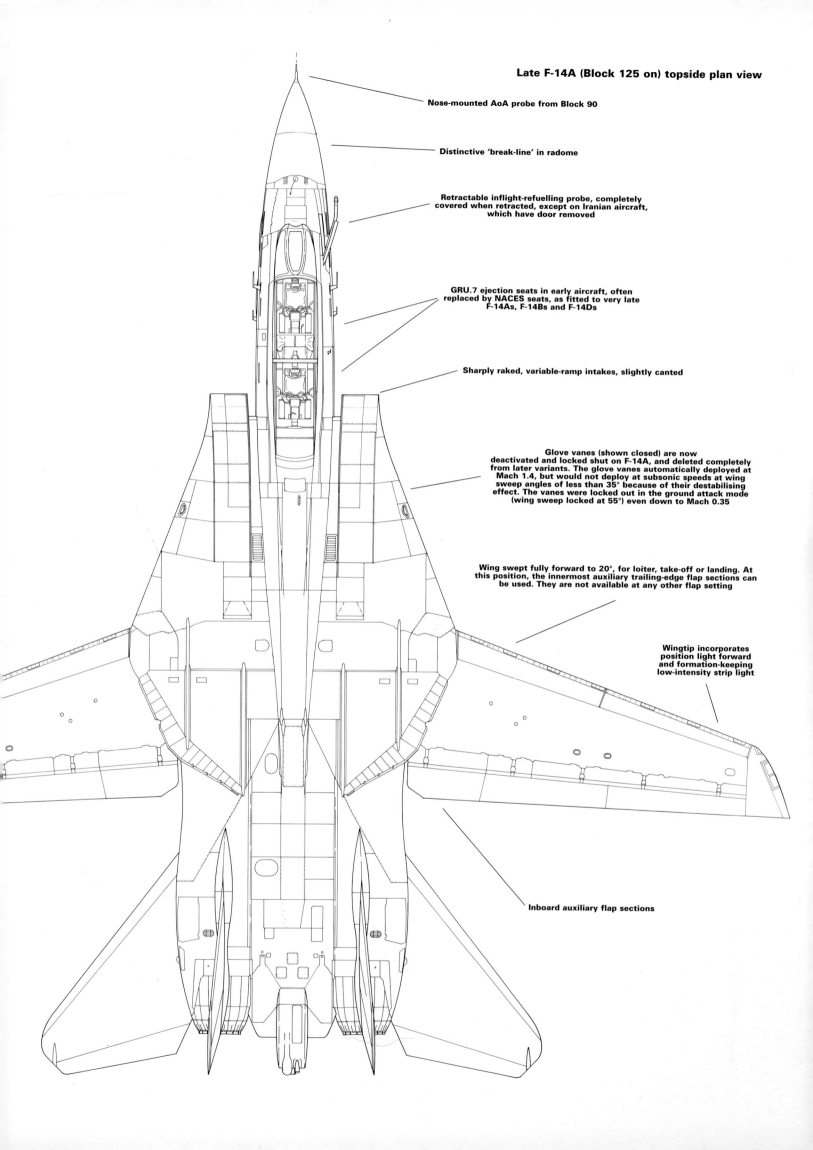

Late F-14A (Block 125 on) topside plan view

Nose-mounted AoA probe from Block 90

Distinctive 'break-line' in radome

Retractable inflight-refuelling probe, completely covered when retracted, except on Iranian aircraft, which have door removed

GRU.7 ejection seats in early aircraft, often replaced by NACES seats, as fitted to very late F-14As, F-14Bs and F-14Ds

Sharply raked, variable-ramp intakes, slightly canted

Glove vanes (shown closed) are now deactivated and locked shut on F-14A, and deleted completely from later variants. The glove vanes automatically deployed at Mach 1.4, but would not deploy at subsonic speeds at wing sweep angles of less than 35° because of their destabilising effect. The vanes were locked out in the ground attack mode (wing sweep locked at 55°) even down to Mach 0.35

Wing swept fully forward to 20°, for loiter, take-off or landing. At this position, the innermost auxiliary trailing-edge flap sections can be used. They are not available at any other flap setting

Wingtip incorporates position light forward and formation-keeping low-intensity strip light

Inboard auxiliary flap sections

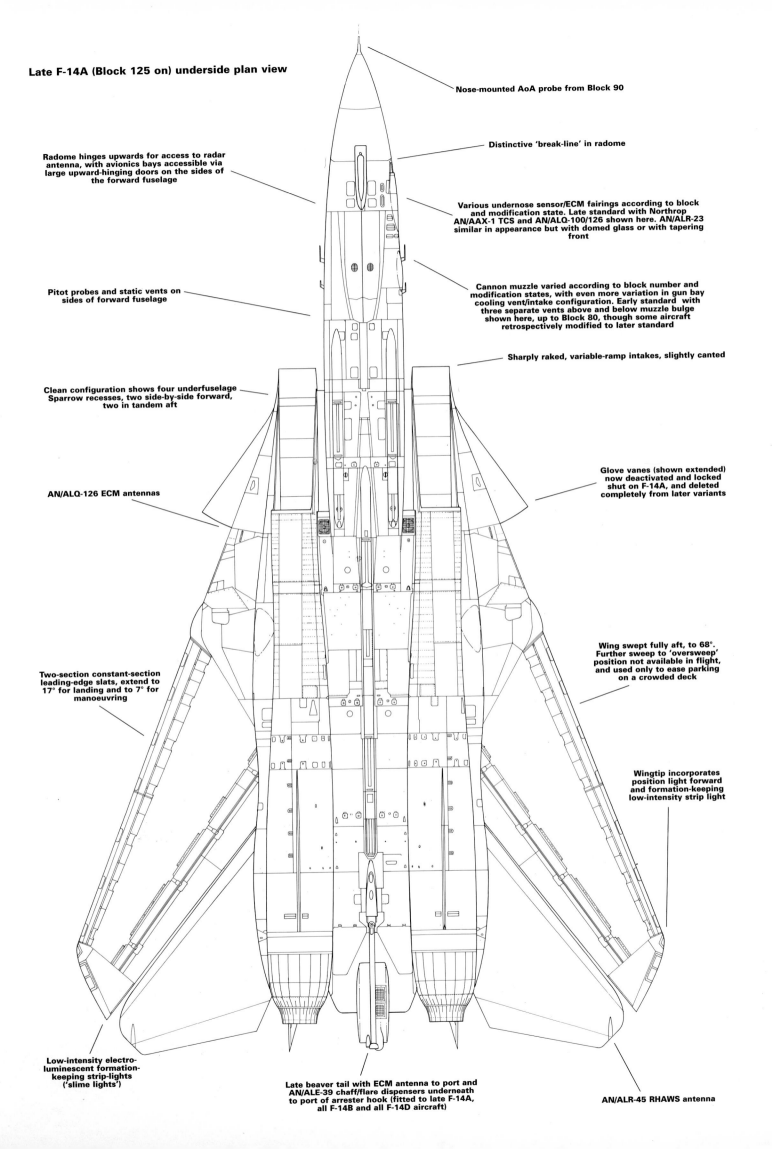

Late F-14A (Block 125 on) underside plan view

Nose-mounted AoA probe from Block 90

Distinctive 'break-line' in radome

Radome hinges upwards for access to radar antenna, with avionics bays accessible via large upward-hinging doors on the sides of the forward fuselage

Various undernose sensor/ECM fairings according to block and modification state. Late standard with Northrop AN/AAX-1 TCS and AN/ALQ-100/126 shown here. AN/ALR-23 similar in appearance but with domed glass or with tapering front

Pitot probes and static vents on sides of forward fuselage

Cannon muzzle varied according to block number and modification states, with even more variation in gun bay cooling vent/intake configuration. Early standard with three separate vents above and below muzzle bulge shown here, up to Block 80, though some aircraft retrospectively modified to later standard

Sharply raked, variable-ramp intakes, slightly canted

Clean configuration shows four underfuselage Sparrow recesses, two side-by-side forward, two in tandem aft

Glove vanes (shown extended) now deactivated and locked shut on F-14A, and deleted completely from later variants

AN/ALQ-126 ECM antennas

Wing swept fully aft, to 68°. Further sweep to 'oversweep' position not available in flight, and used only to ease parking on a crowded deck

Two-section constant-section leading-edge slats, extend to 17° for landing and to 7° for manoeuvring

Wingtip incorporates position light forward and formation-keeping low-intensity strip light

Low-intensity electro-luminescent formation-keeping strip-lights ('slime lights')

Late beaver tail with ECM antenna to port and AN/ALE-39 chaff/flare dispensers underneath to port of arrester hook (fitted to late F-14A, all F-14B and all F-14D aircraft)

AN/ALR-45 RHAWS antenna

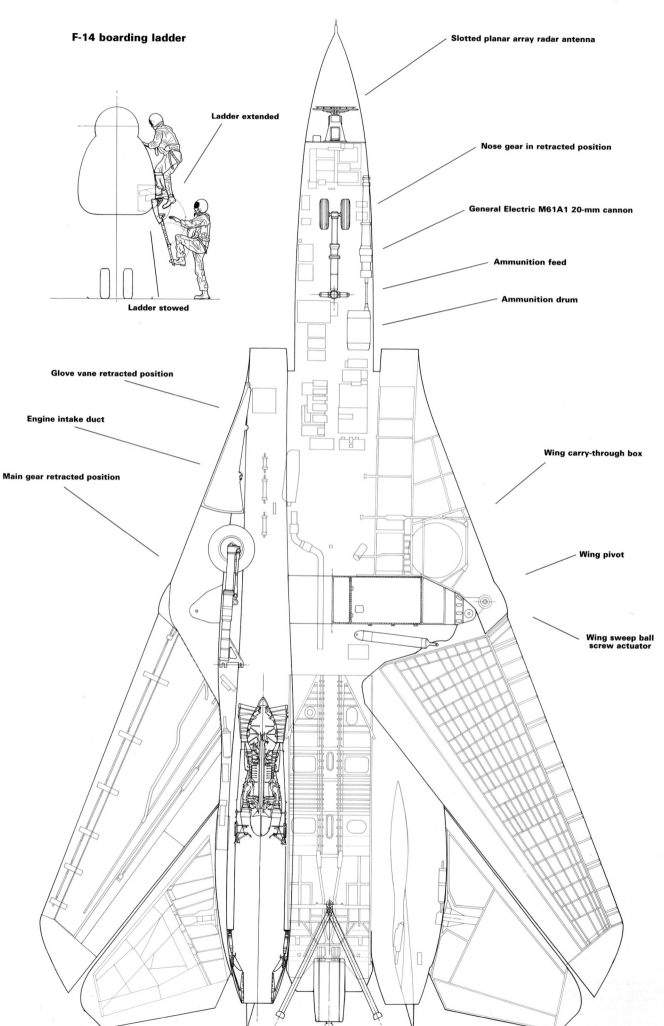

F-14 boarding ladder

F-14A (Block 125 on) underside inboard plan view

Ladder extended

Ladder stowed

Slotted planar array radar antenna

Nose gear in retracted position

General Electric M61A1 20-mm cannon

Ammunition feed

Ammunition drum

Glove vane retracted position

Engine intake duct

Main gear retracted position

Wing carry-through box

Wing pivot

Wing sweep ball screw actuator

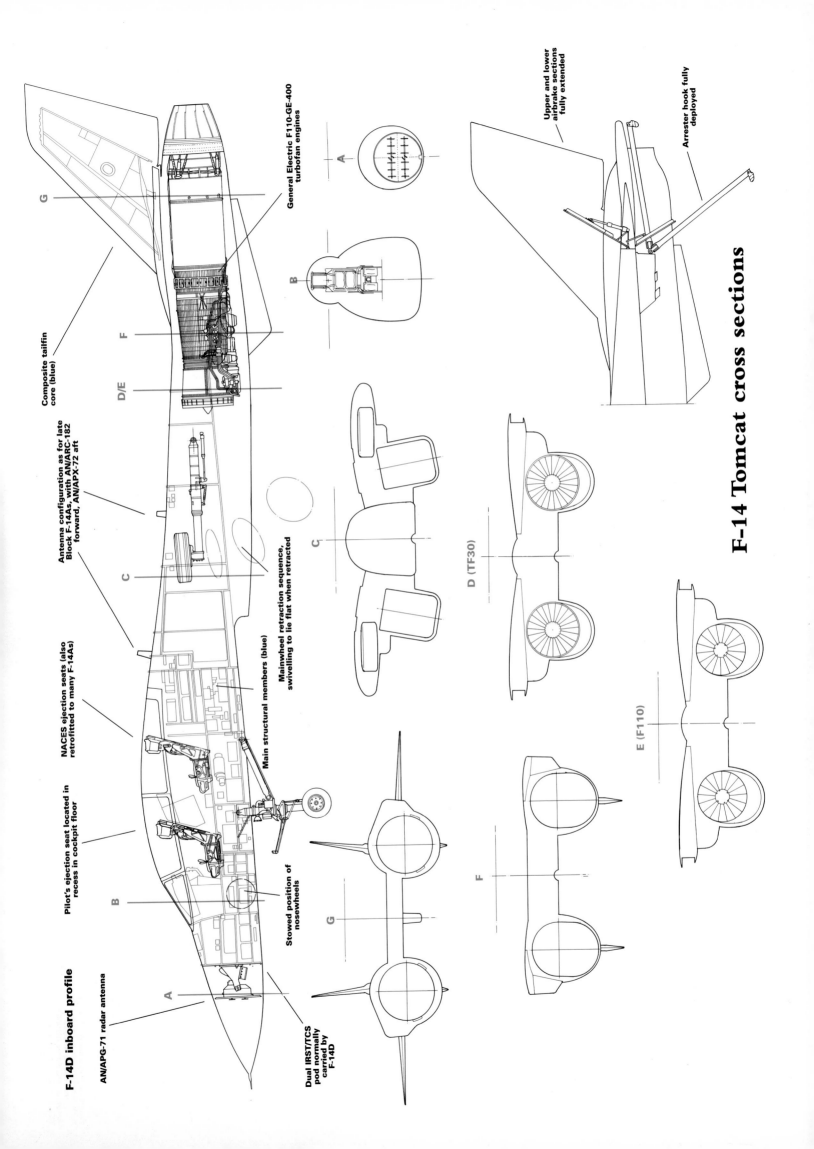

F-14 Tomcat cross sections

F-14D inboard profile

AN/APG-71 radar antenna

Pilot's ejection seat located in recess in cockpit floor

NACES ejection seats (also retrofitted to many F-14As)

Antenna configuration as for late Block F-14As, with AN/ARC-182 forward, AN/APX-72 aft

Composite tailfin core (blue)

General Electric F110-GE-400 turbofan engines

Main structural members (blue)

Mainwheel retraction sequence, swivelling to lie flat when retracted

Stowed position of nosewheels

Dual IRST/TCS pod normally carried by F-14D

Upper and lower airbrake sections fully extended

Arrester hook fully deployed

A

B

C

D/E

F

G

D (TF30)

E (F110)

F-14B Super Tomcat

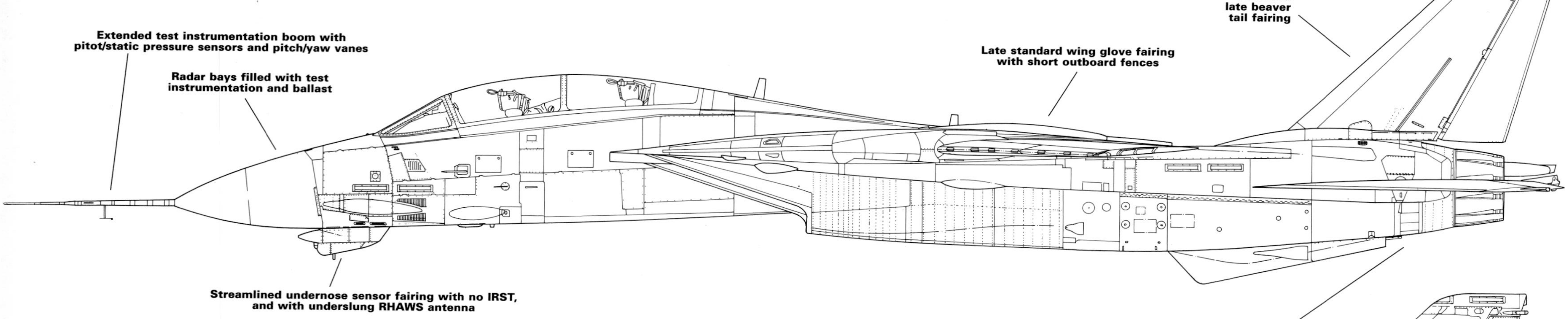

Standard late beaver tail fairing

Late standard wing glove fairing with short outboard fences

Extended test instrumentation boom with pitot/static pressure sensors and pitch/yaw vanes

Radar bays filled with test instrumentation and ballast

Streamlined undernose sensor fairing with no IRST, and with underslung RHAWS antenna

F-14B (F-14A Plus)

Short F101-DFE engines (shown here) fitted after F401-PW-400, eventually replaced by F110-GE-400s

Wing glove vanes deleted

GRU.7 ejection seats

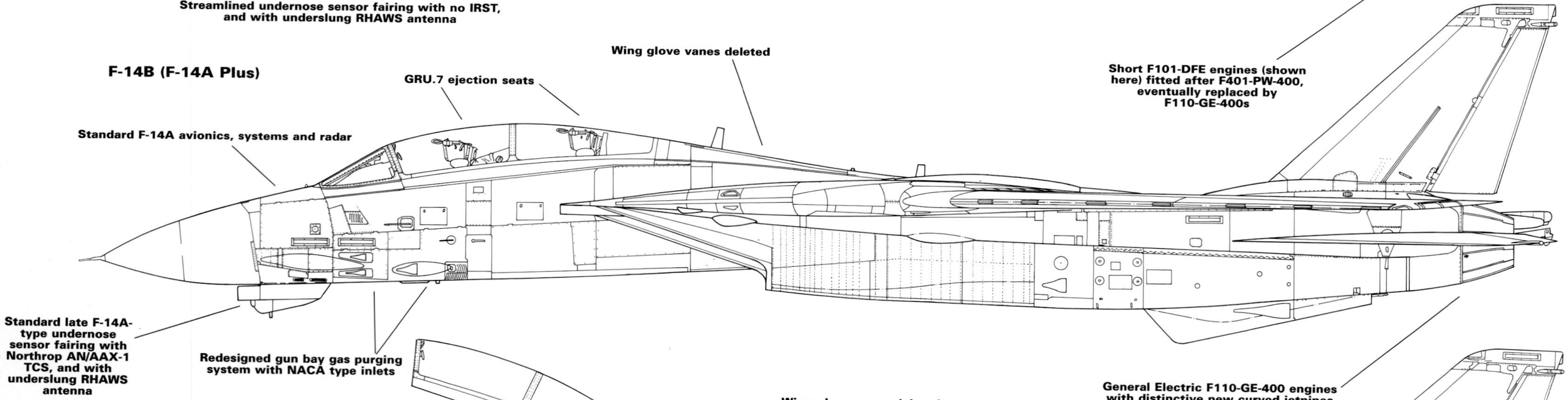

Standard F-14A avionics, systems and radar

Standard late F-14A-type undernose sensor fairing with Northrop AN/AAX-1 TCS, and with underslung RHAWS antenna

F-14D or F-14D(R)

General Electric F110-GE-400 engines with distinctive new curved jetpipes

Wing glove vanes deleted

Redesigned gun bay gas purging system with NACA type inlets

Recontoured wing glove leading edge, incorporating RHAWS antennas

AN/APG-71 radar, but no external change to radome

New undernose sensor fairing with side-by- side sensors and underslung RHAWS antenna. Northrop AN/AAX-1 TCS to starboard and GE IRST to port

Redesigned gun bay gas purging system with NACA type inlets

General Electric F110-GE-400 engines, as for F-14B

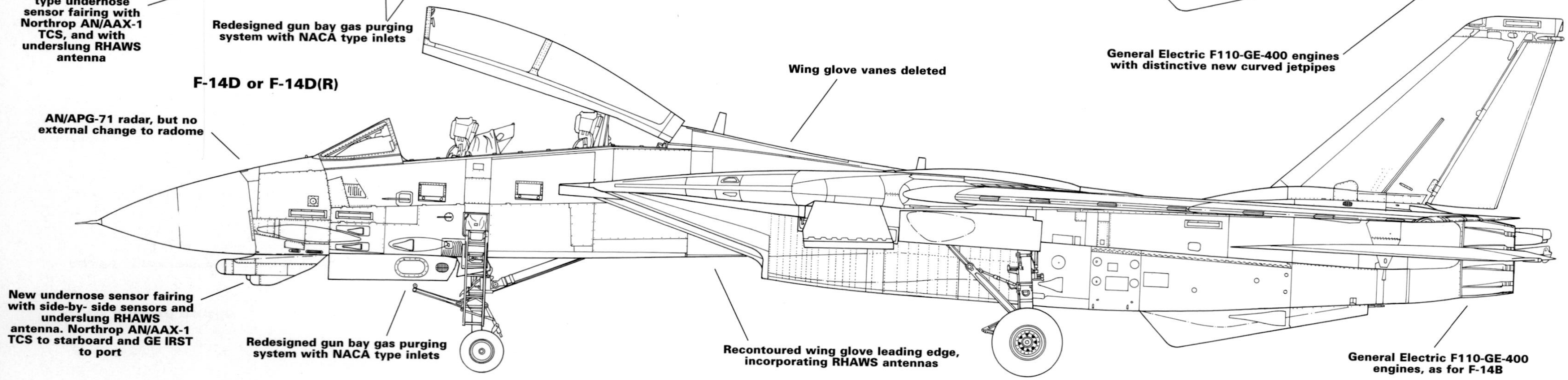

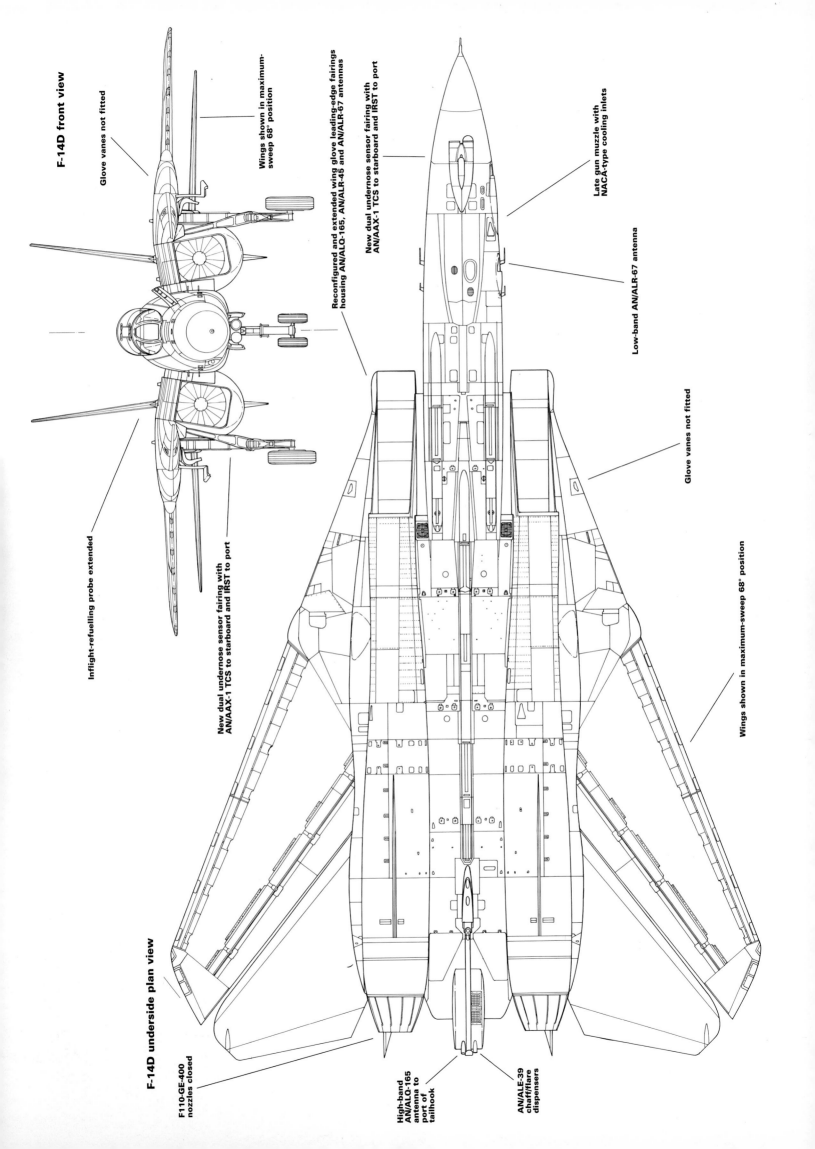

F-14D front view

Glove vanes not fitted

Wings shown in maximum-sweep 68° position

Reconfigured and extended wing glove leading-edge fairings housing AN/ALQ-165, AN/ALR-45 and AN/ALR-67 antennas

New dual undernose sensor fairing with AN/AAX-1 TCS to starboard and IRST to port

Late gun muzzle with NACA-type cooling inlets

Low-band AN/ALR-67 antenna

Inflight-refuelling probe extended

New dual undernose sensor fairing with AN/AAX-1 TCS to starboard and IRST to port

Glove vanes not fitted

F-14D underside plan view

F110-GE-400 nozzles closed

Wings shown in maximum-sweep 68° position

High-band AN/ALQ-165 antenna to port of tailhook

AN/ALE-39 chaff/flare dispensers

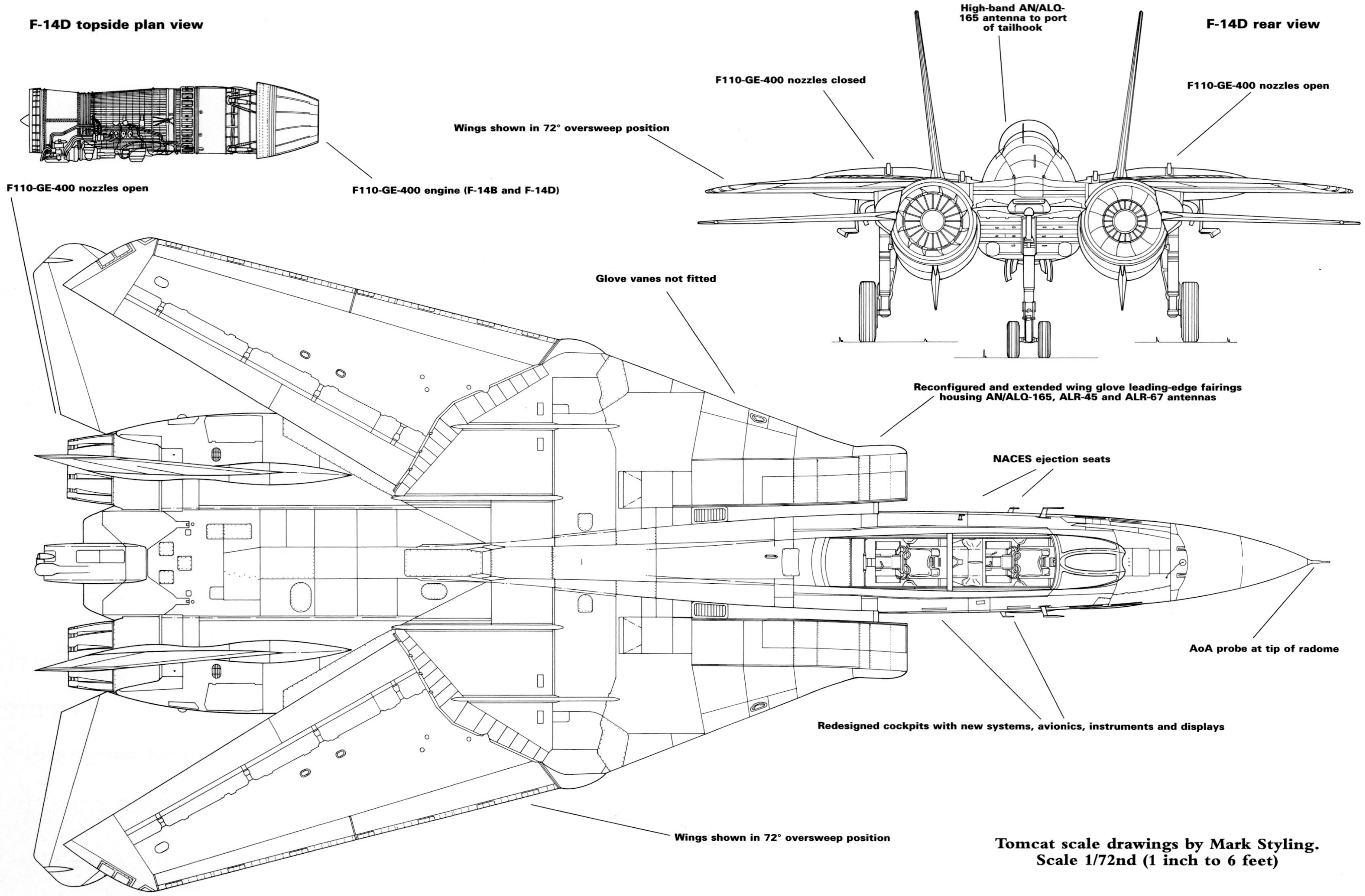

F-14D rear view

F110-GE-400 nozzles open

High-band AN/ALQ-165 antenna to port of tailhook

F110-GE-400 nozzles closed

Wings shown in 72° oversweep position

F-14D topside plan view

F110-GE-400 engine (F-14B and F-14D)

F110-GE-400 nozzles open

Reconfigured and extended wing glove leading-edge fairings housing AN/ALQ-165, ALR-45 and ALR-67 antennas

Glove vanes not fitted

AoA probe at tip of radome

NACES ejection seats

Redesigned cockpits with new systems, avionics, instruments and displays

Wings shown in 72° oversweep position

Tomcat scale drawings by Mark Styling.
Scale 1/72nd (1 inch to 6 feet)

F-14 Tomcat weapons and external stores

Relative positions as carried on aircraft, front pair side-by-side, third missile on centreline slightly behind. Fourth missile shown in relative position of aft centreline recess

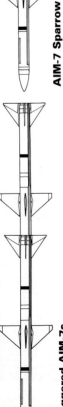

Staggered AIM-7s

AIM-7 Sparrow

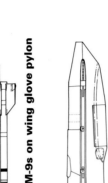
AIM-54 on front underfuselage pallet

Mk 82 500-lb bombs on forward underfuselage pallet

AN/ALQ-167 'Bullwinkle' pod on forward underfuselage pallet (F-14A/B only)

AIM-9 and AIM-7 on wing glove pylon front view

TARPS pod, front view

AIM-54 on rear underfuselage pallet

Mk 83 1,000-lb bomb

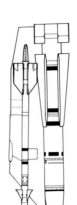
TARPS pod

TARPS pod, underside plan view

KS-87 forward oblique or vertical
KA-99 low-altitude pan camera
AN/AAD-5 IR recce set
AN/ASQ-172 data display set

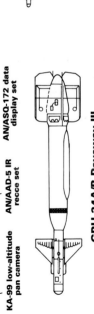
GBU-24A/B Paveway III 2,000-lb laser-guided bomb

AIM-9L/M Sidewinder

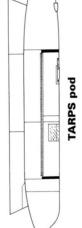  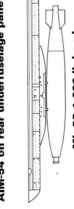 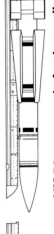

AIM-9 and AIM-7 on wing glove pylon

Twin AIM-9s on wing glove pylon

Wing glove pylon with AIM-7 adaptor rail

AIM-9 and AIM-54 on wing glove pylon

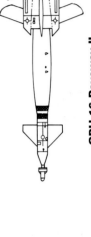
AIM-54C (partially cut away)

GBU-16 Paveway II 1,000-lb laser guided bomb

An AIM-54 falls away from a VX-4 F-14. The motor ignites almost immediately.

Mk 7 cluster dispenser (Mk 20 Rockeye, CBU-59 APAM and CBU-78 Gator)

1,000-lb Mk 83 Low-Drag General Purpose bomb

LANTIRN targeting pod

Tomcat weapon and external stores scale drawings by Mark Styling. Scale 1/72nd (1 inch to 6 feet)

This nose artwork appeared in 1994 on a VF-41 Tomcat in recognition of the F-14's recently-found attack capability.

Specification

F-14A, except where otherwise noted

Dimensions: fuselage length including probe 62 ft 8 in (19.10 m); F-14D 64 ft 4½ in (19.62 m); span (swept) 38 ft 2½ in (11.65 m) (unswept) 64 ft 1½ in (19.54 m); overswept 33 ft 3½ in (10.15 m); aspect ratio 7.28; wing area 565 sq ft (52.49 m²); total area, wing and fuselage 'lifting area' 1,008 sq ft (m²); total slat area 46.2 sq ft (4.29 m²); total flap area 106.3 sq ft (9.87 m²); total spoiler area 21.2 sq ft (1.97 m²); horizontal tail area 140 sq ft (13.01 m²); total fin area 85 sq ft (7.90 m²); total rudder area 33 sq ft (3.06 m²); tailplane span 32 ft 8½ in (9.97 m); gap between fin tips 10 ft 8 in (3.25 m); overall height 16 ft (4.88 m); wheel track 16 ft 5 in (5.00 m); wheelbase 23 ft 0½ in (7.02 m); wing loading 90 lb/sq ft (439 kg/m²); wing/fuselage loading 55 lb/sq ft (268.5 kg/m²)

Powerplant: F-14A – two TF30-P-414A rated at 21,750 lb st (96.78 kN) dry and 34,154 lb st (151.98 kN) with afterburning; F-14B, F-14D – two F110-GE-400 rated at 27,600 lb st (122.82 kN) dry and 55,200 lb st (245.64 kN) with afterburning

Weights: empty operating F-14A 40,104 lb (18191 kg), empty operating F-14B 41,780 lb (18951 kg), empty operating F-14A 43,735 lb (19838 kg), normal take-off, four Sparrow 59,714 lb (27086 kg), normal take-off, six Phoenix 70,764 lb (32098 kg); maximum take-off weight (all versions, service limit) 72,000 lb (32659 kg); maximum take-off weight (manufacturer's limit) 74,349 lb (33724 kg); design landing weight 51,830 lb (23510 kg)

Fuel and load: total internal fuel 16,200 lb (7348 kg) in six main tanks; forward fuselage 4,700 lb (2132 kg), aft fuselage 4,400 lb (1996 kg), left feed (in port side of wing box) 1,500 lb (680 kg), right feed (in starboard side of wing box) 1,600 lb (726 kg), wings 2,000 lb (907 kg) each; External fuel 4,000 lb (1724 kg); Single-point pressure refuelling via port on starboard lower fuselage, below IFR probe. normal weapon load up to 14,500 lb (6577-kg) air-to-ground

Performance: maximum level speed at altitude 1,342 kt (1,544 mph; 2,485 km/h); maximum level speed at low level 792 kt (912 mph; 1468 km/h); limiting Mach no. 2.38 M; Mach 2.4 attained, but initially limited to Mach 2.25 in service; Mach 1.2 at low level; maximum cruising speed 550 kts (633 mph; 1019 km/h); maximum rate of climb at sea level 30,000 ft (9140 m) per minute; absolute ceiling 56,000 ft (17068 m); service ceiling F-14A 50,000 ft (15240 m); service ceiling F-14B, F-14D 53,000 ft (16154 m); normal carrier approach speed 134 kt (154 mph; 248 km/h); stalling speed, landing configuration 115 kt (132 mph; 213 km/h); take-off run (with full fuel, and 4 AIM-7s) 1,400 ft (427 m); landing roll less than 2,000 ft (610 m), minimum 1,600 ft (488 m)

Endurance/radius: CAP endurance with four Phoenix, two Sparrows, two Sidewinders and external fuel 90 minutes at 150 nm (278 km) and one hour at 253 nm (470 km); deck-launched intercept radius with four Phoenix, two Sparrows, two Sidewinders and external fuel 171 nm (317 km) at Mach 1.3; 134 nm (248 km) at Mach 1.5; ferry range F-14A (with two tanks) 1,730 nm (2,000 miles; 3200 km); ferry range F-14B (with two tanks) 2,050 nm (2,360 miles; 3800 km)

Above: A VF-103 F-14A fires an AIM-9G Sidewinder. For the regular missile firing exercises, it is usual practice to use up old stocks of early missile versions.

Below: An F-14 flies with a T-6/Zero conversion during filming for **The Final Countdown.** *In this movie, USS Nimitz was time-warped back to the time of Pearl Harbor.*

Left: A gaggle of F-14As is seen prior to delivery to Iran. All have the glove vanes extended.

Above: The original F-14B Super Tomcat was tested with the AGM-88 HARM missile.

Above: *Proving that the Tomcat is no slouch in air combat, an F-14A pilot makes a point to an adversary F-5. The US Navy's aggressive DACT programme has ensured that F-14 crews are among the best-trained in the world.*

Below: *VF-201 is now the only US Naval Reserve Tomcat squadron. This aircraft is seen carrying Mk 82 GP bombs for a training mission. The aircraft is marked for USS* John C. Stennis, *the Navy's newest fleet carrier.*

An NF-14D of the NAWC-WD 'Bloodhounds' departs Point Mugu for a trials mission over the China Lake ranges. It carries practice bombs on a triple ejector rack under a modified Phoenix pallet.

INDEX